Fundamentals of Object-Oriented Programming in Java

www.oopbook.com

Fundamentals of Object-Oriented Programming in Java

Permanand Mohan
The University of the West Indies

Fundamentals of Object-Oriented Programming in Java™
by Permanand Mohan

Copyright © 2013 Permanand Mohan

ALL RIGHTS RESERVED. No part of this book may be reproduced or transmitted in any form or by any means—graphic, electronic, or mechanical, including photocopying, recording, Web distribution, or information storage and retrieval systems—without the written permission of the author.

Book Design: Shellyann Sooklal and Keshav Bahadoor
Book Web Site: www.oopbook.com

10 9 8 7 6 5 4 3 2 1

ISBN-13: 978-1482587524
ISBN-10: 1482587521

Table of Contents

Preface xix
    Goal of the Book xix
    About the Book xix
    Intended Audience xx
    Pre-requisite Knowledge xx
    Support Materials xxi
    Acknowledgements xxii
    Inspiration for the Book xxiii

About the Author xxv

Chapter 1: Introduction 1
    1.1 Programming Paradigms 1
    1.2 Object-Oriented Programming 3
    1.3 Overview of the Book 4
        1.3.1 Chapter 2 7
        1.3.2 Chapters 3 and 4 7
        1.3.3 Chapters 6 and 7 7
        1.3.4 Chapters 9 and 10 8
        1.3.5 Chapters 12 and 13 8
        1.3.6 Chapter 15 9
        1.3.7 Chapter 17 9
        1.3.8 Remaining Chapters 10
    1.4 Java and the Unified Modelling Language 10
    1.5 Design Patterns 11
    Exercises 11

Chapter 2: Overview of the Java Programming Language 13

   2.1 Java Development Environment 13

   2.2 Hello World 14

   2.3 Comments 15

   2.4 Primitive Data Types 16

   2.5 Variables 17

   2.6 Assignments and Initialisations 17

   2.7 Operators and Expressions 18

       2.7.1 Arithmetic Operators 18

       2.7.2 Comparison Operators 19

       2.7.3 Logical Operators 19

   2.8 Strings 20

   2.9 Input and Output 22

       2.9.1 Output using `System.out` 22

       2.9.2 Formatted Output with `System.out` 23

       2.9.3 Input using the `Scanner` Class 24

   2.10 Control Structures 25

       2.10.1 Conditional Statements 25

       2.10.2 Repetition 27

   2.11 Arrays 28

   Exercises 29

Chapter 3: Objects and Classes 33

   3.1 Understanding Classes 33

       3.1.1 Representing State with Attributes 33

       3.1.2 Implementing Behaviors with Methods 34

       3.1.3 Creating a Class 35

   3.2 UML Notation for a Class 37

   3.3 Creating and Manipulating Instances of a Class 38

       3.3.1 Creating and Manipulating Objects 38

       3.3.2 A Client Class 40

Table of Contents

    3.3.3 Objects in Memory 41

    3.3.4 Assigning One Object Variable to Another 44

3.4 Constructor Methods 45

3.5 Improving the Client Class 48

3.6 Method Signature and Method Overloading 50

3.7 Class Variables and Class Methods 52

    3.7.1 Class Variables 52

    3.7.2 Class Methods 53

3.8 Scope of Variables 55

Exercises 55

Chapter 4: Information Hiding and Design Principles 59

4.1 Encapsulation 59

    4.1.1 Access Modifiers 59

    4.1.2 Hiding the Attributes of an Object 60

    4.1.3 Hiding the Methods of an Object 62

    4.1.4 Effect of Access Modifiers on Instances of the Same Class 63

4.2 Accessing Private Attributes 64

    4.2.1 Accessor and Mutator Methods 64

    4.2.2 Problem with Accessor and Mutator Methods 67

4.3 Immutable Classes 67

    4.3.1 Achieving Immutability 67

    4.3.2 Immutable Classes in Java 68

4.4 Object-Oriented Design Guidelines 70

    4.4.1 Coupling and Cohesion 70

    4.4.2 Law of Demeter 71

4.5 Organizing the Classes of an Application 73

    4.5.1 The Concept of a Package 73

    4.5.2 Three-tier Architecture for Object-Oriented Software 74

    4.5.3 Creating a Package and its Elements 76

    4.5.4 Using the Elements of a Package 77

    4.5.5   Nesting Packages 78
  4.6   Accessing the Attributes and Methods of a Class in a Package 80
  4.7   Controlling Access to a Class 81
    4.7.1   Using Access Modifiers to Declare a Class 81
    4.7.2   Inner Classes 81
  Exercises 83

Chapter 5: First Programming Project 85

  5.1   Requirements of the Application 85
    5.1.1   Overview 85
    5.1.2   UML Diagram of `Student` Class 86
    5.1.3   `Student` Class 86
    5.1.4   User Interface 87
    5.1.5   Implementation Requirements 87
  5.2   Implementation of `Student` Domain Class 87
  5.3   Implementation of the User Interface 89
    5.3.1   Implementation of User Interface Class 90
    5.3.2   Implementation of `choice1()` 91
    5.3.3   Implementation of `choice2()` 92
    5.3.4   Implementation of `choice3()` 92
    5.3.5   Implementation of `choice4()` 93
    5.3.6   Implementation of `getStudent()` Helper Method 93
  5.4   Creating Source Files and Compiling 93
  5.5   Alternative Implementation using Another Domain Class 94

Chapter 6: Unit Testing an Object-Oriented Program 99

  6.1   Classes to Test in the Student Application 99
  6.2   Testing the Student Application 100
    6.2.1   Common Approach to Testing 100
    6.2.2   A Testing Scenario 101
    6.2.3   Weaknesses of the Testing Approach 104

Table of Contents

    6.2.4   The Benefits of Unit Testing 105
  6.3   Testing Individual Classes with JUnit 106
    6.3.1   A Test Class 107
    6.3.2   Annotations 108
    6.3.3   Writing a Test Method 109
    6.3.4   Differentiating a Test from a Test Method 112
  6.4   Unit Testing the `Student` Class 112
    6.4.1   Unit Tests for the `Student` Class 112
    6.4.2   `StudentTest` Class 113
        6.4.2.1   `testCreate()` 114
        6.4.2.2   `testID()` 114
        6.4.2.3   `testSetPhone()` 115
        6.4.2.4   `testToString()` 115
    6.4.3   Executing the Test Methods in `StudentTest` 115
  6.5   Unit Testing the `University` Class 117
    6.5.1   Unit Tests for the `University` Class 117
    6.5.2   `UniversityTest` Class 119
        6.5.2.1   `testCreate()` 119
        6.5.2.2   `testAddStudent()` 119
        6.5.2.3   `testGetStudent()` 120
        6.5.2.4   `testChangePhone()` 120
        6.5.2.5   `testGetStudents()` 121
    6.5.3   Executing the Test Methods in `UniversityTest` 121
  6.6   Combining Unit Tests into a Test Suite 121
  6.7   Testing Scenario Compared to Unit Testing 123
  6.8   Further Testing with JUnit 123
  6.9   Some Guidelines for Unit Testing 127
    6.9.1   `@BeforeClass` and `@AfterClass` Methods 127
    6.9.2   What to Test? 128
    6.9.3   When to Perform Testing? 128
    6.9.4   How to Write a "Good" Test? 128
  Exercises 129

Chapter 7: Relationships between Objects 131

    7.1   Dependencies 131

    7.2   Associations 132

        7.2.1   Multiplicity of an Association 133

        7.2.2   Aggregation 134

        7.2.3   Composition 134

    7.3   Generalizations 135

    7.4   Implementing Dependency Relationships 136

    7.5   Implementing Associations 137

        7.5.1   Implementing One-to-One Associations 137

        7.5.2   Implementing One-to-Many Associations 138

        7.5.3   Implementing Many-to-Many Associations 139

        7.5.4   Using an Association Class 140

        7.5.5   Implementing Aggregation and Composition 143

    Exercises 144

Chapter 8: Second Programming Project 147

    8.1   Requirements of the Application 147

        8.1.1   Overview 147

        8.1.2   UML Diagram of Domain Objects 148

        8.1.3   `Course` 149

        8.1.4   `Student` 149

        8.1.5   `University` 150

        8.1.6   User Interface 152

        8.1.7   Implementation Requirements 152

    8.2   Implementation of Domain Classes 153

        8.2.1   `Course` 153

        8.2.2   `Student` 153

        8.2.3   `University` 155

    8.3   Implementation of the User Interface 157

    8.4   Creating Source Files and Compiling 159

Table of Contents

    8.5   Alternative Implementation Using an Association Class 160

        8.5.1   The `Registration` Association Class 160

        8.5.2   Manipulating Instances of the Association Class 162

        8.5.3   Benefits of Using an Association Class 164

Chapter 9: Inheritance and Polymorphism 167

    9.1   Generalization Relationships and Inheritance 167

    9.2   Creating and Manipulating Child Classes 170

        9.2.1   Writing a Child Class 170

        9.2.2   Inheriting Attributes and Methods from Parent Class 171

        9.2.3   Initialising Instance Variables 172

        9.2.4   Manipulating Child Classes 173

    9.3   Method Refinement and Replacement 174

    9.4   The `Object` Class 176

    9.5   Substitutability and Polymorphism 177

        9.5.1   The Principle of Substitutability 177

        9.5.2   Polymorphism 179

        9.5.3   Method Binding 181

        9.5.4   The Reverse Polymorphism Problem 182

        9.5.5   Parameter Passing and Return Types of Methods 184

    9.6   Preventing Inheritance 185

    9.7   Abstract Classes and Abstract Methods 186

    9.8   Forms of Inheritance 188

    9.9   Benefits and Drawbacks of Inheritance 189

    9.10 Multiple Inheritance 189

    Exercises 192

Chapter 10: Exception Handling 195

    10.1 Exceptions 195

    10.2 Exception Handling in Java 196

    10.3 Checked Exceptions 197

10.3.1 Writing Checked Exceptions 197

10.3.2 Declaring and Throwing Checked Exceptions 198

10.3.3 Catching Checked Exceptions 200

10.3.4 Cleaning Up after Exception Handling 203

10.3.5 Not Handling a Checked Exception 204

10.4 Unchecked Exceptions 206

10.5 Use Exception Handling with Care 207

Exercises 208

Chapter 11: Third Programming Project 211

11.1 Requirements of the Application 211

    11.1.1 Overview 211

    11.1.2 UML Diagram of Domain Objects 212

    11.1.3 `Course` 213

    11.1.4 `Student` 214

    11.1.5 `UndergraduateStudent` 215

    11.1.6 `PostgraduateStudent` 215

    11.1.7 `Registration` 216

    11.1.8 Exception Classes 217

    11.1.9 `University` 217

    11.1.10 User Interface 221

    11.1.11 Implementation Requirements 222

11.2 Implementation of Domain Classes 223

    11.2.1 `Course` 223

    11.2.2 `Student`, `UndergraduateStudent`, and `PostgraduateStudent` 223

    11.2.3 `Registration` 225

    11.2.4 `TooManyCreditsException` and `CourseFullException` 225

    11.2.5 `University` 226

11.3 Implementation of the User Interface 231

11.4 Creating Source Files and Compiling 236

Table of Contents

Chapter 12: Interfaces 239

    12.1   The Concept of an Interface 239

    12.2   A Real-World Example 240

    12.3   Defining an Interface 240

    12.4   Implementing an Interface 241

    12.5   UML Notation for Interfaces 242

    12.6   Properties of Interfaces..243

    12.7   The `Comparable` Interface 245

    12.8   Polymorphism with Interfaces 247

    12.9   Implementing Multiple Interfaces 248

    12.10 Inheritance of Interfaces 249

    Exercises 251

Chapter 13: Container Classes 253

    13.1   The Need for Generics 254

        13.1.1   Linked Lists..254

        13.1.2   A Linked List of Integers...254

        13.1.3   A Linked List of Objects 256

        13.1.4   A Linked List with Generic Types 258

    13.2   Iterators..260

        13.2.1   Iterator Design Pattern 261

        13.2.2   Implementation in Java..261

        13.2.3   Linked List Iterator..262

        13.2.4   *foreach* Statement 263

    13.3   The Java *Collections* Framework 264

        13.3.1   Interfaces in the Java *Collections* Framework 265

            13.3.1.1   The `Collection` Interface...................................265

            13.3.1.2   The `List` Interface 266

            13.3.1.3   The `Set` and `SortedSet` Interfaces.....................267

            13.3.1.4   The `Map` and `SortedMap` Interface 268

        13.3.2   Classes in the Java Collections Framework 269

            13.3.2.1   `LinkedList` 270

    13.3.2.2   `ArrayList` and `Vector` 270
    13.3.2.3   `HashSet` 271
    13.3.2.4   `TreeSet` 273
    13.3.2.5   `HashMap` 274
    13.3.2.6   `TreeMap` 275
  13.4   The `Comparable` Interface (Generics Version) 277
  13.5   The `Comparator` Interface 277
  13.6   Which Collection to Use? 279
  Exercises 280

Chapter 14: Fourth Programming Project 283
  14.1   Requirements of the Application 283
  14.2   Ensuring that at Most One Instance of the `University` Class Exists
         284
  14.3   Using More Efficient Collections to Manage Data in the `University`
          Class 286
    14.3.1   `Comparator`s for `Student` Objects 287
    14.3.2   New Collections for `Course`, `Student`, and `Registration` ...288
    14.3.3   Using the New Collections 291
    14.3.4   Overriding the `hashCode()` and `equals()` Methods 294
  14.4   Using Roles Instead of Inheritance 295
    14.4.1   Problem with Inheritance and a Solution Using Role Objects ..295
    14.4.2   Implementation of Role Objects 298
    14.4.3   Re-design of the Graphical User Interface 301
  14.5   Organizing the Application into Packages 302

Chapter 15: Object Persistence 305
  15.1   Objects to Be Made Persistent 305
  15.2   Classes Used to Describe Object Persistence 306
  15.3   Input / Output Streams in Java 309
  15.4   Using a Text File 309
    15.4.1   Saving `Account` Objects to a Text File 309
    15.4.2   Reading Data for `Account` Objects from a Text File 312

Table of Contents

    15.4.3   Suitability of Text Files for Object Persistence............................314
  15.5   Using a Relational Database 314
    15.5.1   Relational Databases..314
    15.5.2   Java Database Connectivity (JDBC) API...316
    15.5.3   Saving `Account` Objects to a Database 317
    15.5.4   Reading Data for `Account` Objects from a Database 322
    15.5.5   Test Programs...324
    15.5.6   Suitability of Relational Database for Object Persistence 325
  15.6   Using Object Serialization 325
    15.6.1   Saving `Account` Objects using Serialization................................326
    15.6.2   Reading `Account` Objects using Serialization.............................327
    15.6.3   Alternative Approach for Serializing `Account` Objects 328
    15.6.4   Suitability of Serialization for Object Persistence.......................330
  15.7   Objects that Contain Other Objects..330
  15.8   Applying Persistence Techniques to Other Applications..................332
  Exercises...332

Chapter 16: Fifth Programming Project 335

  16.1   Objects to be Made Persistent 335
  16.2   Changes to `StudentApplication` 337
  16.3   Using a Text File 339
    16.3.1   Saving Objects to a Text File 340
    16.3.2   Reading Data for Objects from a Text File...............................341
  16.4   Using a Relational Database 342
    16.4.1   Saving Objects to a Database...344
    16.4.2   Reading Data for Objects from a Database 344
  16.5   Using Object Serialization 345
    16.5.1   Saving Objects using Serialization..346
    16.5.2   Reading Objects Using Serialization 346
    16.5.3   Alternative Approaches for Serialization 347
  16.6   Packaging the Application 348

Chapter 17: Introduction to Graphical User Interface Programming ... 351

    17.1   The Swing Toolkit 352

    17.2   An Empty Window 352

        17.2.1   First Version 352

        17.2.2   Second Version 355

    17.3   Some Simple GUI Components 356

        17.3.1   Label 357

        17.3.2   Text Field 358

        17.3.3   Text Area 358

        17.3.4   Command Button 358

        17.3.5   Layout Manager 359

    17.4   `StudentWindow` 360

        17.4.1   First Version of `StudentWindow` 360

        17.4.2   Second Version of `StudentWindow` 363

    17.5   Three Advanced GUI Components 366

        17.5.1   Combo Box 367

        17.5.2   Radio Button 369

        17.5.3   Check Box 371

        17.5.4   Final Version of `StudentWindow` 372

    17.6   Responding to Events on the `StudentWindow` 375

        17.6.1   Event Handling Mechanism 375

        17.6.2   Clicking on a Command Button 377

        17.6.3   Pressing a Key on the Keyboard 377

        17.6.4   Clicking the Mouse 378

        17.6.5   Attaching Event Handlers to GUI Components 379

    17.7   Communicating with Domain Objects in `StudentWindow` 380

        17.7.1   Model-View Separation 381

        17.7.2   Writing Code that Implements Pull-From-Above 381

    17.8   Enhancing the GUI 385

        17.8.1   Supporting Multiple Windows 386

        17.8.2   Including Menus on the Main Window 389

Table of Contents

    17.8.3 Popup Windows 390

    17.8.4 Completed Student Application 391

  17.9 Is There a Better Way to Develop a GUI? 392

  Exercises 393

Appendix A: Questions on Object-Oriented Programming 395

  A.1 Questions with Answers 395

  A.2 Questions without Answers 407

Appendix B: Answers to Questions 417

Glossary 433

Bibliography 441

Index 443

Preface

Thanks for your interest in this book! Here you will find a detailed introduction to object-oriented programming using the Java programming language. The focus is *not* on the Java programming language; rather, Java is used as a vehicle to implement the object-oriented concepts presented in the book. Object-oriented programming provides a rich set of concepts and techniques that can be used to build more reusable, maintainable, and error-free software compared to traditional approaches. It is my hope that this book will help you along the journey of becoming more knowledgeable of object-oriented concepts and techniques and that ultimately you will become a more highly-skilled software developer.

Goal of the Book

The goal of this book is to present the concepts and techniques of object-oriented programming as simply as possible so that it can be easily understood and mastered by beginners. The emphasis is on presenting concepts at the right time and with the right amount of detail to encourage learning and mastery of the material.

About the Book

To help you get familiar with the Java programming language, the book starts off by describing the basic features of the language. These include data types and variables, arrays, control structures (*if, while, for,* etc.), and performing input and output. Several exercises have been carefully designed so that you can get up to speed with Java as quickly as possible.

This book strikes a good balance between theory and practice. Some object-oriented concepts often require lengthy explanations for beginners to fully understand the concepts. Based on years of experience in teaching object-oriented programming, the book condenses long explanations in favour of providing real examples which show how the concepts are implemented in an object-oriented program. Thus, detailed code examples are liberally interspersed with theoretical descriptions throughout the book. When you have mastered the fundamental concepts of object-oriented programming, you are encouraged to explore the deeper theoretical issues by studying some of the excellent references available.

One of the unique features of the book is that it contains five chapters (called "Programming Projects") which explain how to build a complete object-oriented program based on the material presented in the other chapters. These chapters appear when all the relevant material required for writing the program has been thoroughly discussed in the preceding chapters. Each of the five chapters starts by describing the problem in narrative form. The chapter then gives a detailed definition of the functionality required. Next, the chapter explains how the functionality can be implemented using the object-oriented concepts presented earlier in the book. The chapter ends with a complete working Java program that solves the problem described. Often, alternative solutions are presented so that you will realize that there are competing ways to implement an object-oriented program with different trade-offs.

Another unique feature of the book is that that new material is not used or referenced before it has been discussed. The book is essentially incremental in nature so that new concepts being introduced always build on earlier concepts. Thus, you are only exposed to new concepts or language features when pre-requisite material has been completely discussed. Also, great care has been taken to avoid the use of programming language features which, though very useful for advanced programmers, can make it harder for a beginner to focus on and learn the object-oriented principles being imparted.

This book is based on the experience gained from many years of teaching object-oriented programming to beginners who know another programming language. If you are looking to get a good, practical introduction to object-oriented programming using Java in an easy-to-understand format, this is the book for you!

Intended Audience

This book is suitable for computer professionals who wish to learn the details of object-oriented programming. It is also suitable for students pursuing courses in object-oriented programming or courses that require an in-depth knowledge of the concepts and techniques of object-oriented programming (e.g., object-oriented analysis and design). The material in the book can be covered in a one semester course on object-oriented programming. The book can also be used by software developers who wish to become more proficient in Java from an object-oriented perspective.

Pre-requisite Knowledge

The book assumes that you have already been exposed to computer programming and that you know how to write programs in a programming

Preface

language such as C. It does not matter which programming language you know as long as you are familiar with programming concepts such as:

- Data types and variables
- Arrays
- Control structures such as sequence, selection, and iteration
- Performing input and output using the keyboard and files

If you have never written a computer program before, you may have difficulty in grasping the concepts presented in this book. However, if you understand the basics of computer programming and would like to take your knowledge to another level, you have come to the right place!

Support Materials

The book has an accompanying Web site, www.oopbook.com. The code from each chapter of the book can be downloaded from the Web site. The Web site has several guides which show you how to set up and use popular integrated development environments (IDEs) for Java such as JCreator Lite, Eclipse, and Netbeans. These IDEs simplify the process of writing, compiling, running, and testing object-oriented programs in Java.

The Web site also has several programming guides which show you:

- How to generate automatic documentation for a Java program
- How to test a Java program using JUnit with the IDEs listed above
- How to access a relational database such as MySQL, Microsoft Access®, and Microsoft SQL Server®.

Solutions to several of the exercises are also available for download at the book Web site. In particular, you can download the solutions for the Java programming exercises in Chapter 2 as well as the solutions for the questions in Appendix *A*.

The book Web site has a discussion forum for each chapter of the book. You can go to a particular chapter to enter a comment or question on that chapter or you can go to the *Discussion* section of the Web site where you can post your comments or questions on any chapter of the book or on any of the other topics listed. The book has a Facebook group, "*Object-Oriented Programming in Java Book*". You are welcome to join the group. You can also email your questions or comments to permanand.mohan@oopbook.com. We look forward to hearing from you.

Acknowledgements

I would like to thank Diana Ragbir, Kris Manohar, Phaedra Mohammed, Roger Gajraj, and Jay Coach from the University of the West Indies for reviewing chapters of the book. I am grateful to Shellyann Sooklal from the University of the West Indies for reviewing the entire first draft of the book and picking up things that few would have been able to find. I must also thank Tharaka Ilayperuma from the University of Ruhuna in Sri Lanka and Joel Aragon Valladores from the PUC University in Peru for their quick review and positive feedback of an earlier draft of the book.

I am grateful to the students of COMP 2500 – Object-Oriented Programming at the University of the West Indies who used various draft versions of the book while it was in its formative years.

I wish to acknowledge my colleagues in the Department of Computing and Information Technology at the University of the West Indies who contributed in one way or the other to the book. In particular, Sheik Yussuff shared many valuable insights into object-oriented programming over the years. He also encouraged me to write the chapter on unit testing. Renaldo Jagmohan printed earlier drafts of the book for the students of COMP 2500 and also printed copies of the final text as it was nearing completion. Colleagues such as Wayne Goodridge and Salys Lackan provided feedback on earlier drafts of the book.

I am deeply grateful to my book production crew from the University of the West Indies, incidentally both former students of COMP 2500. First of all, I would like to express my thanks to Shellyann Sooklal for the painstaking hours she spent with the design and layout of the book to make sure that it exceeded my expectations. I am impressed with the quality of work she has delivered. I am greatly indebted to Keshav Bahadoor who has been like a Swiss Army Knife for this book writing project. He was responsible for the design of the book covers, the artwork for the birds on each chapter, development of the book Web site, and writing the programming guides at the book Web site. He also assisted in the book production.

I would like to thank David Siguelnitzky, President of the Herbert Fletcher University and his wife Esther, and Priscilla Pilly from the University of the Southern Caribbean, her husband Vijay and her family, for their friendship as well as their encouragement in pursuing this book writing venture.

I must also thank my personal support team. First, I must thank Rohan Rambally, and friends and associates from the Prayer Command Centre who offered up many prayers and exhortations so that I could finish the book. I am also thankful to Rohan Rambally for his unwavering support and

Preface

friendship over the past few years. He has been a source of continuous encouragement from the first day he heard that I was writing the book. Thanks Rohan, for leading by example rather than with nice words. I must also thank his mother, Taramatie and his brother, Hamenath for their encouragement and support.

Finally, I am greatly indebted to my family for their patience, long-suffering, and support over the many months while I was working on the book. It was a long road but at last, it has come to an end.

Inspiration for the Book

I have been around a long time in the computing industry. During this time, I have seen computer systems, operating systems, and programming languages come and go. Yet, as an observer, practitioner, researcher, and teacher, I continue to be amazed at the changes that computer hardware, software, and telecommunications have brought to this world. I am particularly interested in computer software and the limitless potential it affords to make this world a better place. This book is an effort to crystallize my knowledge and experience in object-oriented programming, and programming in general, in the hope that it will have an impact on the next generation of software developers.

Despite all the wonders made possible by computer technology, I am sure that there are moments in life when we all look to the heavens and wonder, why on earth am I here? I am sure there are moments in life when, despite all that we have done or accomplished, suddenly everything seems to be in vain. A wise man once said that everything on earth is meaningless, completely meaningless. Two years ago, in the comfort of my living room, around 1:30 am in the night, I had no choice but to agree with that wise man. Two burglars had entered the house while my family and I were asleep and here was I, face to face with one of them, as he drew near with a weapon in his hand. The other one had taken my family to another room to interrogate them about any valuables we had. No amount of knowledge or computer technology could save us now.

That night, we all secretly cried out to God for a miracle. We were indeed blessed with a miracle at a time when we desperately needed one. The bandits left us unhurt that night even though they considered kidnapping my son for a ransom. We lost some money, cell phones, and some electronic gadgets. But, the real loss was something inside of me. After that day, keen computer scientist and teacher that I was, I lost a sense of purpose, a reason for being, and drifted along listlessly along the path of life. In the days to come, I would replay those 20 minutes of terror when my family and I were completely at the mercy of two vicious bandits. Sadly, it was an unforgettable experience.

Even though I believed in the existence of a sovereign God and His Son Jesus Christ, I questioned why a loving and Almighty God would allow such things to happen? As I sought answers to these deep questions, the answers came. Under the guidance of Prophet Rohan Rambally from the Prayer Command Centre (www.rohanrambally.org) and others, I found a new sense of being, a new sense of purpose, and started to understand God's will for my life. Another wise man said that the entrance of God's Word brings light to a man. I allowed God's Word to enter my life and since that time, my life has been filled with light. This is the light that has inspired me to write this book. This is the light that now shows me the way forward, little by little, day by day. I am now convinced that life only has meaning to the extent that we are aligned to God's purposes for our lives here on earth.

Dear reader, it is my hope that this book will bring deeper insights and understanding to you in the area of object-oriented programming; I hope that it will be a blessing to you as you strive to become a more knowledgeable and a more highly-skilled software developer. I hope, too, that you will prosper in the field of software development and that you will achieve all that is in your destiny and purpose. However, I hope even more that you, too, will allow the Word of God to enter your heart and flood your life with the light that it needs. It is my desire that you will be all that you were destined to be, by simply giving your creator a chance to become the King, Ruler, Guide, Comforter, and Counsellor of your life. If you would like to make Jesus Christ the Lord of your life, please say this prayer from the depths of your heart:

Jesus, come into my heart.
I believe that you died and rose again on the third day.
Please forgive me of all my sins and iniquities.
Wash me in your precious blood.
Lord Jesus, please write my name in the Lamb's Book of Life.
Fill me with your sweet Holy Spirit.
Lead me to a place of worship where the Word of God is being preached.
Help me to talk to you each day in prayer.
Holy Spirit, please teach me your Word starting with the Gospel of John.
Thank you Lord, for saving my soul,
In the name of Jesus,
Amen.

Permanand Mohan
St. Augustine, Trinidad and Tobago
March 1, 2013

About the Author

Permanand Mohan is a Senior Lecturer in Computer Science at the St. Augustine campus of University of the West Indies in Trinidad and Tobago where he has been teaching full-time for more than 15 years. He has a Ph.D. in Computer Science from the University of the West Indies, an M.Sc. in Computer Science from the University of Saskatchewan, and a B.Sc. in Computer Science from the University of the West Indies. He was previously a Visiting Professor at the Laboratory for Advanced Research in Intelligent Educational Systems (ARIES) at the University of Saskatchewan in Canada and a Fulbright Visiting Scholar to the School of Information Sciences at the University of Pittsburgh in the USA.

Mohan has taught object-oriented programming to hundreds of students over the past ten years. He has also taught courses on computer programming to thousands of students learning to program for the first time. This experience has given him keen insight into the challenges that beginners have when learning new programming concepts. He sought ways to overcome these challenges and developed several strategies that make it easier for a beginner to learn computer programming and object-oriented programming. These strategies focus on simplifying concepts and presenting concrete examples as much as possible. They have been successfully used in his classes over the past few years. These strategies have played in a key role in the organization of the book and in the pedagogical approach taken.

In addition to teaching, Mohan is also an active researcher at the University of the West Indies. One aspect of his research involves using advanced computing technologies for learning. These include intelligent tutoring systems, e-learning, mobile learning, and serious games for learning. He also conducts research in mobile health and telemedicine. He and his research students won an award from Microsoft Research based on its RFP, *Cell Phone as a Platform for Healthcare*. The grant funds were used to develop the MediNet mobile health system for patients in the Caribbean with diabetes and cardiovascular disease.

To

The Lord Jesus Christ, for keeping me safe despite all the times I have slipped and for giving me the health, strength, knowledge, and inspiration to write this book

and to

Fariel, Nishtha, and Sanjiv
The wonderful travelling companions He gave to me along the way

Chapter 1

Introduction

This chapter differentiates between two popular programming paradigms, the procedural paradigm and the object-oriented paradigm, the latter being the focus of this book. It goes on to explain how an object-oriented program can be viewed as a set of objects that collaborate to achieve the purpose of the program. From this view, an overview of the chapters of the book is presented. The chapter then describes the two languages used throughout the book, namely the Java programming language and the graphical Unified Modelling Language. The chapter concludes by discussing the idea of design patterns, which are occasionally used in the book to provide solutions to certain problems that arise.

1.1 Programming Paradigms

The two main paradigms for computer programming are the *procedural paradigm* and the *object-oriented paradigm*. The procedural approach is exemplified by programming languages such as C and Pascal. The object-oriented approach is exemplified by programming languages such as C++, Java, and C#.

In procedural programming, code is modularized based on the processes taking place in the system. For example, in a banking application, typical processes that would be considered include the following:

- Opening accounts for customers
- Performing transactions on accounts
- Generating transaction reports at periodic intervals
- Closing accounts

An application developed using the procedural paradigm consists of a set of processes which are hierarchically connected. Processes are typically implemented as software modules. Figure 1.1 shows an application consisting of a set of processes. As can be seen from the diagram, a process can be further decomposed into a set of sub-processes. An application developed using the procedural paradigm tends to mimic the way a computer works. Thus, the application tends to follow a set of sequential steps structured around the input-processing-output model.

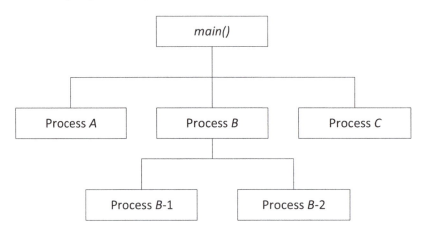

Figure 1.1: Process Decomposition in the Procedural Paradigm

Developing an application using the procedural paradigm typically involves analysing the business processes to discover the procedural tasks that need to be carried out. This is followed by *process modelling* which involves using tools such as *data flow diagrams* to understand how the processes of the application need to work together. Process models highlight the data which needs to flow from one process to another; thus, another activity known as *data modelling* is used to model the data that will be used in the application. From these models, the application is developed consisting of a set of processes and data stores.

In contrast to the procedural paradigm, the object-oriented paradigm views an application as consisting of a set of objects which collaborate to achieve the objectives of the application. An object has both state and behavior. *State* can be regarded as the data/information that is known about an object. *Behavior* can be regarded as the set of operations that manipulates the data of an object and so modifies its state.

Developing an object-oriented application involves discovering the objects that will play a role in the application and understanding how objects interact with each other in the problem space. The object-oriented approach usually results in software that has a closer representation of its real-world problem domain than software built using the procedural approach. Because of this, it is easier to build, debug, and maintain.

Chapter 1: Introduction

In addition, the object-oriented paradigm encourages an iterative, incremental process in developing the application. Thus, an application can be developed in stages with additional functionality being provided as an understanding of the real-world application domain evolves. This is in sharp contrast to the procedural paradigm which tended to be inflexible and required a good understanding of the entire application domain before the application could be developed.

1.2 Object-Oriented Programming

An object-oriented program consists of a set of objects that collaborate to achieve the objectives of the program. Two objects collaborate when one object requests a service from the other. The service is provided by the object receiving the request, perhaps in collaboration with other objects. The term *client object* will sometimes be used to refer to the object requesting the service and the term *server object* will sometimes be used to refer to the object providing the service. Figure 1.2 shows a client object collaborating with a server object.

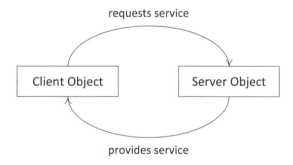

Figure 1.2: Client Object Collaborating with a Server Object

When objects collaborate in an object-oriented program, some objects may be producers of services (server objects) and others may be consumers of services (client objects). However, producer-consumer relationships or client-server relationships are not fixed and the roles may be reversed during the execution of a program. Indeed, an object can be both a service provider and a service consumer.

As an example in the real world, consider a taxi-driver and a banker. A taxi-driver provides a service of transporting a person from one location to another. A banker provides a service of granting loans to persons to purchase things they need. A banker may use the taxi-driver to go from her home to the airport. In this case, the banker is the client and consumes the service provided by the taxi-driver, the server. At some other point in time, the taxi-driver may approach the banker for a loan to purchase a new car for his taxi service. In this case, the taxi-driver is the client and consumes the service provided by the banker, the server. So, the roles of service producer and service consumer are reversed.

Object-oriented programming involves identifying the objects in the real-world problem domain and understanding the relationships between the objects. After this is done, the interactions between objects must be specified. Next, the objects must be implemented in software so that the collaborating objects will provide the functionality required of the application. This book does not cover the process of finding the objects in the real-world problem domain neither does it cover the process of modelling the relationships between objects. Rather, it is a book about writing the code for the collaborating objects in an object-oriented program. Thus, its major concern is to show how to implement objects and their relationships based on established principles and concepts from object-oriented programming.

1.3 Overview of the Book

Since an object-oriented program consists of a community of objects which collaborate to achieve the functionality of the program, the goal of this book is to show how to build this community of collaborating objects using the Java programming language. Figure 1.3 shows a set of objects in an object-oriented application.

Chapter 1: Introduction

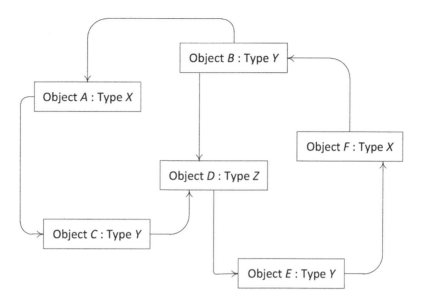

Figure 1.3: Objects Collaborating in an Object-Oriented Application

Figure 1.4 shows how the book is organized. To derive maximum benefit from the book, it should be studied in a sequential manner from the beginning to the end since many concepts must be mastered before moving on to other concepts. The book has been carefully designed to introduce new concepts only after presenting and explaining fully any pre-requisite knowledge and concepts.

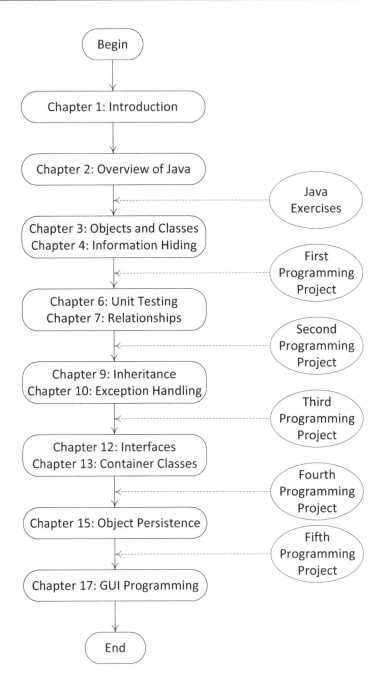

Figure 1.4: Outline of the book

Chapter 1: Introduction

1.3.1 Chapter 2

This book uses Java as the programming language to impart the concepts and principles of object-oriented programming. Thus, before doing anything else, it provides a general overview of the key features of the Java programming language in Chapter 2. It assumes that you already know how to write a program in another programming language. Chapter 2 also contains a number of exercises to get you up to speed with Java as quickly as possible.

1.3.2 Chapters 3 and 4

It is clear from Figure 1.3 that an object is one of the most fundamental concepts in object-oriented programming. The objects in the diagram have different *types*. The types are shown after the colon in each rectangle. For example, the type of object **A** is **X**. There can be more than one object of the same type. For example, the type of object **F** is also **X**. The first object-oriented concept covered in the book is that of objects and their types. The class structure provides a means of creating objects of the same type and this is the subject of Chapter 3.

When objects collaborate with each other, it is important that they don't know too much about each other. Objects that don't know much about other objects are highly desirable from a software development point of view since they can be developed, tested, and debugged in relative isolation from objects of other types. These objects are also easy to reuse in other situations since they don't come with "extra baggage". Thus, an important principle in object-oriented programming is *information hiding* or hiding the internal secrets of an object from other objects. This topic is discussed in Chapter 4. This chapter also shows how to group objects into larger units known as *packages* to promote a more coarse-grained kind of information hiding. In terms of information hiding, a class is something like a house and a package is something like a gated-community.

1.3.3 Chapters 6 and 7

Regardless of the programming paradigm used to develop an application, the application must be tested to ensure that it is fit for use and that it achieves its intended objectives. The object-oriented approach results in the compartmentalization of an application into a set of collaborating objects where the objects know very little about each other. This provides an opportunity to test objects separately from each other. The process can also be automated, ensuring that the testing procedure can be saved and repeated in the future. This type of automated testing is called *unit testing* and can be undertaken using a unit testing framework. Chapter 6 gives a thorough description of testing an object-oriented application using the well-known JUnit testing framework.

In order for two objects to collaborate, they must be related in some way. Looking again at the diagram in Figure 1.3, we see that **A** and **B** are related in some way (because of the connecting line) but **A** and **E** are not related to each other. When two objects are related, it is important to ask the question: how many of one object can be related to the other object? The *relationships* in an object-oriented program are important because they must be implemented correctly in code in order for the program to preserve the relationships which currently exist in the real world. For example, if a customer can hold more than one account in a bank, it is important to choose the right data structures to implement the relationship so that at any point in time we can find all the accounts that belong to a particular customer. Relationships between objects are discussed in detail in Chapter 7.

1.3.4 Chapters 9 and 10

Figure 1.3 shows a set of collaborating objects in an application. An important question that comes to mind is: is it possible to reuse code from one object when developing another object? In the procedural paradigm, functions are often written that can be used in many different modules. It is highly desirable if the features which are programmed for one object can somehow be utilized when writing another object. This is indeed attainable in object-oriented programming; in fact, it is referred to as *inheritance* and is one of the hallmarks of object-oriented programming. Chapter 9 discusses the principle of inheritance and provides detailed examples showing how it is implemented in Java. It also discusses the related topic of *polymorphism*.

When objects are collaborating in an object-oriented program, things can go wrong; unexpected things can happen. An object-oriented program (and indeed, any program) should be able to deal gracefully with the exceptional conditions that can occur while the program is executing. Chapter 10 discusses how to build robust programs using the *exception handling* mechanism in Java. This mechanism allows exception objects to be created and thrown when an error condition occurs. These exception objects can be caught and dealt with by other objects resulting in errors being handled in a graceful manner.

1.3.5 Chapters 12 and 13

Chapter 12 of the book describes one of the most powerful features of object-oriented programming known as an *interface*. An interface allows a group of unrelated objects to be treated in a similar manner which simplifies the writing

Chapter 1: Introduction

of code. The chapter also gives an appreciation of the kinds of polymorphic behavior that are made possible when multiple interfaces are implemented. Interfaces also make it possible to write code to handle objects about which nothing is known, except that they implement the features of an interface. Thus, code can be written in an extensible manner to facilitate future enhancements.

As previously discussed, objects can relate to other objects in many ways. Some objects contain collections of other objects. For example, in a banking application, a bank object can contain thousands of customer objects. A data structure for storing a set of objects is called a *collection*. An important issue in object-oriented programming is how to store the objects in a collection to facilitate the type of access required by the application. The Java *Collections* Framework provides a number of built-in objects that are specially designed to store collections of other objects. These include objects such as linked lists, hash tables, trees, etc. Chapter 13 discusses the Java *Collections* Framework. It also shows how to generalize a collection so that it can store any kind of object using a feature known as *generics*.

1.3.6 Chapter 15

A software application needs to store data in some *persistence medium* so that it is available for future use after the application shuts down. Chapter 15 explains how to store the objects in an object-oriented application in a persistence medium. Three types of persistence are discussed: a text file, a relational database, and Java object serialization. Persistence using a relational database is particularly valuable since databases are widely used by organizations around the world. Additional information on accessing several popular relational databases is available at the book Web site.

1.3.7 Chapter 17

Chapter 3 of the book discusses the idea of an object-oriented application consisting of three layers. These layers are the user interface, the business processing, and data storage layer. Most of the chapters of the book are concerned with the objects in the business processing layer and the data storage layer. To complete the picture of an object-oriented application, the last chapter of the book explains how to develop a *graphical user interface* that interacts with objects from the business processing layer and the data storage layer. Incidentally, building a GUI requires knowledge of the material covered in most of the other chapters of the book. Thus, Chapter 17 takes the opportunity to link together all the important concepts in object-oriented programming covered throughout the book.

1.3.8 Remaining Chapters

There are five other chapters in the book which have not yet been mentioned. These chapters are called "Programming Projects" and they explain how to build a complete object-oriented program based on the material presented in the other chapters. These chapters appear when all the relevant material required for writing the program has been thoroughly discussed in the preceding chapters. Each of the five chapters starts by describing the problem in narrative form. The chapter then gives a detailed definition of the functionality required. Next, the chapter gives a detailed explanation of how the functionality can be implemented using the object-oriented concepts presented earlier in the book. The chapter ends with a complete working Java program that solves the problem described. Often, alternative solutions are presented so that you will realize that there are competing ways to implement an object-oriented program with different trade-offs. Of course, all the source code is available for download from this Web site.

1.4 Java and the Unified Modelling Language

This book discusses object-oriented programming using two languages. One is the programming language, Java. The other is a graphical language known as the *Unified Modelling Language* (UML). The book does not focus exclusively on the Java programming language; rather, Java is used as a vehicle for implementing the object-oriented concepts presented in the book. Thus, it avoids many features of the Java programming language which can detract a beginner from learning object-oriented principles. The book assumes that readers already have experience in writing programs in another programming language (including Java). Chapter 2 of the book provides an overview of the Java programming language so that you can get up to speed with the language as quickly as possible.

In writing an object-oriented program, it is useful to have a visual understanding of the objects that collaborate to provide the functionality of the program. Throughout the book, whenever it is appropriate to illustrate an object-oriented concept, this is done using the symbols and notation of the UML. The UML diagrams show the collaborating objects in an application as well as the relationships between these objects. The diagrams provide sufficient information about the collaborating objects in an application so that you can get a good idea of how the objects will collaborate in the actual program. The UML is a widely used modelling language for object-oriented applications. Although only a small subset of the UML is used in this book, it is enough for you to get a very good understanding of how it can be used as a modelling tool.

1.5 Design Patterns

The book occasionally refers to design patterns, a well-known concept in object-oriented software engineering. A *design pattern* is a reusable solution to a commonly occurring problem in object-oriented software development in a given context. The book does not attempt to cover design patterns in a meaningful way. There are many good books that already do that especially the landmark book on Design Patterns [Gamma et al, 1995]. Occasionally, some of the problems addressed by existing design patterns show up in the book; when they do, a design pattern is presented which can be used to solve the problem. In particular, the book highlights the usefulness of design patterns such as Singleton, Iterator, and Model-View Separation when developing object-oriented applications.

Exercises

1. How is the object-oriented paradigm for software development different from the procedural paradigm?

2. Why is an object-oriented program a closer representation of a real-world problem than a procedural program?

3. Differentiate between a client object and server object in an object-oriented program. Explain why objects can be both producers and consumers of services in the same object-oriented program.

4. What is the Unified Modelling Language (UML)? Why is it an important tool in object-oriented software development?

5. Typical processes in a banking application that would result from using the procedural approach are listed in Section 1.1. Suggest a set of objects that could provide the same functionality in an object-oriented application.

6. A design pattern is a solution to a commonly occurring problem in object-oriented programming (in a given context). How do you think design patterns can be useful to a software developer?

Chapter 2

Overview of the Java Programming Language

This chapter provides a general overview of the key features of the Java programming language. It assumes that you have already been exposed to computer programming and that you know how to write programs in a programming language such as C or Visual Basic®. It does not matter which programming language you know; however, you should be familiar with concepts such as data types, variables, arrays, control structures, and performing input and output.

The chapter starts by explaining how to create, compile, and execute a Java program from within an integrated development environment. It then presents a simple *Hello World* program and gives the steps necessary to create an executable version of this program on your computer. The chapter goes on to describe features such as data types, variables, control structures, and arrays in Java. Numerous examples are given throughout the chapter to reinforce the descriptions. The chapter also contains several exercises carefully designed to get you up and running with Java as quickly as possible. Programming hints and solutions for these exercises can be downloaded from the book Web site.

2.1 Java Development Environment

In order to compile and run a Java program, it is necessary to download the Java compiler and run-time environment. Editing and compiling a Java program can be simplified by using one of the integrated development environments (IDEs) available for Java. These include *JCreator*, *Eclipse*, and *NetBeans*. These IDEs provide facilities for editing, compiling, and running a Java program from within a single environment.

The book Web site provides instructions for installing the Java compiler and run-time environment. It also provides instructions for downloading and installing the three IDEs mentioned above. At the book Web site, you can also get detailed instructions for editing, compiling, and running a Java program in each of the IDEs. The remainder of this chapter assumes that you have installed the Java compiler and run-time environment and that you know how to edit, compile, and run a Java program.

2.2 Hello World

Consider the following Java code:

```java
public class HelloWorld
{
    public static void main(String[] args) {
        System.out.println ("Hello World!");
        System.out.println ("This is my first Java program.");
        System.out.println
            ("Now I am ready for object-oriented programming!");
    }
}
```

The above code comprises a complete Java program[1]. You should type the program in an IDE and save it as `HelloWorld.java`. Note that Java is case sensitive so `HelloWorld.java` is different from `helloworld.java`.

Classes are the building blocks with which all Java programs are built. They are discussed in detail in Chapter 3. Almost everything in a Java program must be inside a class. The name of the class must follow the keyword `class`. In the code above, the name of the class is `HelloWorld`. A class name can have any combination of letters and digits (and a few special characters). However, it must begin with a letter.

The name of the file containing the source code must be the same as the name of the class with the word `.java` appended. For example, the `HelloWorld` class must be saved in the file `HelloWorld.java`.

A Java program consists of one or more classes. One of the classes in the program must contain a `main()` method[2]. The `main()` method is automatically called when the program is executed and serves as the entry point into the program.

---

[1] The term *Java program* is sometimes used in this book to refer to what is formally called a *Java application*.
[2] Classes and methods are discussed in detail in Chapter 3. For the time being, consider a method as a programming feature that is similar to a function.

Chapter 2: Overview of the Java Programming Language

Braces (curly brackets) are used to delineate the parts or blocks in a Java program just like in C or C++. They are similar to the **begin/end** pairs in Pascal and the **Sub/End Sub** pairs in Visual Basic®.

When the `HelloWorld` program is compiled, a file `HelloWorld.class` is produced if compilation is successful. This is the "executable" version of the source code[3]. If compilation is not successful, the compilation error/s will be displayed on one of the screens of the IDE. These errors must be corrected until a successful compilation is obtained.

When the `HelloWorld` program is executed, the following output is generated:

```
Hello World!
This is my first Java program.
Now I am ready for object-oriented programming!
```

The remainder of this chapter will explore features in Java that you are likely to have encountered in some other programming language. Of course, the object-oriented features of Java are covered throughout the book.

2.3 Comments

Comments in Java, like comments in most programming languages, are ignored by the compiler in producing the executable code. The most common way to write a comment is to use `//` for a comment that will span only one line:

```java
System.out.println ("Hi There!");    //this is a one line comment
```

When longer comments are needed, it is more convenient to use the `/*` and `*/` symbols to block off the comment. For example,

```java
/* ---------------------------------------------
   This is a longer comment that spans more than
   one line.
   ---------------------------------------------
*/
```

There is a third kind of comment that can be used to generate source code documentation which is formatted for viewing on a Web browser. This type of

---

[3] The `.class` file is not directly executable on a computer like the `.exe` file generated by a C compiler. It must be interpreted by the Java run-time system.

comment starts with the /** symbol and ends with the */ symbol. More information on this kind of comment is available at the book Web site.

2.4 Primitive Data Types

Java is a *strongly typed language*. This means that every variable must have a declared type. There are eight *primitive* types in Java. Six of them are number types, one is the character type `char`, and one is the `boolean` type for truth values.

The integer types are for numbers without fractional parts. Negative values are allowed. Four integer types are provided: `byte`, `short`, `int`, and `long`. The range of an `int` is just over 2 billion. Bigger integers can be stored in a variable of type `long`. A `byte` requires 1 byte of storage, a `short` 2 bytes, an `int` 4 bytes, and a `long`, 8 bytes.

The floating-point types are used for numbers with fractional parts. There are two floating-point types: `float` and `double`. The range of a `float` is 7 significant digits, and that of a `double` is 15 significant digits. A `float` requires 4 bytes of storage while a `double` requires 8 bytes.

The `char` type uses 2 bytes to store characters represented in the Unicode encoding scheme. Since 16 bits are used to store a character, 2^{16} or 65,536 different characters can be stored in a variable of type `char`. Note that the first 128 characters in Unicode correspond to ASCII characters.

The `boolean` type has two values, `true` and `false`. It can be used for flags which keep track of `true`/`false` conditions. It can also be used for storing the results of logical expressions.

Table 2.1 lists the primitive types in Java.

Chapter 2: Overview of the Java Programming Language

Name of Type	Data Stored	Size	Range of Values
byte	An integer	1 byte	-128 to 127
short	An integer	2 bytes	-32,768 to 32,767
int	An integer	4 bytes	-2,147,483,648 to 2,147,483,647 (-2^{31} to $2^{31} - 1$)
long	An integer	8 bytes	-2^{63} to $2^{63} - 1$
float	A floating point number	4 bytes	Single-precision 32-bit floating point
double	A floating point number	8 bytes	Double-precision 64-bit floating point
char	A single Unicode character	2 bytes	0 to 65,535
boolean	A Boolean value	Is not precisely defined by the Java specification	true, false

Table 2.1: Primitive Types in Java

2.5 Variables

To declare a variable, the type of the variable must be written first followed by the name of the variable. A variable name must begin with a letter and can be a sequence of letters or digits. Declarations can be placed anywhere in a block of Java code. Here are some examples:

```
int anIntegerVariable;      // declares an integer variable
long aLongVariable;         // declares a long variable
char ch;                    // declares a character variable
float aFraction;            // declares a float variable
int x, y, z;                // declares several variables at once
```

2.6 Assignments and Initialisations

Assigning a value to a variable is done in the normal way in Java. For example,

```
anIntegerVariable = 56;     // assigns 56 to anIntegerVariable
ch = 'Y';                   // assigns 'Y' to ch
```

In Java, it is possible to declare and initialise a variable on the same line. For example,

```
int i = 10;
char ch = '@';
```

2.7 Operators and Expressions

This section describes the arithmetic operators in Java and shows how to form arithmetic expressions with them. It also describes the comparison and logical operators in Java and shows how to form Boolean expressions with them.

2.7.1 Arithmetic Operators

The usual arithmetic operators + - * / are used in Java for addition, subtraction, multiplication, and division. The / operator denotes integer division if both operands are integers.

Arithmetic expressions are formed by combining literals, variables, and other arithmetic expressions with arithmetic operators. The following are some examples of arithmetic expressions:

```
x + 1
(x - y) * 3
(9.0 * celcius) / 5.0 + 32.0
```

Arithmetic expressions can be used to assign values to variables. For example,

```
x = x + 1;
z = (x - y) * 3;
fahrenheit = (9.0 * celcius) / 5.0 + 32.0;
```

Java provides a shortcut for using arithmetic operators in an assignment statement. For example,

```
x += 4;                    // equivalent to x = x + 4
y -= 1;                    // equivalent to y = y - 1
```

When using the shortcut, the arithmetic operator should be placed to the left of the = sign.

Java provides an operator for integer remainder (also known as the *modulus* operator); it is denoted by %. To find the remainder when 14 is divided by 5, the modulus operator can be used:

```
x = 14 % 5;                // x is 4 after modulus operation
```

Chapter 2: Overview of the Java Programming Language

Java has no operator for exponentiation—the built-in `pow()` function in the `Math` library should be used for this purpose. For example,

```
y = Math.pow (x, 5.0);     // y is x raised to the power of 5.0
```

Java has both increment and decrement operators: `x++` adds one to the current value of the variable `x`, and `x--` subtracts one from it. For example,

```
int n = 7;        // n is assigned the value 7
n++;              // n now has the value 8
```

2.7.2 Comparison Operators

Comparison operators are used to compare two values. A comparison operator can be used to form a Boolean expression. A *Boolean expression* is an expression which evaluates to either `true` or `false`. Table 2.2 lists the comparison operators in Java and gives some Boolean expressions formed with them. The Boolean expressions in Table 2.2 only contain literals such as 3, 4 and 5. However, a Boolean expression can contain literals as well as variables and arithmetic expressions. For example,

```
(b * b >= 4 * a * c)       // to determine if equation has real roots
```

Comparison Operator	Java Symbol	Boolean Expression	Evaluates To
Less than	<	(3 < 4)	True
Greater than	>	(5 > 5)	False
Equal to	==	(3 == 4)	False
Not equal to	!=	(3 != 5)	True
Less than or equal to	<=	(5 <= 5)	True
Greater than or equal to	>=	(3 >= 4)	False

Table 2.2: Comparison Operators

2.7.3 Logical Operators

Logical operators operate on Boolean values and Boolean expressions. Like comparison operators, logical operators can be used to form Boolean expressions. Table 2.3 lists the three logical operators in Java and gives some Boolean expressions formed with them.

Logical Operator	Java Symbol	Boolean Expression	Evaluates To
And	&&	(3 < 4 && 5 <= 5)	True
Or	||	(5 < 5 || 4 == 5)	False
Not	!	(!(3 == 4))	True

Table 2.3: Logical Operators

An expression with the *and* operator evaluates to `true` if both operands are `true`. An expression with the *or* operator evaluates to `true` if at least one of its operands is `true`. An expression with the *not* operator evaluates to `true` if its operand is `false`; it evaluates to `false` if its operand is `true`.

2.8 Strings

Strings are sequences of characters such as "Hello World". Java does not have a built-in string type. However, the standard Java library contains a predefined *class* called `String`. A variable of type `String` can be declared as follows:

```
String greeting;
```

A variable of type `String` can be used like a primitive type. For example, it can be assigned a value as follows:

```
greeting = "Hello";    // greeting is assigned the string "Hello"
```

Two strings can be concatenated using the + operator. For example,

```
String firstName, lastName, name;

firstName = "John";    // firstName is assigned the string "John"
lastName = "Doe";      // lastName is assigned the string "Doe"

name = firstName + " " + lastName;
                       // firstName is concatenated with lastName
```

After the concatenation operation, the `name` string has the value "John Doe".

The `String` class has several useful methods which can be called to find out information about a string and to manipulate it in various ways. Table 2.4 lists some methods of the `String` class.

Chapter 2: Overview of the Java Programming Language

Method	Description
length()	Returns the number of characters in the given string.
isEmpty()	Returns **true** if the length of the given string is zero.
substring(startIndex, endIndex)	Returns a string that is a substring of the given string (from `startIndex` to `endIndex-1`).
toCharArray()	Returns an array of characters corresponding to the given string.
equals(anotherString)	Returns `true` if `anotherString` is exactly the same as the given string and `false` otherwise.
equalsIgnoreCase(anotherString)	Returns `true` if `anotherString` is the same as the given string, ignoring case considerations; returns `false` otherwise.
toLowerCase()	Returns a new string which consists of the characters in the given string in lower case.
toUpperCase()	Returns a new string which consists of the characters in the given string in upper case.

Table 2.4: Some Useful Methods of the `String` Class

To use the methods in Table 2.4, the name of the variable containing the string must be written first, followed by a dot ("."), followed by the method name and the argument list. For example, to find out the length of the `greeting` string, the `length()` method can be used as follows:

```
int length = greeting.length();
            // length is 5 since greeting is "Hello"
```

To extract a substring from a larger string, the `substring()` method can be used as follows:

```
String telephone = "1-868-123-4567";
String countryCode = telephone.substring(2, 5);
            // countryCode is "868"
```

The first argument of the `substring()` method specifies the starting index from which characters are extracted. The second argument specifies the index *one beyond* the last character to be extracted. Note that 0 is the index of the first character in the string.

To test two strings for equality, the `equals()` method should be used instead of the `==` operator. For example, the following Boolean expression can be used to check if the `countryCode` is 876:

```
(countryCode.equals("876"))
```

To test if two strings are identical except for the upper case/lower case distinction, the `equalsIgnoreCase()` method should be used. For example, if `greeting` is "Hello", "HELLO", "hello", etc., the following Boolean expression evaluates to `true`:

```
(greeting.equalsIgnoreCase("Hello"))
```

2.9 Input and Output

2.9.1 Output using `System.out`

For console-based programs, the `System.out.println()` method can be used to display output on the console. The output is sent to the terminal or to one of the windows in an IDE. Any type of variable can be printed using the `System.out.println()` method. For example,

```
int x = 43;
boolean flag = true;

System.out.println (x);
System.out.println (flag);
```

The output of the above statements is:

```
43
true
```

The variable to be printed can be concatenated with a string to produce more descriptive output as follows:

```
System.out.println ("x = " + x);
System.out.println ("Flag is: " + flag);
```

The output of the above statements now becomes:

Chapter 2: Overview of the Java Programming Language

```
x = 43
Flag is: true
```

Note that `System.out.println()` positions the output cursor to the beginning of a new line after its output has been printed. To print output without advancing the output cursor to a new line, the `System.out.print()` method can be used.

2.9.2 Formatted Output with `System.out`

In the C programming language, the `printf()` function is used with various format strings to control the appearance of output on a console. A similar approach can be taken in Java using the `System.out.printf()` method. For example,

```
int number = 10;
double balance = 2000.00;
String owner = "John Doe";

System.out.printf ("Account Number: %5d ", number);
          // 5 spaces allocated for number

System.out.printf ("Balance: %8.2f ", balance);
          // 8 spaces allocated for balance (2 d.p.)

System.out.printf ("Account Holder: %s\n", owner);
          // prints a string followed by a new line
```

The first argument of the `System.out.printf()` statement is referred to as a *format string*. A format string can contain plain text and/or format specifiers such "%8.2f" (meaning that the variable will be printed with a field width of 8 characters in which two decimal places are reserved for the fractional part). If the actual value of a variable requires fewer characters than the field width, it is padded to left with spaces. The code above generates the following output:

```
Account Number:    10 Balance:  2000.00 Account Holder: John Doe
```

Format strings are beyond the scope of this chapter. You can consult the Java documentation or a C reference for more information.

2.9.3 Input using the Scanner Class

One way to obtain user input from the keyboard is to use the built-in Scanner class. To indicate that this class will be used, the first line of the source file must contain the following statement:

```
import java.util.Scanner;
          // required in order to use Scanner class
```

To use the Scanner class for input, a Scanner object must first be created as follows:

```
Scanner scanner = new Scanner(System.in);
```

Next, methods from the Scanner class must be used to read specific types of data from the keyboard such as integer values and double values. For example, nextInt(), nextDouble(), and next() must be used to read an integer, a double, and a string from the keyboard, respectively.

The following program uses the Scanner class to obtain three values entered by the user at the keyboard (an integer, a double, and a string):

```
import java.util.Scanner;
          // required in order to use Scanner class

public class Input
{
   public static void main(String[] args) {
      int number;
      double balance;
      String owner;

      Scanner scanner = new Scanner(System.in);
             // create Scanner object to input data

      System.out.print ("Please enter the account number: ");
      number = scanner.nextInt();
             // obtain an integer from keyboard input

      System.out.print ("Please enter the account balance: ");
      balance = scanner.nextDouble();
             // obtain a double from keyboard input

      System.out.print
          ("Please enter the name of the account holder: ");
```

Chapter 2: Overview of the Java Programming Language

```
        owner = scanner.next();
            // obtain a string from keyboard input

        System.out.println ("Account Number: " + number);
        System.out.println ("Balance: " + balance);
        System.out.println ("Account Holder: " + owner);
    }
}
```

It is also possible to use the `Scanner` class to read data from a file. However, this is beyond the scope of this chapter.

2.10 Control Structures

2.10.1 Conditional Statements

The general form of the conditional statement in Java is:

> *if (condition)*
>   *{ block1 }*
> *else*
>   *{ block2 };*

where *block1* and *block2* contain one or more statements, enclosed in braces. If there is only one statement in a block, it is easier to write that statement without braces, followed by a semicolon. The `else` part is optional; if it is used, it may itself contain nested `if` statements. Note that the condition is written as a Boolean expression.

An `if-then-else` statement to find the maximum of two values `x` and `y` is given below:

```
if (x > y)
   max = x;
else
   max = y;
```

For multiple selections with many alternatives, a `switch` statement is available. The type of the selection variable for the `switch` statement is normally `byte`, `short`, `int`, or `char`. However, a recent release of Java allows the selection variable to be of type `String`.

An example of a `switch` statement is given below:

```java
Scanner scanner = new Scanner(System.in);

System.out.print ("Please enter the discount code: ");
int discountCode = scanner.nextInt();

double discount;

switch (discountCode)
{
   case 636:
      discount = 15.0;
      break;

   case 662:
      discount = 20.0;
      break;

   case 672: case 673:
      discount = 25.0;
      break;

   default:
      discount = 10.0;
      break;
}
```

The body of a **switch** statement is called the **switch** block. A statement in the **switch** block can be labeled with a **case** label. The **switch** statement evaluates its expression (the value of **discountCode** in the example above) and then executes the statements that follow the matching **case** label. For example, if the **discountCode** is 636, the **discount** is set to 15.0 percent.

Note that each **case** section must conclude with a **break** statement; otherwise execution of the statements in a matching case label will flow (or fall through) into the next **case** section even if the **case** label of this latter section does not match.

The **default** section is the last section of the case statement and handles all values that are not explicitly handled by one of the **case** sections. For example, a **discountCode** of 681 would end up in the **default** section, resulting in the **discount** being set to 10.0 percent.

Chapter 2: Overview of the Java Programming Language

Finally, it should be mentioned that a statement in the `switch` block can be labeled with more than one case label (e.g., 672 and 673 in the example above). Thus, the `discount` is set to 25.0 percent if the `discountCode` is 672 or 673.

2.10.2 Repetition

For determinate looping, Java provides a for loop. An example of its use is:

```
for (int i=1; i<=10; i++)
   System.out.println (i);   // can be a block enclosed with braces
```

The first slot of the `for` statement (`i=1`) initializes the loop control variable, `i`. The second slot (`i<=10`) specifies the condition that must be true for the loop to continue executing. The third slot (`i++`) is an expression for changing the loop control variable on each iteration of the loop.

For indeterminate looping, the `while` loop statement is provided. The general form is:

> *while (condition)*
> *{ block };*

The `while` loop version of the `for` loop above can be written as follows:

```
int i = 1;
while (i <= 10) {
   System.out.println (i);
   i++;
}
```

To ensure that the block is executed at least once, the `do` version of the `while` loop can be used:

> *do*
> *{ block }*
> *while (condition);*

For example, the `do while` version of the `while` loop above is:

```
int i = 1;
do {
   System.out.println (i);
   i++;
} while (i <= 10);
```

2.11 Arrays

Arrays in Java are different from arrays in other programming languages. Three steps are required to create and use an array: declaration, creation, and initialization. To *declare* an array of type `int`, the following syntax should be used:

```
int[] arrayOfInt;        // declares array variable of type int
```

The square brackets after the type `int` declares that `arrayOfInt` is an *array variable* of type `int`. Arrays of the other primitive types can be declared in a similar fashion. To actually *create* the array, the `new` keyword should be used. The follow statement creates the array to hold 100 integer quantities and assigns it to the array variable:

```
arrayOfInt = new int[100];   // creates an array of 100 integers
```

Once the array is assigned to the array variable, the array variable can be treated exactly like an array declared in another programming language. If the array consists of *n* elements, the first element is in location 0 and the last element is in location (*n-1*), similar to an array in C. In the example above, the first element of the array is `arrayOfInt[0]`, and the last element is `arrayOfInt[99]`.

An interesting feature in Java is the ability to create a new array while the program is executing and assign it to an array variable which already "contains" an array. This makes it seem as if the array has been re-sized. For example,

```
arrayOfInt = new int[1000]; // creates a new array of 1000 integers
```

When the above statement is executed, the original array is lost. However, `arrayOfInt` can now store 1000 integers instead of 100.

A `for` loop is commonly used to initialize an array. For example,

```
for (int i=0; i<100; i++)
   arrayOfInt[i] = 0;
```

To find out the size of an array, the `length` *attribute* of the array can be used as follows:

```
int length = arrayOfInt.length;
                   // size is 100
                   // NB: there are no brackets after length
```

Chapter 2: Overview of the Java Programming Language

It should be noted that the `length` attribute gives the capacity of the array, not the amount of elements that are currently stored. To find out how many elements are currently stored, the program must maintain a count in a separate variable. This variable must be updated accordingly when elements are added to or deleted from the array.

If an array is completely filled, a version of the `for` statement (known as the *foreach* statement) can be used to access all the elements, one at a time. For example,

```
sum = 0;
for (int i: arrayOfInt)
   sum = sum + i;
```

The above code goes through each element `i` in the array and adds its value to `sum`. So, at the end of the loop, `sum` is the total of all the elements in `arrayOfInt`.

Java has a shorthand way to declare, create, and initialize an array at the same time. For example,

```
int[] discountCodes = {636, 662, 672, 673, 681, 682, 725, 727};
```

The above statement causes the `discountCodes` array to be created consisting of 8 elements. The first element of the array is 636 and the last element is 727.

Two-dimensional arrays can also be used in Java. A two-dimensional array can be declared and created as follows:

```
double[][] matrix = new double[5][6];
               // matrix has 5 rows and 6 columns
```

It is possible to have arrays of objects (i.e., non-primitive types). These types of arrays are discussed in different parts of the book such as in Chapter 3.

Exercises

1. Monica wants to buy a new car. She has saved up a certain amount of money for this purpose but needs to borrow the remaining money from a bank (the principal, p) for a certain number of years (the time, t) at a certain interest rate (the rate, r). The bank will charge Monica interest on the loan using the formula for simple interest:

$$Interest = (p * r * t) / 100$$

The interest calculated is added to the principal and Monica will have to repay the total amount of money in equal monthly installments over the period of the loan.

Write a program that inputs p, r, and t from the user and calculates the interest that will be charged on the loan. Your program should also calculate the monthly installment that Monica will have to pay.

2. Instead of buying a new car, Monica prefers to use public transportation and invest her money in the bank. The bank is offering her an interest rate of r if she invests her money for a certain number of years, t. Interest will be paid on a monthly basis and compounded.

Write a program that inputs the principal amount invested (p), the interest rate (r) and the time in years (t) from the user and calculates the total value of Monica's investment after t years. Use the following formula for compound interest:

$$\text{Value of investment after } t \text{ years} = p * [1 + (r / 100) / 12]^{12 * t}$$

NB: You will need to use the `Math.pow()` function to calculate the exponent, $12 * t$.

3. Write a program which accepts a student's mark for a course in the range 0 to 100 and calculates the student's grade according to the following scheme:

```
67- 100:    A
60 - 66:    B+
50 - 59:    B
43 - 49:    C
40 - 42:    D
0 - 39:     Fail
```

Your program should generate an error message if the mark is outside the range.

4. Write a program that accepts as input three integer values representing three angles in degrees, and determines if the angles form a triangle. If the angles form a triangle, the type of triangle is determined based on the following categories:

Chapter 2: Overview of the Java Programming Language

> Equilateral: Three angles are the same
> Isosceles: Two angles are the same
> Scalene: No angles are the same

NB: Three angles form a triangle if their sum is equal to 180 degrees.

5. A leap year is one that is:

   - evenly divisible by 400 or
   - evenly divisible by four and not evenly divisible by 100

   For example, the year 2000 was a leap year since 2000 is evenly divisible by 400. Similarly, the year 2012 was a leap year since 2012 is evenly divisible by four but not by 100. However, the year 2100 will not be a leap year since it does not satisfy any of the two conditions above.

   Write a program that accepts an integer *year* as input and determines if *year* is a leap year.

6. Write a program that accepts as input an integer *year* and an integer *month* in the range 1 to 12 and prints out the name of the month and the number of days in the month. You must cater for leap years.

   Hint: It is easier to use a **switch** statement instead of a series of nested **if** statements.

7. (a) Write a program that accepts as input two integers *m* and *n* and prints a table of squares from *m* to *n* using a **for** loop. For example, if *m* is 2 and *n* is 5, the table should be:

   ```
   Number     Number Squared
   ======     ==============
   2          4
   3          9
   4          16
   5          25
   ```

   (b) Modify the program in 7(a) to print the table of squares in reverse order from *n* down to *m*, skipping every other number.

   (c) Write the program in 7(a) using a **while** loop and a **do while** loop.

8. A certain tank has w litres of water. A fixed *percentage* of water, p, is taken out from the tank each day. Write a program that accepts as input w and p, and starting from the first day, displays the number of the day, the amount of water taken out on that day, and the amount of water remaining in the tank at the end of that day. Your program should stop after 30 days have been displayed or when the amount of water remaining is less than 100 litres, whichever comes first.

   For example, if $w = 1000$, and $p = 10$, the output should start as follows:

DAY	AMT TAKEN	AMT REMAINING
===	=========	=============
1	100.00	900.00
2	90.00	810.00
3	81.00	729.00
4	72.90	656.10

9. Write a program that inputs a set of student marks in an array and then finds the maximum, minimum and average of the set of marks. Your program should also find the amount of marks that were greater than or equal to the average mark.

   The marks must be entered at the keyboard. The number of marks is not known beforehand but input is terminated with a mark of -1. Assume that the marks are in the range 0 to 100.

10. A string is a *palindrome* if it is spelled the same way forwards and backwards. Some examples of string palindromes are: "radar", "able was i ere i saw elba", and "a man a plan a canal panama". Write a program that accepts as input a string s and determines if s is a palindrome. You should ignore spaces in the string during input.

    Hint: Use a variable s of type **String** to store the string entered by the user. Next, convert s into an array of characters which can then be examined to find out if the characters form a palindrome. To convert s into an array of characters, use the following code:

    ```
    char[] stringChars = s.toCharArray();
                // stringChars is an array of characters
                // corresponding to the input string
    ```

Chapter 3

Objects and Classes

In object-oriented programming, the principal modeling element is an *object*. An object is a distinct entity with a current state and a well-defined bevaviour. Objects are created from classes; thus, a *class* is a template for creating objects of the same type. This chapter explains how to write classes and how to create objects from these classes. It uses the concept of an account in a banking application to show how classes are written and how objects can be created and manipulated.

3.1 Understanding Classes

In object-oriented programming, a class is a template for creating objects of the same type. A class has a set of properties called *attributes*. Individual objects of the class have different values for the attributes. A class also defines a set of *behaviors* that are common to all members of the class. This section describes the attributes and behaviors of a class and shows how they are implemented in Java.

3.1.1 Representing State with Attributes

Attributes are properties of an object. They are used to store data about an object. The *state* of an object is the set of values for each of its attributes. Attributes are usually given noun-like names such as `number`, `balance`, `firstName`, `address`, etc. Attributes have types since the data they represent have types such as `int`, `double`, `String`, etc.

Consider an `Account` object in a banking application. This object will have attributes such as the following:

- **number**: a number which uniquely identifies the given `Account` object (an `int` value which serves as the *primary key*)

- `balance`: the current balance in the `Account` (a `double` value)

Attributes are usually given names that match the purpose they serve in an application. It is common to give names that closely match the real-world concepts being represented. Unintuitive or abbreviated names which are hard to decipher are generally not recommended since they are not considered good programming style.

The two attributes of an `Account` object can be declared as follows:

```
int number;          // number attribute is of type int
double balance;      // balance attribute is of type double
```

3.1.2 Implementing Behaviors with Methods

An object has a set of behaviors. A *behavior* is a particular action or task that the object performs. A behavior depends on the current state of the object and will often result in the modification of that state. Behaviors are implemented by methods. A *method* is like a *function* of procedural programming languages and causes a certain action or operation to take place. A method usually has a verb-like name since it represents a particular task being done.

A method can be regarded as a *service* provided by an object. The object providing the service can be referred to as a *service provider* or *server object*. The object requesting the service can be referred to as a *service consumer* or a *client object*. A service can be requested by calling or invoking the corresponding method on the server object, sending any arguments that are required to provide the service.

Five behaviors of an `Account` object are listed in Table 3.1.

Behavior	Description
Deposit	Deposits a certain amount of money to an account.
Withdraw	Withdraws a certain amount of money from an account.
Set Number	Changes the account number of an account.
Get Balance	Finds out what is the balance in an account.
To String	Gives a string representation of the information available on an account.

Table 3.1: Five Behaviors of an `Account` Object

The code below shows how each of the behaviors listed in Table 3.1 can be implemented as a method in Java.

Chapter 3: Objects and Classes

```java
public void deposit(double amount) {           // Deposit behavior
   balance = balance + amount;
}

public void withdraw(double amount) {          // Withdraw behavior
   if (balance >= amount)
      balance = balance - amount;
}

public void setNumber(int n) {                 // Set Number behavior
   number = n;
}

public double getBalance() {                   // Get Balance behavior
   return balance;
}

public String toString() {                     // To String behavior
   String s;

   s = "Number: " + number + " Balance: " + balance;
   return s;
}
```

As can be observed from the code, the methods of an `Account` object can access the attributes of the object and can read and/or update the values of these attributes depending on their specific behaviors.

3.1.3 Creating a Class

A *class* is something like a template from which "real" objects are created. Thus, it is not really something tangible. An analogy is the pans that are used for baking. If it is shaped a certain way, all the cakes take on the shape of the pan. Thus, all the objects of the same class have the same set of attributes and the same set of behaviors. It is the combination of attribute values of an object which gives each object its state and differentiates objects from each other. It is not possible for an object to "leave out" an attribute of the class (though it is possible to not assign a value to the attribute in question). An object of a class is also referred to as an *instance* of the class.

In Java, the *class* structure combines the attributes and behaviors of an object into one unit. So, the attributes and methods described above can be combined together in an `Account` class as follows:

```java
public class Account
{
   // declaration of attributes

   int number;
   double balance;

   // declaration and definition of methods

   public void deposit(double amount) {
      balance = balance + amount;
   }

   public void withdraw(double amount) {
      if (balance >= amount)
         balance = balance - amount;
   }

   public void setNumber(int n) {
      number = n;
   }

   public double getBalance() {
      return balance;
   }

   public String toString() {
      String s;

      s = "Number: " + number + " Balance: " + balance;
      return s;
   }
}
```

The keyword `public` used in the code above is referred to as an *access modifier*. Access modifiers are used to restrict access to the features of an object; they are discussed in more detail in Chapter 4. The `public` access modifier is used before a class declaration to specify that the class as a whole can be accessed by objects of any other class. This implies that objects of other classes can create and manipulate objects of the class whenever they require. The `public` access modifier is used before a method declaration to specify that the method can be invoked by an object of any other class.

Chapter 3: Objects and Classes

As mentioned in Chapter 2, the file containing the source code for a class must have the same name as the name of the class, with the keyword `.java` appended. Thus, the file containing the `Account` class must be called `Account.java`. When `Account.java` is compiled, the `Account.class` file is produced if there are no compilation errors. If there are compilation errors, these must be fixed before the `Account.class` file is produced. Note that the `Account.class` file cannot be executed on its own since it does not contain a `main()` method.

It should be noted that the development of an object-oriented program is usually an incremental process. It is not necessary to write the code for all the methods of a class before compiling and testing the source code. A class can actually compile successfully with no attributes and no methods! So, if you are now starting out with object-oriented programming, you will find it very useful to write the code for methods incrementally as your understanding of the problem grows.

3.2 UML Notation for a Class

The UML notation for a class is a diagram consisting of three components. The top component is reserved for the name of the class. The middle component is used for the attributes of the class (with type specifiers if necessary). The bottom component is used to list the methods of the class. Figure 3.1 is a UML diagram of the `Account` class containing the attributes and methods discussed so far in this chapter.

The attribute component or the method component of a class may be left empty if the list of attributes or methods is not of interest at the moment. In addition, a single rectangle containing only the name of the class can be used to represent a class if there is no interest at the moment on attributes and methods. These variations of the UML diagram of the `Account` class are shown in Figure 3.2. The four types of UML diagrams shown in Figure 3.1 and Figure 3.2 will be used throughout the book to represent a class.

It should be noted that the UML supports the specification of primitive data types as well as user-defined types, just like in Java and other object-oriented programming languages. Each primitive type is named as a complete word in English, beginning with an upper case letter; for example, `Integer`, `Double`, `Boolean`, etc. The type of an element such as an attribute, a parameter name, or a return value of a method is specified *after* the name of the element. Types can be omitted from a UML diagram in the interest of space or if the information provided does not add significant value to the diagram.

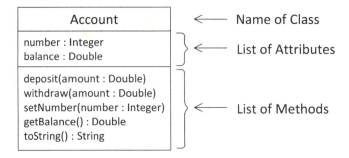

Figure 3.1: UML Diagram of **Account** Class

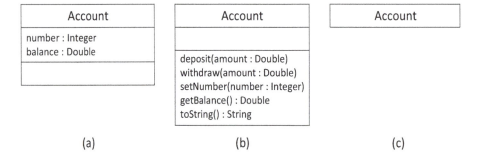

Figure 3.2: Variations of UML Diagram of **Account** Class (a) Methods are omitted (b) Attributes are omitted (c) Both methods and attributes are omitted

3.3 Creating and Manipulating Instances of a Class

This section shows how to create and manipulate instances of a class. In particular, it shows how to create **Account** objects and how to invoke methods on the **Account** objects. It uses various diagrams to show how client code modifies the state of an object in memory.

3.3.1 Creating and Manipulating Objects

In order to use the services of an object, an instance of the class must first be created. This is referred to as *instantiating* the class. An instance or object of the class can be created using the **new** keyword, followed by the name of the class,

Chapter 3: Objects and Classes

followed by a pair of parentheses. For example, to create an instance of the `Account` class, the following code can be used:

```
new Account();
```

This statement creates an `Account` object in memory. However, the object is lost immediately since there is no way to refer to the object just created. Thus, there is need for a variable which can refer to the object in memory. This variable is called an *object variable* and it holds a reference to an actual object in memory. (One can think of an object variable as containing the memory address of the created object.)

An object variable must be declared to be of the same type as the object to which it will refer. So, if an object variable is required to refer to an `Account` object, it must be declared to be of type `Account`:

```
Account a;          // a is an object variable of type Account
```

This statement declares `a` to be an object variable that will refer to a specific `Account` object. While the program is executing, `a` can refer to different `Account` objects. However, at any point in time, `a` can refer to at most one `Account` object. If `a` does not currently refer to a specific `Account` object, it should be set to `null` as follows:

```
a = null;
```

To assign a newly created `Account` object to `a`, the following code should be used:

```
a = new Account();
```

Once an object variable contains a reference to an instance of a class, services can be requested from that instance using method invocations on the object variable. Services are requested by specifying the name of the object variable, followed by a dot, followed by the name of the method, followed by a list of arguments (if any). For example, a client object can request the following services from the `Account` object, `a`:

Line 1:
```
a.setNumber(10);     // give the newly created account a number
```

Line 2:
```
a.deposit(1000.00);  // deposit $1000.00 to the account
```

Line 3:
```
System.out.println(a.toString());
                // display contents of the account
```

Note that arguments must be supplied by the client object in Lines 1 and 2. The `toString()` method does not have any parameters so the argument list is empty.

Requesting a service from `a` when it does not currently refer to any object (i.e., `a` is `null`) results in a serious programming error. The compiler is sometimes able to detect this situation before it occurs. However, if it occurs at run-time, Java generates a `NullPointerException` and halts the program. Thus, it is important to ensure that object variables are not `null` (i.e., they refer to valid objects in memory) before requesting a service.

Throughout the book, whenever an object variable is used in the text, it refers to either the actual declared variable (e.g., `a` above) or to the object referred to by the object variable. The meaning will be clear from the context in which the object variable is used.

3.3.2 A Client Class

The code given in the previous sub-section is referred to as client code since it uses the services of the `Account` class. The client code can be written in another class, `BankApplication`. The code for the `BankApplication` class is given below:

```
public class BankApplication
{
   public static void main(String[] args) {

      Account a;       // declare object variable

      a = new Account();
                // let a refer to object created

      a.setNumber(10);
                // give the newly created account a number

      a.deposit(1000.00);
                // deposit $1000.00 to the account

      System.out.println(a.toString());
                // display contents of the account
```

Chapter 3: Objects and Classes

```
   }
}
```

The `BankApplication` class must be saved in the file `BankApplication.java`. After compilation, the `BankApplication.class` file is produced. The `BankApplication` class *uses* the `Account` class since it creates an instance of the `Account` class and then proceeds to request services (invoke methods) from the instance. Thus, we now have a complete program where the functionality is achieved through the collaboration of two classes, `BankApplication` and `Account`. The program is available for download at the book Web site.

When the program is run, the following output is produced (generated from the `toString()` method of `a`):

```
Number: 10 Balance: 1000.0
```

3.3.3 Objects in Memory

The state of memory before the `BankApplication` program terminates is shown in Figure 3.3 (note that this is a variation of an actual UML diagram). The diagram shows that the object variable `a` refers to an instance of `Account` where the `number` attribute has the value 10 and the `balance` attribute has the value $1000.00.

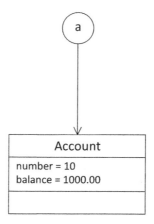

Figure 3.3: An Object Variable Referring to an Instance of `Account`

Suppose that the client code in `BankApplication` is extended to include code which creates another `Account` object and then proceeds to invoke methods on this object:

```
Account a2;                    // declare another object variable, a2

a2 = new Account();            // let a2 refer to object created
a2.setNumber(20);              // give the newly created account a number
a2.deposit(2000.00);           // deposit $2000.00 to the account
System.out.println(a2.toString());
                               // display contents of the account
```

When the program is run, the following output is produced:

```
Number: 10 Balance: 1000.0
Number: 20 Balance: 2000.0
```

The situation in memory before the program terminates is as follows. There are now two object variables, a and a2. a refers to one Account object in memory where the number attribute is 10 and the balance attribute is $1000.00. a2 refers to another Account object in memory where the number attribute is 20 and the balance attribute is $2000.00. The state of memory is shown in Figure 3.4.

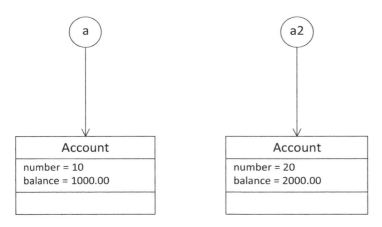

Figure 3.4: Two Object Variables Referring to Two Account Instances

So, there are two physical objects in memory, each one having its own state as determined by the values of its attributes. Each object will act independently of the other when services are requested of them. For example, consider the following code in a client:

```
a.withdraw(500.00);            // withdraw $500.00 from account #10
a2.withdraw(500.00);           // withdraw $500.00 from account #20
System.out.println(a.toString());
                               // display contents of account #10
```

Chapter 3: Objects and Classes

```
System.out.println(a2.toString());
                        // display contents of account #20
```

The output generated from the above statements is as follows:

```
Number: 10 Balance: 500.0
Number: 20 Balance: 1500.0
```

When the **withdraw()** method is invoked on **a**, the withdrawal is successful and its **balance** is updated to $500.00 since its initial **balance** was $1000.00. However, when the **withdraw()** method is invoked on *a2*, its **balance** is updated to $1500.00 since its initial **balance** was $2000.00. Thus, even though the same **withdraw()** request was made of the two **Account** objects, the end result was different since the state of the objects was different. The state of the **Account** objects after the withdrawal is shown in Figure 3.5.

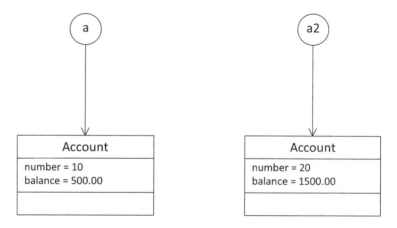

Figure 3.5: **Account** Objects after Withdrawal of $500.00

The behavior of individual objects in response to the same **withdraw()** request can be different as well. Consider the following code, given the state of the **Account** objects shown in Figure 3.5:

```
a.withdraw(600.00);         // withdraw $600.00 from account #10
a2.withdraw(600.00);        // withdraw $600.00 from account #20
System.out.println(a.toString());
                        // display contents of account #10
System.out.println(a2.toString());
                        // display contents of account #20
```

The output generated from the above statements is as follows:

```
Number: 10 Balance: 500.0
Number: 20 Balance: 900.0
```

The state of memory after the code is executed in shown in Figure 3.6.

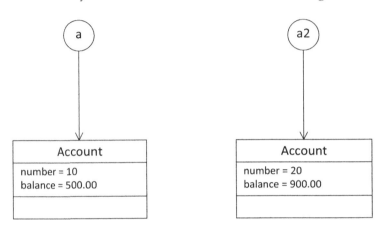

Figure 3.6: `Account` Objects after Withdrawal of Additional $600.00

Notice that the **balance** of **a** is unchanged. This is because the withdrawal amount is greater than the **balance** so the withdrawal did not take place. However, withdrawal of the $600.00 from **a2** is successful and its **balance** is updated to $900.00. This shows that different objects of the same class can behave differently when asked to do the same thing for a client since behaviors are governed by the state of an object. This is a key concept in object-oriented programming.

3.3.4 Assigning One Object Variable to Another

Consider what happens when we assign one object variable to another. For example,

```
a2 = a;
```

Assigning **a** to **a2** causes **a2** to have the same value as **a**. Thus, **a2** will now refer to the same object in memory as **a**. This is shown in Figure 3.7. It is important to note that assigning **a** to **a2** does not create a copy of the object referred to by **a**; only the object variable is copied.

Chapter 3: Objects and Classes

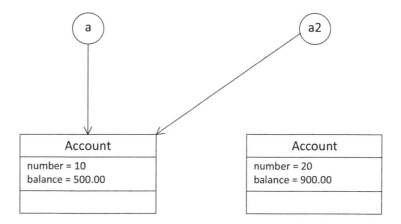

Figure 3.7: Both Object Variables Refer to the Same Object

If a method is invoked on either **a** or **a2**, the effect is the same since the same object in memory is being manipulated.

Eventually, the object formerly referred to by **a2** will be removed from the memory space of the application (by something known as the Java *garbage collector*) if there is no other object variable that refers to it.

3.4 Constructor Methods

A *constructor method* is a method that is used to initialize the attributes of an object after it has been created with the **new** keyword. The following is a constructor method for the **Account** class:

```
public Account(int n, double b) {
   number = n;
   balance = b;
}
```

Constructor methods always carry the same name as the class for which they are written (and must match exactly in terms of upper case and lower case characters). Thus, a constructor method for the **Account** class must have the name **Account**. Note that a constructor method does not have a return type. Constructor methods are the only kind of methods which do not have return types since they cannot be called like other methods.

The only time a constructor method comes into action is when an instance of a class is created with the **new** keyword. For example, after an **Account** instance is created, the constructor above sets its **number** and **balance** attributes to the arguments that were supplied when the constructor was called with the **new** keyword:

```
Account a = new Account(10, 1000.00);
```

This statement causes the value 10 to be assigned to the **number** attribute and the value 1000.00 to be assigned to the **balance** attribute of the newly created **Account** object.

Since a constructor method is just like a normal method (except that it does not specify a return type) it may take zero, one, or more arguments. The constructor above takes two arguments. If a constructor takes no arguments, it is called a *no-argument* constructor.

It is not necessary for a constructor method to have parameters for all the attributes of a class. For example, the following constructor for **Account** only accepts a parameter for the **number** attribute and sets the **balance** attribute to zero:

```
public Account(int n) {
    number = n;
    balance = 0.0;
}
```

In general, a constructor method should have parameters for attributes that a client can reasonably be expected to send when an instance is created. The other attributes are set to meaningful default values (like setting **balance** to zero in the example above).

A no-argument constructor enables clients to create an instance of a class without supplying any arguments. For example, consider the following no-argument constructor for the **Account** class:

```
public Account() {
    number = 0;
    balance = 0.0;
}
```

This constructor sets the **number** and **balance** attributes of an **Account** object to default values. When writing a no-argument constructor, the requirements of the application should be carefully considered. For example, in a banking application it probably makes no sense to have an **Account** object that does not have meaningful values for its **number** and **balance** attributes.

Chapter 3: Objects and Classes

Consider the following code which was used in the previous section to create an instance of **Account**:

```
Account a;
a = new Account();
```

Account() is really a no-argument constructor that is used to initialize an **Account** object after it has been created by the **new** keyword. However, in the previous section, the **Account** class did not have any constructor methods. So, where did the no-argument constructor come from?

If a class contains no constructors, Java provides a *default no-argument constructor*. This constructor sets all the instance variables to default values which are appropriate for their type. So, numeric attributes (e.g. **double**, **int**, **long**, etc.) are set to zero, **boolean** attributes are set to **false**, character attributes are set to '*u0000*' (the Unicode representation of a **null** character—which sometimes prints incorrectly as a space), and object references are set to **null**. Thus, the **Account()** constructor is a default no-argument constructor supplied by Java. Note that Java will not supply the default no-argument constructor if one or more constructors are written for a class.

In specifying a parameter for a constructor method, programmers are often careful to use a name that does not conflict with name of the attribute being set. This results in parameter names that are sometimes quite meaningless. For example, the parameter **n** in the constructor method above is rather meaningless. To improve on this situation, one might consider using the name of the attribute as the parameter name. For example:

```
public Account(int number, double balance) {
   number = number;
   balance = balance;
}
```

This improves the readability of the parameter name; unfortunately, it results in a run-time error that often goes undetected. Since **number** and **balance** were declared in the parameter list, the reference to **number** and **balance** in the body of the method is actually a reference to the parameters, not the attributes of **Account**. This situation can be fixed by using the **this** keyword followed by a dot ('. ') as follows:

```
public Account(int number, double balance) {
   this.number = number;
   this.balance = balance;
}
```

The **this** keyword refers to the object of the class that contains the method that is currently being executed. Thus, **this**, followed by a dot, followed by the name of an attribute is a reference to an attribute of the current object. The use of **this** followed by a dot distinguishes the attribute name from the parameter name. In general, the **this** keyword can be used to distinguish the attributes of an object from the other variables declared in a method. This can be done in a constructor method as well as in the other methods of a class.

3.5 Improving the Client Class

The **BankApplication** class can be re-written to take advantage of the new constructor. In the following example, the **main()** method of **BankApplication** creates three **Account** objects and initializes them using the constructor. It then invokes methods on each object.

```java
public class BankApplication
{
   public static void main(String[] args) {
      Account a1 = new Account(10, 1000.00);
      Account a2 = new Account(20, 2000.00);
      Account a3 = new Account(30, 3000.00);

      System.out.println (a1.getBalance());
      System.out.println (a2.toString());
      System.out.println (a3.getNumber());
   }
}
```

Since the constructor sets the account number to the value supplied as an argument, a **setNumber()** method is no longer required in the **Account** class. Indeed, having a **setNumber()** method is potentially dangerous since it is now possible for a client to modify **number**, the unique identifier of an **Account** object. So, the **setNumber()** method is removed from the **Account** class.

Instead of using three separate object variables in the code above, an array can be used to store the three **Account** objects. First, an array variable of type **Account** must be declared:

```java
Account[] accounts;
```

The array is then created and assigned to the array variable as follows:

```java
accounts = new Account[3];
```

Chapter 3: Objects and Classes

Each **Account** object is created and initialized using the **new** keyword in conjunction with the constructor. The newly created **Account** object is then assigned to a specific location of the array using a subscript. The code below shows how the array is created and manipulated.

```
public class BankApplication
{
   public static void main(String[] args) {

      Account[] accounts;     // declare array variable

      accounts = new Account[3];
                              // create array

      accounts[0] = new Account(10, 1000.00);
                              // store account #10 in location 0

      accounts[1] = new Account(20, 2000.00);
                              // store account #20 in location 1

      accounts[2] = new Account(30, 3000.00);
                              // store account #30 in location 2

      for (int i=0; i<accounts.length; i++)
                              // display contents of each account

        System.out.println (accounts[i].toString());
   }
}
```

It should be noted that when the **accounts** array is created, the object variables are set to the default value of **null** since there are currently no **Account** objects in the array. This situation is depicted in Figure 3.8. Note that the *earth (ground)* symbol is used to indicate that an object reference is **null**.

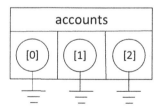

Figure 3.8: **accounts** Array Does Not Currently Refer to **Account** Objects

When an `Account` object is created, it is assigned to one of the array locations (just as if it were assigned to an ordinary object variable). To refer to a specific object variable in the array, the name of the array must be used, followed by the location of the `Account` object in the array. For example,

```
accounts[2]
```

Figure 3.9 depicts the `accounts` array after three instances of `Account` have been created and assigned to locations in the array:

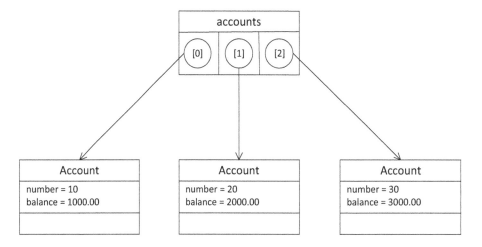

Figure 3.9: accounts Array Refers to Three Account Objects

Once the `accounts` array has been populated with references to actual `Account` objects, methods can be invoked on individual objects by using the object reference, followed by a dot, followed by the method name, followed by a list of arguments (if any). For example,

```
accounts[2].toString();
```

The `for` loop in the `main()` method of `BankApplication` uses an index variable `i` to traverse through each object variable in the array.

3.6 Method Signature and Method Overloading

Given the declaration of a method, the *method signature* consists of the name of the method, and the number, types, and order of its parameters. Consider the `deposit()` method of the `Account` class:

Chapter 3: Objects and Classes

```
public void deposit(double amount) {
   balance = balance + amount;
}
```

The method signature of the `deposit()` method (underlined in the code above) is:

```
deposit(double amount)
```

Note that this method signature is identical to the following method signature since only the name of the dummy parameter has changed:

```
deposit(double value)
```

In Java, it is possible to define two or more methods in the same class with the same name but with different method signatures. When this is done, the methods are said to be *overloaded*. The process of writing methods with the same name is called *method overloading*. As an example, consider the `withdraw()` method of the `Account` class which is overloaded as follows:

```
// Version 1
public void withdraw(double amount) {
   balance = balance - amount;
}

// Version 2
public void withdraw(double amount, double fee) {
   balance = balance - amount - fee;
}
```

Suppose `a` is an instance of `Account`. The overloaded methods can be called as follows:

Line 1:
```
a.withdraw(100.00);
```

Line 2:
```
a.withdraw(200.00, 1.00);
```

When the `withdraw()` method in Line 1 is called, the `withdraw()` method that is used is the one with the single parameter (Version 1). When the `withdraw()` method in Line 2 is called, the `withdraw()` method that is used is the one with the two parameters (Version 2). It is easy for the compiler to resolve overloaded methods since the argument list in the method invocation is matched with the method signature in the declaration.

It is possible to write another version of the `withdraw()` method where the return type is changed from `void` to `int`. The code for this version is given below.

```
// Version 3
public int withdraw(double amount) {
                    // return type changed from void to int

   balance = balance - amount;
   return 0;
}
```

Notice that the signature of this method is the same as the `withdraw()` method in Version 1. A compile time error occurs indicating that the method in Version 1 is being re-declared. To fix the problem, one of the methods must be deleted. Alternatively, the signature of one of the methods must be changed so that the signatures of the two methods are different.

Constructor methods can also be overloaded. This makes it possible to create an instance of a class using different sets of initial values. Thus, the three constructors of the `Account` class which were previously described can all be used in the same class definition.

3.7 Class Variables and Class Methods

The attributes of a class can have different values for each instance of the class. Also, the methods of a class require an instance of the class to be present before a service can be requested (i.e., before invoking a method). A class can also have attributes that pertain to the class as a whole instead of individual instances. These are referred to as *class variables*. Similarly, a class can have methods that provide a service even if no instance of the class is available. These methods are referred to as *class methods*. This section discusses class variables and class methods.

3.7.1 Class Variables

Variables such as `number` and `balance` in the `Account` class are called *instance variables* since each instance of the class has its own set of values for these variables. If there are 100 instances of the `Account` class, there would be 100 sets of instance variables, each set containing its own values for the variables.

Chapter 3: Objects and Classes

A *class variable* is a variable that is shared among all the instances of a class. Suppose the `Account` class needs a variable, `generator`, which is to be shared among all the instances of the `Account` class. `generator` is a class variable and is declared as follows:

```
static int generator;
```

The keyword `static` is used to distinguish a class variable from an instance variable. If there are 100 instances of the `Account` class, there is only one copy of `generator`, so there is only one value for the variable. If this value is modified by an object from the `Account` class, the changed value is immediately available to all the other objects of the `Account` class.

It is common to give a class variable an initial value when it is being declared. For example,

```
static int generator = 10000;
```

Class variables are useful for sharing data among instances of a class. For example, suppose that we wish to generate `Account` numbers automatically starting from 10000. We would like the `number` of each `Account` to be 10 higher than the `number` previously generated. We can share the `generator` among all instances of `Account` using a class variable. Whenever an `Account` instance is created, the `number` assigned is the value of the `generator`. The `generator` is then updated by 10 so the next instance will be assigned the incremented `generator` value. An example of a constructor method of `Account` which uses the `generator` class variable is given below:

```
public Account(double balance) {
        // NB: number is not a parameter

  number = generator;
        // account number assigned the value of generator

  this.balance = balance;
  generator = generator + 10;
        // prepare generator for next instance

}
```

3.7.2 Class Methods

All the methods described in the previous sections of this chapter can be called *instance methods* since they require an instance of a class to be present before they can be invoked. For example, the `deposit()` method of the `Account` class can only be invoked on an instance of `Account`:

```
Account a;
a = new Account(1000);
a.deposit(2000.00);
```

As previously mentioned, if `a` is not a valid reference to an `Account` instance, a run-time error occurs.

Unlike instance methods, *class methods* can be invoked without an instance of the class being present. A class method is declared just like an instance method except that the keyword `static` is used to indicate that it is a class method. For example, the `setGenerator()` method below is a class method:

```
public static void setGenerator (int newValue) {
    generator = newValue;
}
```

The `setGenerator()` method allows resetting of the `generator` value to a new starting value. Since it is a class method, it can be called without an instance of the class present.

In order to call a class method, you must specify the name of the class, followed by a dot, followed by the name of the class method and the argument list (if any). For example, the `setGenerator()` class method can be called as follows:

```
Account.setGenerator(20000);
```

A class method cannot refer to instance variables. Since it can be invoked without an instance present, no assumptions can be made about any instance of the class (and its associated instance variables). However, as can be seen from the `setGenerator()` method, a class method can refer to class variables. It can also refer to variables declared locally in the class method (see next section).

The client class, `BankApplication`, has a `main()` method which is declared with the `static` keyword. This implies that the `main()` method is a class method. Notice that `main()` only refers to variables declared locally in `main()`, e.g., `a1`, `a2`, etc.

Chapter 3: Objects and Classes

3.8 Scope of Variables

An instance variable stores the value of an attribute of an object. In the `Account` class, `balance` is an instance variable. A *local variable* is a variable declared inside a method. For example, in the `calculateInterest()` method of the `Account` class shown below, `interest` is a local variable.

```
public void calculateInterest(double interestRate) {

  double interest;   // local variable declared inside method

  interest = balance * (interestRate / 12.0);

  // other processing
}
```

An instance variable of an object maintains its value as long as the object is "alive". In Java, "alive" is interpreted to mean that at least one other object in the program is currently referring to the given object. Of course, a client can change that value during the course of execution of the program. However, the important point to note about the state of an instance variable is that whenever a client accesses an object, the state of an instance variable is exactly the same as when the last client left it.

On the other hand, a local variable declared inside a method comes into existence when a method is invoked and "dies" when the method terminates (i.e., its former value cannot be accessed). The next time the method is invoked (from the same or from some other client), the local variable comes into existence again and dies when the method terminates. So, the value of a local variable does not persist from execution to execution of a method.

A class variable is "alive" from the first moment the class is referenced in the program and stays "alive" until the program terminates. Whenever a client (or the `this` object) accesses a class variable, the value of the class variable is the same as when the last client left it.

Exercises

1. A class has attributes and behaviors. How are these two aspects of a class implemented in Java?

2. Draw the UML diagram for an `Employee` class which has attributes such as `number`, `name`, and `salary`, and methods such as

raiseSalary(percentage), which raises an employee's **salary** by a certain percentage.

3. Two **Employee** objects have the same value for the **salary** attribute. The **raiseSalary()** method is invoked on each of them with a **percentage** argument of 5.0. Will the **salary** attribute of both objects have the same value after the **raiseSalary()** method is invoked? State any assumptions you make.

4. Figure 3.7 shows the result of copying an object variable **a** to another object variable **a2**. This results in a *shallow copy* of **Account** #10 being made since **a2** simply refers to the same **Account** #10. Explain how you would create a *deep copy* of **Account** #10, i.e., create a separate object which has the same attributes as **Account** #10. Write a method **deepCopy()** which returns a deep copy of the **Account** object on which it is invoked.

5. Explain why a class variable should not be initialized in a constructor method.

6. The methods of a class can be invoked on any instance of the class. Suppose a class has two types of instances for which certain methods are not applicable to all instances. For example, suppose that the **Employee** class has certain methods that are apply to only male instances and some that apply to only female instances. Suggest a technique for accomplishing this functionality in an object-oriented program (even in a limited way).

7. An array has been declared as follows:

```
Employees[] employees = new Employee[100];
```

Determine if the following code will run successfully:

```
for (int i=0; i<employees.length; i++)
    System.out.println(employees[i].toString());
```

8. A fraction is a number represented by two integer values: one for the numerator and the other for the denominator. For example, the fraction 3/5 is represented by the numerator 3 and the denominator 5. A **Fraction** class is required for storing and manipulating fractions. It should have methods such as **addFraction()**, **substractFraction()**, **multiplyFraction()**, and **divideFraction()** (each of which takes two arguments of type

Chapter 3: Objects and Classes

Fraction and returns a new Fraction object). It should also have a toString() method which returns a string representation of the fraction.

(a) Draw a UML diagram of the Fraction class.

(b) Write the code for the Fraction class.

(c) Write the code for a client of Fraction that inputs several fractions from the user and performs various operations on the fractions.

9. Suppose that the constructor of the Fraction class receives a denominator of 0. Since a fraction cannot contain a denominator of 0, suggest a technique for dealing with this situation.

10. The withdraw() method of the Account class only performs the withdrawal if there are sufficient funds in an account. Suppose that an Account object does not have enough funds to perform a withdrawal. How can the Account object notify its client about this?

Chapter 4

Information Hiding and Design Principles

In an object-oriented program, objects of different classes interact in many different ways. Good software engineering practice recommends that these interactions be properly controlled; otherwise, the program will be difficult to understand, debug, and maintain. *Information hiding* is the process of hiding all the secrets of an object that do not contribute to its essential characteristics. This chapter explains how information hiding can be achieved in object-oriented programming. It also discusses some design principles that are pertinent to the development of object-oriented software.

4.1 Encapsulation

The previous chapter has shown how to combine the attributes and behaviors of an object into a single unit called a class. Attributes and behaviors are said to be *encapsulated* in the class. Encapsulation provides the first level of information hiding in an object-oriented application since it separates the external aspects of an object (its interface) from the internal implementation details of the object. Another level of information hiding is to control access to the individual attributes and methods of an object by the use of access modifiers. This kind of information hiding is the subject of this section.

4.1.1 Access Modifiers

Access modifiers are used in Java to control access to the individual members of a class such as its attributes and methods. There are three access modifiers that can be used when declaring the attributes and methods of a class:

- `private`
- `protected`   Increasing level of access
- `public`

These access modifiers permit an increasing amount of access going down the list. For example, `private` members are accessible only by objects of the same class. However, `public` members can be accessed by objects of any other class. If none of the above access modifiers is used to declare a member of a class, Java provides a default level of access to the member being declared. The following sub-sections describe how access modifiers are used to control access to the members of a class.

4.1.2 Hiding the Attributes of an Object

It is a good idea to hide the attributes of an object from its clients. When this is done, client code will not be able to directly access the value of an instance variable. Direct access implies that a client can get hold of an object through an object variable and then use the variable name, followed by a dot, followed by the name of the instance variable, to either read or change the variable. For example, suppose that `a` is a reference to an `Account` object. Direct access to the `balance` attribute of an `Account` object means that a client can do things such as the following:

```
double currentBalance = a.balance;   // client can read balance
a.balance = 10000.00;                // client can change balance
```

Giving clients uncontrolled access to the `balance` attribute makes code maintenance very difficult. If there is a change in the `Account` class involving the `balance` attribute, it is necessary to find and change all the clients which may have accessed this attribute directly. Debugging is also more difficult since an error involving the `balance` attribute requires several other classes to be examined. If no client is able to directly access an attribute of another class, changes involving that attribute are isolated to its own class, simplifying program maintenance and debugging. This is the reason why clients should not be able to directly access the values of attributes as in the examples above.

Access modifiers are used to selectively control access to each attribute of an object. An attribute declared as `private` is only visible to the methods of the object. For example, the instance variable `balance` of the `Account` class can be declared `private` as follows:

```
private double balance;
```

Chapter 4: Information Hiding and Design Principles

Since the `balance` instance variable is declared as `private`, it can only be seen and manipulated by methods of the `Account` class. For example, the `deposit()` method of the `Account` class adds the value of the `amount` parameter to the current `balance` and updates the `balance` attribute to this value:

```
public void deposit(double amount) {
   balance = balance + amount;    // read and update balance
}
```

It is not possible for clients of an object to view an instance variable that has been declared as `private`. Thus, client code such as the following will not compile successfully since the client does not have direct access to the `balance` instance variable:

```
Account a;                           // declaration OK
a = new Account(10, 1000.00);        // creation of Account instance OK

System.out.println("Account balance: " + a.balance);
                                     // cannot access balance directly
```

The access permitted to a `public` instance variable is completely opposite to that which is permitted to a `private` instance variable. A `public` instance variable is visible to objects of every class and thus can be seen and modified directly by these objects. For example, suppose that the `balance` instance variable of `Account` is declared `public` as follows:

```
public double balance;
```

It is now possible for a client object of some other class to create an instance of `Account` and then directly change the value of `balance`. This can be done as follows:

```
Account a;

a = new Account(10, 1000.00);         // create account instance

System.out.println("Old balance: " + a.balance);
                                      // read value of balance

a.balance = 5000.00;                  // change value of balance

System.out.println("New balance: " + a.balance);
                                      // read value of balance
```

Allowing client objects to directly access the **balance** instance variable is not recommended for the reasons given earlier. In addition, it is possible for client code to change the variable in undesirable ways. For example, clients may not be aware of validation checks that have to be performed before changing an instance variable (e.g., ensuring that the **balance** is within a certain range). As part of the practice of information hiding, instance variables are normally declared as **private**.

The third access modifier, **protected**, is discussed later in this chapter after the section on packages. When no access modifier is specified, a default type of access is permitted referred to as *friendly* or *package-private*. Recall that the instance variables of the **Account** class discussed in Chapter 3 were not declared with access modifiers. Thus, the type of access permitted is *friendly*. *Friendly* access is discussed later in the chapter.

4.1.3 Hiding the Methods of an Object

The access modifiers **private**, **protected** and **public** can also be used to control access to methods, i.e., the services offered by an object. A **private** method defined in a class can only be invoked by methods of that class. This type of access to a method is normally used if the method provides services that are not required by objects of other classes. This often happens when a method performs a task that is not particularly useful to other classes (e.g., "helper" methods).

A client object can invoke a **public** method by using the name of the object variable which refers to the object, followed by a dot, followed by the method name and list of arguments (if any). We saw numerous examples of this in Chapter 3 in the **BankApplication** client code. For example,

```
Account a;                  // declare object variable

a = new Account();          // let a refer to object created
a.setNumber(10);            // invoke setNumber() method of Account
a.deposit(1000.00);         // invoke deposit() method of Account

System.out.println(a.toString());
                            // invoke toString() method of Account
```

The methods of a class are generally declared as **public**, since their purpose is to provide services to other objects. For example, the methods of the **Account** class in Chapter 3 are all declared as **public**.

Chapter 4: Information Hiding and Design Principles

`Protected` methods are discussed later in this chapter, after the section dealing with packages. When no access modifier is specified when declaring a method, a default type of access is permitted referred to as *friendly* or *package-private*. Methods that provide *friendly* access are discussed later in the chapter.

It should be noted that clients do not need to be aware of how a method is implemented (i.e., the logic and data structures that are used to achieve the behavior of the method). Clients are only responsible for invoking methods with the appropriate arguments. As a result, when a client object requests a service from another object, the service is provided, yet the client is unaware of what is involved in providing that service. In other words, clients should know the interface to an object (i.e., they should know how to access its services), but they should not be concerned with the implementation of these services. This enables the service provider to alter the way its services are provided without clients being affected.

4.1.4 Effect of Access Modifiers on Instances of the Same Class

Access modifiers determine the extent to which client code can read and/or modify the individual members of a class. However, in Java, access modifiers have no effect when a client object belongs to the same class as the object being manipulated. Thus, an instance of a class is always permitted complete access to the attributes and methods of another object of the *same* class, regardless of the access modifiers used to declare these members. For example, consider the following method of the `Account` class:

```java
public boolean isEqual(Account account) {
   if (this.number == account.number)
      return true;
   else
      return false;
}
```

The `isEqual()` method returns `true` if the `Account` parameter has the same `number` as the object on which the `isEqual()` method is acting (the `this` object). Observe how it is possible to refer directly to the `number` variable of the `Account` parameter despite the fact that the `number` variable was declared `private` in `Account`:

```java
if (this.number == account.number)
   // direct access to number attribute permitted
```

4.2 Accessing Private Attributes

It is not possible for a client to directly access a `private` attribute of a class. However, in an object-oriented program, a client will often need to view or modify the value of a `private` attribute. Thus, a class must provide a means for client objects to view and/or modify the value of a `private` attribute. This is achieved by writing special methods that allow client objects to read or change the values of instance variables. These methods are called accessor and mutator methods, respectively.

4.2.1 Accessor and Mutator Methods

An *accessor* method simply returns the value of an instance variable. It is sometimes called a *getter*. An example is the `getBalance()` method of the `Account` class which returns the current value of the `balance` attribute. A *mutator* method changes the value of an instance variable. The simplest mutator method is one that accepts a parameter and changes the value of an instance variable to the value of the parameter. This type of mutator is often called a *setter*. An example is the `setNumber()` method of the `Account` class (before constructor methods were introduced). This method changes the value of the `number` attribute of an `Account` object to a new value supplied as an argument. Mutators may be more complex such as the `withdraw()` method of the `Account` class which changes the value of the `balance` attribute under certain conditions.

Getter methods are usually named by preceding the name of the instance variable with the prefix "*get*"; the first letter of the variable name is also capitalized. For example, `getBalance()` returns the value of the `balance` attribute of an `Account` object. A getter method for an instance variable `x` of type `T` is generally written as follows:

```
public T getX() {        // x is the instance variable, T is its type
   return x;             // simply return value of x
}
```

If `x` is of type `boolean`, the getter method is written with an "*is*" prefix instead of "*get*" as follows:

```
public boolean isX() {   // x is an instance variable of type boolean
   return x;             // return value of x
}
```

Chapter 4: Information Hiding and Design Principles

isX() is a more natural name to find out the value of a **boolean** variable. For example, if **empty** is an instance variable of type **boolean**, it is more readable to name the accessor method isEmpty() rather than getEmpty().

Setter methods are similarly named, except that the prefix "*set*" is used. For example, setNumber(n) changes the value of the **number** attribute of an **Account** object to **n**. The new value is supplied as an argument to the setter method.

A setter method for an instance variable **x** of type **T** is generally written as follows:

```
public void setX (T newValue) {
                // x is the instance variable, T is its type

   x = newValue;      // change x to value of parameter
}
```

Consider Figure 4.1 which is a UML diagram of a **Customer** class:

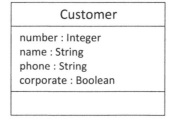

Figure 4.1: UML Diagram of a **Customer** Class

Getter methods for all the instance variables of the **Customer** class are given below:

```
public int getNumber() {
   return number;
}

public String getName() {
   return name;
}

public String getPhone() {
   return phone;
}
```

```java
public boolean isCorporate() {
   return corporate;
}
```

The corresponding setter methods for the `Customer` class are given below:

```java
public void setNumber(int number) {
   this.number = number;
}

public void setName(String name) {
   this.name = name;
}

public void setPhone(String phone) {
   this.phone = phone;
}

public void setCorporate(boolean corporate) {
   this.corporate = corporate;
}
```

A setter method can apply validation checks before modifying the value of an instance variable. For example, suppose there is a requirement that the `name` attribute of `Customer` should be at most fifteen characters long. This constraint can be implemented in the `setName()` method as follows:

```java
public void setName(String name) {
   if (name.length() > 15)
      this.name = name.substring(0, 15);
                // take first 15 characters & ignore the rest

   else
      this.name = name;
                // take all the characters
}
```

It should be noted that accessor and mutator methods are not normally shown in a UML diagram. Also, some integrated development environments (IDEs) and tools that generate code from UML diagrams automatically generate getter and setter methods for all the attributes of a class. This feature should be used with caution, as the next section explains.

4.2.2 Problem with Accessor and Mutator Methods

It is not necessary to have getter and setter methods for all the attributes of a class. Getter and setter methods should only be provided for attributes when it is expected that client objects will need to view and/or modify the values of these attributes. If a client object only needs to view the value of a particular attribute, only a getter method should be provided for that attribute. Care must also be taken in providing a setter method for an attribute which acts as a primary key. If this attribute is modified, it will become disconnected from other objects which are still referring to the old primary key.

It should be noted that getter and setter methods violate information hiding to a certain degree. Consider the `number` instance variable of the `Customer` class. This variable is of type `int`. So, the getter method returns a value of type `int` and the setter method accepts a parameter of type `int`. Suppose a decision is made later to change the type of the variable to `String`. This requires changes in the getter and setter methods to accommodate the new type. More importantly, every client object which uses the getter and setter methods must change to deal with the new type as well. This happens because the getter and setter methods did not completely encapsulate all the details of the `number` attribute so client objects were not shielded from modifications to this setter methods should be used with caution.

4.3 Immutable Classes

If a class has at least one mutator (either a setter method or a more complex method that modifies the value of an instance variable) it is said to be *mutable*. If a class has no mutators and all its instance variables are `private`, it is impossible for clients to modify objects of that class after they have been created. Such a class is called *immutable*. Objects of an immutable class can be freely shared with other client objects without the danger of the objects being modified. Some authors suggest that you should make a class immutable whenever you can do so (Horstmann, 2002).

4.3.1 Achieving Immutability

To ensure that an object is immutable, its attributes should be declared as `final` in the class definition. For example, the attributes of the `Customer` class can be declared `final` as follows:

```
private final int number;
private final String name;
private final String phone;
private final boolean corporate;
```

However, when this is done, the attributes can only be modified in the constructor. Thus, the four setter methods must be removed from the `Customer` class.

It is possible to assign a value to a `final` attribute in the declaration statement itself. For example,

```
private final int number = 100;   // assigns 100 to number
```

Once this is done, `number` cannot be subsequently modified, not even in a constructor method. Clearly this approach for setting the value of a `final` attribute has very limited use. So, the recommended approach for creating an immutable class is to declare all the instance variables as `final` and use a constructor to set the instance variables. Since the attributes are `final`, Java ensures that no subsequent modification of the instance variables takes place.

4.3.2 Immutable Classes in Java

There are several classes in Java that are immutable. For example, the `String` class is immutable. Consider the following code which creates a `String` object:

```
String greeting = "Hello There!";
```

An equivalent `String` object can be created with the following code:

```
String greeting = new String("Hello There!");
```

The object variable `greeting` refers to a `String` object which contains twelve characters. It is impossible to modify the characters in the `String` object. However, the object variable can be re-assigned to another `String` object as follows:

```
greeting = "Bye!";
```

Eventually, the `String` object corresponding to the string "Hello There!" will be removed from the memory space of the application, if no other variable refers to it.

Consider the following code:

Line 1:
```
greeting = "John";
```

Chapter 4: Information Hiding and Design Principles

Line 2:
```
greeting = "Hello there " + greeting + "!";
```

It might seem as if the **String** object referred to by **greeting** is being modified in Line 2. However, what is really happening is that a new **String** object is created after applying the concatenation operator on the right hand side of the equals sign. A reference to this new **String** object is assigned to **greeting** in Line 2. Thus, the original **String** object containing "John" remains unmodified in memory.

Java also has a set of *wrapper* classes for each of the eight primitive types. A wrapper class is used in situations where an object is required instead of a primitive value. Objects of the wrapper classes are immutable.

Suppose that **x** is a variable of type **int**. To create an *object* which contains the value of **x**, the **Integer** wrapper class is used. For example,

```
int x = 10;
Integer xWrapper = new Integer(x);
```

Once the instance **xWrapper** is created, its contents cannot be modified. The only way to change **xWrapper** is to create another instance of **Integer**. For example,

```
x = 25;
xWrapper = new Integer(x);
```

Methods such as **intValue()** can be used to obtain the value of the **int** stored in **xWrapper**. For example,

```
System.out.println("Value of x: " + xWrapper.intValue());
```

The wrapper classes for the eight primitive types are listed in Table 4.1. A constructor method for each class is also given, together with the method used to retrieve the primitive value stored in a wrapper object.

Primitive Type	Wrapper Class	Constructor	Method to Retrieve Primitive Value
byte	Byte	Byte(byte b)	byteValue()
short	Short	Short(short s)	shortValue()
int	Integer	Integer(int i)	intValue()
long	Long	Long(long l)	longValue()
float	Float	Float(float f)	floatValue()
double	Double	Double(double d)	doubleValue()
char	Character	Character(char c)	charValue()
boolean	Boolean	Boolean(boolean b)	booleanValue()

Table 4.1: Wrapper Classes in Java

In passing, it should be mentioned that the wrapper classes in Table 4.1 have class methods which can be used to convert a primitive value stored as a string to a value of the corresponding primitive type. For example, the `parseInt()` method of the `Integer` class can be used to convert the string "25" to an `int` value:

```
String numberString = "25";
int accountNumber = Integer.parseInt(numberString);
```

The methods of the other wrapper classes have similar names. These conversion methods will often be used in the book to obtain the primitive value stored in a string.

4.4 Object-Oriented Design Guidelines

This section discusses some design guidelines for building an object-oriented application. It explains how coupling and cohesion, two fundamental concepts in software design, are applicable to the design of an object-oriented application. It also describes the Law of Demeter, a guideline for reducing the coupling among objects.

4.4.1 Coupling and Cohesion

An object-oriented program consists of a set of objects that collaborate to achieve some goal. Two objects collaborate when one object requests a service from the other. As mentioned at the beginning of this chapter, objects of different classes interact in many different ways and it is important to control these interactions to create high quality programs. Two notions that affect the quality of object-oriented programs are *coupling* and *cohesion*.

Chapter 4: Information Hiding and Design Principles

Object-oriented coupling refers to the degree or strength of interconnection among classes. Loosely coupled classes (as opposed to tightly coupled classes) are desirable since each class can be handled in a relatively independent manner. A class can become coupled to another class, **C**, if it knows about **C** in some way. For example, it may create an object of **C** or one of its methods may accept an object of class **C** as a parameter. An object-oriented program with loosely coupled classes facilitates:

- The replacement of one class by another so that only a few classes are affected by the change
- The speedy debugging of errors since it is easier to track down an error and isolate the defective class causing the error

One extreme in coupling is to have the classes in an application totally uncoupled. When this is done, there is no way for objects to collaborate with each other. This defeats the fundamental notion of an object-oriented program. The other extreme is to have all the classes coupled to each other so there is a high degree of dependence between each pair of classes. This makes it extremely difficult to replace classes and to debug and maintain programs. Between these two extremes, there are many degrees of coupling. A desirable goal in object-oriented programming is to reduce any excess or unnecessary coupling among classes. This reduces maintenance and debugging costs and promotes reusability of classes.

The notion of *cohesion* concerns the internal strength of a class, i.e., how strongly related the parts of a class are. A class whose parts are strongly related to each other and to the concept being represented is said to be *strongly cohesive*. In contrast, a class whose parts are hardly related to each other is said to be *weakly cohesive*. Strongly cohesive classes are easier to understand, debug, and maintain.

An example of a weakly cohesive class is one where the class embodies more than one unrelated concept and thus takes on responsibilities that could be best handled by another class. For example, if customer information such as customer name and telephone number are stored in an **Account** class, then the **Account** class is weakly cohesive.

4.4.2 Law of Demeter

The *Law of Demeter* is a guideline for reducing the amount of coupling between objects in an object-oriented application. Consider again the **Account** class. The **Account** class has two attributes, **number** and **balance**. Suppose we wanted an **Account** object to store information on the customer who owns the account. An additional attribute of **Account** can be used to store a reference to the corresponding **Customer** object. This attribute is called **customer** and is of type **Customer**. Figure 4.2 is a UML diagram showing the enhanced **Account** class.

Account
number : Integer balance : Double customer : Customer

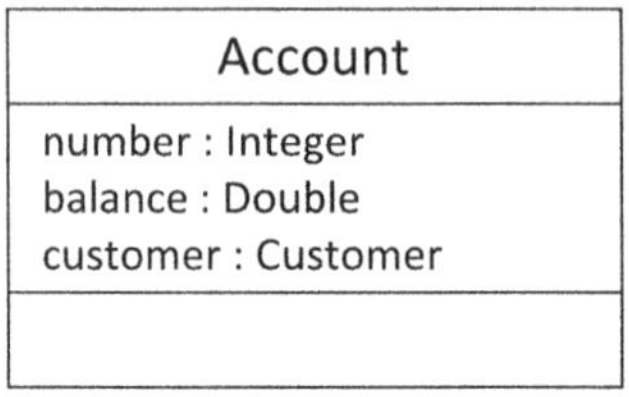

Figure 4.2 UML Diagram of the Enhanced Account Class

A getter method, **getCustomer()**, can be written in **Account** that returns the **Customer** instance:

```
public Customer getCustomer() {
   return customer;
}
```

Now, suppose that a client object obtains a reference to an **Account** object. Let this reference be **a**. The client object can then invoke the **getCustomer()** method on **a** as follows:

```
Customer accountHolder;
accountHolder = a.getCustomer();
```

The client object now has a reference to a **Customer** object in its hands. Since **Customer** is a mutable class, the client object is free to invoke any of its setter methods and modify the **Customer** object as it pleases. If this is done, it means that an attribute of **Account** (i.e., its **Customer** object) can be modified without the **Account** object knowing about it. This is a violation of encapsulation. The **getCustomer()** method was designed to give information about the **Customer** object, not to permit modification of it.

The problem just described can be reduced or eliminated by following the *Law of Demeter*. This law states that a method **m()** of an object **o** should only invoke methods from the following kinds of objects:

- Methods from **o** itself
- Methods from objects passed to **m()** as arguments
- Methods of objects created within **m()**

Chapter 4: Information Hiding and Design Principles

A client object that follows the Law of Demeter does not invoke methods on objects that are part of another object. Thus, the client object should not operate on the `Customer` instance returned by the `getCustomer()` method since this violates the Law of Demeter. The Law of Demeter is sometimes called the *Principle of Least Knowledge* since its purpose is to make objects know as little as possible about other types of objects.

The Law of Demeter is not a natural or mathematical law. It is simply a guideline to be considered when designing an object-oriented program. Following the guideline often requires client objects to request services from server objects instead of directly manipulating objects managed by the server objects (e.g., the `Customer` instance above). Server objects must be enlarged to provide these services. The next section gives a few more guidelines for developing an object-oriented application.

4.5 Organizing the Classes of an Application

An object-oriented application usually consists of several layers of software where each layer is composed of several classes. As the complexity of the application increases, it is convenient to organize the classes into different units. These units are known as packages in Java. This section describes the concept of a package and explains how a package can be created and manipulated. The section also presents a three-layered architecture of an object-oriented application in which the layers consist of a set of packages which interact with each other.

4.5.1 The Concept of a Package

A *package* is a way of grouping related classes into a single unit. So, instead of an object-oriented program consisting all of its classes lumped together in one place, it can consist of a group of packages each containing a set of related classes.

So far in this book, all the classes that have been created reside in a single unit. This unit is referred to as the *default package* and corresponds to the folder on your computer where the classes are stored and compiled. Since no package was specified when the classes were created, they were automatically placed in the default package. However, as the number of classes in an application increases, it is more convenient to group the classes into packages.

Suppose in a banking application it is decided to keep all the classes related to accounts in a package called `CustomerAccount`. This package may contain classes such as `Account`, `SavingsAccount`, `ChequingAccount`,

MutualFundAccount, FixedDepositAccount, etc. Figure 4.3 shows how the CustomerAccount package can be drawn using the UML. The package diagram is drawn as a tabbed folder where the name of the package is specified in the tab and the folder specifies the names of the classes which belong to the package".

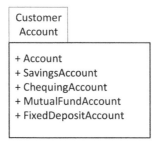

Figure 4.3: UML Diagram of CustomerAccount Package

The **public** parts of a package are called its exports (i.e., its class members declared with the **public** keyword). The '+' symbol preceding each class name indicates that the class is exported from CustomerAccount and is thus available to classes in other packages.

Packages promote information hiding since the members of the classes in one package (instance variables and methods) can be selectively exported to other packages. Thus, there may be elements in one package that are not accessible by other packages.

The notions of coupling and cohesion are also applicable to the decomposition of an object-oriented application into packages. A desirable goal is to have loosely coupled packages. Thus, packages should be independent as far as possible. The classes within a package should also be highly cohesive. Thus, the classes in a package should be related to each other as much as possible.

4.5.2 Three-tier Architecture for Object-Oriented Software

Except for small applications, an object-oriented program does not usually consist of one layer of software grouped together in one unit or package. It is common to employ a three-layered architecture when designing object-oriented programs. This is known as the *three-tiered architecture* and consists of the following three vertical layers:

Chapter 4: Information Hiding and Design Principles

1. User Services—visual interface for presenting information and gathering data
2. Business Services—tasks and rules that govern application processing
3. Data Services—persistent storage mechanism to maintain, access, and update data

The unique quality of the three-tier architecture is the separation of the application (business) logic into a distinct logical middle tier of software. The *User Services* tier is relatively free of application processing and forwards task requests to the *Business Services* tier. The *Business Services* tier communicates with the back-end *Data Services* tier. The classes in the *Business Services* tier will often be referred to as *domain classes* in the book

The three-tier architecture for an object-oriented application can be designed as a set of packages as shown in Figure 4.4 below. Depending on the complexity of different applications, the packages may be further decomposed into sub-packages representing finer layers in the architecture.

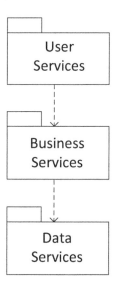

Figure 4.4: An Object-Oriented Program as a Set of Packages

Note that the dashed lines between packages indicate a dependency relationship between the packages (this type of relationship is described further in the next chapter). So, the `UserServices` package depends on the `BusinessServices` package which, in turn, depends on the `DataServices` package.

4.5.3 Creating a Package and its Elements

Suppose that the `Account` class must be part of the `BusinessServices` package. This must be indicated at the top of the source file containing `Account`. The keyword `package` is used followed by the name of the package in lower case:

```
package business;        // 'services' has been omitted from the name
```

The folder structure corresponding to the packages in an application is shown in Figure 4.5. Notice that all the folders are sub-folders of the top level `application` folder.

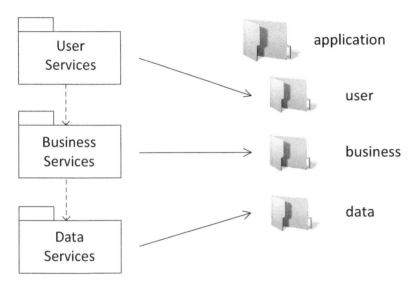

Figure 4.5: Correspondence between Packages and Folders

After the `Account` class has been compiled, the class file must be placed in the `business` folder. Since the `BankApplication` class from Chapter 3 belongs to the `UserServices` package, it must be placed in the `user` folder. The `package` statement must be placed at the top of the source file to indicate that the class belongs to the `UserServices` package:

```
package user;            // 'services' has been omitted from the name
```

The next section discusses the changes that are necessary in `BankApplication` so that it can access the `Account` class in the `BusinessServices` package.

Chapter 4: Information Hiding and Design Principles

4.5.4 Using the Elements of a Package

The `Account` class is now in the `BusinessServices` package. Classes in the same package can access each other depending on the levels of access permitted. For example, suppose that a `Bank` class belongs to the `BusinessServices` package. An instance of `Bank` can create an instance of `Account` in the normal manner:

```
Account a;
a = new Account(10, 1000.00);
```

However, consider the `BankApplication` class which has been placed in the `UserServices` package. The `BankApplication` class needs to create and manipulate instances of the `Account` class which now resides in the business folder. To do so, it needs to specify the full name and path of the package containing `Account`, relative to the root `application` folder. Thus, the `BankApplication` class requires the following code in order to create an instance of `Account`:

```
business.Account a;
a = new business.Account(10, 1000.00);
```

To access the `Account` class, the `BusinessServices` package (abbreviated to `business`) must be specified, followed by a dot, followed by the name of the class. This can be rather cumbersome. The code can be considerably simplified by placing the path to the `Account` class in an `import` statement. The `import` statement that is required to use the `Account` class is written as follows:

```
import business.Account;
```

If there are other classes from the `BusinessServices` package that will be needed by the `BankApplication` class (or some other client), each one can be listed in a separate `import` statement. Alternatively, the following statement can be used to import all the classes from the `BusinessServices` package:

```
import business.*;   // '*' specifies all the classes in the package
```

The `import` statement must be placed at the top of the source file, before the client class is declared. Now, whenever the client class wishes to access the `Account` class, it simply uses the name of the class. For example,

```
Account a;
a = new Account(10, 1000.00);
```

4.5.5 Nesting Packages

It is possible for packages to be nested. For example, the `BusinessServices` package may contain three sub-packages called `CustomerAccount`, `Loan`, and `Mortgage`. Each of the sub-packages contains classes that manage the business operations for each category of business in a bank. This is shown in the UML diagram in Figure 4.6:

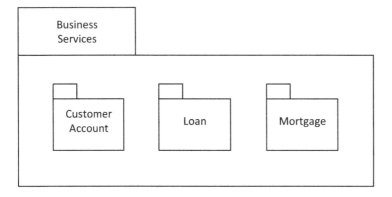

Figure 4.6 Nested Packages

Nested packages correspond to a nested folder structure. So, the three sub-packages would be stored as sub-folders of the **business** folder. Figure 4.7 shows the folder structure corresponding to the nested packages:

Chapter 4: Information Hiding and Design Principles

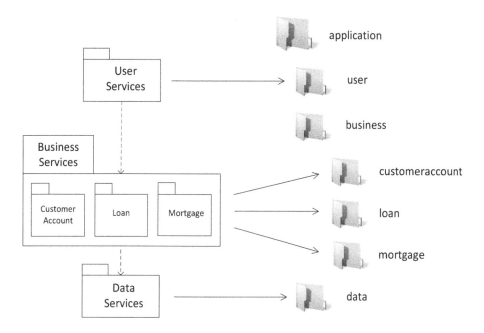

Figure 4.7: Folder Structure Corresponding to Nested Packages

Suppose that the **Account** class must now belong to the **CustomerAccount** sub-package. The **package** statement in **Account** must change to reflect this:

```
package business.customeraccount;
```

After compiling the **Account** class, it must be placed in the **customeraccount** sub-folder of **business**. A similar procedure must be followed for all the classes belonging to a particular package.

If the **BankApplication** class needs to create an instance of the **Account** class, the following code is required:

```
business.customeraccount.Account a;
a = new business.customeraccount.Account(10, 1000.00);
```

Again, the code in **BankApplication** can be simplified by placing the path to the **customeraccount** package in an **import** statement. The **import** statement required to use the **Account** class is written as follows:

```
import business.customeraccount.Account;
```

Now, whenever the `BankApplication` class wishes to access the `Account` class, it simply uses the name of the class, as before.

4.6 Accessing the Attributes and Methods of a Class in a Package

Within a package, the `private` and `public` access modifiers permit the same level of access to the attributes and methods of a class as previously described. However, if no access modifier is used to declare an instance variable of a class, client objects in the *same* package are automatically granted *friendly* (*package-private*) access to this variable. For example, the following statement declares *name* to be a *friendly* instance variable of the `Customer` class:

```
String name;                    // no access modifier specified
```

Granting *friendly* access to an instance variable is equivalent to granting `public` access to all objects in the same package. So, declaring an instance variable with no access modifier is equivalent to declaring that instance variable as `public`; however, `public` access is restricted to classes in the same package. The instance variable is `private` to all classes outside the package.

Similarly, if no access modifier is used to declare a method of a class, client objects in the same package are automatically granted *friendly* access to this method. For example, if the `setName()` method of the `Customer` class is defined as follows, then `setName()` is a *friendly* method:

```
void setName (String name) {    // no access modifier specified
   this.name = name;
}
```

Declaring a method with no access modifier is equivalent to declaring that method as `public`; however, `public` access is restricted to classes in the same package. The method is `private` to all classes outside the package.

If an instance variable is declared as `protected`, it is accessible to all the classes in the same package. Thus, a `protected` instance variable permits the same type of access as a *friendly* instance variable. Similarly, a method declared as `protected` provides the same type of access as a *friendly* method. An example of a `protected` instance variable is the `number` attribute of the `Customer` class which is declared as follows:

```
protected int number;
```

Chapter 4: Information Hiding and Design Principles

`protected` instance variables are different from *friendly* instance variables since they can also be accessed by objects of another kind of class. This type of class is referred to as a *subclass* and is discussed further in Chapter 9.

4.7 Controlling Access to a Class

This chapter has shown how access modifiers permit different degrees of access to the individual members of a class such as its attributes and methods. It is also possible to control access to the class as a whole using the same set of access modifiers. In addition, it is possible to declare a class as an inner class to restrict its visibility to client objects.

4.7.1 Using Access Modifiers to Declare a Class

A class is declared using the `public` access modifier. This makes the class accessible to objects of any other class. It is not possible to declare a class as `private` or `protected` (*except* for inner classes which are discussed in the next sub-section). If no access modifier is used to declare a class, *friendly* (package-private) access is permitted. *Friendly* access means that objects of the same package can access the class. Two examples of a class declaration are as follows:

```
public class Account { … }      // public access permitted
class Account { … }             // friendly access permitted
```

4.7.2 Inner Classes

An *inner class* is a class that is written inside another class. An inner class is written the same way as any other class. However, an inner class is normally declared as `private` so that it can only be accessed by the class in which it is contained. Inner classes provide a level of encapsulation that is similar to `private` methods which are written for the exclusive use of the class in which they are contained. Thus, a `private` inner class is written for the sole benefit of the containing class.

The only time an inner class is used in this book is in Chapter 13, where a `LinkedList` class contains a `private` inner class called `Node`. The following code is part of the `LinkedList` class:

```
public class LinkedList
{
   private Node head;         // first node of the linked list
   private int count;         // amount of nodes in the linked list
```

```
public LinkedList() {
   head = null;
   count = 0;
}

public void addFirst(int element) {
   Node newNode = new Node(element);
   newNode.next = head;   // can access next attribute of Node
   head = newNode;
   count++;
}

// Other linked list methods

// Node inner class

private class Node {
   private int element;
   private Node next;

   public Node(int element) {
      this.element = element;
   }
}
}
```

As can be seen from the **addFirst()** method in the code above, the class containing the inner class (**LinkedList**) can access the attributes and methods of the inner class (**Node**) regardless of the access modifiers used to declare these members. Similarly, an inner class can access the attributes and methods of the containing class regardless of the access modifiers used to declare these members (not shown in the code above).

To reduce coupling, it is better for the containing class to be coupled to the inner class only rather than for both classes to be coupled to each other. However, this is unavoidable at times if the inner class needs to access data from its containing class.

An inner class can be declared using the **protected** or **public** access modifiers. This permits other objects to access the inner class using the name of the outer class, followed by a dot, followed by the name of the inner class. For example, assume that the **Node** inner class was declared **protected**. This

Chapter 4: Information Hiding and Design Principles

means that a client in the same package can declare an object variable to access a **Node** instance as follows:

```
LinkedList.Node node;
```

The client can then obtain a reference to an instance of **Node** or create a **Node** object on its own. However, the coding is not only cumbersome and error-prone, but it also assumes that a client knows what to do with a **Node** object. If it is intended that an inner class should be accessible to other clients, it is probably better to make it an independent class.

Exercises

1. Explain why the attributes of a class are usually **private** and the methods are usually **public**. Of what use is a **private** method? What is an appropriate use of a **public** instance variable?

2. Why should a class provide accessor and mutator methods? Is it necessary to provide accessor and mutator methods for *all* the attributes of a class? If not, which attributes should be omitted?

3. What is an inner class? What are the implications of declaring an inner class as **public**?

4. What do you think will happen if all the constructors of a class are declared with the **private** access modifier?

5. The attributes and methods of a certain class are declared without any access modifiers. Explain the type of access that will be permitted to objects in the same package and to objects in other packages.

6. What are the advantages of having low coupling among classes? What are the disadvantages of having weakly cohesive classes?

7. Describe the three-tiered architecture for an object-oriented application and explain how the classes of the application can be partitioned into packages.

8. Suppose that an attribute, **a**, of a class **C** is declared **private**. Is it possible in Java for an instance of **C** to view and/or modify attribute **a** of another instance of **C**?

Chapter 5

First Programming Project

This chapter discusses how to go about building a simple object-oriented application based on the concepts presented in Chapters 3 and 4. The application consists of a single domain class and a user interface that manipulates the objects of this class to achieve the functionality required. The chapter first describes the requirements of the application and then presents a UML diagram showing the only domain class in the application. The implementation of this class is then explained. Next, a user interface is written that manipulates the domain objects using a text-based menu structure. The chapter explains how to go about creating and compiling the necessary source files in Java. Finally, an alternative implementation of the application is presented in which there are two domain classes instead of one.

5.1 Requirements of the Application

An object-oriented application is required to manage information on students at a certain university. This section describes the functionality desired of the application.

5.1.1 Overview

The application must manage information on the students enrolled at a university. It must also provide a user interface that allows a user to perform the following operations:

- Enroll new students at the university
- Query for a particular student
- Change a student's telephone number
- List all the students at the university

Fundamentals of Object-Oriented Programming in Java

The application will consist of a single domain class, **Student**. The user interface of the application will be provided by another class, **StudentApplication**. The next section gives a UML diagram of the **Student** class and this is followed by a detailed description of the functionality required of the two classes in the application.

5.1.2 UML Diagram of **Student** Class

Figure 5.1 is a UML diagram of the single domain class, **Student**, in the application.

Student
ID : Integer firstName : String lastName : String phone : String
setPhone(newPhone : String) toString() : String

Figure 5.1: UML Diagram of **Student** Class

5.1.3 **Student** Class

The **Student** class models the concept of a student at the university. Table 5.1 shows the list of attributes of **Student**.

Attribute	Type	Purpose
ID	int	Unique identifier for the student.
firstName	String	First name of the student.
lastName	String	Last name of the student.
phone	String	Telephone number of the student.

Table 5.1: Attributes of **Student**

The **ID** attribute of each student should be automatically generated. The first student **ID** should be 10 and each new student should increment the previous **ID** by 10. So, the second student will have an **ID** of 20, the third will have an **ID** of 30, and so on.

Table 5.2 shows the methods that should be provided by the **Student** class.

Chapter 5: First Programming Project

Method	Return Type	Purpose
Student (String firstName, String lastName, String phone)		Constructor (NB: the student ID is not a parameter since it is automatically generated).
setPhone(String newPhone)	void	Changes the student's telephone number to the one in the parameter list.
toString()	String	Returns a string representation of the Student object.

Table 5.2: Methods of Student

5.1.4 User Interface

The user interface must enable the user to perform several operations such as:

- Add a new student to the system
- Display information about the student with a given student ID
- Change a student's telephone number
- List all the students in the system

The user interface should accept input from the keyboard and generate textual output to the console. The class, StudentApplication, should provide the functionality of the user interface.

5.1.5 Implementation Requirements

The Student class and the StudentApplication class must be in the same package. Also, accessors must be provided for the attributes of the Student class (although they are not used in the application). An array should be used to store the collection of Student objects. Information hiding should be enforced as much as possible.

5.2 Implementation of Student Domain Class

The Student class can be implemented in a similar manner to the Account class described in Chapters 3 and 4. It has four attributes which are declared as private instance variables in the following code:

```
private int ID;
```

```
private String firstName;
private String lastName;
private String phone;
```

There is a requirement that the ID numbers of the Student objects should be generated in increments of 10, starting from 10. One way to do this is to let the client (e.g., the user interface) manage the creation of the ID numbers. This will work if there is only one client of the Student class. If there are more clients (e.g., in a networked system), clients will have to synchronize themselves in some way in order to generate a unique sequence of ID numbers.

An easier approach is to use a class variable. Recall from Chapter 3 that a class variable is shared among all the instances of a class. Thus, the class variable can keep track of the next student ID to be assigned.

An IDGenerator class variable is declared in the Student class as follows:

```
private static int IDGenerator = 10;
```

Its value is set to 10 which is the value of the first student ID. In the constructor of the Student class, the ID attribute of the new Student instance is set to the current value of the IDGenerator. The IDGenerator is then incremented by 10. Thus, if another instance of Student is created, the current value of IDGenerator will be the incremented value.

Apart from the code to generate a student ID using a class variable, the rest of the code for the constructor is fairly straightforward:

```
public Student (String firstName, String lastName, String phone) {
   ID = IDGenerator;
   this.firstName = firstName;
   this.lastName = lastName;
   this.phone = phone;

   IDGenerator = IDGenerator + 10;
}
```

Note the use of the this keyword to distinguish an instance variable of the class from a variable declared in the parameter list. For example, this.firstName refers to the instance variable firstName, while firstName by itself refers to the parameter of the method.

The accessor methods are also straightforward to implement. All that has to be done is to return the value of the corresponding instance variable:

Chapter 5: First Programming Project

```
public int getID() {
   return ID;
}

public String getFirstName() {
   return firstName;
}

public String getLastName() {
   return lastName;
}

public String getPhone() {
   return phone;
}
```

The **toString()** method concatenates the values of all the instance variables of the **Student** object in a **String** and returns the **String** object:

```
public String toString() {
   String s;

   s =  "ID: " + ID +
        " Name: " + firstName + " " + lastName +
        " Telephone: " + phone;

   return s;
}
```

The **setPhone()** method accepts a new telephone number as a parameter and replaces the existing telephone number with this new number:

```
public void setSetPhone(String newPhone) {
   phone = newPhone;
}
```

Note that all the methods of **Student** are declared as **public** since they must be made available to client classes such as the user interface.

5.3 Implementation of the User Interface

The user interface can be implemented as a menu containing a list of choices generated by output statements (using **System.out.println()**). The **Scanner** class can be used to obtain user input from the keyboard. Methods of the `Scanner` class obtain the selection made by the user from the menu and read the data required for that selection.

Figure 5.2 shows a menu structure for implementing the user interface:

```
1. Add a new student to the system
2. Display information about a student with a given student ID
3. Change a student's telephone number
4. List all the students in the system
5. Exit

Please make a selection:
```

Figure 5.2: User Interface

The user interface class contains methods that provide the functionality required of menu options 1 to 4 above. The methods that have to be invoked for each menu option and the input values that must be entered by the user are listed in Table 5.3:

Menu option	Method to invoke from user interface class	Values to be input by the user
1	choice1()	First name, last name, and telephone number
2	choice2()	ID
3	choice3()	ID, new telephone number
4	choice4()	<none>
5	None; exit application.	<none>

Table 5.3: Methods and Input Values Corresponding to Menu Options

5.3.1 Implementation of User Interface Class

The user interface class needs to keep a collection of `Student` objects. An array is used for this purpose. A variable, `numStudents`, keeps track of the number of `Student` objects currently in the array.

The `main()` method of the user interface class calls the `menu()` method which generates the menu shown in Figure 5.2. The `main()` method then calls

Chapter 5: First Programming Project

`choice1()`, `choice2()`, `choice3()`, and `choice4()` based on the options selected by the user. Since `main()` is a class method, these methods must also be class methods so they are declared with the `static` keyword.

Now, `choice1()`, `choice2()`, `choice3()`, and `choice4()` need to manipulate the array of `Student` objects to do their work. Since class methods cannot access instance variables, the array of `Student` objects and the `numStudents` instance variable must be declared as class variables using the `static` keyword:

```
private static Student[] students;
private static int numStudents;
```

The instance of the `Scanner` class that is used to obtain user input must also be declared as a class variable since it is used by the class methods above. The declaration is as follows:

```
private static Scanner scanner;
```

The `main()` method of the user interface class creates the `students` array, initialises `numStudents` to zero, and creates the instance of `Scanner`:

```
students = new Student[100];
numStudents = 0;
scanner = new Scanner(System.in);
```

5.3.2 Implementation of `choice1()`

After obtaining the student's first name, last name, and telephone number from the user, the `choice1()` method creates an instance of `Student` with these values, inserts the instance into the collection of `Student` objects, and updates the `numStudents` variable. The code for the `choice1()` method is given below:

```
public static void choice1() {
   String firstName, lastName;
   String phone;

   System.out.println
      ("Enter the student's first name, last name, and telephone
      number: ");

   firstName = scanner.next();
   lastName = scanner.next();
```

```java
    phone = scanner.next();

    students[numStudents] = new Student(firstName, lastName, phone);
    numStudents++;
}
```

5.3.3 Implementation of choice2()

After obtaining the student's ID from the user, the `choice2()` method checks the collection of Student objects to see if there is a student with the given ID (using a helper method, `getStudent()`). If so, it displays the student information on the console using the `toString()` method; otherwise, it displays an error message. A portion of the code for the `choice2()` method is given below:

```java
student = getStudent(studentID);

if (student == null)
   System.out.println ("There is no student with this ID.");
else
   System.out.println (student.toString());
```

5.3.4 Implementation of choice3()

Like `choice2()`, `choice3()` first determines if there is a student with the given ID using the `getStudent()` helper method. If so, the new telephone number is obtained from the user and the student's telephone number is updated to the new number using the `setPhone()` method; otherwise, an error message is displayed:

```java
student = getStudent(studentID);

if (student == null)
   System.out.println ("There is no student with this ID.");
else {
   String newPhone;

   System.out.print ("Please enter the new telephone number: ");
   newPhone = scanner.next();
   student.setPhone(newPhone);

   System.out.println
       ("Student's telephone number has been updated.");
}
```

5.3.5 Implementation of `choice4()`

The `choice4()` method is implemented by traversing the collection of `Student` objects and displaying information on each `Student` object using its `toString()` method:

```
for (int i=0; i<numStudents; i++) {
   System.out.println(students[i].toString());
}
```

5.3.6 Implementation of `getStudent()` Helper Method

In order to display information about a particular student or to change the telephone number of a particular student, the `choice2()` and `choice3()` methods must first determine if there is a `Student` object corresponding to the `ID` that is input by the user. This is accomplished through the `getStudent()` helper method which traverses the collection of `Student` objects to check whether there is a `Student` object with the same `ID` as the parameter. The code is given below:

```
public static Student getStudent(int studentID) {

   for(int i=0; i<numStudents; i++) {
      if (students[i].getID() == studentID)
         return students[i];
   }

   return null;
}
```

5.4 Creating Source Files and Compiling

The code for each class in the application should be written in a separate source file as follows:

        `Student` class   : `Student.java`
        User interface class : `StudentApplication.java`

Compiling `StudentApplication.java` will initially cause `Student.java` to be compiled as well since it is coupled to the `Student` class. However, it is better to compile the `Student` class separately since it is not coupled to any other class. After it has been successfully compiled, the `StudentApplication` class can be compiled. Once `StudentApplication` compiles successfully, the application is ready to run. Please note that the complete application is available for download at the book Web site.

5.5 Alternative Implementation using Another Domain Class

A closer look at the code segments of the user interface class given above reveals that the user interface is performing a number of tasks that are best undertaken by a domain class. For example, it maintains a collection of **Student** objects and manipulates this collection in various ways. Ideally, the user interface should receive input from the user, send requests to domain objects based on this input, receive output from the domain objects, and display this output to the user. Clearly, the user interface is doing more than it should in this application.

A better approach is to extract the domain-related tasks that are being performed by the user interface and create a domain class that is responsible for performing these tasks. The new domain class is called **University** since it seems natural that a **University** class should manage instances of a **Student** class. A UML diagram of the **University** class is given in Figure 5.3.

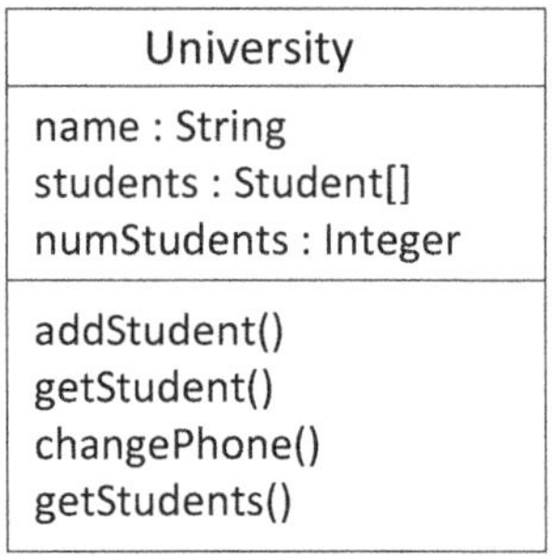

University
name : String students : Student[] numStudents : Integer
addStudent() getStudent() changePhone() getStudents()

Figure 5.3: **University** Class

The **University** class is now responsible for managing the **Student** objects. Thus, it stores a collection of **Student** objects and uses a variable **numStudents** to keep track of the number of **Student** objects in the collection. **University** contains the list of attributes shown in Table 5.4.

Chapter 5: First Programming Project

Attribute	Type	Purpose
name	String	The name of the university.
students	Collection of `Student` objects	A list of all the students at the university.
numStudents	int	The number of students at the university.

Table 5.4: Attributes of `University`

The `University` class must also provide the methods shown in Table 5.5.

Method	Return Type	Purpose
University()		Constructor method.

addStudent(
    String firstName,
    String lastName,
    String phone)
	void	Creates a `Student` object and adds it to its collection of students.

getStudent(int studentID)	Student	Finds and returns the `Student` object with the given `ID`; if none exists, returns `null`.

changePhone(
    int studentID,
    String newPhone)
	boolean	Changes the telephone number of the given student to the new telephone number; returns `true` if successful and `false` otherwise.

getStudents ()	String	Returns a string representation of all the `Student` objects.

Table 5.5: Methods of `University`

It can be observed that the `University` class is now responsible for several of the tasks that were previously being performed by the user interface.

In the new application, the user interface first creates an instance of the `University` class as follows:

```
university = new University("The University of Computing");
```

After it receives user input, it forwards requests to domain objects instead of doing the work by itself. For example, `choice4()` (which displays a list of all the students in the system) is implemented as follows:

```
public static void choice4() {
   System.out.println(university.getStudents());
```

}

Thus, the user interface is now solely responsible for receiving input from the user, forwarding requests to the domain objects based on the input, and displaying output to the user.

There are now two domain classes in the application, **University** and **Student**. These two classes are related to each other through an *"enrolls"* relationship since a university enrolls students. Alternatively, the relationship can be called *"is enrolled at"* since a student is enrolled at a university. To illustrate that there is a relationship between **University** and **Student** in a UML diagram, we draw a solid line with the label *"enrolls"* between the **University** class and the **Student** class:

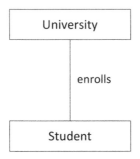

Figure 5.4: University is Related to Student

The relationship between **University** and **Student** can be more precisely specified as being a relationship of *containment* (or *aggregation*) since a **University** object contains and manages a collection of several **Student** objects. Containment relationships are drawn with an open diamond at the object that contains the other object. Thus, the relationship between **University** and **Student** can be more accurately drawn in the UML diagram below:

Chapter 5: First Programming Project

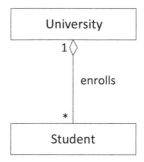

Figure 5.5: **University** is Related to **Student** by a Containment Relationship

The "1" at the University end of the relationship and the "*" at the Student end indicates that one University object is related to several Student objects; however, a given Student object is related to only one University object.

At this point, we have an application that seems to work. But, how do we know if the application is fit for use and achieves its intended purpose? How do we know if the methods described in the previous sections work correctly under all circumstances? If we write an application we want to ensure that it does what is required and that it works correctly. It makes no sense to write an application that does not achieve its objectives or generates errors all the time. This is the reason why applications are tested. The next chapter explains how to test an object-oriented application. In particular, it focuses on unit testing the University and Student classes which were developed in this chapter for the student application.

Chapter 6

Unit Testing an Object-Oriented Program

This chapter discusses the need to unit test an object-oriented program and explains how it can be achieved using the JUnit testing framework. Unit testing ensures that a class is fit for use and behaves as intended. Unit testing is not the kind of testing where a programmer uses a console application or some other user interface to test the functionality of a program. Rather, a unit test is an automated piece of code which invokes the method or class being tested and checks some assumptions about the logical behavior of that method or class (Osherove, 2009). A good unit test is automated and repeatable. Once written, it is available for future use and can be run at the push of a button. This chapter discusses how to unit test the domain classes created in the first programming project. In particular, it explains how to write unit tests for the `Student` and `University` classes and how to run them using the JUnit framework.

6.1 Classes to Test in the Student Application

Figure 6.1 is a UML diagram of the domain classes from the Student application in the first programming project. There are two classes, `University` and `Student`. `University` is related to `Student` through an "enrolls" relationship.

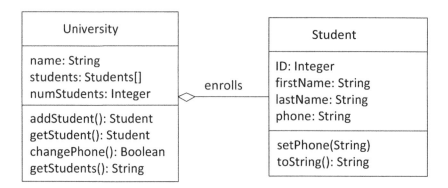

Figure 6.1: **University** and **Student** Classes

This chapter describes how to unit test the two domain classes in Figure 6.1. It does not cover the testing of the user interface.

6.2 Testing the Student Application

This section first describes an approach that is commonly used by developers to test an object-oriented application. In particular, it is an approach used by developers who are not familiar with automated testing techniques. A detailed testing scenario with the Student application is presented, highlighting some of the weaknesses of this testing approach. The section then explains how unit testing with a unit testing framework can make the testing process more robust and efficient. This section may be omitted if you are already familiar with automated tested techniques.

6.2.1 Common Approach to Testing

A common approach to testing an object-oriented application involves using the user interface to exercise different features of the application. The user interface of the Student application is shown in Figure 6.2.

Chapter 6: Unit Testing an Object-Oriented Program

```
1. Add a new student to the system
2. Display information about a student with a given student ID
3. Change a student's telephone number
4. List all the students in the system
5. Exit

Please make a selection:
```

Figure 6.2: User Interface of Student Application

A common approach to testing the application is to run the user interface and execute its options one by one, verifying manually that the results are correct. Using this approach, a typical set of steps a developer might follow to test the application is:

- Use Option 1 to add a few students to the system.
- Use Option 2 to test that the student information displayed is the same as that which was used to create the student in Option 1; supply a valid student ID as well as a student ID which does not correspond to any student.
- Use Option 3 to change a student's telephone number; supply a valid student ID as well as a student ID which does not correspond to any student.
- Use Option 2 to test whether the telephone number was correctly changed.
- After using Option 1 to add several students to the system, use Option 4 to test whether the list of students displayed is consistent with the actual students which were added.

6.2.2 A Testing Scenario

This sub-section describes a testing scenario where the approach described in the previous section is used to test the Student application. The scenario is a little drawn out; however, this is done so that you will appreciate the need for an alternative approach to testing. This alternative approach is automated testing using a unit testing framework. Three programming errors have been introduced in the **University** class to make the discussion more interesting. The errors are located in the **addStudent()**, **getStudent()**, and **getStudents()** methods.

We start by executing the Student application which causes the user interface shown in Figure 6.2 to be displayed. We then choose Option 1 to enter information on a student. When the system prompts for the first name, last name, and telephone number of the student, the following data is entered:

```
John Doe 123-4567
```

The system then generates the following output and re-displays the user interface:

```
Student added to the system. Student ID is 10.
```

Naturally, before proceeding, we would like to ensure that we can correctly retrieve the **Student** object just added. So, Option 2 is chosen. When the system prompts for a student ID, 10 is entered. Interestingly, the following output is displayed:

```
There is no student with this ID.
```

This is cause for concern. So, we abort the testing process and start debugging. Which methods should we examine? Since Option 2 uses the **getStudent()** method to search for a student, we study this method first:

```
public Student getStudent(int studentID) {

   for(int i=0; i<numStudents-1; i++) {
      if (students[i].getID() == studentID)
         return students[i];
   }

   return null;
}
```

The method looks correct but after examining the code several times, we discover the error: the condition for staying in the loop should not be (**i <numStudents-1**). Since (**numStudents-1**) evaluates to 0, the loop would not be entered and **getStudent()** will return **null**. Hastily, we change the condition to (**i<=numStudents**) and recompile the **University** class.

Once again, we execute the Student application and choose Option 1. We enter the same information as before and choose Option 2. When 10 is entered for the student ID, the program crashes unexpectedly with the following message:

Chapter 6: Unit Testing an Object-Oriented Program

```
Exception in thread "main" java.lang.NullPointerException
   at University.getStudent(University.java:32)
   at StudentApplication.choice2(StudentApplication.java:77)
   at StudentApplication.main(StudentApplication.java:20)
```

Now, this is even more serious. The error message indicates that the `NullPointerException` occurred in the `getStudent()` method of the `University` class. But, we just checked through `getStudent()` several times and there were no more errors. Where could the error be? We look again at Line number 32 of `University.java`, as indicated by the error message:

```
if (students[i].getID() == studentID)
```

Now, a `NullPointerException` occurs if an object variable is not currently referring to an object in memory. So, somehow, `students[0]` does not refer to a `Student` object. But, how could that be? Recall that after we entered the data for a student in Option 1, we got a message that the student was added to the system and the ID was 10.

Since there doesn't seem to be anything wrong with `getStudent()`, we turn our attention to the `addStudent()` method:

```
public Student addStudent
   (String firstName, String lastName, String phone) {

   Student student = new Student (firstName, lastName, phone);
   numStudents++;
   students[numStudents] = student;
   return student;
}
```

The `addStudent()` method creates a `Student` object and inserts it in an appropriate location of the array. Unable to figure out what might be causing the problem, we do a manual execution. First, we verify that the initial value of the `numStudents` instance variable is zero. This is indeed so, since the constructor assigned `numStudents` to zero. After creating the `Student` object, `numStudents` is incremented to 1. Then, the `Student` object is assigned to location 1 of the array. Location 0 is empty, i.e., it has a `null` reference. This is the error! So, we fix the error by moving the statement which increments `numStudents` *after* the array assignment statement.

We re-compile the `University` class and continue the testing process. Once again we execute the `Student` application and choose Option 1. Once again we enter the same information as before and choose Option 2. This time, the information for the student is correctly displayed:

```
ID: 10 Name: John Doe Telephone: 123-4567
```

Now that things seem to be working, we choose Option 1 and enter data for another student. The system generates the following output and re-displays the user interface:

```
Student added to the system. Student ID is 20.
```

So, it looks like the automatic generation of student **ID**s in increments of 10 is working properly as well. We then choose Option 2 and enter 20 to ensure that the **Student** object can be correctly retrieved. Happily, the system displays the correct data for the student:

```
ID: 20 Name: Peter Pan Telephone: 111-4444
```

To continue testing, we choose Option 2 and supply an invalid student **ID** to ensure that the system says that there is no such student. So, we supply 30 for the student **ID**. Rather weirdly, we get the same **NullPointerException** again, in exactly the same line of the source code.

So, we re-examine the source code once again. After some time, we find the error. In our haste to correct the first error, we had set the condition of the **for** loop to (**i<=numStudents**) instead of (**i<numStudents**). So, we fix the error and resume testing. Again, we need to create two new students, verify that the **Student** objects can be retrieved, and ensure that the system gives a correct message for an invalid student. The tests succeed and we proceed to test Option 4.

There are two students in the system, one with **ID** 10 and the other with **ID** 20. When Option 4 is selected, the system displays the following information:

```
List of Students:
ID: 10 Name: John Doe Telephone: 123-4567
```

This is rather surprising. Why wasn't the information for the second student displayed? So we start the debugging process all over again ...

6.2.3 Weaknesses of the Testing Approach

The testing scenario described above highlights several weaknesses of the approach taken. If the program "crashes" while being tested, the error must be fixed and the testing process has to be repeated. To determine if the error has been corrected, it is necessary to re-create the scenario that caused the program to crash and this can be very time-consuming. If other errors are detected, these must be noted and the testing process has to be repeated, again going through the tedious process of re-entering data and re-creating the scenarios that led to the errors in the first place. Even after testing is completed, there may be a need later on to change one or more of the classes in the application. After making the necessary changes, the application needs to be tested from scratch since the results of the previous testing may not be available.

When the final application is tested instead of individual classes, it is easy to omit the testing of certain functionality provided by the domain classes since the methods of the underlying domain classes may not correspond directly to the options of the user interface. In addition, the tests are often not documented properly and developers who were not involved in the initial testing may not know how the application was tested previously.

There is also the problem of finding and fixing errors identified by the testing process. The Student application has two underlying domain classes. If an error occurs, it could be due to a problem in one of the classes or in both of them. It could also be due to one or more methods in a class. As the testing scenario unfolded, errors which we thought were due to one method were eventually traced to another method. Indeed, Osherove (2009) observes that the kind of testing performed in the testing scenario is not really unit testing; rather, it is a form of testing done at a later stage known as *integration testing*.

The weaknesses of the non-automated approach to testing are highlighted below:

- Need to re-create testing scenarios each time an error occurs
- Difficult to identify source of error
- Not possible to re-use tests previously conducted
- Does not exhaustively test the methods of the domain classes
- Tests are often not documented

6.2.4 The Benefits of Unit Testing

A better approach to testing is to first test the individual classes of the application independently of each other and then perform the integration testing. It is also desirable to automate the testing process so that tests are repeatable and are available for future use. Thus, if an error occurs, the previous tests are simply re-executed without the need to re-create the scenario that led to the error. This approach to testing is known as *unit testing*. A unit test can be defined as follows:

"A *unit test* is an automated piece of code that invokes the method or class being tested and then checks some assumptions about the logical behavior of that method or class. A unit test is almost always written using a unit-testing framework. It can be written easily and runs quickly. It's fully automated, trustworthy, readable, and maintainable." (Osherove, 2009, p.11)

The remainder of this chapter explains how to write unit tests using the JUnit testing framework. JUnit is the most popular unit testing framework for the Java language. As an example, the chapter shows how to write unit tests for the classes from the Student application in the first programming project. It also describes a set of unit tests for a `Triangle` class to show the range of testing that is possible with JUnit.

6.3 Testing Individual Classes with JUnit

In order to unit test the `Student` class, a test class called `StudentTest` is written. Similarly, in order to unit test the `University` class, a test class called `UniversityTest` is written. The `StudentTest` class consists of a number of test methods which test the methods of the corresponding `Student` class. Typically, a test method will invoke methods on an instance of the class being tested and verify that the methods have been correctly written. The `StudentTest` and `UniversityTest` classes must be compiled like other Java classes. The compiled version of each class is supplied as input to the JUnit testing framework. Figure 6.3 illustrates the testing process with JUnit using `StudentTest` as an example.

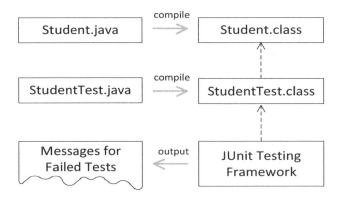

Figure 6.3: Testing Process with JUnit

6.3.1 A Test Class

A test class is similar to any other class. The following code is an outline of a test class. Note that a colon is used to indicate places where code must be inserted. Also, the name of the test class and the name of the methods are user-defined. Specific naming conventions may be adopted as needed.

```
import org.junit.*;    // import package with JUnit classes

import static org.junit.Assert.*;
                      // import package with JUnit classes

public class NameOfClassTest {
                     // class containing test methods

  // declare instance variables for test class

  @BeforeClass      // perform one time test initialization
                    // before all tests

  public void runOnceBeforeTests() {
     :
  }

  @Before           // perform initialization before each test
  public void runBeforeEachTest() {
     :
  }

  @Test             // test method 1
  public void testMethod1() {
     :
  }

  @Test             // test method 2
  public void testMethod2() {
     :
  }
  :

  @Test             // test method N
  public void testMethodN() {
     :
  }
```

```
    @After              // perform cleanup after each test
    public void runAfterEachTest() {
        :
    }

    @AfterClass         // perform one time test cleanup
                        // after all tests
    public void runOnceAfterTests()  {
        :
    }
}
```

As can be seen, the individual methods of a test class are annotated with a word prefixed with the "@" symbol (e.g., `@Test`). This is done so that the methods can be recognized by the JUnit testing framework. The next subsection discusses the concept of an annotation and explains how different types of test methods can be annotated for the JUnit testing framework.

When a test class is executed, the test methods are executed one by one by the JUnit testing framework. JUnit does not guarantee the order of execution of the test methods in a test class. Since the test methods are executed in an arbitrary manner, the test methods can be placed in any order in the test class. The approach taken in this book is to use the same order as the corresponding methods in the class being tested. Since the order in which two test methods are executed cannot be known beforehand, a test method should not depend on another test method.

Note that a test class can contain instance variables like any other class. Since test methods should not depend on each other, one might ask, what is the purpose of an instance variable in a test class? An instance variable can be set to a value by the methods that perform test initialization. Thus, through the use of instance variables, a test initialization method can set up a test environment that is available to each test method. This environment can be destroyed at the end of each test method by the methods that perform test cleanup.

6.3.2 Annotations

In Java, *annotations* are a form of metadata which provides data about the source code. Classes, methods, variables, and other program elements can be annotated. Annotations are somewhat like comments in a program. Like comments, they have no direct effect on the source code. Annotations have a number of uses in programming. They can provide information to the

Chapter 6: Unit Testing an Object-Oriented Program

compiler to take some action such as detecting certain types of errors or suppressing warnings. Annotations can also be embedded in compiled Java classes; thus, they can be examined at run-time. The JUnit testing framework uses the annotations in a compiled test class to know how to execute the test methods defined in the class.

An annotation begins with the "@" symbol. By convention, it appears on its own line before the program element being annotated. Table 6.1 lists some of the annotations that can be used to annotate the methods of a test class for JUnit.

Annotation	*Purpose*
@BeforeClass	The method that follows is executed once, before all the other methods of the class have executed. It is used to establish an environment in which all the test methods will operate (one time test initialization).
@AfterClass	The method that follows is executed once, after all the other methods of the class have finished executing. It is used to destroy the testing environment (one time test cleanup).
@Before	The method that follows is executed before each test method is executed (test initialization).
@After	The method that follows is executed after each test method is executed (test cleanup).
@Test	The method that follows is a test method.

Table 6.1: Some Annotations Used By JUnit

6.3.3 Writing a Test Method

JUnit provides various *assert* methods that can be used for writing tests. Four of them are listed in Table 6.2.

Assert Methods	Description
assertEquals(expected, actual)	The test passes if `expected` is equal to `actual` and fails otherwise.
assertTrue(booleanCondition)	The test passes if the `booleanCondition` evaluates to `true` and fails otherwise.
assertNull(object)	The test passes if the object is `null` and fails otherwise.
assertNotNull(object)	The test passes if the object is not `null` and fails otherwise.

Table 6.2: *Assert* Methods

It should be noted that the methods in Table 6.2 are overloaded for different types of data. For example, the `assertEquals()` method can be used to check if values of the same type are equal. It can be used with integer values as follows:

```
assertEquals(10, 10);   // test passes since values are equal
```

It can also be used with character or string values as follows:

```
assertEquals('a', 'b');
                // test fails since values are not the same
assertEquals("John", "John");
                // test passes since values are equal
```

Table 6.3 gives ten examples of tests written using the *assert* methods. The results of these tests are also given. The tests in Table 6.3 contain supporting code such as declarations and assignments. They are contained in a class called `ExampleTest` which is available for download at the book Web site. `ExampleTest` contains a test method for each of the tests shown in Table 6.3.

Chapter 6: Unit Testing an Object-Oriented Program

Test with Supporting Code	Result of Test
assertEquals(10, 10);	Test passes since 10 is equal to 10.
int x = 10; assertEquals(x, 15);	Test fails since the value of **x** is not equal to 15.
char c = 'a'; assertEquals(c, 'a');	Test passes since the value of **c** is equal to 'a'.
String actual = "John"; String expected = "Doe"; assertEquals(expected, actual);	Test fails since the two strings are different.
int x = 10; assertTrue((x%2) == 1);	Test passes for odd numbers. Since 10 is an even number, test fails.
double balance = -5.00; assertTrue(balance >= 0.0);	Test fails since **balance** is less than 0.0.
boolean success = true; assertTrue(success);	Test passes since **success** evaluates to **true**.
Student student = new Student("John", "Doe", "123-4567"); assertNull(student);	Test fails since **student** contains a reference to an object so it is not **null**.
University university = new University("The University of Computing"); assertNotNull(university);	Test passes since **university** contains a reference to an object so it is not **null**.
Student student = null; assertNull(student);	Test passes since the **student** object variable is **null**.

Table 6.3: Examples of Tests with Results

The first test in Table 6.3 is quite simple and can be implemented in a test method as follows:

```
@Test
public void test1()
{
   assertEquals(10, 10);
}
```

The test methods for the other tests in Table 6.3 are written in a similar manner to `test1()` above. Each test method contains the code shown in the left-hand column of Table 6.3. It should be noted that a test method is generally not as simple as `test1()` or the other test methods in `ExampleTest`. A test method will usually obtain data for the test (or tests) it performs by invoking methods on the class being tested.

6.3.4 Differentiating a Test from a Test Method

It is important to distinguish between the terms test and test method, as used in this book. A *test* is written using one of the *assert* methods in Table 6.2. A test will either pass or fail as indicated in Table 6.3. A *test method* is a method that is preceded by the @Test annotation such as the `test1()` method. A test method can contain any number of tests.

6.4 Unit Testing the Student Class

This section explains how to unit test the Student class using the JUnit testing framework. It describes some tests that can be carried out and then shows how each of these tests can be implemented as a test method. It also explains how to use JUnit to run the test methods.

6.4.1 Unit Tests for the Student Class

As mentioned earlier in the chapter, in order to test the Student class with JUnit, a test class called StudentTest is written. The Student class is fairly straightforward to test. Table 6.4 lists the four tests that are carried out on the Student class together with the names of the corresponding test methods in StudentTest.

Description of Test	Corresponding Test Method
Test whether a Student object has been correctly created and initialized.	testCreate()
Test whether the student ID is being generated automatically in increments of 10.	testID()
Test whether the phone attribute of a Student object is being correctly updated.	testSetPhone()
Test whether the toString() method of Student is returning the correct string representation.	testToString()

Table 6.4: Unit Tests for the Student Class

Figure 6.4 is a UML diagram of the StudentTest class and the corresponding Student class. Since StudentTest uses instances of Student to perform its tests, there is a dependency arrow between StudentTest and Student.

Chapter 6: Unit Testing an Object-Oriented Program

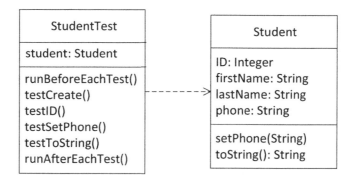

Figure 6.4: **StudentTest** Class and Corresponding **Student** Class

6.4.2 StudentTest Class

The **StudentTest** class contains an instance variable **student** which is declared as follows:

```
private Student student;
                // instance of Student
```

The instance variable is assigned a reference to a **Student** object by the **runBeforeEachTest()** initialization method which is executed before each test method:

```
@Before           // perform test initialization before each test
public void runBeforeEachTest()  {
   student = new Student ("John", "Doe", "123-4567");
}
```

Thus, each test method has access to a **Student** object which can be used to perform any type of testing required. The **runAfterEachTest()** method performs test cleanup by setting the reference to the **Student** object to **null** after each test so that it can be garbage collected:

```
@After            // perform test cleanup after each test
public void runAfterEachTest() {
   student = null;
}
```

There are no **@BeforeClass** and **@AfterClass** methods in **StudentTest**. The details of each test method in **StudentTest** will now be given.

6.4.2.1 testCreate()

The `testCreate()` method tests that a `Student` object has been correctly created and initialized using the `new` operator in conjunction with the constructor. The `Student` object is the same one that was created using the `runBeforeEachTest()` method since this method is guaranteed to execute before the `testCreate()` method (because of the `@Before` annotation). The `testCreate()` method is written as follows:

```
@Test
public void testCreate() {
   String firstName = student.getFirstName();
   String lastName = student.getLastName();
   String phone = student.getPhone();

   assertEquals("John", firstName);
   assertEquals("Doe", lastName);
   assertEquals("123-4567", phone);
}
```

The values of the attributes of the `Student` object are obtained using the accessor methods of `Student`. The first test in `testCreate()` checks to see if the `firstName` is equal to "John". The second test checks to see if the `lastName` is equal to "Doe". The third test checks to see if the telephone number is equal to "123-4567". Overall, the three tests check to see if the `Student` object was correctly initialized by the constructor. All three tests are written using the `assertEquals()` method.

6.4.2.2 testID()

The `testID()` method creates a `Student` object of its own to ensure that the `ID` numbers are being generated in increments of 10. It compares the `ID` of the already created `Student` object with the `ID` of the newly created `Student` object to see if the difference is 10.

```
@Test
public void testID()
{
   Student newStudent;
   int ID1, ID2;

   newStudent = new Student ("Peter", "Pan", "111-4444");

   ID1 = student.getID();
   ID2 = newStudent.getID();
```

Chapter 6: Unit Testing an Object-Oriented Program

```
    assertTrue(ID2 == (ID1 + 10));
}
```

6.4.2.3 testSetPhone()

The `testSetPhone()` method ensures that the `phone` attribute of a `Student` object is being correctly updated by the `setPhone()` method. It changes the `phone` attribute to a new value and verifies that the actual value obtained from `getPhone()` is the same as the new value.

```
@Test
public void testSetPhone()
{
    String newPhone = "111-4444";
    String phone;

    student.setPhone(newPhone);
    phone = student.getPhone();

    assertEquals(newPhone, phone);
}
```

6.4.2.4 testToString()

The `testToString()` method checks to see if the `toString()` method in `Student` is accurately producing a string based on the attribute values of a `Student` object. It compares an expected string with the actual string returned by the `toString()` method. It is written as follows:

```
@Test
public void testToString()
{
    int ID = student.getID();
    String actual = student.toString();
    String expected = "ID: " + ID +
                    " Name: John Doe Telephone: 123-4567";
    assertEquals(expected, actual);
}
```

6.4.3 Executing the Test Methods in StudentTest

The `StudentTest` class must be compiled and supplied as input to the JUnit testing framework. JUnit invokes the test methods in the test class one by one.

As mentioned before, JUnit does not guarantee the order of execution of the test methods in a test class. For example, the test methods in `StudentTest` may be executed in the following order:

testToString() → testCreate() → testID() → testSetPhone()

After executing a test class, JUnit provides a summary of the test methods executed, if none of the tests failed. Since `StudentTest` has already been successfully tested, the summary is as follows (note that the time will vary from computer to computer):

```
JUnit version 4.10
....
Time: 0.006

OK (4 tests)
```

To see what happens when there are testing errors, let's introduce a deliberate error in `Student`, the class being tested. Instead of simply returning the value of the `firstName` instance variable in `getFirstName()`, the `firstName` string is converted to upper case and then returned:

```java
public String getFirstName() {
   return firstName.toUpperCase();
}
```

When the test class is executed, JUnit displays the following summary and gives details of the test that failed:

```
JUnit version 4.10
..E..
Time: 0.007
There was 1 failure:
1) testCreate(StudentTest)
org.junit.ComparisonFailure: expected:<J[ohn]> but was:<J[OHN]>
:
FAILURES!!!
Tests run: 4,  Failures: 1
```

The error message gives a good indication of the source of the error. It states that there is one failure occurring in the `testCreate()` method of the `StudentTest` class. The failure occurred because of a comparison mismatch. The error message also shows exactly where the mismatch occurred in the strings being compared. To fix the error, the `testCreate()` method in `StudentTest` should be analysed.

There are two statements in the `testCreate()` method which are relevant to the error:

```
String firstName = student.getFirstName();
:
assertEquals("John", firstName);
```

The *assert* statement expects the `firstName` variable to have a value of "John" since this was the value supplied to the constructor of the `Student` object (created in the `runBeforeEachTest()` method). However, the value returned by `getFirstName()` is "JOHN", as indicated in the error message. So, the next step is to examine the `getFirstName()` method of `Student` to see why the string returned is not "John". The source of the error becomes apparent when it is observed that the `firstName` attribute is converted to upper case before it is returned by `getFirstName()`. The error is fixed in the `Student` class and then the test class is executed again.

There is a small possibility that the error could have been due to a problem in the `testCreate()` method itself. Generally, test methods should be written as simple as possible and should avoid logic statements to reduce the chance of introducing errors.

It should be noted that when the assert statement failed, JUnit immediately exited the method as if it encountered a `return` statement. Thus, the two other assert statements in `testCreate()` were not executed by JUnit. However, JUnit continues to execute the remaining test methods that were not yet executed. The test class needs to be run repeatedly with JUnit until no failures result.

6.5 Unit Testing the `University` Class

This section explains how to unit test the `University` class. It first describes the tests that are carried out and then shows how each test can be implemented as a test method in the `UniversityTest` class. The test methods in `UniversityTest` are executed in a similar manner to those in `StudentTest`.

6.5.1 Unit Tests for the `University` Class

Table 6.5 gives a brief description of the test methods that are written in `UniversityTest`.

Fundamentals of Object-Oriented Programming in Java

Test Method	Purpose
testCreate()	Tests whether a `University` object has been correctly created and initialized.
testAddStudent()	Tests whether the `addStudent()` method is correctly creating a `Student` object and storing it properly.
testGetStudent()	Tests whether the `getStudent()` method is correctly returning a `Student` object corresponding to the `ID` supplied as a parameter.
testChangePhone()	Tests whether the `changePhone()` method is correctly updating the `phone` attribute of the given `Student` object.
testGetStudents()	Tests whether the `getStudents()` method is correctly returning a string representation of all the `Student` objects in the system.

Table 6.5: Test Methods in `UniversityTest`

In addition to the test methods in Table 6.5, the `runBeforeEachTest()` method performs test initialization by creating an instance of `University` before each test begins. This is assigned to the `university` instance variable. Also, the `runAfterEachTest()` method performs test cleanup by setting the reference to the `University` object to `null` after each test so that it can be garbage collected. There are no `@BeforeClass` and `@AfterClass` methods in `UniversityTest`.

Figure 6.5 is a UML diagram showing the `UniversityTest` class and the corresponding `University` class.

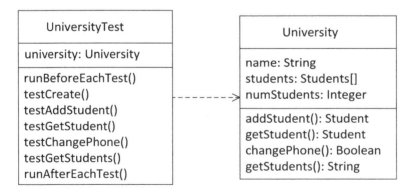

Figure 6.5: `UniversityTest` Class and Corresponding `University` Class

Chapter 6: Unit Testing an Object-Oriented Program

6.5.2 `UniversityTest` Class

The `UniversityTest` class is written in a similar way to the `StudentTest` class. The details of each test method will now be given.

6.5.2.1 `testCreate()`

The constructor for `University` sets the `name` instance variable to the value supplied as an argument and creates an array to store `Student` objects. The number of students is initialized to zero.

The `testCreate()` method checks to see if the `name` instance variable has been correctly initialized and if the number of students is indeed zero. It is written as follows:

```
@Test
public void testCreate() {

  String name = university.getName();
  int numStudents = university.getNumStudents();

  assertEquals("University of Computing", name);
  assertEquals(0, numStudents);

}
```

6.5.2.2 `testAddStudent()`

The `addStudent()` method creates a `Student` object and initializes it with the data supplied as arguments. The `Student` object is stored in the `University` object and the number of students is incremented by one. The method returns the `Student` object created. The `testAddStudent()` method checks to see if the `Student` object returned is not `null` and if the number of students is being correctly updated. Two students are added by the test method. The code for the `testAddStudent()` method is given below.

```
@Test
public void testAddStudent() {

  int numStudents;
  Student student;

  student = university.addStudent("John", "Doe", "123-4567");
  numStudents = university.getNumStudents();
```

```
    assertNotNull(student);
    assertEquals(1, numStudents);

    student = university.addStudent ("Peter", "Pan", "765-4321");
    numStudents = university.getNumStudents();
    assertNotNull(student);
    assertEquals(2, numStudents);

}
```

6.5.2.3 testGetStudent()

The getStudent() method accepts an ID as an argument and returns the Student object with the corresponding ID or null, if there is no such student. The testGetStudent() method uses the addStudent() method to add a student to the system. It then checks to see if the getStudent() method returns the same Student object as the one added. The testGetStudent() method also checks to see if getStudent() returns null if there is no student with the given ID. It is written as follows:

```
@Test
public void testGetStudent() {

    Student student, student2;

    student = university.addStudent("John", "Doe", "123-4567");

    student2 = university.getStudent(student.getID());
    assertNotNull(student2);
    assertEquals(student, student2);

    student2 = university.getStudent(student.getID() + 10);
    assertNull(student2)
}
```

6.5.2.4 testChangePhone()

The changePhone() method changes the telephone number of the student with the given ID. It returns true if the telephone number was successfully changed and false otherwise. The testChangePhone() method creates a Student object and then changes the telephone number of the student. It checks to see if the changePhone() method returns true and if the telephone number was successfully changed. It also attempts to change the telephone

Chapter 6: Unit Testing an Object-Oriented Program

number of a non-existent student to ensure that the `changePhone()` method returns `false`. The code for the `testChangePhone()` method is given below.

```
@Test
public void testChangePhone() {

  Student student;
  int ID;
  boolean success;

  student = university.addStudent("John", "Doe", "123-4567");
  ID = student.getID();

  success = university.changePhone(ID, "111-4444");
  assertEquals (true, success);
  assertEquals ("111-4444", student.getPhone());

  success = university.changePhone(ID + 10, "777-3333");
  assertEquals (false, success);
}
```

6.5.2.5 testGetStudents()

The `testGetStudents()` method creates two `Student` objects and generates a string which the `getStudents()` method of `University` is expected to produce. This string is compared with the actual string returned by the `getStudents()` method to test whether the `getStudents()` method is working correctly. The code is rather bulky so it is not included here. However, the complete code for `UniversityTest` can be downloaded from the book Web site.

6.5.3 Executing the Test Methods in `UniversityTest`

The `UniversityTest` class must be compiled and supplied as input to the JUnit testing framework. The same procedure that was used for running the test methods in `StudentTest` should be followed to run the test methods in `UniversityTest`.

6.6 Combining Unit Tests into a Test Suite

Test classes can be written for each domain class in an application, e.g., `Student` and `University`. The test classes can be executed individually using the JUnit framework. After each class has been tested, it is tedious to use this approach to test all the classes in the application. JUnit provides a means of running a collection of test classes as one unit. The collection of test classes is referred to as a *test suite*. A test suite is appropriate when all the classes of the application have already been tested individually. In order to use a test suite, two additional annotations are required. They are listed in Table 6.6.

Annotation	Purpose
@RunWith	Used with the name of a class (which contains a "runner") to tell JUnit to use the runner specified rather than the one that is built into JUnit.
@SuiteClasses	Used to specify the class files that comprise a test suite.

Table 6.6 Annotations Required for Creating a Test Suite

To specify that the `Suite` runner should be used instead of the built-in runner in JUnit, the `@RunWith` annotation should specify `Suite.class` in parentheses:

```
@RunWith(Suite.class)
```

The `@SuiteClasses` annotation can be used to specify the test classes that comprise the test suite. For example, the following `@SuiteClasses` annotation specifies that the test suite is made up of `StudentTest.class` and `UniversityTest.class`:

```
@SuiteClasses({StudentTest.class, UniversityTest.class})
```

The actual class where the test suite is specified does not need to contain any code since all we want to do is to run the test classes as a suite. However, a new set of JUnit packages must be imported for the `@RunWith` and `@SuiteClasses` annotations.

The test suite for the first programming project is written as follows:

```
import org.junit.runner.RunWith;
import org.junit.runners.Suite;
import org.junit.runners.Suite.SuiteClasses;

@RunWith(Suite.class)
@SuiteClasses( { StudentTest.class, UniversityTest.class } )

public class Project1Test
{
   // class does not contain any code
```

Chapter 6: Unit Testing an Object-Oriented Program

```
}
```

When the class `Project1Test` is executed with `JUnit`, the tests in `StudentTest` are executed first followed by the tests in `UniversityTest`. If there are more test classes, these can be easily added to the `@SuiteClasses` annotation.

6.7 Testing Scenario Compared to Unit Testing

The testing scenario described in Section 6.2 is an inefficient attempt to test the domain classes of the Student application. Indeed, the testing concentrates on testing the methods of the `University` class rather than the `Student` class. The test classes created for the JUnit testing framework automate the testing process so there is no need to go through the tedious process of creating a test environment whenever a feature must be tested. The automated tests also make it easy to re-run all the tests that previously succeeded, resulting in huge savings in time. The unit tests document the testing process for current and future developers. The tests can be executed as many times as required and can be executed long into the future without change.

6.8 Further Testing with JUnit

The Student application from the first programming project has been used in this chapter to demonstrate how test methods can be written to test the individual classes of an application. The classes in the application have been deliberately kept simple to focus on creating and linking objects together. The methods of `Student` and `University` do not perform many calculations and are not very "algorithmic" in nature. In order to broaden the range of testing covered in this chapter, this section shows how to write test methods for objects that perform many calculations or which use various algorithms to make decisions.

The class that will be tested is a `Triangle` class. The `Triangle` class has three instance variables, `side1`, `side2`, and `side3`, all of type integer. It provides the methods described in Table 6.5.

Fundamentals of Object-Oriented Programming in Java

Method	Return Type	Description
isTriangle()	boolean	Determines if the three sides can form a triangle using the fact that in a triangle, the sum of any two sides must be greater than the third side.
getType()	String	If it is a triangle, determines what kind of triangle is formed (equilateral, isosceles, or scalene).
isRightAngled()	boolean	If it is a triangle, determines if it is a right-angled triangle using Pythagoras' Theorem.
getPerimeter()	int	If it is a triangle, finds the perimeter of the triangle by adding the length of each side.
getArea()	double	If it is a triangle, finds the area of the triangle using Heron's formula ($area = \sqrt{[p \times (p - \texttt{side1}) \times (p - \texttt{side2}) \times (p - \texttt{side3})]}$ where $p = perimeter/2$).
toString()	String	Returns a string representation of the data on each side of the triangle.

Table 6.5: Methods of **Triangle** Class

A **TriangleTest** class is written to test the methods of the **Triangle** class. Figure 6.6 is a UML diagram showing the **TriangleTest** class and the corresponding **Triangle** class.

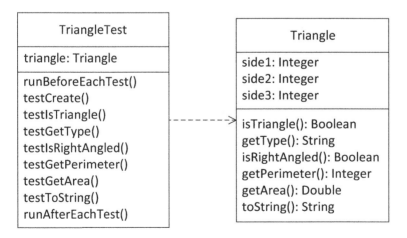

Figure 6.6: **TriangleTest** Class and Corresponding **Triangle** Class

Chapter 6: Unit Testing an Object-Oriented Program

The `runBeforeEachTest()` method is similar to the one written in `StudentTest` and `UniversityTest`. It simply creates an instance of `Triangle` and assigns it to the `triangle` instance variable. Thus, it is available to all the test methods. The code is as follows:

```
@Before
public void runBeforeEachTest() {
   triangle = new Triangle (8, 10, 6);
}
```

The `Triangle` object created by the `runBeforeEachTest()` method is indeed a triangle. Its type is "Scalene" and it is right-angled. Both its perimeter and its area are 24.

The `runAfterEachTest()` method sets the instance to `null` so that it can be removed from the memory space of the application. `testCreate()` is similar to the `testCreate()` methods in `StudentTest` and `UniversityTest`; it checks to see if the `Triangle` object has been correctly created and initialized.

The `testIsTriangle()` method checks to see if `isTriangle()` will return `true` for the `Triangle` object since it is indeed a triangle. It also creates a `Triangle` object of its own where the sides do not form a triangle and checks to see if `isTriangle()` will return `false` for this `Triangle`. The `testIsTriangle()` test method is given below:

```
@Test
public void testIsTriangle() {

   Triangle triangle2 = new Triangle(10, 20, 50);
                   // sides do not form triangle

   boolean isTriangle1 = triangle.isTriangle();
   boolean isTriangle2 = triangle2.isTriangle();

   assertEquals(true, isTriangle1);
   assertEquals(false, isTriangle2);

}
```

The `Triangle` object created by the `runBeforeEachTest()` method is a scalene triangle. The `testGetType()` method checks to see if the `getType()` method will return "Scalene" for this triangle. However, this is not sufficient to test the `getType()` method. Other types of triangles must also be tested. So, the `testGetType()` method creates an equilateral triangle and an isosceles triangle and checks the result obtained by the `getType()` method. It also checks that an appropriate result is returned when the sides do not form a triangle. The code for the `testGetType()` method is given below:

```
@Test
public void testGetType() {

  Triangle triangle2 = new Triangle(10, 10, 10);
                 // type is equilateral

  Triangle triangle3 = new Triangle(10, 15, 10);
                 // type is isosceles

  Triangle triangle4 = new Triangle(10, 20, 50);
                 // sides do not form a triangle

  assertEquals("Scalene", triangle.getType());
  assertEquals("Equilateral", triangle2.getType());
  assertEquals("Isosceles", triangle3.getType());
  assertEquals("Not a triangle", triangle4.getType());

}
```

The `testIsRightAngled()` method checks to see if the `isRightAngled()` method of `Triangle` returns `true` for the `triangle` instance variable. It also creates two instances of `Triangle` (one of which is not a triangle and the other is a triangle but not right-angled) and checks to see if the `isRightAngled()` method returns `false` in both cases.

The `testGetPerimeter()` method is fairly straightforward. It checks to see if the perimeter returned by the `getPerimeter()` method is equal to the sum of the three sides which were used as arguments for the constructor. The code is given below:

```
@Test
public void testGetPerimeter() {
   assertEquals(24, triangle.getPerimeter());
}
```

In order to write the `testGetArea()` method, the area of the `triangle` instance variable is calculated manually using Heron's formula. This value is compared with the value returned by the `getArea()` method of `Triangle`. Since floating point representations are not exact, there is the possibility of the test failing even though the values seem to be the same. To avoid this problem, the double value returned by `getArea()` is rounded to the nearest integer and

Chapter 6: Unit Testing an Object-Oriented Program

compared. If more precise comparisons are required, the numbers can be rounded to a fixed number of decimal places.

Just for good measure, the `testGetArea()` method creates another `Triangle` object and compares the value returned by its `getArea()` method with the value obtained by manual calculation. The `testGetArea()` method is shown below:

```
@Test
public void testGetArea() {

   Triangle triangle2 = new Triangle(10, 10, 10);

   int area1 = (int) Math.round(triangle.getArea());
   int area2 = (int) Math.round(triangle2.getArea());

   assertEquals(24, area1);
   assertEquals(43, area2);

}
```

The `testToString()` method is written in a similar manner to the ones in `StudentTest` and `UniversityTest`. It generates an expected string based on the values of the instance variables of `Triangle` and compares this string with the one returned by the `toString()` method of `Triangle`.

6.9 Some Guidelines for Unit Testing

This section concludes the chapter by providing some guidelines for unit testing an object-oriented application.

6.9.1 @BeforeClass and @AfterClass Methods

As previously noted, a method annotated with `@BeforeClass` in a test class performs one-time initialization in the test class. This method is executed once, before all the other methods of the test class have executed. Similarly, a method annotated with `@AfterClass` is executed once, after all the other methods of the test class have executed. None of the test classes described in this chapter contains methods annotated with `@BeforeClass` or `@AfterClass`.

The need for `@BeforeClass` and `@AfterClass` methods in a test class may indicate that the classes being tested have some undesirable dependencies. It may be better to remove the dependencies rather than write `@BeforeClass` and `@AfterClass` methods. However, dependencies are sometimes unavoidable. For example, if all the test methods need to use an expensive resource such as a database connection, it is better to set up the resource in a `@BeforeClass` method so that it is available to all the test methods.

6.9.2 What to Test?

Consider an accessor method of a class **X** which simply returns the value of an instance variable of an instance of **X**. There is no real need to test this accessor method since it cannot fail. Similarly, if a mutator method simply changes the value of an instance variable, there is no need to test this mutator method since it cannot fail. However, if the mutator method performs some validation then it can be tested. In general, test methods should only be written for methods which can reasonably be expected to fail.

6.9.3 When to Perform Testing?

An important question in unit testing is when to write the unit tests for the classes of an application? It is common to write the unit tests *after* the classes have been written. The unit tests are then run and any bugs are fixed. This is the approach that was followed in this chapter. However, writing the unit tests *before* the classes have been written is becoming more and more popular. This approach is known as *test-first* or *test-driven development* (TDD). TDD involves the following two steps:

- Write a test that fails; this proves that code or functionality is missing from the class being tested
- Write the code for the class being tested so that the test will pass

The purpose of this chapter has been to show how unit tests can be written for a testing framework such as JUnit. It is outside the scope of this chapter to discuss the merits of the different approaches to unit testing an object-oriented application. However, you are encouraged to study the TDD approach to better appreciate the advantages of the test-first approach to development.

6.9.4 How to Write a "Good" Test?

Osergrove (2009) highlights three properties which make a unit test "good":

- Trustworthiness: trustworthy tests don't have bugs and test the right things.

Chapter 6: Unit Testing an Object-Oriented Program

- Maintainability: maintainable tests can be easily changed depending on the needs of the application.
- Readability: readable tests are easy to read; it is also easy to find the problem if a test fails; readability affects maintainability and trustworthiness.

Together, these three properties are described as "the pillars of good tests" in Osergrove (2009). The focus on this chapter has been on showing how to write unit tests for an object-oriented application as simply as possible. Some of the tests described may not have all the properties recommended by Osergrove (2009). The interested reader can consult this excellent resource on unit testing to understand how to write good unit tests.

Exercises

1. Discuss three benefits of unit testing with a unit testing framework such as JUnit.

2. Describe the purpose of each of the following annotations in a test class: `@BeforeClass`, `@AfterClass`, `@Before`, `@After`, and `@Test`.

3. Write two tests using each of the following *assert* methods: `assertEquals()`, `assertTrue()`, `assertNull()`, and `assertNotNull()`. One of the tests should succeed and the other should fail.

4. Distinguish between a test and a test method.

5. Explain how you would go about testing the `Account` class from Chapter 3.

6. Explain what is involved in creating a test suite.

7. Discuss why it is not advisable to have `@BeforeClass` and `@AfterClass` methods in a test class. Under what conditions are these methods appropriate?

8. Explain why test methods should not contain logic statements.

9. Suggest an approach that could be adopted for testing accessors and mutators in a test class.

10. Describe the approach to unit testing known as *test-driven development* (TDD).

Chapter 7

Relationships between Objects

An object-oriented program consists of a set of objects that collaborate to achieve the objectives of the program. As a result, very few objects in an object-oriented program stand alone. Most of them collaborate with other objects in a number of ways. For an object to collaborate with another object, it must be related to that object in some way. Thus, it is important to understand how objects relate to each other and how to implement these relationships in an object-oriented program.

A relationship is a connection among objects. The three most important relationships in an object-oriented program are *dependencies*, *associations*, and *generalizations*. In a UML diagram, a relationship is typically drawn as a line between two objects. Different kinds of lines are used to distinguish the kinds of relationships possible. This chapter describes the three main types of relationships in an object-oriented program and explains how to implement each type of relationship in Java.

7.1 Dependencies

A class **A** *depends* on a class **B** if objects of class **A** manipulate objects of class **B** in any way. For example, a `Mailbox` class in a voice mail system depends on a `Message` class because the `Mailbox` class manipulates `Message` objects (Horstmann, 2004). A *dependency* is essentially a *using* relationship that states that a change in specification of the class being used (e.g., the `Message` class) may affect the other class that uses it (e.g., the `Mailbox` class). However, the converse is not necessarily true.

It is sometimes helpful to consider when a class does not depend on another class. If a class can carry out all of its tasks without being aware that some other class exists, then it does not depend on that class. Also, a dependency relationship between two classes **A** and **B** implies that **A** is coupled to **B**. Thus, a dependency relationship between the `Mailbox` class and the `Message` class indicates that the `Mailbox` class is coupled to the `Message` class. Consequently, the goal of low coupling can be achieved by minimizing the number of dependency relationships in an object-oriented program.

In a UML diagram, a dependency relationship is drawn as a dashed directed line, with the arrow pointing to the class being depended on. Figure 7.1 shows the dependency relationship between a `Mailbox` class and a `Message` class in a voice mail system (Horstmann, 2004).

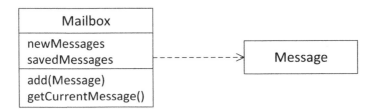

Figure 7.1: Dependency between `Mailbox` and `Message`

7.2 Associations

An *association* is a structural relationship between two classes that specifies that objects of one class are connected to objects of the other class. Given an association connecting two classes, it is possible to navigate from an object of one class to an object of the other class, and vice versa (Booch, Rumbaugh, and Jacobson, 1999). An association that connects exactly two classes is called a *binary association*. The classes involved in a binary association are usually distinct; however, it can sometimes be the same. Associations that connect more than two classes are called *n-ary associations* where *n* is the number of classes involved in the association; however, these are not as common as binary associations.

In the UML, a binary association is drawn as a solid line connecting the same or two different classes. Consider the association between a `Person` class and a `Company` class (Booch, Rumbaugh, and Jacobson, 1999). This association is shown in Figure 7.2.

Figure 7.2: Association between a `Person` class and a `Company` Class

Chapter 7: Relationships between Objects

The association is given a name, **works for**, which is written just above the association line. To remove ambiguity, a direction reading arrow is used to indicate the direction in which the association name should be read. So, the association in Figure 7.2 can be expressed as, *"Person works for Company"*.

7.2.1 Multiplicity of an Association

Since an association is a structural relationship between objects, it is important to state how many objects may be connected across an instance of an association. This value is called the *multiplicity* of an association and is written as an expression that evaluates to a range of values or an explicit value. The UML symbols used for common multiplicity values are shown in Table 7.1:

Multiplicity Value	Symbol Used
Exactly one	1
Zero or one	0..1
Many	0..*, *
One or more	1..*
An exact number	e.g., 5

Table 7.1: Symbols Used for Multiplicity Values

Figure 7.3 shows three associations where the multiplicity of the association from one object to the other is (a) one-to-one, (b) one-to-many, and (c) many-to-many, respectively.

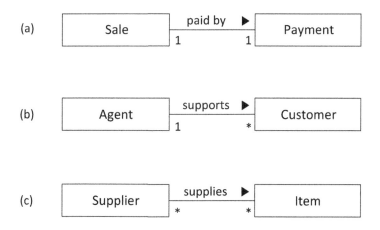

Figure 7.3: Associations with Different Multiplicity Values

Figure 7.3(a) indicates that a **Sale** is paid for by one **Payment** in a point-of-sale application (Larman, 1998). Figure 7.3(b) says that one **Agent** supports many **Customer**s in an insurance application. Figure 7.3(c) says that one **Supplier** can supply many **Item**s and that one **Item** can be supplied by many **Supplier**s in an inventory application (Date, 1995).

7.2.2 Aggregation

An *aggregation* relationship models a *"whole/part"* relationship between two classes **A** and **B**, in which an instance of **A** (the "whole") consists of instances of **B** (the "parts"). Aggregation represents a *"has-a"* relationship, meaning that an object of the whole *has* objects of the part. Aggregation is really just a special kind of association. It is drawn using an association line with an open diamond at the "whole" end. Figure 7.4 shows how to draw the aggregation relationship between a **Company** and its **Department**s (Booch, Rumbaugh, and Jacobson, 1999).

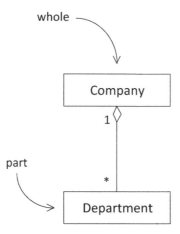

Figure 7.4: Aggregation Relationship between **Company** and **Department**

7.2.3 Composition

Composition is a form of aggregation with strong ownership between the "whole" and its "parts". In a composite aggregation, the "whole" is responsible for the creation and destruction of the "parts". The "parts" in the association live and die with the "whole". The "parts" can belong to only one composite at any point in time.

In the UML, composition is drawn exactly like aggregation except that the diamond at the "whole" end is shaded. Figure 7.5 shows a composition

Chapter 7: Relationships between Objects

relationship between a `Customer` and his/her `Account`s at a financial institution. A `Customer` object can be associated with many `Account` objects over a period of time. However, the lifetime of the related `Account` objects is dependent on the lifetime of the `Customer`. So, if a `Customer` object is removed, the `Account` objects corresponding to that `Customer` must also be removed.

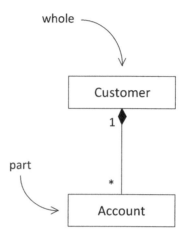

Figure 7.5: Composition Relationship between a `Customer` and `Account`

7.3 Generalizations

A *generalization* is a relationship between a general class (called the *superclass* or *parent class*) and a more specific class (called the *subclass* or *child class*). Generalization relationships are often called "*is-a*" or "*is-a-kind-of*" relationship since the child class *is-a-kind-of* the parent class. In a generalization relationship, the child class inherits the state and behavior of its parent. So, at the least, an instance of the child class can act like an instance of the parent.

As an example, consider the generalization relationship between a `Person` class and a `Customer` class. The `Customer` class inherits the state and behavior of its parent class `Person`. However, it may also add state and behavior of its own. The relationship is shown in Figure 7.6.

Observe that the line for the generalization relationship has a hollow arrow at one end pointing to the parent class, `Person`. The other end of the line is connected to the child class, `Customer`.

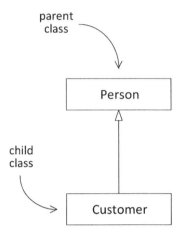

Figure 7.6: Generalization Relationship between **Customer** and **Person**

Generalizations will not be discussed further in this chapter. This is an important topic in object-oriented programming and it is covered in detail in Chapter 9.

7.4 Implementing Dependency Relationships

If instances of a class **A** is dependent on (or uses) instances of a class **B**, it follows that **B** provides a service (through a method) that is required by instances of class **A**. This service can be requested by invoking the appropriate method on an instance of class **B**, and sending the appropriate arguments.

Suppose that **a** is an instance of **A,** and that **b** is an instance of **B**. Suppose further, that **a** has access to **b**. If **a** wishes to request a service, **s()** of **b**, this can be done as follows:

```
b.s();
```

In general, the above statement can be used to request any service **s()** from an instance **b** of any class **B**, except that it will have to be modified when arguments are required. For example, suppose that **s()** requires an integer argument. Then, **s()** can be requested as follows:

```
b.s(10);            // argument is an integer value
```

There are several ways in which **a** can get access to **b**:
- **a** can create an instance of **B** and assign it to **b**

Chapter 7: Relationships between Objects

- **b** can be passed as a parameter to a method **m()** of the class **A** (the parameter must be of type **B**)
- **b** can be returned by a method **m()** of another class **C** that is called by a. **m()** can be an instance method or a class method.

Examples of these three ways in which **a** can get access to an instance of **B** are shown in Table 7.2 below. As would be expected, these also correspond to three common ways for **A** to be coupled to **B**.

How to get access to an instance of B	*Sample code*
An instance of **B** is created by **A**	B b; b = new B();

An instance of **B** is a parameter of a method of **A**	public void m (B b) {
	　// body of method
	}

An instance of **B** is returned by a method **m()** of a class **C** (an instance of **C** is required)	B b;
	C c; // assign c to an
	　　// instance of C
	b = c.m();

An instance of **B** is returned by a class method **m()** of a class **C**	B b; b = C.m();

Table 7.2: Getting Access to an Instance of Class **B** from Class **A**

7.5 Implementing Associations

This section explains how to implement binary associations. Implementing a binary association depends on the multiplicity of the relationship between the participating objects; thus, the common multiplicities are discussed separately. The section also explains how an association class can be used to implement a binary association of any multiplicity.

7.5.1 Implementing One-to-One Associations

Consider the one-to-one association between a **Sale** object and a **Payment** object shown in Figure 7.3. A **Sale** represents the event of a purchase transaction and a **Payment** represents payment for the items that make up the **Sale**.

Suppose that we are given a **Sale** object and we wish to find the corresponding Payment object. All that is needed is to store a reference to the **Payment** object in the **Sale** object. However, given a **Payment** object, it will not be possible to find the corresponding **Sale** object. If bi-directional navigability is required of the `paid by` relationship (i.e., the ability to navigate the relationship from both ends), a reference to the `Sale` object must also be stored in the `Payment` object. This makes it possible to traverse the `paid by` relationship from either a `Sale` object or a `Payment` object.

The object references that are required to implement bi-directional navigability are illustrated in Figure 7.7. An object reference is denoted as a small circle with an arrow that points to the actual object in memory. Note that accessor and mutator methods may now have to be written to view and modify the object references in `Sale` and `Payment` (giving due consideration to design guidelines such as the Law of Demeter).

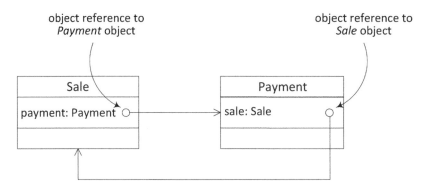

Figure 7.7: Implementation of the One-to-One `paid by` Association

7.5.2 Implementing One-to-Many Associations

Consider the one-to-many association between an insurance **Agent** class and a **Customer** class based on the **supports** relationship shown in Figure 7.3. The one-to-many association from **Agent** to **Customer** can be implemented as a collection of references to **Customer** objects in **Agent** (Rumbaugh et al. 1991). The simplest collection to use is an array of **Customer** objects. The **Agent** class will now have to provide methods to add and remove **Customer** objects from the array as well as methods to query the **Customer** objects in the array.

If, given a **Customer**, we wish to find out who is the **Agent** who supports that **Customer**, an object reference to an **Agent** object must be stored in **Customer**. Implementation of the object references for the **supports** relationship is shown in Figure 7.8. In the diagram, there are three **Customer** objects currently being supported by the given **Agent** object. The collection of **Customer** objects in **Agent** therefore contains three references to **Customer** objects. Each **Customer** object contains a single reference to the **Agent** they are supported by.

Chapter 7: Relationships between Objects

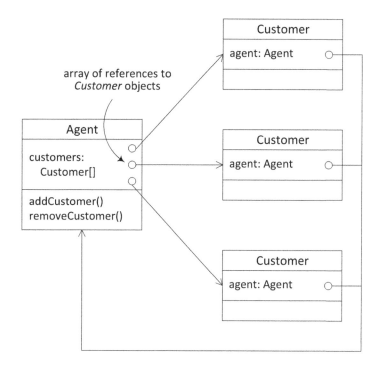

Figure 7.8: Implementation of the One-to-Many **supports** Association

7.5.3 Implementing Many-to-Many Associations

Consider the many-to-many association between `Supplier` and `Item` based on the `supplies` relationship shown in Figure 7.3. One way to implement the association is to maintain a collection of object references to `Item` objects in a related `Supplier` object, and to maintain a collection of object references to `Supplier` objects in a related `Item` object. Implementation of the `supplies` relationship using this approach is illustrated in Figure 7.9. The diagram shows a `Supplier` object that is related to five `Item` objects (only one `Item` object is drawn) and an `Item` object that is related to three `Supplier` objects (only one `Supplier` object is drawn).

Fundamentals of Object-Oriented Programming in Java

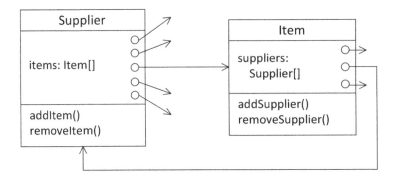

Figure 7.9: Implementation of the Many-to-Many `supplies` Association

Note that both `Supplier` and `Item` need to have methods that will enable objects to be added and removed from their respective collections as well as methods that allow the collections to be queried. Whenever a `Supplier` supplies a particular `Item`, the instance of the `Item` must be added to the collection of `Item`s in the given `Supplier` and the instance of the `Supplier` must be added to the collection of `Supplier`s in the given `Item`.

An alternative way to implement a many-to-many association is to use an *association class* (Rumbaugh et al. 1991; Booch, Rumbaugh, and Jacobson 1998). The use of an association class is discussed in the next sub-section.

7.5.4 Using an Association Class

It is possible to model and implement any relationship using an *association class*. An association class contains attributes and methods that pertain to the association between two or more objects. Thus, it can be viewed as an association that also has class properties. It is required in some many-to-many associations where *link attributes* (which pertain to an instance of a relationship) cannot be attached to one of the objects participating in the relationship without losing information (Rumbaugh et al. 1991).

The previous sections have shown that the implementation of a one-to-one association is different from the implementation of a one-to-many association, and this in turn is different from the implementation of a many-to-many association. If the multiplicity of the association between two classes changes over the lifetime of an application, at least one of the classes has to be modified. For example, if a one-to-one association changes to a one-to-many association, the object at the "one" side of the association must be re-designed with a collection of object references to the objects at the "many" end. Additional code must be written to handle retrieval, insertion, and deletion of

Chapter 7: Relationships between Objects

object references to and from the collection. Thus, a change to an association is expensive and requires the modification of existing classes.

Given the inconvenience and error-prone nature of making changes to existing classes, some authors suggest that *all* associations should be treated like many-to-many associations with link attributes (Date, 1995). Thus, association classes can be used to implement one-to-one, one-to-many, and many-to-many relationships. Figure 7.10 shows how an association class can be used to model the many-to-many association between a `Supplier` class and an `Item` class based on the `supplies` relationship.

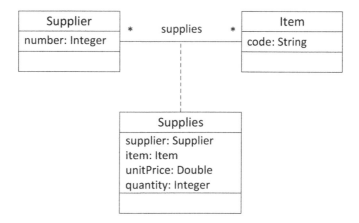

Figure 7.10: The Supplies Association Class

Figure 7.11 shows three cases of the `supplies` association where a `Supplier` object is linked to an `Item` object. Figure 7.11(a) shows that Supplier 10 supplies Item A100. Figure 7.11(b) shows that Supplier 10 also supplies Item B300. This is possible since a given `Supplier` can supply more than one `Item`. Figure 7.11(c) shows that Item A100 is also supplied by Supplier 20. This is possible since a given `Item` can be supplied by more than one `Supplier`.

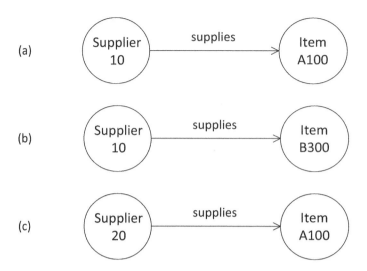

Figure 7.11: Cases of the supplies Association

Each case in Figure 7.11 is really an instance of the supplies association. Since an association class is now being used to represent the association, each case corresponds to an instance of the Supplies association class.

An instance of the Supplies association class may have attributes of its own. These are the link attributes mentioned earlier which store information on the "coming together" or linking of a Supplier instance and an Item instance. For example, the *quantity* of items supplied and the *unit price* at which they were supplied are link attributes. Note that the instance of the association class will always contain a reference to both the Supplier instance and the Item instance that it is linking together.

The instances of the association class must be stored somewhere. A good place to store the instances of the association class is the same place where the Supplier instances and Item instances are stored. Also, an appropriate collection should be used to store the instances of Supplier, Item, and Supplies based on the type of access desired. The class that manages the collections must also provide methods for client objects to query the collections. For example, a client may wish to find out how many times a particular Item was supplied by a particular Supplier. This query can be satisfied by traversing the collection of Supplies instances, checking to see which ones correspond to the given Item and the given Supplier.

The code below shows how the query can be implemented. It assumes that an array is used to store the collection of Supplies instances and that numSupplies is the amount of elements in the array.

Chapter 7: Relationships between Objects

```
public int numSupplied(Item item, Supplier supplier) {

  // supplies is an array of Supplies instances
  // numSupplies is the amount of elements in supplies

  int count = 0;

  for (int i=0; i<numSupplies; i++) {
    Supplies assoc = supplies[i];
                // get instance of association

    Item assocItem = assoc.getItem();
                // get Item object in association

    Supplier assocSupplier = assoc.getSupplier();
                // get Supplier object in association

    if ((assocItem.getCode().equals(item.getCode())) &&
       (assocSupplier.getNumber() == supplier.getNumber()))
                // check to see if supplier and item match

      count = count + 1;
                // update count by 1
  }

  return count;
}
```

Note that when an association class is used, there is no longer a need to store a collection of references in **Supplier** or **Item** to maintain a one-to-one, one-to-many, or many-to-many association.

7.5.5 Implementing Aggregation and Composition

If an instance of a class **A** contains instances of a class **B**, there are various ways to implement the association, depending on the multiplicity of the association. If the instance of **A** contains only one instance of **B**, the association can be implemented by storing the reference to an instance of **B** in **A**. An instance variable of type **B** must first be declared in **A** as follows:

```
B b;
```

One of the methods of **A** is then responsible for creating b, or perhaps accepting a reference to b from an external source (see Table 7.2).

If an instance of **A** contains more than one instances of a class **B**, a collection is needed to hold all the instances contained. Similar to when implementing a one-to-many association, an array is a simple collection that can be used for this purpose. The array is declared as an instance variable of **A**:

```
B[] b;                  // elements to be stored are instances of B
```

The array is created as follows by some method of **A** (normally the constructor), or is supplied by an external source:

```
b = new B[size];        // create array of B with 'size' elements
```

Note that after creating the array, the instances of **B** do not yet exist and must be created individually. Thus, class **A** will have methods to add instances of **B** to the array as well as methods to delete instances and make queries on the objects contained.

Instead of using arrays, there are "collection" classes that are specially designed to store multiple objects such as the "parts" of an aggregation association or the objects at the "many" end of a one-to-many or many-to-many association. Collection classes facilitate different types of access (e.g., linear, tree-based) with different performance characteristics (e.g., $O(n)$, $O(n \log n)$). They belong to the Java *Collections* Framework and are discussed in Chapter 13.

Exercises

1. By giving suitable examples, explain what is meant by an association between two classes.

2. Explain what is meant by the multiplicity of an association. What are three typical multiplicities of a binary association? Give an example of each one.

3. By giving suitable examples, distinguish between aggregation and composition. Describe one way to implement each association.

4. Describe two ways in which a many-to-many association can be implemented.

5. Describe three ways in which an instance of a class **A** can get access to an instance of another class **B**.

Chapter 7: Relationships between Objects

6. In the context of an association class, explain what is a *link* attribute. Why does an instance of the association class always have a reference to the objects at both ends of the association?

7. Using appropriate classes, draw a UML diagram illustrating each of the following types of relationships: dependency, aggregation, and composition.

Chapter 8
Second Programming Project

This chapter explains how to go about developing a more advanced object-oriented application by building on the first programming project and the material on relationships discussed in Chapter 7. It first describes the requirements of the application and then presents a UML diagram showing the collaborating objects in the application. The implementation of each class in the UML diagram is then explained. Next, a user interface is written that manipulates the objects shown in the UML diagram using a text-based menu structure. The chapter explains how to go about creating and compiling the necessary source files in Java. Finally, an alternative implementation of the application is presented using the concept of an association class discussed in Chapter 7.

8.1 Requirements of the Application

An object-oriented application is required to manage information on students and the courses they register for at a certain university. This section describes the functionality desired of the application.

8.1.1 Overview

Students who are enrolled at the university register for courses at different times in order to fulfil the requirements of their academic program. The application must manage information on students and the courses they register for. It must also provide a user interface that allows a user to perform the following operations:

- Create and view information on the courses that are offered at the university
- Create and view student records

- Register a student for a course and view information on the courses that a student has registered for

The application will consist of three domain classes, **Course**, **Student**, and **University** which work together to provide the desired functionality. A fourth class, **StudentApplication**, will provide the user interface of the application. The next sub-section gives a UML diagram of the domain classes and this is followed by a detailed description of each class in the application.

The **Student** class and the **University** class from the first programming project will be extended to accommodate the new functionality required. The existing attributes and methods of these classes will be left unchanged.

8.1.2 UML Diagram of Domain Objects

Figure 8.1 is a UML diagram of the domain classes in the second programming project.

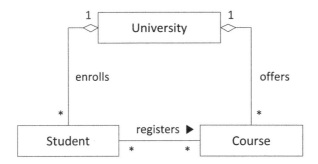

Figure 8.1: UML Diagram of Domain Classes

There are two aggregation relationships in the diagram and the multiplicity of each one is one-to-many. The "enrolls" relationship was already discussed in the first programming project where a single instance of the **University** class is related to many instances of the **Student** class. The UML diagram shows the new class, **Course**. An instance of the **University** class is related to many instances of the **Course** class through an "offers" relationship. This relationship expresses the fact that a university can offer many courses.

The UML diagram also shows a many-to-many relationship between **Student** and **Course**. One **Student** object can be associated with many **Course** objects through the "registers" relationship. Conversely, one **Course** object can be associated with many **Student** objects through the same relationship.

Chapter 8: Second Programming Project

Details of each class in the UML diagram are given in the following subsections.

8.1.3 Course

The `Course` class models the concept of a course offered at the university. Table 8.1 shows the list of attributes of `Course`.

Attribute	Type	Purpose
code	String	Unique identifier for the course.
title	String	The name of the course.
numCredits	int	Amount of credit hours.

Table 8.1: Attributes of `Course`

`Course` should provide the methods listed in Table 8.2.

Method	Return Type	Purpose
Course (String code, String title, int numCredits)		Constructor.
toString()	String	Returns a string representation of the `Course` object.

Table 8.2: Methods of `Course`

Given the attributes and methods listed above, there is no need for the `Course` class to refer to any other class in its attributes or methods. Thus, it is not coupled to any other class.

8.1.4 Student

The `Student` class models the concept of a student in the system. The `Student` class has the same set of attributes as in the first programming project as well as those listed in Table 8.3.

Attribute	Type	Purpose
courses	Collection of `Course` objects	Keeps a list of the courses the student has registered for.
numCourses	int	Number of courses the student has registered for.

Table 8.3: Additional Attributes of `Student`

Table 8.4 shows the additional methods that should be provided by the `Student` class.

Method	Return Type	Purpose
register(Course course)	boolean	Registers the student for a course; returns `true` if successful and `false` otherwise.
getCourses()	String	Returns a string representation of all the courses the student has registered for.

Table 8.4: Additional Methods of `Student`

The UML diagram in Figure 8.1 shows that the association between `Student` and `Course` is many-to-many. Assuming that the association only has to be traversed from `Student` to `Course` (e.g., to find the `Course` objects that are associated with a given `Student` object), the association can be implemented in a one-to-many fashion. This can be accomplished by using an array, `courses`, in `Student` to store the collection of `Course` objects a particular `Student` is associated with. The attribute `numCourses` keeps track of the amount of elements in the `courses` array. The method `register()` is used to insert a `Course` object in the array and `getCourses()` returns a string representation of all the `Course` objects stored in the array.

Since `Student` objects maintain a collection of `Course` objects, the `Student` class is coupled to the `Course` class.

8.1.5 University

The `University` class is responsible for managing students and the courses they register for at the university. It contains the same set of attributes as in the first programming project as well as those listed in Table 8.5.

Chapter 8: Second Programming Project

Attribute	Type	Purpose
courses	Collection of `Course` objects	A list of all the courses that are offered at the university.
numCourses	int	Number of courses that are offered at the university.

Table 8.5: Additional Attributes of `University`

The `University` class must provide the methods shown in Table 8.6 in addition to those provided in the first programming project.

Method	Return Type	Purpose
addCourse(String courseCode, String title, int numCredits)	void	Creates a `Course` object and adds it to its collection of courses.
getCourse(String courseCode)	Course	Finds and returns the `Course` object with the given `courseCode`; if none exists, returns `null`.
registerStudent(int studentID, String courseCode)	boolean	Registers the given student for the course specified; returns `true` if successful and `false` otherwise.
getCourses()	String	Returns a string representation of all the `Course` objects.
getCourses(int studentID)	String	Returns a string representation of all the `Course` objects that are associated with the given student; if the student is not found, returns `null`. (Note that this is an overloaded method.)

Table 8.6: Additional Methods of `University`

The UML diagram of Figure 8.1 shows two aggregation relationships: one between `University` and `Course` and the other between `University` and `Student`. The multiplicity of each relationship is one-to-many. It is assumed that traversal is only required from the "one" end of each relationship to the "many" end. Thus, the aggregation relationships can be implemented using an array in the object at the "one" end, i.e., `University`.

Consequently, `University` has an attribute, `courses`, which stores the `Course` objects that are offered at the university. The `courses` attribute is implemented as an array. The `numCourses` attribute keeps track of the number of elements in this array. These two attributes are similar to the attributes `students` and `numStudents` which were used in the first programming project. There are also similar methods to facilitate the insertion and querying of the objects in the `courses` array (e.g., `addCourse()` and `getCourse()`).

The aggregation relationship between `University` and `Course` and between `University` and `Student` cause the `University` class to be coupled to both the `Course` class and the `Student` class.

8.1.6 User Interface

The user interface should allow the user to perform several operations such as:

- Add a new course to the system
- Add a new student to the system
- Display information about a course with a given course code
- Display information about a student with a given student ID
- Register a student for a course
- List all the courses offered at the university
- List all the students in the system
- List all the courses a given student has registered for

Similar to the first programming project, the user interface should accept input from the keyboard and generate textual output to the console. The class, `StudentApplication`, should provide the functionality of the user interface.

Since it needs to interact with all the domain classes, the user interface class is coupled to the `Course`, `Student`, and `University` classes.

8.1.7 Implementation Requirements

All the classes must be in the same package. Also, accessors should be provided for the attributes of the three domain classes (`Course`, `Student`, and `University`) which have primitive values. As previously mentioned, arrays should be used to store the collection of `Course` objects and the collection of `Student` objects in `University`. Also, an array should be used to store the collection of `Course` objects in `Student`. Information hiding should be enforced as much as possible.

8.2 Implementation of Domain Classes

8.2.1 Course

Since the `Course` class is not coupled to any other class, its implementation is fairly straightforward. All that is required is to declare the attributes listed in Table 8.1 as instance variables and to implement the methods listed in Table 8.2. To enforce information hiding, the instance variables are declared as `private`. The constructor, accessor, and `toString()` methods are also straightforward to implement. These methods are declared as `public` since they must be made available to the other classes.

8.2.2 Student

The implementation of the `Student` class is quite similar to that of the `Course` class except for the attributes `courses` and `numCourses`, and the methods, `register()` and `getCourses()`. The `courses` attribute is used to store a collection of courses the student has registered for. According to the requirements, `courses` must be implemented using an array. Thus, `courses` is an array of `Course` objects. It is declared as follows:

```
private Course[] courses;
```

The instance variable, `numCourses`, keeps track of the number of `Course` objects that are stored in the array. A constant, `MAX_COURSES`, is used to specify the maximum amount of courses that a student can register for.

The constructor of the `Student` class is essentially the same as in the first programming project. However, it also needs to create the `courses` array and initialise the `numCourses` instance variable to zero. The code is as follows:

```
public Student() {

    ID = IDGenerator;
    this.firstName = firstName;
    this.lastName = lastName;
    this.phone = phone;

    IDGenerator = IDGenerator + 10;

    courses = new Course [MAX_COURSES];
    numCourses = 0;

}
```

The Student class must provide a register() method to enable a Course object to be added to its collection of Course objects. This corresponds to the real-world scenario of a student registering for a course. The register() method checks to see if there is space in the array for the new Course object and if the Course object is not already present in the array. If so, it inserts the Course object in the courses array, updates the numCourses instance variable, and returns true. Otherwise, it returns false. The code for the register() method is as follows:

```
public boolean register (Course course) {

   if (numCourses == MAX_COURSES)
      return false;

   for (int i=0; i<numCourses; i++) {
      if (courses[i] == course)
         return false; // student already registered for this course
   }

   courses[numCourses] = course;
   numCourses++;

   return true;

}
```

The getCourses() method of the Student class needs to return a list of all the courses that the student has registered for. This method traverses the courses array and invokes the toString() method on each Course object stored in the array. The results are concatenated and returned by getCourses():

```
public String getCourses() {
   String s;

   s = "Courses registered for:\n";

   for (int i=0; i<numCourses; i++) {
      s = s + courses[i].toString() + "\n";
   }

   return s;
}
```

Chapter 8: Second Programming Project

It should be noted that **Student** is a client of **Course** in the above code since it uses the **toString()** service of **Course**.

8.2.3 University

The **University** class uses an array, **courses**, to maintain its collection of **Course** objects, similar to the **students** array which is used to store **Student** objects. The array is declared as an instance variable of **University**. The instance variable, **numCourses** is used to keep track of the amount of objects in the array. These new instance variables of **University** are declared as follows:

```
private Course[] courses;
private int numCourses;
```

In the constructor of **University**, the **courses** array is created and **numCourses** is initialized to zero:

```
public University(String name) {
   this.name = name;
   students = new Student [1000];
   numStudents = 0;

   courses = new Course [100];
   numCourses = 0;
}
```

The **addCourse()** method of **University** first creates an instance of **Course** using the data supplied as arguments. It then adds the newly created **Course** object to its **courses** array and updates the **numCourses** instance variable:

```
public void addCourse(String code, String title, int numCredits) {
   courses[numCourses] = new Course (code, title, numCredits);
   numCourses++;
}
```

The **getCourse()** method traverses the **courses** array searching for the **courseCode** supplied as a parameter. If it finds one with the given **courseCode**, it returns the **Course** object. If there is no **Course** object with the given **courseCode**, **null** is returned. It is implemented as follows:

```
public Course getCourse(String courseCode) {

   for(int i=0; i<numCourses; i++) {
```

```
        if (courses[i].getCode().equals(courseCode))
            return courses[i];
    }

    return null;
}
```

The `registerStudent()` method is a little more complicated. It must first find the `Student` object and the `Course` object corresponding to the `studentID` and `courseCode` parameters. This can be done using the `getStudent()` and `getCourse()` methods. It must then invoke the `register()` method on the given `Student` object so that the course will be added to the collection of `Course` objects maintained by the given `Student`. The code for `registerStudent()` is given below:

```
public boolean registerStudent(int studentID, String courseCode) {

    Student student = getStudent(studentID);
    Course course = getCourse(courseCode);

    if (student == null || course == null)
        return false;

    boolean success = student.register(course);
    return success;

}
```

The `getCourses()` method is implemented in a similar manner to the `getStudents()` method. It traverses the collection of `Course` objects and invokes the `toString()` method on each one. The results are concatenated in a string and returned.

Finally, the `getCourses(studentID)` method searches for the `Student` object corresponding to the `studentID` supplied as a parameter. If it is found, it invokes the `getCourses()` method of the `Student` object and returns the result; otherwise, it returns `null`. The method is shown below:

```
public String getCourses(int studentID) {

    Student student;

    student = getStudent(studentID);
```

```
    if (student == null)
       return null;
    else
       return student.getCourses();
}
```

It should be observed that the `getCourses(studentID)` method of **Student** is different from the `getCourses()` method of **University**. The former requires a specific instance of **Student** on which to invoke the method. The latter requires a **studentID** to be supplied to the **University** instance.

8.3 Implementation of the User Interface

The user interface can be implemented as a menu containing a list of choices generated by output statements. As in the first programming project, the **Scanner** class is used to obtain user input from the keyboard. Essentially, methods of the **Scanner** class make it possible for the user to make a selection from the menu and to enter data required for that selection.

The user interface code firsts create an instance of **University** since **University** knows about the two other domain classes. Based on the choices made by the user, the user interface then invokes methods on **University**, **Student**, and **Course**.

Figure 8.2 shows a menu structure for implementing the user interface:

```
1. Add a new course to the system
2. Add a new student to the system
3. Display information about a course with a given course code
4. Display information about a student with a given student ID
6. Register a student for a course
6. List all the courses offered at the university
7. List all the students in the system
8. List all the courses a given student has registered for
9. Exit

Please make a selection:
```

Figure 8.2: User Interface

The values that have to be input by the user when a particular menu option is selected and the corresponding method of `University` that has to be invoked are listed in Table 8.7:

Chapter 8: Second Programming Project

Menu option	Values to be input by the user	Method to invoke from University
1	course code, title, number of credits	addCourse(code, title, numCredits)
2	first name, last name, phone number	addStudent(firstName, lastName, phone)
3	course code	Call getCourse(courseCode) to find **Course** object and then invoke **toString()** method of **Course** object.
4	student ID	Call getStudent(studentID) to find **Student** object and then invoke **toString()** method of **Student** object.
5	student ID, course code	registerStudent(studentID, courseCode)
6	<none>	getCourses()
7	<none>	getStudents()
8	student ID	getCourses(studentID)
9	<none>	None; exit application.

Table 8.7: Input Values and Methods Corresponding to Menu Options

8.4 Creating Source Files and Compiling

The code for each domain class must be written in a separate source file as follows:

Course class	: Course.java
Student class	: Student.java
University class	: University.java

In addition, the user interface class containing the `main()` method must be written in the source file, `StudentApplication.java`.

Compiling `StudentApplication.java` will initially cause all its dependent classes (`University`, `Student`, and `Course`) to be compiled as well. However, it is recommended that you compile the classes one at a time, in the following order:

- **Course**, since it is not coupled to any other class
- **Student**, since it is coupled to only the **Course** class
- **University**, since it is coupled to both **Course** and **Student**

- `StudentApplication`, since it is coupled to the three domain classes

Once `StudentApplication` compiles successfully, the application is ready to run.

8.5 Alternative Implementation Using an Association Class

The many-to-many association between `Student` and `Course` can be implemented as an association class if we wish to keep additional information about the association such as the academic year and semester in which the student registered for the course. Figure 8.3 shows the association class, `Registration`:

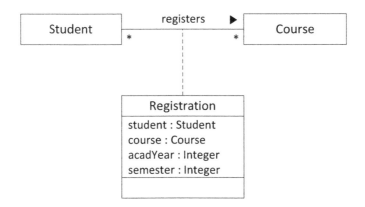

Figure 8.3: Modelling the `registers` Association with an Association Class

8.5.1 The `Registration` Association Class

An instance of the `Registration` association class links a specific instance of `Student` with a specific instance of `Course` (e.g., the student with ID 10 who registers for the course, COMP2500). Thus, the `Registration` class has two attributes, `student` and `course`, which refer to the specific instances of `Student` and `Course` being linked.

It is possible to have another instance of `Registration` linking the same `Student` with another instance of `Course` (e.g., the student with ID 10 who registers for the course, COMP2000) or linking the same `Course` with another instance of `Student` (e.g., the student with ID 20 who registers for the course, COMP2500). These instances of the association class are shown in Figure 8.4.

Chapter 8: Second Programming Project

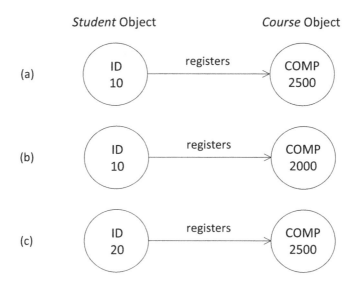

Figure 8.4: Instances of the **Registration** Association Class

The other attributes of **Registration** are referred to as *link* attributes since they pertain to the specific linking relationship. In this case, **acadYear** and **semester** provide more information about the link between **Student** and **Course**, indicating in what year and semester the two were linked.

The implementation of the Registration association class is given below:

```
public class Registration
{
   private Student student;
   private Course course;
   private int acadYear;
   private int semester;

   public Registration(Student student, Course course, int acadYear,
      int semester) {

      this.student = student;
      this.course = course;
      this.acadYear = acadYear;
      this.semester = semester;
   }

   public Student getStudent() {
      return student;
```

```
}

public Course getCourse() {
    return course;
}

public int getAcadYear() {
    return acadYear;
}

public int getSemester() {
    return semester;
}
}
```

8.5.2 Manipulating Instances of the Association Class

When an association class is used, instances of the association class must be stored somewhere. For this application, a good place to store the instances of `Registration` is in a collection maintained by `University`, just like the collections of `Course` and `Student` objects. So, `University` now has two additional instance variables to manage instances of the association class:

```
private Registration[] registrations;
            // stores collection of Registration objects

private int numRegistrations;
            // keeps track of number of Registration objects
```

These variables are initialized in the constructor of `University` in a similar manner to the `courses` and `students` collections.

When the association class is used, there is no need to store a collection of `Course` objects in each `Student` object. Thus, the collection of `Course` objects in `Student` is removed as well as the related methods, `register()` and `getCourses()`.

The signature and implementation of the `registerStudent()` method of `University` have to change to accommodate the association class. The signature must change to include parameters for any additional data required for creating an instance of the association class (e.g., academic year and semester). This data is supplied by the user interface class when calling the `registerStudent()` method.

Chapter 8: Second Programming Project

Previously, the `registerStudent()` method obtained the corresponding Student and Course objects and invoked the `register()` method of Student to insert the Course object in the collection maintained by the given Student object. Now, there is no collection of Course objects maintained by each Student object. So, the `registerStudent()` method must first create an instance of the association class, Registration, and then insert this instance into the registrations collection maintained by University.

The code for the `registerStudent()` method is given below:

```
public boolean registerStudent(int studentID, String courseCode,
   int acadYear, int semester) {

   Student student = getStudent(studentID);
   Course course = getCourse(courseCode);

   if (student == null || course == null)
      return false;

   Registration registration =
      new Registration (student, course, acadYear, semester);
         // create instance of association class

   registrations [numRegistrations] = registration;
         // insert instance in collection

   numRegistrations++;

   return true;

}
```

The `getCourses(studentID)` method must also be changed. Previously, to find all the courses a student registered for, the `getCourses(studentID)` method invoked the `getCourses()` method on the corresponding Student object. However, when the association class is used, Student objects no longer maintain a collection of Course objects. So, the query must be fulfilled by manipulating the registrations collection in University:

```
public String getCourses(int studentID) {

   Student student = getStudent(studentID);

   if (student == null)
```

```
      return null;
   else {
      String s = "Courses registered for:\n";
      for (int i=0; i<numRegistrations; i++) {
         if (registrations[i].getStudent() == student) {
            Course course = registrations[i].getCourse();
            s = s + course.toString() + "\n";
         }
      }
      return s;
   }
}
```

In the code above, the **registrations** array is traversed from beginning to end. Each **Registration** object in the array is checked to see if its **Student** object is the same as the one being queried. If so, the corresponding **Course** object is obtained. In this way, all the **Course** objects that are associated with the given **Student** object are obtained.

It should be noted that the **Registration** association class can still be used to implement the many-to-many association between **Student** and **Course** even if there is no need to store link attributes such as academic year and semester.

Table 8.8 summarizes the changes that have to be made when an association class is used.

• There is no need to maintain a list of courses a student has registered for in the **Student** class
• A new class, **Registration**, must be implemented, with link attributes, if necessary
• The **University** class is completely responsible for registering a student for a course

Table 8.8 Summary of Changes Due to Association Class

8.5.3 Benefits of Using an Association Class

There are several benefits of using an association class such as **Registration**:

Chapter 8: Second Programming Project

- The **Student** class is no longer coupled to the **Course** class and it is simpler to write. Indeed, it becomes exactly as it was at the end of the first programming project.

- If bi-directional navigability of the **registers** association is required (e.g., to find all the students who have registered for a particular course), there is no need to change **Course** to maintain a collection of **Student** objects. All that is needed is to write a method in **University** (like **getCourses()**) which traverses the collection of instances of the association class to perform the desired query.

If there is a large amount of instances of the association class, the performance of the application may be affected by the time it takes to search the collection. Thus, appropriate data structures should be chosen to make the insertion, search, and retrieval process more efficient when association classes are used. This topic is explored further in Chapter 13 when the collection classes in Java are discussed.

Chapter 9

Inheritance and Polymorphism

Inheritance is a mechanism that allows one class to incorporate the state and behavior of another class. This makes it possible to build new classes out of existing classes thereby promoting code sharing and reusability. This chapter describes how inheritance is achieved in object-oriented programming. It also discusses an important related concept known as polymorphism which allows classes that inherit from a common class to be treated in a uniform manner.

9.1 Generalization Relationships and Inheritance

The `Account` class implements the concept of an account in a bank. In the real world, banks offer various types of accounts to customers. For example, customers can open accounts such as the following:

- Savings account: This type of account is generally intended for saving funds; interest is usually paid to the account at specified intervals (e.g., monthly).

- Chequing account: This type of account is generally intended for day-to-day transactions. The customer may be allowed to write a certain amount of free cheques in a certain period; any amount of cheques beyond this amount is charged a fee. No interest is payable on this type of account.

Each type of account has an account number and a balance. Each type of account also enables deposits and withdrawals. Thus, the concept of a savings account is really an extension of the concept of an account. Similarly, the concept of a chequing account is an extension of the concept of an account. Inheritance makes it possible to create a `SavingsAccount` class and a `ChequingAccount` class by extending the `Account` class. Before explaining how this is achieved, some terminology is presented.

Fundamentals of Object-Oriented Programming in Java

Generalization is used to model a relationship between classes in which one class represents a more general concept (e.g., Account) and another class represents a more specialized concept (e.g., SavingsAccount). The more general class is called the *superclass* or *parent class* and the more specialized class is called the *subclass* or *child class*. Each subclass is said to inherit the features (attributes and operations) of its superclass. Generalization is sometimes called the "is-a" relationship because an instance of a subclass is an instance of the superclass as well. For example, an instance of SavingsAccount "is-a" instance of Account.

Generalization and specialization are two different viewpoints of the same relationship. Generalization refers to the fact that the superclass generalizes the subclasses while specialization refers to the fact that subclasses specialize the superclass. *Inheritance* refers to the mechanism of sharing attributes and operations (state and behavior) using the generalization relationship.

A subclass extends the capabilities of the superclass with additional methods and attributes. For example, consider the generalization relationships between Account, SavingsAccount, and ChequingAccount, shown in the UML diagram in Figure 9.1 below.

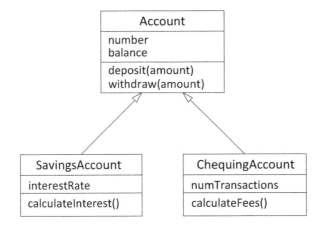

Figure 9.1: Generalization Relationships between Account, SavingsAccount, and ChequingAccount

SavingsAccount adds one attribute, interestRate, and one method, calculateInterest(), to the Account class. ChequingAccount also adds one attribute, numTransactions, and one method, calculateFees(), to the Account class. Using the terminology, Account is a generalization of SavingsAccount and ChequingAccount. Conversely, SavingsAccount is a

Chapter 9: Inheritance and Polymorphism

specialization of `Account`; `ChequingAccount` is also a specialization of `Account`.

It is possible to specialize the subclasses in Figure 9.1 even further. For example, suppose that there are three types of savings accounts in a bank. We can create three new classes, `A`, `B`, and `C`, which are subclasses of `SavingsAccount`. Suppose further that there are two types of chequing accounts in a bank. We can create two new classes, `D`, and `E`, which are subclasses of `ChequingAccount`. A UML diagram with the new classes is shown in Figure 9.2.

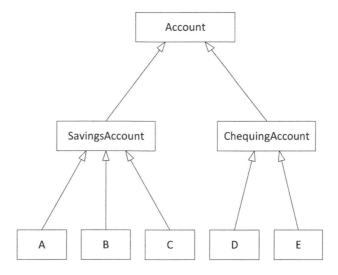

Figure 9.2: Specializing `SavingsAccount` and `ChequingAccount`

The UML diagrams in Figure 9.1 and Figure 9.2 are examples of an inheritance hierarchy. An *inheritance hierarchy* consists of a set of classes which are connected by generalization relationships. The *depth* of an inheritance hierarchy is the length of the path from the root to the deepest class in the hierarchy; it varies from application to application. The inheritance hierarchy in Figure 9.1 has a depth of one. The inheritance hierarchy in Figure 9.2 has a depth of two.

Since `SavingsAccount` is a child class of `Account`, it is said to be a *direct subclass* of `Account`. Now, class `A` is a direct subclass of `SavingsAccount` since it is a child class of `SavingsAccount`. However, `A` has all the features of `Account` since `SavingsAccount` inherits all the features of `Account`. Thus, `A` is also a subclass of `Account`, even though there is an intervening class between `A` and `Account` in the inheritance hierarchy. In this situation, `A` is said to be an *indirect subclass* of `Account`. Note that since an inheritance hierarchy can be as deep as required, there may be several intervening classes between `Account` and one of its indirect subclasses.

9.2 Creating and Manipulating Child Classes

This section explains how to write the code for a child class. In particular, it shows how to write the code for the two child classes, `SavingsAccount` and `ChequingAccount`, shown in Figure 9.1. It also explains how instances of a child class can be manipulated by clients.

9.2.1 Writing a Child Class

To create a subclass of `Account`, the `extends` keyword is used to indicate that a subclass/superclass relationship is being established. The attributes and methods that belong to the subclass are written the same way as in any other class. The `SavingsAccount` subclass is written as follows:

```java
public class SavingsAccount extends Account {

    private double interestRate;    // new attribute of subclass

    public SavingsAccount(int number, double balance,
        double interestRate) {

        // code for constructor
    }

    public void calculateInterest() {
        // code for calculateInterest()
    }
}
```

Similarly, the `ChequingAccount` class is written as follows:

```java
public class ChequingAccount extends Account {

    private int numTransactions;

    public ChequingAccount(int number, double balance) {
        // code for constructor
    }

    public void calculateFees() {
        // code for calculateFees()
```

Chapter 9: Inheritance and Polymorphism

```
   }
}
```

Note that the instance variables of `Account` are not re-declared in `SavingsAccount` or `ChequingAccount` since a subclass inherits all the instance variables of its superclass. Also, the methods of `Account` are not rewritten since each subclass inherits the methods of its superclass as well. This is what inheritance is all about. A subclass automatically acquires the attributes and methods of its superclass.

9.2.2 Inheriting Attributes and Methods from Parent Class

Consider the `calculateInterest()` method of the `SavingsAccount` class. This method should calculate the monthly interest based on the current balance in the account. Since `balance` is an attribute of `Account` which is inherited by `SavingsAccount`, the following seems to be a reasonable implementation of the `calculateInterest()` method:

```
public void calculateInterest() {
   double interest;

   interest = balance * (interestRate / 12.0);
   deposit(interest); // method inherited from Account superclass
}
```

However, the above code will not compile. Although `balance` is an attribute of `SavingsAccount` by inheritance, it has been declared as `private` in its parent class, `Account`. So, the `balance` attribute is only visible within the `Account` class. To make the `balance` attribute visible to subclasses, it should be declared as `protected` in `Account`. Of course, declaring the `balance` instance variable as `public` makes it accessible to any other class, including subclasses of `Account`.

Note that even though the `SavingsAccount` class does not have a `deposit()` method, the following statement is valid since the `deposit()` method is inherited from `Account`:

```
deposit(interest);
```

Inheritance of methods provides another way to fix the `calculateInterest()` method instead of changing the access modifier for `balance` in `Account`. In this case, the accessor for the `balance` instance variable in `Account` is called from the `calculateInterest()` method as follows:

```
public void calculateInterest() {
   double interest;

   interest = getBalance() * (interestRate / 12.0);
   deposit(interest);
}
```

The `getBalance()` accessor from `Account` is inherited by `SavingsAccount` so it can be used by the `calculateInterest()` method, just like any other method in the `SavingsAccount` class.

9.2.3 Initialising Instance Variables

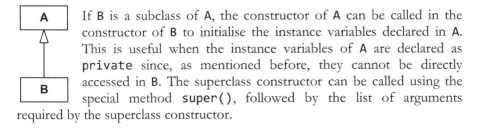

If B is a subclass of A, the constructor of A can be called in the constructor of B to initialise the instance variables declared in A. This is useful when the instance variables of A are declared as `private` since, as mentioned before, they cannot be directly accessed in B. The superclass constructor can be called using the special method `super()`, followed by the list of arguments required by the superclass constructor.

For example, the constructor of the `ChequingAccount` class can be written as follows:

```
public ChequingAccount(int number, double balance) {
   super(number, balance);
                // call superclass constructor

   numTransactions = 0;
                // set attributes declared in ChequingAccount
}
```

The call to `super()` initializes the `number` and `balance` attributes using the superclass constructor. Note that the call to `super()` must be the first statement in the constructor of `ChequingAccount`.

Suppose that the call to `super(number, balance)` is omitted from the `ChequingAccount` constructor. The compiler attempts to insert code which invokes the default no-argument constructor in the superclass, `Account`. It will generate an error if the superclass does not contain a no-argument constructor

Chapter 9: Inheritance and Polymorphism

(either explicitly written in the superclass or provided as a default constructor by the compiler).

If there is no constructor in the subclass, the compiler attempts to provide the default no-argument constructor. This no-argument constructor in the subclass needs to invoke the no-argument constructor in the superclass to initialize the instance variables of the superclass. Again, the compiler will generate an error if the superclass does not contain a no-argument constructor.

9.2.4 Manipulating Child Classes

A child class can be manipulated like any other class. A client object can create an instance of the child class using the **new** keyword and then proceed to invoke methods on the child class using the object variable. For example, consider a client object performing the following operations on the `ChequingAccount` child class:

Line 1:
```
ChequingAccount ca = new ChequingAccount(10, 2000.00);
```

Line 2:
```
ca.withdraw(500.00);
```

Line 3:
```
System.out.println(ca.getBalance());
```

Line 4:
```
ca.calculateFees();
```

Line 1 creates an instance of `ChequingAccount` and assigns it to a variable of type `ChequingAccount`. Line 2 invokes the `withdraw()` method on the instance of `ChequingAccount`. Even though the `ChequingAccount` class does not have a `withdraw()` method defined, this is valid since the method is inherited from `Account`. Similarly, the `getBalance()` method is inherited from `Account` in Line 3 and can be used as if it were defined in `ChequingAccount`. Since the `calculateFees()` method is defined in `ChequingAccount` it is legal to invoke this method on an instance of `ChequingAccount` so Line 4 is also valid.

It is helpful to visualize the superclass and subclass as a fused structure that contains all the methods and attributes of the superclass as well as all the methods and attributes of the subclass. The subclass contains all the methods and attributes of the fused structure and thus an instance of the subclass contains all the attributes of the fused structure. All the methods of the fused structure can be invoked on an instance of the subclass. This fused structure is shown in Figure 9.3.

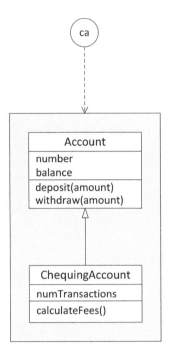

Figure 9.3: Fusing of Superclass and Subclass

9.3 Method Refinement and Replacement

So far we have assumed that the attributes and methods added by a subclass to those inherited from its superclass are always distinct. However, it is possible for a child class to define a method with the same signature (method name and parameter list) as a method in the parent class. The method in the child class is said to *override* the method in the parent class and it effectively hides the method in the parent class.

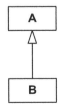

Suppose that B is a subclass of A. A method defined in B can override a method inherited from A in one of two ways: method refinement and method replacement. In *method refinement*, the method inherited from the parent class is executed as part of the behavior of the child class method. Thus, the behavior of the parent class is preserved and augmented with method refinement. In *method replacement*, the code of the parent class method is never

Chapter 9: Inheritance and Polymorphism

executed when instances of the child class are manipulated. This requires the overridden method to be completely rewritten in **B**.

As an example of method refinement, consider the **toString()** method of the **Account** class:

```
public String toString() {
   String s;
   s = "Account number: " + number + " Balance: " + balance;
   return s;
}
```

A reasonable attempt to refine the **toString()** method in **ChequingAccount** is as follows:

Line 1:
```
public String toString() {
```

Line 2:
```
   String s;
```

Line 3:
```
   s = toString() + " Transaction Count: " + numTransactions;
```

Line 4:
```
   return s;
```

Line 5:
```
}
```

In Line 3, an attempt is made to call the **toString()** method of the parent and augment the string obtained with the **numTransactions** attribute of **ChequingAccount**. However, this results in a recursive call to the **toString()** method being defined. This problem can be solved by preceding the call to the **toString()** method in Line 3 with the keyword **super** as follows:

```
s = super.toString() + " Transaction Count: " + numTransactions;
```

In general, when a superclass method is being refined in a subclass, the keyword **super** should be used to distinguish the method in the superclass from the method being defined in the subclass.

As an example of method replacement, suppose that the `SavingsAccount` class wishes to override the `toString()` method of `Account` using replacement. The `toString()` method must be written without using the services of the `toString()` method from the parent class, `Account`. For example, it can be written as follows:

```java
public String toString() {
   String s;

   s =  "Savings Account ->" + " Number: " + getNumber() +
        " Interest rate: " + interestRate;

   return s;
}
```

In the example, the `toString()` method uses the `getNumber()` method to find the value of the `number` attribute of the `SavingsAccount` object since it is a `private` instance variable in `Account`.

Finally, it should be mentioned that if a method is re-defined in a subclass **B** with a different signature from the superclass **A**, this is really *method overloading* which is not related to inheritance and polymorphism.

9.4 The `Object` Class

All Java classes are automatically subclasses of the `Object` class. A class that does not explicitly inherit from another class is a direct subclass of `Object`. For example, although it wasn't mentioned before, the `Account` class is really a direct subclass of the `Object` class. Consequently, every class in Java is either a direct or an indirect subclass of `Object`. Thus, the methods of the `Object` class are available to every class in Java.

Three methods of the `Object` class that are frequently used in this book are listed in Table 9.1.

Chapter 9: Inheritance and Polymorphism

Method	Description
public String toString()	Returns a string representation of the state of the object.
public boolean equals(Object obj)	Returns `true` if the current object is equal to `obj` and `false`, otherwise.
public int hashCode()	Returns a hash code for use in data structures that employ hash tables.

Table 9.1: Commonly Used Methods of the `Object` Class

The methods of the `Object` class are meant to be overridden in user-defined classes. If they are not overridden in a class, they return the values described in Table 9.2.

Method	Value Returned When Method is not Overridden
public String toString()	Returns a string with the memory address of the object, prefixed with the name of the class and the '@' symbol, e.g., `Account@19821f`.
public boolean equals(Object obj)	Returns `true` if the current object is stored at the same memory address as `obj` and `false`, otherwise. In other words, the `equals()` method in `Object` behaves as "==".
public int hashCode()	Generates a hash code which is based on the memory address of the object.

Table 9.2: Not Overriding Methods of `Object` Class

9.5 Substitutability and Polymorphism

This section describes the concept of substitutability which enables an object variable to refer to different types of objects in an inheritance hierarchy. It also discusses an important concept in object-oriented programming known as polymorphism.

9.5.1 The Principle of Substitutability

The Principle of Substitutability says that if we have two classes **A** and **B**, such that **B** is a subclass of **A** (even indirectly), it should be possible to substitute instances of class **B** for instances of class **A** in *any situation* with *no observable effect*.

Subtype refers to a subclass relationship in which the Principle of Substitutability is maintained. This is distinguished from the general *subclass* relationship, which may or may not satisfy this principle.

Consider the following declarations:

```
Account account;
ChequingAccount ca;
```

By the Principle of Substitutability, it is possible to create an instance of `ChequingAccount` and assign it to a variable of type `Account`:

```
ca = new ChequingAccount(10, 5000.00);
account = ca;
```

The `ChequingAccount` instance has all the features of an `Account` plus additional features of its own (this is what specialization is all about). It is safe to refer to the `ChequingAccount` instance using a variable of type `Account` since all the `Account` features are present in `ChequingAccount`. However, the converse is not true. It is not possible to create an instance of `Account` and assign it to a variable of type `ChequingAccount`:

```
account = new Account(10, 5000.00);
ca = account;
```

Suppose it is possible to refer to an `Account` instance using a variable of type `ChequingAccount`. An `Account` instance has less features than a `ChequingAccount` instance (it does not have the `numTransactions` attribute neither does it have the `calculateFees()` method). If a `ChequingAccount` feature is requested which is not present in `Account` (e.g., `calculateFees()`), the request would fail. For this reason, substituting an instance of the parent class where an instance of the child class is expected is not allowed.

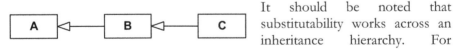

It should be noted that substitutability works across an inheritance hierarchy. For example, suppose that B is a direct subclass of A and C is a direct subclass of B. Since C is an indirect subclass of A, it is still possible to substitute an instance of C whenever an instance of A is expected. So, if we have an inheritance hierarchy rooted at A, an object variable of type A can be used to refer to an instance of any class in the hierarchy.

9.5.2 Polymorphism

Before discussing polymorphism, the terms static type and dynamic type will now be defined. *Static type* is the type assigned to an object variable by means of a declaration statement. Consider the following declarations:

```
Account account;
SavingsAccount sa;
```

Based on the definition, the static type of `account` is `Account` and the static type of `sa` is `SavingsAccount`.

Dynamic type is the actual type associated with an object variable at run-time. Consider the following code which uses the Principle of Substitutability:

```
sa = new SavingsAccount(10, 5000.00, 5.50);
account = sa;
```

The dynamic type of the `account` object variable is `SavingsAccount` since it is actually referring to an instance of `SavingsAccount` at run-time. The `account` variable is said to be *polymorphic* since its dynamic type does not match its static type.

Now, recall that `SavingsAccount` defines a method of its own, `calculateInterest()`, which is declared as follows:

```
public void calculateInterest() {
    :
}
```

It is instructive to consider what happens when the following call is made:

```
account.calculateInterest();
```

This line of code generates a compilation error. Even though the `account` variable is actually referring to a `SavingsAccount` instance at run-time (which has the `calculateInterest()` method defined), the compiler does not know this (because it happens at run-time). Thus, the compiler uses the static type of an object variable to determine if a method call is legal. Since the static type of `account` is `Account` and there is no `calculateInterest()` method in `Account`, the compiler generates an error to the effect that there is no such method in the `Account` class. Thus, it is only possible to invoke methods defined in the class corresponding to the static type of an object variable, even though there may be additional methods in the class corresponding to the dynamic type.

Figure 9.4 depicts this situation using the fused superclass/subclass diagram introduced earlier. The features of the subclass have been shaded to indicate that, while they are actually present in the object being referred to, they cannot be accessed. Only the features defined in the static type (superclass) can be accessed.

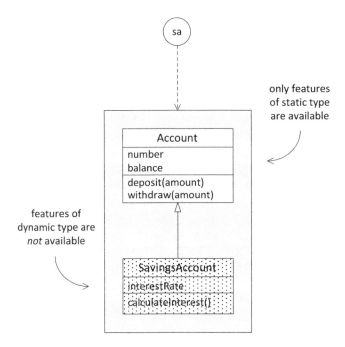

Figure 9.4: Polymorphic Variables Can Only Access Features of Static Type

Substitutability and polymorphism make it possible to treat instances of a parent class and instances of child classes in a uniform manner. For example, consider the following code:

```
Account[] accounts = new Account[3];
accounts[0] = new Account(10, 3500.00);
accounts[1] = new ChequingAccount(20, 5000.00);
accounts[2] = new SavingsAccount(30, 1500.00, 5.50);

for (int i=0; i<accounts.length; i++)
   System.out.println(accounts[i].toString());
```

Chapter 9: Inheritance and Polymorphism

In this example, instances of `Account`, `ChequingAccount`, and `SavingsAccount` are created and stored in an array of type `Account` since they are all `Account` instances based on the generalization hierarchy. The `for` loop then processes the objects in the array as if they were all `Account` instances.

Recall that the `toString()` method of the `Account` class implemented as follows:

```
public String toString() {
   String s;
   s = "Account number: " + number + " Balance: " + balance;
   return s;
}
```

Given this implementation, it is reasonable to assume that the following output will be generated from the code above:

```
Account number: 10 Balance: 3500.00
Account number: 20 Balance: 5000.00
Account number: 30 Balance: 1500.00
```

However, it may come as a surprise to find out that the actual output generated is the following:

```
Account number: 10 Balance: 3500.00
Account number: 20 Balance: 5000.00 Transaction Count: 0
Account number: 30 Balance: 1500.00
```

Somehow, it seems that the `toString()` method of `ChequingAccount` was used to generate the second line of output, even though the static type of the object is `Account`. To understand why this happened, the concept of *method binding* will now be discussed.

9.5.3 Method Binding

Consider the `withdraw()` method of the `Account` class. This method is declared as follows:

```
public void withdraw(double amount) {
   :
}
```

Suppose the `withdraw()` method is overridden in `ChequingAccount` using refinement:

```
public void withdraw(double amount) {
   super.withdraw(amount);
   numTransactions++;
}
```

Let's re-examine the following client code which was given in a previous section:

```
Account account;
ChequingAccount ca;
ca = new ChequingAccount(10, 5000.00);
account = ca;
```

After this code is executed, the `account` object variable refers to an instance of `ChequingAccount`. Consider now what happens when the `withdraw()` method is invoked on the `account` object variable:

```
account.withdraw(200.00);
```

Which `withdraw()` method is invoked at run-time? Will it be the one in `Account` or the one in `ChequingAccount`? In Java, method binding (i.e., choosing which method to execute) is based on the dynamic type of the object variable. This means that although the static type of `account` is `Account`, the `withdraw()` method that will be invoked is the one defined in the dynamic type, `ChequingAccount`. This makes sense since the `account` object variable is currently referring to a `ChequingAccount` instance.

If there is no `withdraw()` method in the dynamic type, the search for a `withdraw()` method continues upwards along the generalization hierarchy. The first `withdraw()` method found with the matching signature is selected. Note that a `withdraw()` method is guaranteed to be found somewhere along the generalization hierarchy; otherwise, the compiler would have generated an error.

9.5.4 The Reverse Polymorphism Problem

Consider the `accounts` array which was previously introduced to store `Account`, `ChequingAccount`, and `SavingsAccount` objects:

```
Account[] accounts = new Account[3];
```

Using substitutability, the array was populated with an instance of `Account`, an instance of `ChequingAccount`, and an instance of `SavingsAccount`.

Chapter 9: Inheritance and Polymorphism

Suppose we are given the `accounts` array and we don't know what is stored in the array. Certainly, all the objects can be considered to be of type `Account`. But, can we tell if an object is really an `Account`, a `ChequingAccount`, or a `SavingsAccount`? Also, if an object is indeed a `ChequingAccount` or a `SavingsAccount`, how can we get back the original object that was placed in the array? This problem is called the *reverse polymorphism problem*.

The reverse polymorphism problem is solved in Java in two stages:

- Finding out what is the type of an object using the `instanceof` operator[1]
- Casting an object whose type is higher in a generalization hierarchy to a type lower in the hierarchy (i.e., the reverse of substitutability).

Suppose that `o` is a reference to an object whose type is not known. The `instanceof` operator can be used as follows to determine the actual type of `o`:

```
if (o instanceof Account)
    // A: do something based on Account
else
if (o instanceof ChequingAccount)
    // B: do something based on ChequingAccount
```

The intention behind the code is that if `o` is an `Account` object, the code denoted by `A` in the example will be executed; and, if `o` is a `ChequingAccount` object, the code denoted by `B` will be executed. However, this does not happen. If `o` is an `Account` object *or* a `ChequingAccount` object, only the code denoted by `A` will be executed. This is because `ChequingAccount` inherits from `Account` so an instance of `ChequingAccount` can be considered to be an instance of `Account`. The same thing happens if `o` is replaced by the polymorphic variable `account` discussed in the previous section.

To handle situations such as these, the check for the more specific type (in this case, `ChequingAccount`) should be placed *before* the check for the more general type (`Account`). So, the code above should be written as follows:

```
if (o instanceof ChequingAccount)
    // B: do something based on ChequingAccount
else
if (o instanceof Account)
```

---

[1] It is also possible to use `o.getClass().getName()` to find out the class name of an object, `o`, in Java. However, this approach is not discussed in this chapter.

```
// A: do something based on Account
```

Once we know the type of an object, we can cast it to this type. The following code shows how the `instanceof` operator together with casting can be used to solve the reverse polymorphism problem:

```
if (o instanceof ChequingAccount) {
   ChequingAccount ca = (ChequingAccount) o;
            // cast is perfectly safe

   // perform ChequingAccount operations with ca
}
else
if (o instanceof Account) {
   Account a = (Account) o;
            // cast is perfectly safe

   // perform Account operations with a
}
```

However, if the client code contains a number of `instanceof` checks with classes in a generalization hierarchy (such as `Account` and `ChequingAccount` above) it is likely that the code can be optimized using method overriding and polymorphism. This requires an examination of the specific behavior that is taking place inside the `if` statements. This behavior can be incorporated into a method. Using method overriding, different versions of the method can be written for each class in the hierarchy. Once this is done, polymorphic behavior is used to select the correct method to execute at run-time.

9.5.5 Parameter Passing and Return Types of Methods

We know that `SavingsAccount` is a subclass of `Account`. Suppose that a class `Bank` has a method `method1()` which accepts a parameter of type `Account` and returns nothing:

```
public void method1 (Account a) {
   // code for method1()
}
```

Suppose also that `b` is an instance of `Bank`. It is possible to invoke `method1()` on `b` using an instance of `SavingsAccount` rather than an instance of `Account`. This is the Principle of Substitutability at work:

```
SavingsAccount sa = new SavingsAccount(10, 1500.00, 5.50);
```

Chapter 9: Inheritance and Polymorphism

```
b.method1(sa);
```

`method1()` can make no assumptions about the parameter `a` and must treat it as an instance of `Account`. Of course, it can use the `instanceof` operator to find out the type of `a`.

Suppose that `Bank` has a method `method2()` which accepts a parameter of type `int` and returns an `Account` instance:

```
public Account method2 (int x) {
   // code for method2()
}
```

Using substitutability, `method2()` can return an instance of `Account` or an instance of any subclass of `Account` such as `SavingsAccount` (even indirectly). If the client code that invokes `method2()` wishes to use the return value, it must use an object variable of type `Account`. Again type checking with casting can be used to obtain the original type of the object:

```
Account a;
SavingsAccount sa;

a = b.method2(0);
if (a instanceof SavingsAccount) {
   sa = (SavingsAccount) a;   // cast a to SavingsAccount instance

   // perform SavingsAccount operations with sa
}
```

9.6 Preventing Inheritance

In Java it is possible to prevent a method from being overridden in a subclass by using the keyword `final` when defining the method. For example, the following method `deposit()` from the `Account` class cannot be overridden in a subclass:

```
public final void deposit(double amount) {
   balance = balance + amount;
}
```

Note that other methods of the parent class (or its ancestors) can be overridden as long as they are not declared as `final`.

It is also possible to prevent a class from having subclasses by using the keyword **final**. For example, to prevent subclasses of **Account** from being defined, the keyword **final** can be used as follows:

```
public final class Account {
   // body of Account class
}
```

It is not possible to define a class that inherits from a **final** class. So, the following cannot be done if **Account** is a **final** class:

```
public class SavingsAccount extends Account {
   // body of SavingsAccount class
}
```

9.7 Abstract Classes and Abstract Methods

For various reasons, it is sometimes necessary for client objects *not* to be able to create instances of a class. To prevent instances of a class from being created, it can be made *abstract*. For example, the **Account** class can be made abstract as follows:

```
public abstract class Account {
   // method body is the same as before
}
```

The **abstract** keyword prevents instances of **Account** from being created. However, the **Account** class can have attributes and methods such as those already discussed in this chapter.

An abstract class can be useful in situations where we want to factor out common attributes and behavior from several classes. An abstract class can be used to represent the factored-out attributes and behavior. The original classes can then inherit from the abstract class simplifying their design, development, and maintenance.

For example, suppose we didn't have an **Account** class but we had a **ChequingAccount** class and a **SavingsAccount** class, each with their own attributes and behavior. After factoring out the attributes and behavior in a new class **Account**, **ChequingAccount** and **SavingsAccount** can be created as subclasses of **Account**. All the attributes and methods of the **Account** class will be inherited by **ChequingAccount** and **SavingsAccount** in the way previously described.

Chapter 9: Inheritance and Polymorphism

Since it is not possible to create instances of an abstract class, we will use the term *concrete class* to describe a class from which instances can be created. The term *concrete method* will be used to denote the implementation of a method in a class (which is done by writing statements in the body of the method enclosed with braces). A concrete method is different from an *abstract method* which is simply a method declaration without a method body (or implementation). The following is an abstract method `withdraw()` in the `Account` class:

```
public abstract void withdraw (double amount);
```

Suppose the `withdraw()` method is present in the abstract class `Account` and that `ChequingAccount` inherits from `Account`. Since the `withdraw()` method is abstract in the `Account` class, it must be implemented in `ChequingAccount` if `ChequingAccount` is a concrete subclass of `Account`. If `ChequingAccount` does not implement the `withdraw()` method (by writing code in the method body), it must itself be declared as abstract.

An abstract method in a superclass enforces a protocol in all its subclasses without specifying how the protocol is implemented. Thus, the `withdraw()` method above forces all the subclasses of `Account` to have a `withdraw()` method which accepts a `double` parameter and returns nothing. However, each subclass is free to implement the `withdraw()` method according to its needs.

It should be noted that the name of an abstract class is written in italics in the UML. Abstract methods are also written in italics. Figure 9.5 shows how to specify in the UML that the `Account` class is abstract and that it contains an abstract `withdraw()` method.

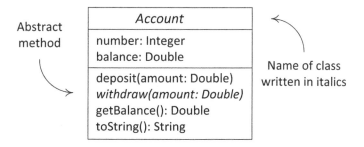

Figure 9.5: Abstract Class with an Abstract Method

Using substitutability, an abstract class can also be used as a type, simplifying the manipulation of child classes. For example, the following is possible in a client class:

```
Account[] accounts = new Account[2];
accounts[0] = new ChequingAccount(10, 5000.00);
accounts[1] = new SavingsAccount(20, 3500.00, 5.25);

for (int i=0; i<accounts.length; i++)
   System.out.println(accounts[i].toString());
```

In this example, the object references of the `ChequingAccount` instance and the `SavingsAccount` instance are of type `Account`. The object references can therefore be stored in an array of type `Account` and can be processed based on this general type instead of based on their specific types.

An abstract class can have zero or more concrete methods. It can also have zero or more abstract methods. A concrete class cannot contain an abstract method since if an instance is created, there will be no method implementation of that method. Finally, it should be mentioned that an abstract class can be a subclass of a concrete class.

9.8 Forms of Inheritance

Inheritance can be used in number of different ways. This section gives a short summary of the ways in which inheritance can be used (Budd, 1998).

- *Specialization.* The new class is a specialized form of the parent class but satisfies the specifications of the parent class in all relevant aspects. Thus, the Principle of Substitutability is explicitly upheld and the new class is a subtype of the parent class. This is the most ideal form of inheritance.

- *Specification.* The parent class defines behavior that is implemented in its child classes but not in the parent class. This guarantees that the child classes maintain a common interface. In Java, this is accomplished by using abstract methods in the parent class.

- *Construction.* The child class makes use of the behavior provided by the parent class but is not a subtype of the parent class. It is often a fast and easy route to developing new classes from existing ones.

- *Extension.* The child class adds new functionality to the parent class, but does not change any inherited behavior. Since the functionality of the parent is not modified, inheritance for extension does not violate the Principle of Substitutability and child classes are always subtypes.

Chapter 9: Inheritance and Polymorphism

- *Combination*. The child class inherits features from more than one parent class. This is known as *multiple inheritance* and is discussed in a later section of this chapter.

9.9 Benefits and Drawbacks of Inheritance

There are many benefits that can be gained by using inheritance when developing an object-oriented application. A major benefit is that of software reusability. When a class inherits behavior from another class, the code that provides the behavior does not have to be rewritten. Reusable code is also more reliable since there are more opportunities for discovering errors.

Another important benefit of inheritance is that of code sharing when two or more classes inherit from a single parent class. The code in the parent class only has to be written once resulting in more reliable code that requires less maintenance. Also, when two or more classes inherit from the same parent class, the behavior they inherit will be the same in all cases. This makes it easier to guarantee that interfaces to similar objects are indeed similar.

There are various problems associated with using inheritance in an object-oriented application. These include the following:

- Inheritance introduces inheritance coupling; instead of features being encapsulated in one class, they are scattered throughout classes in the inheritance hierarchy, increasing the coupling between classes.

- In medium-sized and large inheritance hierarchies, it is often difficult to understand what features are present in the classes that are lower in the hierarchy.

- Modifications to ancestor classes may cause unexpected effects on descendant classes thereby reducing reliability.

9.10 Multiple Inheritance

Multiple inheritance permits a class to have more than one parent class and to inherit features from all its parents. This permits mixing of information from two or more sources. A class with two or more parent classes is called a *join class*. Figure 9.6 is a UML diagram showing how a `VestedHourlyEmployee` class inherits from both an `HourlyEmployee` class and a `VestedEmployee` class (Rumbaugh et al, 1991). `VestedHourlyEmployee` is therefore a join class.

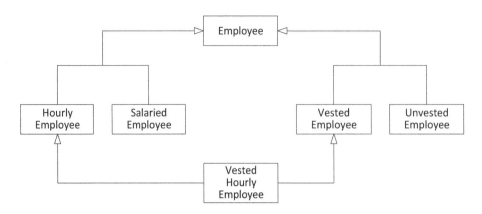

Figure 9.6: Multiple Inheritance

Note that a *salaried employee* is one who is paid at an annual or monthly rate. An *hourly employee* is one who is paid by the hour. A *vested employee* is one who has worked for an organization for a certain period of time and becomes entitled to full pension benefits. An *unvested employee* is one who is not yet entitled to full pension benefits.

Multiple inheritance can be useful in practical programming situations. However, it can be very complex to implement in an object-oriented programming language. Two major challenges in implementing multiple inheritance are:

1. How to deal with name clashes where features with the same name (e.g., instance variables and methods) are inherited from different parent classes. The solution usually involves a combination of *renaming* and *redefinition* (Budd, 1998).

2. How to inherit from two classes that themselves inherit from a common parent class. The major issue here is the sharing of data from the common parent: do we want two copies of the data or only one copy?

The designers of Java decided that the complexity of multiple inheritance outweighed the benefits so Java only supports single inheritance. Two workarounds will now be presented for achieving the effects of multiple inheritance in Java. These workarounds make use of *delegation*, an implementation mechanism by which an object forwards an operation to another object for execution.

Chapter 9: Inheritance and Polymorphism

The first workaround is *delegation using aggregation of roles* (Rumbaugh et al, 1991). A superclass in a generalization hierarchy with multiple inheritance is converted to an aggregate in which each component replaces a generalization relationship. Figure 9.7 shows how the model of Figure 9.6 can be restructured using delegation.

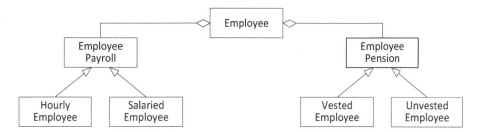

Figure 9.7: Multiple Inheritance Using Delegation

Two new parent classes are created, `EmployeePayroll` and `EmployeePension`. `EmployeePayroll` becomes the parent class of `HourlyEmployee` and `SalariedEmployee`. `EmployeePension` becomes the parent class of `VestedEmployee` and `UnvestedEmployee`. `Employee` can now be modeled as an aggregation of `EmployeePayroll` and `EmployeePension`.

Note that the join class, `VestedHourlyEmployee` is not explicitly created. Its functionality is obtained by combining the functionality of `HourlyEmployee` with the functionality of `VestedEmployee`, both of which are stored as instances in the `Employee` class. Behaviors from the `HourlyEmployee` class are delegated to the `EmployeePayroll` component by the `Employee` class. Similarly, behaviors from the `VestedEmployee` class are delegated to the `EmployeePension` component.

The second workaround is to *inherit from the most important class in the hierarchy and delegate the rest through aggregation* (Rumbaugh et al, 1991). This is illustrated in Figure 9.8 where the most important superclass is `Employee`. `Employee` is also an aggregation of `EmployeePension` just like in the first workaround. The `HourlyEmployee` class inherits from `Employee` as in Figure 9.6. The functionality of the join class, `VestedHourlyEmployee`, is achieved by combining the functionality of `HourlyEmployee` with delegation to the `VestedEmployee` aggregate.

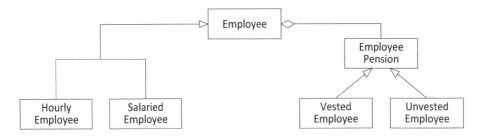

Figure 9.8: Multiple Inheritance Using Inheritance and Delegation

It should be mentioned that the semantics of substitutability are lost when delegation is used. For example, it is expected that an instance of `VestedHourlyEmployee` can take the place of an instance of `HourlyEmployee` or an instance of `VestedEmployee`. Using the workarounds above, there is no explicit `VestedHourlyEmployee` class so substitutability is impossible.

Exercises

1. Explain what is meant by an inheritance hierarchy. How is generalization different from specialization?

2. Distinguish between a direct subclass of a class **A** and an indirect subclass of a class **A**.

3. Suppose that **B** is a subclass of **A**. An instance of **B** is stored in a polymorphic variable of type **A**. With respect to the polymorphic variable, explain how method binding takes place at run-time.

4. Describe the reverse polymorphism problem and explain how it is usually solved in an object-oriented program.

5. Suppose we would like to create a subclass **C** which inherits from two classes **A** and **B**. Since multiple inheritance is not possible in Java, describe a workaround that can provide almost the same functionality.

6. Discuss two benefits and two drawbacks of inheritance.

7. `SavingsAccount` is a subclass of Account. Suppose a method of a **Bank** class has a parameter of type `Account`. Can a `SavingsAccount` object be supplied as an argument to this method? Should **Bank** be allowed to have another method that takes a parameter of type `SavingsAccount`? Investigate how Java deals with this issue.

Chapter 9: Inheritance and Polymorphism

8. If **X** is an immutable class, it is possible for a class to inherit from **X** and add attributes which are mutable. Explain how this can be prevented.

Chapter 10

Exception Handling

This chapter discusses the need for exception handling in writing robust, reliable software. It defines several terms commonly used with exception handling. It then presents the exception handling facilities in Java and shows how to write code that takes advantage of these facilities. This chapter does not aim to give an exhaustive treatment of exception handling; rather, its intention is to give the reader a basic appreciation of the fundamental concepts.

10.1 Exceptions

Exceptional conditions (or simply *exceptions*) are things that occur in an application that are not expected or that are not part of the application's normal operation (Shelton, 1999). If exceptions are not handled properly by the application, it can lead to failures and system crashes. Many exceptional conditions can be anticipated when an application is being designed and protection against these conditions can be incorporated into the application.

Broadly speaking, there are three main types of exceptions that can occur when an object-oriented application is executing (Doshi, 2003). These are listed in Table 10.1.

Cause of Exception	How to Recover from Exception	Example
Exceptions due to programming errors in objects which provide services to other objects.	A client object can do very little to recover from this type of exception.	`NullPointerException` (which occurs when an attempt is made to reference an object variable which does not refer to an actual object) and `ArrayIndexOutOfBoundsException` (which occurs when an attempt is made to access an array element outside the bounds of an array).
Exceptions due to errors in a client object where a client object attempts to do something not allowed by a server object.	A client object can recover from the exception by taking an alternative course of action if there is sufficient information available on what caused the exception.	An attempt to withdraw funds from an `Account` which would cause the account balance to become less than zero (or another pre-defined value).
Exceptions due to resource failures.	A client object can re-try the operation after some time or bring the system to a halt.	The system running out of memory.

Table 10.1: Main Types of Exceptions

10.2 Exception Handling in Java

Exception handling is the method of building an application to detect and recover from exceptional conditions (Shelton, 1999). In Java, exception handling is implemented using two kinds of exceptions, *checked exceptions* and *unchecked exceptions*. Both types of exceptions are first-class objects. If an object providing a service generates a checked exception, a client object must handle the checked exception. However, it is not necessary for a client object to handle unchecked exceptions.

Object-oriented programming languages generally support only unchecked exceptions. However, Java is the first mainstream programming language to support checked exceptions. There are numerous arguments for and against

Chapter 10: Exception Handling

the use of checked exceptions. A checked exception generated by an object which provides a service to clients is a forced contract on client objects to deal with it. This contract can become an unwanted burden if client objects are unable to deal with the exception effectively (Doshi, 2003).

In deciding whether to use checked or unchecked exceptions in Java, the question should be asked, "What should a client object do when an exception occurs?" If the client object can take an alternative course of action to deal with the exception, a checked exception should be used. If the client object cannot do anything useful with the exception, an unchecked exception should be used.

10.3 Checked Exceptions

This section explains how to incorporate checked exceptions in an object-oriented program. It shows how to write the code for a checked exception class and how to write exception handling code in a client object.

10.3.1 Writing Checked Exceptions

Suppose we wanted to write a checked exception, `InsufficientFundsException`, for the situation where an attempt is made to withdraw funds from an account which would leave the account with a balance that is not allowed. Since checked exceptions inherit from the built-in `Exception` class, we must first inherit from the `Exception` class as shown in Figure 10.1.

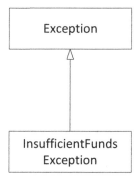

Figure 10.1: `InsufficientFundsException` is a Subclass of `Exception`

The code for a basic `InsufficientFundsException` class is given below:

```
public class InsufficientFundsException extends Exception {
```

```
   public InsufficientFundsException () {
      super ("Not enough funds to permit operation.");
   }

   public InsufficientFundsException (String message) {
      super (message);
   }
}
```

The no-argument constructor of the `InsufficientFundsException` class calls the superclass constructor with an error message that is specific to the situation. The second constructor takes an error message as a parameter and uses this message in the call to the superclass constructor.

The `InsufficientFundsException` class can be made more sophisticated with attributes and methods of its own. However, the remainder of this chapter uses the basic class shown above.

10.3.2 Declaring and Throwing Checked Exceptions

Suppose a checked exception occurs in an object which is providing a service to a client object. To raise an exception, it is necessary to create an instance of the checked exception at the point where the exception occurred. The exception object is then passed to the Java run-time system which sends it to the calling method in the client object. The process of creating an exception object and passing it to the run-time system (which then sends it to the client object requesting the service) is referred to as *throwing an exception*.

As an example, consider the situation where a client object attempts to make a withdrawal which would cause the balance in an account to fall below a pre-determined threshold. This is an exception condition and the `Account` object providing the withdrawal service must not allow the withdrawal to proceed. So, the `Account` object must throw an exception. To do this, the `Account` object first creates an instance of `InsufficientFundsException` using one of the two available constructors. Next, the `Account` object uses the `throws` statement to throw the `InsufficientFundsException` to the client object, without performing the withdrawal.

The code below shows how the `withdraw()` method can be written to deal with the exception condition:

```
public void withdraw (double amount) throws
   InsufficientFundsException {
```

Chapter 10: Exception Handling

```
    if (balance >= amount)
        balance = balance - amount;
    else
        throw new InsufficientFundsException();

}
```

The code above uses the no-argument constructor when creating the exception object. However, the second constructor can be used to send a customised message when creating the exception object as follows:

```
String message = "Withdrawal of " + amount + " exceeds balance of "
    + balance;
throw new InsufficientFundsException(message);
```

Two points should be noted about throwing checked exceptions. First, the method which could potentially throw the exception must state in its declaration that the exception can be thrown. For example, the following declaration states that the **withdraw()** method can throw an **InsufficientFundsException**:

```
public void withdraw (double amount) throws
    InsufficientFundsException {
    :
}
```

Second, whenever an exception object is thrown from a method, the method is exited immediately and control returns to the client object which invoked the method. So, any remaining statements in the execution path of the method are ignored. In this regard, the **throw** statement is similar to a **return** statement.

Figure 10.2 shows a client object requesting a service from an object (via a method invocation); an exception condition occurs in the object providing the service so it creates and throws an exception object.

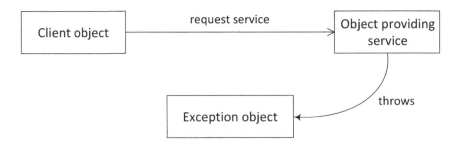

Figure 10.2 Throwing an Exception

10.3.3 Catching Checked Exceptions

The process of identifying an exception and dealing with it in a specific way is referred to as *catching an exception*. When a checked exception is thrown by a server object, a client object can take two courses of action: it can catch the exception and deal with it in a meaningful way or it can throw the exception to its own client. Figure 10.3 shows how a client object can catch an exception and deal with it.

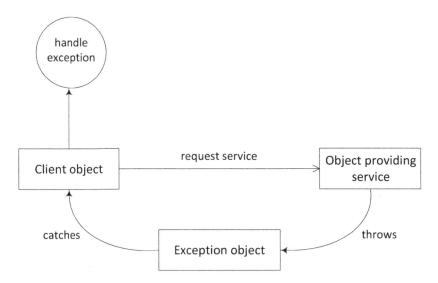

Figure 10.3 Catching and Handling an Exception

In order to catch an exception and perform exception handling, a client object must use a `try-catch` block. The following example shows how a client object can catch the `InsufficientFundsException` thrown by an `Account` object and perform exception handling. In the code, `account` refers to an instance of an `Account` created earlier.

Chapter 10: Exception Handling

```
try {
   account.withdraw(2000.00);
}
catch (InsufficientFundsException ife) {
   System.out.println (ife.getMessage());
   System.out.println ("Repeat operation with smaller amount.\n");
}
```

The statement in the `try` block is executed first. If the `InsufficientFundsException` is thrown, it is caught in the `catch` block and exception handling is performed according to the statements in the `catch` block. Note that the statement,

```
catch (InsufficientFundsException ife) {
```

catches the `InsufficientFundsException` object (thrown by the `Account` object) and gives it the variable name `ife`. Any variable name can be used instead of `ife`. The variable name allows the exception object to be referred to in the `catch` block, for example, to access the error message. After the statements in the `catch` block are executed, execution of the method continues to the next statement following the `try-catch` block. Of course, if the exception is not caught, the method is exited as soon as the exception occurs.

It is possible to have more than one statement in the `try` block. For example, suppose that $1000.00 has to be transferred from one account instance, `account1`, to another account instance, `account2`. The following `try` block can be used:

```
try {
   account1.withdraw(1000.00);
   account2.deposit(1000.00);
}
```

If the `withdraw()` statement generates an exception, an immediate exit of the `try` block occurs and control is transferred to the statements in the `catch` block. Thus, the `deposit()` statement is not executed. In general, if there is more than one statement in the `try` block, the block is exited as soon as an exception occurs.

It is also possible to have more than one `catch` blocks in the exception handling code. For example, suppose that a checked exception, `TooLargeWithdrawalException`, is written to deal with situations where the withdrawal amount exceeds a certain amount. The `try-catch` block can be written as follows:

```
try {
   a.withdraw(2000.00);
}
catch (InsufficientFundsException ife) {
   System.out.println (ife.getMessage());
   System.out.println ("Repeat operation with smaller amount.\n");
}
catch (TooLargeWithdrawalException tlwe) {
   System.out.println (tlwe.getMessage());
   System.out.println ("Repeat operation with smaller amount.\n");
}
```

Of course, the `withdraw()` method in `Account` must throw the `TooLargeWithdrawalException` when the condition for the exception is met.

When there are multiple `catch` blocks, the exception is caught in the first `catch` block which matches the type of the exception object thrown and all other `catch` blocks are ignored. So, if the `TooLargeWithdrawalException` is thrown, only the code in the second `catch` block is executed.

Since both exceptions inherit from `Exception` (and through substitutability, they can be referred to using a variable of type `Exception`), it is possible to catch both exceptions in a single `catch` block by specifying the exception type as `Exception`:

```
try {
   a.withdraw(2000.00);
}
catch (Exception e) {
   System.out.println (e.getMessage());
   System.out.println ("Repeat operation with smaller amount.\n");
}
```

This gives rise to the possibility of designing an exception inheritance hierarchy for any application. A parent exception class is written for the entire application and child exception classes inherit from this class and so on until an inheritance hierarchy of exceptions is obtained. If exception handling based on specific types is required, child type exception objects can be thrown and caught. However, if the exception handling needs to be generalized, child type

Chapter 10: Exception Handling

exception objects can be thrown but parent type exception objects can be caught to simplify the exception handling.

10.3.4 Cleaning Up after Exception Handling

The `try-catch` statement has one other block which allows cleanup operations to be performed. This block is the `finally` block. An exception generated by one statement in a `try` block may leave the application in an inconsistent state due to statements which may have already executed in the `try` block. These statements may have resulted in resources being held that should now be released since the `try` block as a whole was unsuccessful.

Consider the following code which is responsible for saving `Account` objects to a relational database. This code is discussed in detail in Chapter 15. It is not necessary to fully understand the code to appreciate the exception handling mechanism employed.

```
public void saveAccounts() throws Exception {

   Connection connection = null;
   Statement stmt = null;

   try {
      Class.forName(JdbcDriver);
      connection = DriverManager.getConnection(connectionStr);

      stmt = connection.createStatement();

      :

   }
   catch (SQLException sqle) {
      :
   }

}
```

The `try` block contains code which informs Java about the database driver to be used to connect to the database (`Class.forName(…)`). The code then makes a connection to the database, storing the connection in a `Connection` object. A `Statement` object is then created which is used to send SQL commands to the database. The checked exception, `SQLException` can be thrown several times in the try block. However, if it occurs in the code which creates the `Statement` object, the resources held by the `Connection` object should be released.

Code can be written in the `catch` block to close the `Connection` object and the `Statement` object (which will release the resources held):

```
if (stmt != null)
   stmt.close();

if (connection != null)
   connection.close();
```

If the `SQLException` is thrown, the code in the `catch` block will cause the database resources to be released. However, if the `saveAccounts()` method terminates normally, it still needs to release the resources held by the `Connection` object and the `Statement` object. So, it is necessary to have another set of statements after the `try` block which closes the `Connection` object and the `Statement` object.

Instead of writing two sets of code that perform cleanup activities, the cleanup code can be written once in a `finally` block of the `try-catch` statement:

```
finally {

   if (stmt != null)
      stmt.close();

   if (connection != null)
      connection.close();
}
```

The `finally` block is guaranteed to be executed just before the method exits, regardless of what happens inside the method. There is no need to have separate cleanup statements inside the `catch` block and outside the `try-catch` statement. In essence, a `finally` clause acts like a miniature function within a method that is guaranteed to be executed before the method is exited.

10.3.5 Not Handling a Checked Exception

If a client object does not intend to deal with an exception thrown by an object providing a service, it should not provide an exception handler using the `try-catch` statement. Instead, the client object should simply allow the exception to be passed on to its own caller. For this to work, the method in the client

Chapter 10: Exception Handling

class must declare that it will not be handling the exception and thus will be indirectly re-throwing the exception to its own caller.

For example, assume that the method in the client which invokes the `withdraw()` method on an `Account` object is called `clientMethod()`. If `clientMethod()` does not intend to handle the `InsufficientFundsException`, it must be declared as follows:

```
public <return-type> clientMethod (<parameter-list>) throws
   InsufficientFundsException
```

If an `InsufficientFundsException` is thrown by the object providing the service (an `Account` object in this case), control returns immediately to `clientMethod()`. However, since `clientMethod()` has declared that it does not want to deal with the exception, `clientMethod()` is terminated immediately and control is transferred to its own caller. Other methods in the calling sequence can also declare that they do not want to deal with the exception. This will cause the exception to be re-thrown several times from one object to the next in the calling sequence.

However, it is necessary for some method along the calling sequence to eventually catch the exception. If not, the `main()` method must declare that it, too, throws the exception. In the latter case, if the exception is generated by the object providing the service, it is thrown all the way up to `main()` which then throws it to the run-time system resulting in the termination of the program. The re-throwing of the `InsufficientFundsException` is illustrated in Figure 10.4.

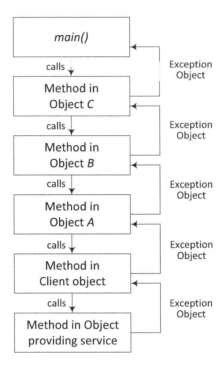

Figure 10.4: Not Handling a Checked Exception

Figure 10.4 shows the call stack of a program up to the point where the object providing a service to the client object throws an exception. The client object does not handle the exception so it is propagated to its own caller. This is repeated until an exception handler is found somewhere in the one of the methods in the call stack or until `main()` is reached, at which point the program is terminated.

10.4 Unchecked Exceptions

The class for an unchecked exception can be written just like the class for a checked exception. However, an unchecked exception inherits from the `RuntimeException` class which itself inherits from the `Exception` class. `NullPointerException` is an example of an unchecked exception. A UML diagram showing the exception hierarchy of a `NullPointerException` is given in Figure 10.5.

Chapter 10: Exception Handling

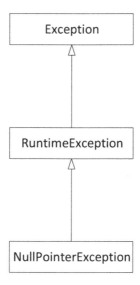

Figure 10.5: Exception Hierarchy of `NullPointerException`

The checked exception, `InsufficientFundsException`, can be easily converted to an unchecked exception by changing the class it inherits from:

```
public class InsufficientFundsException extends RuntimeException {
   // body is the same as before
}
```

An unchecked exception can be thrown and caught just like a checked exception. However, it is not necessary to catch an unchecked exception and it is not necessary to declare that a method will throw an unchecked exception.

If an unchecked exception occurs in an object providing a service and it is not caught in the method of the client object that requests the service, execution returns immediately to the caller of the client method. If the exception is not caught eventually by an object in the calling sequence, it will be re-thrown all the way up to the `main()` method resulting in the termination of the program.

10.5 Use Exception Handling with Care

Exception handling is a key to writing robust, reliable software systems. However, creating, throwing, and catching exceptions require memory and CPU processing cycles. Thus, exception handling can slow down a system. Also, too much exception handling can make code difficult to read and frustrating for programmers using the objects which can throw exceptions.

Moreover, exception handling forces a tight coupling between objects providing services and their clients. For these reasons, care must be taken when writing exception handling code.

Exercises

1. Explain how a checked exception is different from an unchecked exception.

2. A certain method `m()` of a class `C` can potentially throw a checked exception. Describe the code that needs to be written in `m()` to facilitate the throwing of the exception.

3. Explain what is involved in writing an event handler for a client object.

4. A client object is requesting services from another object which can potentially throw a checked exception. What is needed in the client method if it does not wish to provide an event handler?

5. Why is the `finally` block an important block in the event-handling code?

6. Suppose that a `try` block contains five statements. An exception was thrown in the fourth statement. Will the fifth statement be executed? How can the effects of the first three statements be undone?

7. Suppose a `try-catch` statement has two `catch` blocks. An exception is generated in the `try` block and matches the exception type in both of the `catch` blocks. Which of the `catch` blocks will be executed?

8. Although not discussed in this chapter, the exception handling code in a client can re-throw a checked exception or even throw a new exception to its own client. What code changes are necessary in the client method which performs the exception handling?

9. Suppose that the exception handling code in a `catch` block can potentially generate an exception itself. Suggest an approach to handle this situation.

10. Now that you know about exceptions, let's re-visit Question 9 at the end of Chapter 3:

Chapter 10: Exception Handling

Suppose that the constructor of the `Fraction` class receives a denominator of 0. Since a fraction cannot contain a denominator of 0, suggest a technique for dealing with this situation.

Chapter 11

Third Programming Project

This chapter builds on the concepts covered in the second programming project by showing how to develop an application using inheritance and exception handling. It first describes the requirements of the application and then presents a UML diagram showing the collaborating objects in the application. The implementation of each class in the UML diagram is then discussed. Next, the chapter presents a graphical user interface (GUI) which manipulates the domain objects to provide the functionality required. The classes that manage the GUI do not have to be written and are supplied at the book Web site. Finally, the chapter explains how to go about creating and compiling the necessary source files in Java.

11.1 Requirements of the Application

An object-oriented application is required to manage information on students and the courses they register for at a certain university. There are two types of students, undergraduate students and postgraduate students. The application must deal with exceptional conditions such as the enrolment limit for a particular course being exceeded. This section describes the functionality required of the application.

11.1.1 Overview

Students at the university register for courses at different times of the academic year. There are two kinds of students, undergraduate students and postgraduate students. Each course has a credit weighting and there is a limit to the amount of credits a student can register for. Each course can accommodate a certain number of students and once this limit is reached, no more students can be registered for the course. In both cases, exceptions must be thrown to indicate that the registration cannot proceed.

A graphical user interface (GUI) is supplied at the book Web site which performs the following operations on the domain objects:

- Create, view, and update information on the students at the university
- Create, view, and update information on the courses offered at the university
- Register and de-register students from courses
- View the courses a student is currently registered for
- View the students currently registered for a course

The next sub-section gives a UML diagram of the domain classes. This is followed by a detailed description of each class in the application.

11.1.2 UML Diagram of Domain Objects

Figure 11.1 is a UML diagram of the set of collaborating domain objects in the application.

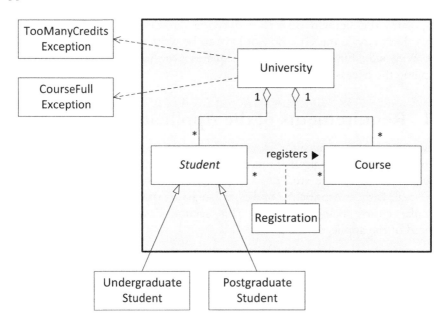

Figure 11.1: UML Diagram of Domain Objects

The shaded part of the UML diagram shows classes that have already been developed in the second programming project. Thus, the third programming project is essentially an extension of the second programming project to include the following:

Chapter 11: Third Programming Project

- Using inheritance to create subclasses of the **Student** class (which is now abstract)
- Performing exception handling when the relevant conditions occur

Details of each class in the UML diagram are given in the following subsections. It should be noted that there is some duplication in the description of classes already discussed in the second programming project. This is done in order to keep the class descriptions for this project in one place. It should also be mentioned that most of the classes in the second programming project have been enhanced in some way.

11.1.3 Course

The **Course** class models the concept of a course at the university. It is a concrete class. Table 11.1 shows the list of attributes of **Course**:

Attribute	Type	Purpose
code	String	Unique identifier for the course.
title	String	The title of the course.
numCredits	int	The number of credit hours corresponding to the course.
maxStudents	int	The maximum number of students who can register for the course.

Table 11.1: Attributes of **Course**

Course should provide the new or updated methods listed in Table 11.2.

Method	Return Type	Purpose
Course(String code, String title, int numCredits, int maxStudents)		Constructor.
equals(Object obj)	boolean	Returns **true** if the current course is equal to **obj**; otherwise, returns **false**. Equality is based on the course **code**.
toString()	String	Returns the string representation of a **Course** object.

Table 11.2: Methods of **Course**

The `Course` class should provide accessors for all its instance variables. It should provide mutators for all its instance variables except `code` (which serves as the primary key).

11.1.4 Student

The `Student` class models the concept of a student at the university. It is an abstract class. Table 11.3 shows the list of attributes of `Student`:

Attribute	Type	Purpose
ID	long	Unique identifier for the student.
name	String	The name of the student.
address	String	The address of the student.
phone	String	The telephone contact of the student.
email	String	The email address of the student.

Table 11.3: Attributes of `Student`

`Student` should provide the new or updated methods listed in Table 11.4.

Method	Return Type	Purpose
Student (long ID, String name, String address, String phone, String email)		Constructor.
equals(Object obj)	boolean	Returns `true` if the current student is equal to `obj`; otherwise, returns `false`. Equality is based on the student ID.
toString()	String	Returns the string representation of a `Student` object.

Table 11.4: Methods of `Student`

The `Student` class should provide accessors for all its instance variables. It should provide mutators for all its instance variables except `ID` (which serves as the primary key). It should be noted that the requirement to automatically generate the student IDs is removed in this programming project.

Chapter 11: Third Programming Project

11.1.5 UndergraduateStudent

The `UndergraduateStudent` class models the concept of an undergraduate student at the university. It is a concrete class that inherits from the `Student` class. Table 11.5 shows the list of attributes of `UndergraduateStudent`.

Attribute	Type	Purpose
major	String	Major degree being pursued by the student.
minor	String	Minor degree being pursued by the student.

Table 11.5: Attributes of `UndergraduateStudent`

Table 11.6 shows the methods that should be provided by the `UndergraduateStudent` class.

Method	Return Type	Purpose
UndergraduateStudent(long ID, String name, String address, String phone, String email, String major, String minor)		Constructor.
toString()	String	Returns a string representation of the undergraduate student.

Table 11.6: Methods of `UndergraduateStudent`

The `UndergraduateStudent` class should provide accessors for the two instance variables listed in Table 11.5. Since `UndergraduateStudent` inherits from `Student`, there is no need to declare the attributes of `UndergraduateStudent` that have already been declared in `Student`. So, an `UndergraduateStudent` object will contain seven instance variables: five declared in `Student` and two declared in `UndergraduateStudent`. Note also that the `toString()` method uses method refinement to override the `toString()` method defined in `Student`.

11.1.6 PostgraduateStudent

The `PostgraduateStudent` class models the concept of a postgraduate student at the university. It is a concrete class that inherits from the `Student` class. Table 11.7 shows the list of attributes of `PostgraduateStudent`.

Attribute	Type	Purpose
thesisTitle	String	Title of the thesis the student is working on.
supervisor	String	Name of person who is supervising the thesis.

Table 11.7: List of Attributes of `PostgraduateStudent`

Table 11.8 shows the methods that should be provided by the `PostgraduateStudent` class.

Method	Return Type	Purpose
PostgraduateStudent(long ID, String name, String address, String phone, String email, String thesisTitle, String supervisor)		Constructor.
toString()	String	Returns a string representation of the postgraduate student.

Table 11.8: Methods of `PostgraduateStudent`

The `PostgraduateStudent` class should provide accessors for the two instance variables listed in Table 11.7. Since `PostgraduateStudent` inherits from `Student`, there is no need to declare the attributes of `PostgraduateStudent` that have already been declared in `Student`. Like an `UndergraduateStudent` object, a `PostgraduateStudent` object will contain seven instance variables: five declared in `Student` and two declared in `PostgraduateStudent`. Note also that the `toString()` method overrides the `toString()` method defined in `Student` using method refinement.

11.1.7 Registration

`Registration` is an association class linking instances of `Student` with instances of `Course`. It is basically the same as in the second programming project except that the link attributes, `acadYear` and `semester`, have been omitted to simplify the coding.

Chapter 11: Third Programming Project

11.1.8 Exception Classes

From Figure 11.1, it can be observed that there is a *using* relationship between `University` and the two exception classes, `TooManyCreditsException` and `CourseFullException`. A *using* relationship is appropriate since the `University` will throw instances of these exceptions when the exception conditions are met. An instance of `TooManyCreditsException` should be thrown if an attempt is made to register a student for a course which will exceed the maximum amount of credits that the student is allowed to register for. An instance of `CourseFullException` should be thrown when an attempt is made to register a student for a course for which the enrolment limit has been reached.

`TooManyCreditsException` and `CourseFullException` are checked exceptions so they must inherit from the class `Exception`. Each class will contain two constructors: a no-argument constructor, and a constructor that accepts a `message` argument to be associated with the given instance of the exception class. No other methods or attributes are required of the exception classes in this project.

11.1.9 `University`

The `University` class is responsible for managing information on students and courses and for registering and de-registering students from courses. It must also provide services that make it possible for clients to query the information stored in the system. It contains the list of attributes shown in Table 11.10 (these are conceptually the same as in the second programming project).

Attribute	*Type*	*Purpose*
name	String	Name of the university.
courses	Collection of `Course` objects	A list of all the courses being offered at the university.
students	Collection of `Student` objects	A list of all the students at the university (both undergraduate and postgraduate).
registrations	Collection of `Registration` objects	A list of all the `Registration` objects in the system (each one represents a link between a particular student and a particular course).

Table 11.10: Attributes of `University`

In the second programming project, an array was used to implement each of the three collections of objects listed in Table 11.10. In this project, a new type of collection called the `ArrayList` will be used for this purpose; it is discussed in the next sub-section.

The `University` class must provide the new or updated methods shown in Table 11.11.

Method	Return Type	Purpose
University(String name)		Constructor.
addCourse(String code, String title, int numCredits, int maxStudents)	Course	Creates a `Course` object and adds it to its collection of courses.
updateCourse(String code, String title, int numCredits, int maxStudents)	Course	Updates the attributes of the `Course` object identified by the course `code`.
addUndergraduateStudent(long ID, String name, String address, String phone, String email, String major, String minor)	UndergraduateStudent	Creates an `UndergraduateStudent` object and adds it to its collection of students
updateUndergraduateStudent(long ID, String name, String address, String phone, String email, String major, String minor)	UndergraduateStudent	Updates the attributes of the `UndergraduateStudent` object identified by the student ID.
addPostgraduateStudent(long ID, String name, String address, String phone, String email, String thesisTitle, String supervisor)	PostgraduateStudent	Creates a `PostgraduateStudent` object and adds it to its collection of students.
updatePostgraduateStudent(long ID, String name, String address, String phone, String email, String thesisTitle, String supervisor)	PostgraduateStudent	Updates the attributes of the `PostgraduateStudent` object identified by the student ID.
getCourse(String code)	Course	Finds and returns the `Course` object

Chapter 11: Third Programming Project

Method	Return Type	Purpose
		with the given `code`; if none exists, returns `null`.
getStudent(long ID)	Student	Finds and returns the `Student` object with the given student `ID`; if none exists, returns `null`.
getCourses(long studentID)	Collection of `Course` objects	Finds the courses which the student with the given `ID` has registered for; returns the result in a collection (see next sub-section).
getStudents(String courseCode)	Collection of `Student` objects	Finds the students who are registered for the course with the given `code`; returns the result in a collection (see next sub-section).
getRegistration(long studentID, String courseCode)	Registration	Finds the `Registration` object corresponding to the given student `ID` and course `code`.
registerStudent(long studentID, String courseCode)	boolean	Registers the student with the given `ID` for the course with the given course `code`; returns `true` if successful and `false` otherwise. Throws `TooManyCreditsException` or `CourseFullExcep`

Method	Return Type	Purpose
		tion if exception conditions are met.
deRegisterStudent(long studentID, String courseCode)	boolean	De-registers the student with the given ID from the course with the given course code; returns true if successful and false otherwise.
getCourses()	String	Returns a list of all the courses in the system (note that this is an overloaded method).
getStudents()	String	Returns a list of all the students in the system; data from only a few attributes of Student is shown (note that this is an overloaded method).
getUndergraduateStudents()	String	Returns a list of all the undergraduate students; data from only a few attributes of UndergraduateStudent is shown.

Chapter 11: Third Programming Project

Method	Return Type	Purpose
getPostgraduateStudents()	String	Returns a list of all the postgraduate students; data from only a few attributes of `PostgraduateStudent` is shown.

Table 11.11: Methods of `University`

Note that there is no `addStudent()` method in `University` since `Student` is an abstract class. Also, an accessor and mutator must be provided for the `name` instance variable. No other accessors and mutators are required.

11.1.10 User Interface

In this application, the user interacts with a graphical user interface (GUI) instead of the text-based menu structure used in the first two programming projects. The GUI manipulates the domain objects to provide the functionality required. The GUI consists of three screens as follows:

Students

- Add a new student to the system
- Update information on an existing student
- Query for a student with a particular student ID
- Register a student for a course
- De-register a student from a course

Courses

- Add a new course to the system
- Update information on an existing course
- Query for a course with a particular course code
- Register a student for a course
- De-register a student from a course

View All

- List all the courses offered by the university
- List all the students at the university

- List all the undergraduate students at the university
- List all the postgraduate students at the university

It should be noted that in order to simplify the user interface, the *Students* screen allows the user to manipulate information on both undergraduate and postgraduate students.

11.1.11 Implementation Requirements

The `University` class maintains three collections: `courses`, `students`, and `registrations`. Two of its methods also return collections of objects (`getCourses(long ID)` and `getStudents(String code)`). In this programming project, an `ArrayList` object is used for each collection instead of an array. `ArrayList` is a built-in collection class in Java. The built-in collection classes in Java are discussed in detail in Chapter 13. Table 11.12 lists the methods of `ArrayList` that will be required in this programming project:

Method	Return Type	Purpose
ArrayList()		Constructor.
add(Object obj)	boolean	Appends `obj` to the end of the list; returns `true` if successful and `false` otherwise.
get(int index)	Object	Returns the element at position `index` in the list.
remove(Object obj)	boolean	Removes `obj` from the list if it is present; returns `true` if successful and `false` otherwise.
size()	int	Returns the number of elements in the list.

Table 11.12: Methods of `ArrayList` Required for this Project

The `ArrayList` class is located in the `java.util` package. Thus, in order to use the `ArrayList` class, the following line must be placed at the top of the source file containing the `University` class:

```
import java.util.*;
```

An instance of `ArrayList` is created for each collection and its `add()` method is used to insert objects into the collection. The `get()` method is used to retrieve the object at a specific location in the `ArrayList`. The `remove()` method is used to remove an object from the `ArrayList`. Observe that the `add()`, `get()`, and `remove()` methods operate on objects of type `Object`.

Chapter 11: Third Programming Project

Since `Object` is the superclass of all user-defined classes in Java, an instance of any user-defined class can be inserted into an `ArrayList` (through substitutability). However, the `get()` method returns an object of type `Object` from the `ArrayList`. Thus, casting will be necessary to recover the original object inserted into the `ArrayList`.

When using an `ArrayList`, there is no need to have an integer variable that keeps track of the number of objects in the collection (which is required when an array is used). An instance of `ArrayList` automatically keeps track of the number of objects in the `ArrayList`. This number can be obtained at any time by calling its `size()` method.

11.2 Implementation of Domain Classes

11.2.1 Course

The `Course` class enhances the `Course` class in the second programming project by including the `maxStudents` instance variable and implementing the `equals()` method. The `equals()` method checks for equality based on the course `code`. It is implemented as follows:

```java
public boolean equals(Object obj) {

   if (obj instanceof Course) {
      Course c = (Course) obj;
      if (this.code.equals(c.getCode()))
         return true;
      else
         return false;
   }
   else
      throw new IllegalArgumentException
         ("Argument not of type Course.");

}
```

11.2.2 Student, UndergraduateStudent, and PostgraduateStudent

The `Student` class is implemented almost exactly as in the second programming project except that it now has an additional instance variable, `email`, and it implements the `equals()` method. The `ID` instance variable is also declared as `long` instead of `int`. Since `Student` is an abstract class, it is declared as follows:

```
public abstract class Student
{
   private long ID;
   private String name;
   private String address;
   private String phone;
   private String email;

   :

}
```

`UndergraduateStudent` inherits from `Student`. It also declares two additional instance variables, `major` and `minor`. Part of the implementation of the `UndergraduateStudent` class is given below:

```
public class UndergraduateStudent extends Student
{
   private String major;
   private String minor;

   public UndergraduateStudent(long ID, String name, String address,
      String phone, String email, String major, String minor) {

      super(ID, name, address, phone, email);
      this.major = major;
      this.minor = minor;
   }

   public String toString() {
      String s;

      s = super.toString() + "  Major: " + major +
         "  Minor: " + minor;

      return s;
   }

   // accessor and mutator methods

}
```

Chapter 11: Third Programming Project

Note that the `extends` keyword is used to specify that `UndergraduateStudent` is a subclass of `Student`. Although `UndergraduateStudent` has seven instance variables, five are already declared in `Student`. So, only the two instance variables that are specific to `UndergraduateStudent` are declared.

The constructor for `UndergraduateStudent` accepts values for all seven instance variables. It uses `super()` in the first line to call the superclass constructor to initialise the five instance variables declared in `Student`. The remaining two are initialised in the constructor itself.

The `toString()` method of `UndergraduateStudent` overrides the `toString()` method of `Student` using *refinement*. It calls the `toString()` method of the parent class, `Student`, using the keyword `super`. The results of this call are concatenated to the values of the `major` and `minor` instance variables to get the final result.

The implementation of the `PostgraduateStudent` class is similar to the implementation of `UndergraduateStudent` so it is not discussed further in this section.

11.2.3 Registration

The implementation of the `Registration` association class was discussed in the second programming project. An instance of `Registration` is created whenever an object of type `Student` is linked to an instance of `Course`. Since `UndergraduateStudent` and `PostgraduateStudent` are subclasses of `Student`, an instance of either one of these classes can take the place of `Student` by substitutability. Thus, a `Registration` object can link an instance of `UndergraduateStudent` to an instance of `Course`. Similarly, it can link an instance of `PostgraduateStudent` to an instance of `Course`. Note that since `Student` is an abstract class, it is not possible for an instance of `Student` to be linked to an instance of `Course`.

11.2.4 TooManyCreditsException and CourseFullException

The two exceptions are checked exceptions so the corresponding exception classes inherit from `Exception` as explained in Chapter 10. The following is the implementation of the `CourseFullException` class:

```
public class CourseFullException extends Exception
{
```

```
  public CourseFullException() {
    super
        ("Enrollment limit reached. No more students can be
        registered.");
  }

  public CourseFullException(String message) {
    super(message);
  }
}
```

The implementation of the `TooManyCreditsException` class is similar.

11.2.5 University

The `University` class is essentially an extension of the `University` class developed in the second programming project. However, `ArrayList` objects are used instead of arrays to maintain collections of objects. Thus, the three collections described in Table 11.10 are declared as follows:

```
private ArrayList students;
private ArrayList courses;
private ArrayList registrations;
```

The `students ArrayList` is used to store both `UndergraduateStudent` objects and `PostgraduateStudent` objects. The objects in this array can be regarded as being of type `Student` since `UndergraduateStudent` and `PostgraduateStudent` are subclasses of `Student`.

The constructor of `University` creates the actual collections as follows:

```
students = new ArrayList();
courses = new ArrayList();
registrations = new ArrayList();
```

The `addCourse()` method is implemented as follows:

```
public Course addCourse(String code, String title,
    int numCredits, int maxStudents) {

  Course course;
```

Chapter 11: Third Programming Project

```
        course = getCourse(code);
                    // check if course already exists

    if (course == null) {
                    // course does not exist

        course = new Course(code, title, numCredits, maxStudents);
        courses.add(course);
                    // add course object to courses ArrayList

        return course;
    }
    else              // course already exists
        return null;
}
```

The addCourse() method first calls the getCourse() method to determine if a course with the given code already exists. If not, a new instance of Course is created and added to the courses collection using the add() method of ArrayList. Otherwise, null is returned.

The updateCourse() method first calls the getCourse() method to determine if indeed a course with the given code already exists. If not, null is returned. Otherwise, the instance of Course is updated using the setter methods of its instance variables. The code instance variable cannot be changed.

The getCourse() method traverses the courses ArrayList from the beginning (element 0) to the end (element courses.size() - 1) searching for the course that has an identical code. Since the ArrayList consists of objects of type Object, it is necessary to cast the objects to Course when they are taken out of the ArrayList with the get() method. If this is not done, it will not be possible to use methods like getCode() (since there is no getCode() method in the Object class). The following is the code for the getCourse() method:

```
public Course getCourse(String code) {

  for (int i=0; i<courses.size(); i++) {
    Course c = (Course) courses.get(i);
    if (c.getCode().equals(code))
      return c;
  }
```

```
    return null;
}
```

The `getStudent()` and `getRegistration()` methods are implemented in a similar manner to `getCourse()`.

The methods to add and update undergraduate and postgraduate students are implemented in a similar manner to the `addCourse()` and `updateCourse()` methods.

The `getCourses(long studentID)` method returns an `ArrayList` object containing a collection of `Course` objects which the student with the given ID has registered for. To find the courses for which a student is registered, it is necessary to traverse the instances of the association class, `Registration` (which are stored in the `registrations` collection). The `Student` object is obtained from each `Registration` instance and its `ID` attribute is compared with the `studentID` parameter. If they are the same, it means that the `Registration` object is associated with the given student. The `Course` object is then obtained from the `Registration` object and inserted in the `result` `ArrayList`. This `ArrayList` is returned by the `getCourses()` method after all the `Registration` objects have been examined. The code for the `getCourses()` method is given below.

```
public ArrayList getCourses(long studentID) {

   ArrayList result;

   result = new ArrayList();

   for (int i=0; i<registrations.size(); i++) {
      Registration r = (Registration) registrations.get(i);
      if (r.getStudent().getID() == studentID)
         result.add(r.getCourse());
   }

   return result;
}
```

The `getStudents(String courseCode)` method behaves in a similar manner to the `getCourses(long studentID)` except that the search is made for a course with the given `code`.

The `getCourses(long studentID)` and `getStudents(String courseCode)` methods show how an association can be traversed in both

Chapter 11: Third Programming Project

directions. `getCourses(long studentID)` traverses the `Student-Course` association in the direction `Student` to `Course`. `getStudents(String courseCode)` traverses the association in the direction `Course` to `Student`. Using the `Registration` association class makes it simpler to traverse the association in both directions.

If the `Registration` association class was not used, to support bi-directional navigability between `Student` and `Course` it would be necessary to (1) store a collection of `Course` objects in each instance of `Student` and (2) store a collection of `Student` objects in each instance of `Course`.

The `registerStudent()` method does a little more work than the other methods of `University`. It must first verify that the given student `ID` and course `code` correspond to valid `Student` and `Course` objects. It also needs to know how many credits the given student has already registered for and the amount of students who have already registered for the given course. So, it calls the `getCourses(long studentID)` and `getStudents(String courseCode)` methods to obtain this information.

If the maximum amount of credits that the student can register for is exceeded, `registerStudent()` throws an instance of `TooManyCreditsException`. If the maximum number of students who can register for a course is exceeded, `registerStudent()` throws an instance of `CourseFullException`. Observe that the method declaration of `registerStudent()` specifies that both of these exceptions can be thrown. The two exceptions are caught by the user interface classes.

If no exceptions are thrown, `registerStudent()` proceeds to create an instance of the association class and inserts this instance into the `registrations` collection. The code for `registerStudent()` is given below.

```
public boolean registerStudent(long studentID, String courseCode)
   throws TooManyCoursesException, CourseFullException {

  ArrayList studentCourses;
            // list of courses already registered by student

  ArrayList courseStudents;
            // list of students already registered for course

  Student student = getStudent(studentID);
  Course course = getCourse(courseCode);
```

```
    if (student == null || course == null)
        return false;
                    // can't find student ID or course code

    studentCourses = getCourses(ID);
    courseStudents = getStudents(code);

    if (getCredits(studentCourses) + course.getNumCredits() >
        MAX_CREDITS)
        throw new TooManyCoursesException();

    if (courseStudents.size() == course.getMaxStudents())
        throw new CourseFullException();

    Registration registration = new Registration (student, course);
    registrations.add(registration);
    return true;
}
```

Note that `getCredits()` is a `private` method that calculates the number of credits the student is currently registered for.

The `deRegisterStudent()` method is easier to implement. Once it finds the corresponding instance of the association class using `getRegistration()`, it removes this instance from the `registrations` collection using the `remove()` method:

```
public boolean deRegisterStudent(long studentID, String courseCode){

    Registration registration;

    registration = getRegistration(studentID, courseCode);
    if (registration == null)  // can't find registration object
        return false;

    registrations.remove(registration);
                    // remove it from the collection

    return true;
}
```

The `getCourses()`, `getStudents()`, `getUndergraduateStudents()`, and `getPostgraduateStudents()` methods are almost identical in functionality. They traverse the respective collections and generate a string representation of all the `Course` objects, `Student` objects, etc. Note that the `getUndergraduateStudents()` and `getPostgraduateStudents()` methods must traverse the same `students ArrayList` to find the `UndergraduateStudent` objects and `PostgraduateStudent` objects in the collection, respectively. The `instanceof` operator is used to distinguish between the two types of objects.

11.3 Implementation of the User Interface

It is not necessary to understand how the user interface is implemented at this point in time. However, an overview will now be given so that you can appreciate how the implementation is based on several of the concepts already covered in previous chapters. For example, inheritance and composition are heavily used in implementing the user interface.

The user interface is implemented as a tabbed pane consisting of three panels: `StudentPanel`, `CoursePanel`, and `ViewAllPanel`. Each panel is implemented as a separate class with the same name. The panels provide the following functionality:

> `StudentPanel`: Used to perform *Student* operations
> `CoursePanel`: Used to perform *Course* operations
> `ViewAllPanel`: Used to perform *View All* operations

The window containing the tabbed pane is generated by the `StudentApplication` class. `StudentApplication` contains the `main()` method of the application.

The classes for the GUI can be downloaded from the book Web site. A User's Guide is also available which gives some more details on interacting with the GUI.

Figure 11.2 is a UML diagram of the major GUI objects that collaborate to provide the functionality of the user interface. `JFrame`, `JTabbedPane`, and `JPanel` are built-in GUI objects in Java; they are shaded in the diagram. The application window in `StudentApplication` is built by inheriting from `JFrame` and by composing the functionality of a `JTabbedPane`. Each of the panels displayed on the `JTabbedPane` inherits from `JPanel`. Chapter 17 describes these GUI elements in more detail and explains how you can build a user interface similar to this one.

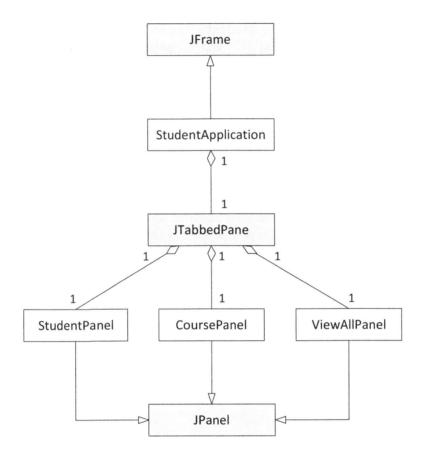

Figure 11.2: UML Diagram of User Interface Objects

Figure 11.3 is a screen shot of the `StudentPanel` displayed on the tabbed pane of `StudentApplication`. Figure 11.4 is a screen shot of the `CoursePanel` and Figure 11.5 is a screen shot of the `ViewAllPanel`.

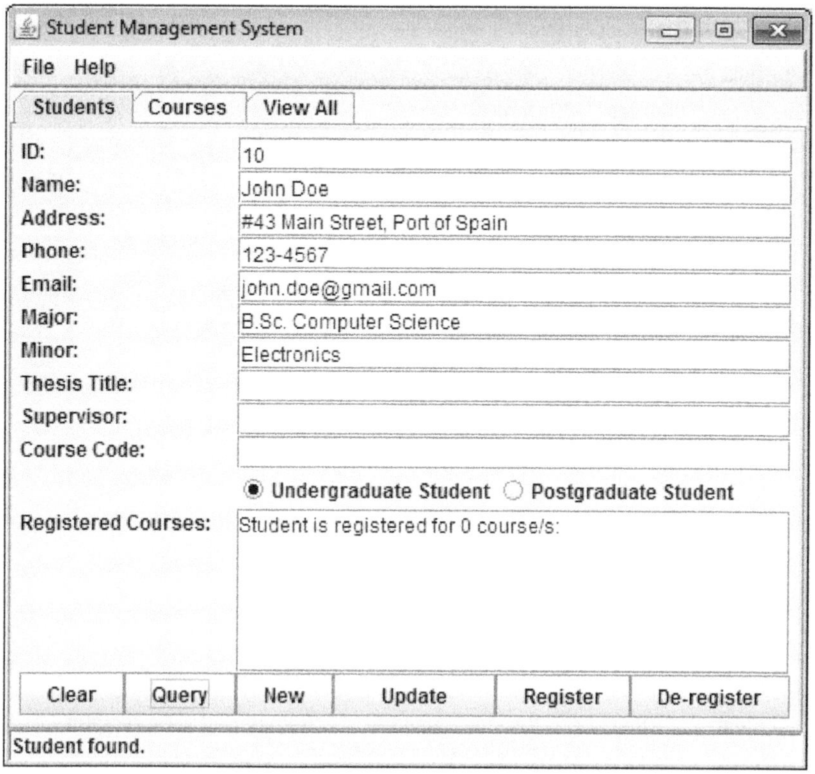

Chapter 11: Third Programming Project

Figure 11.3: Screenshot of the `StudentPanel`

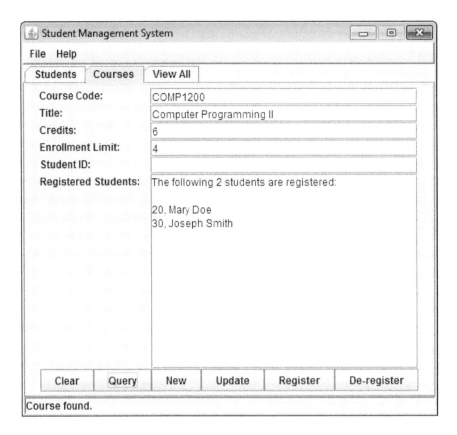

Figure 11.4: Screenshot of the `CoursePanel`

Chapter 11: Third Programming Project

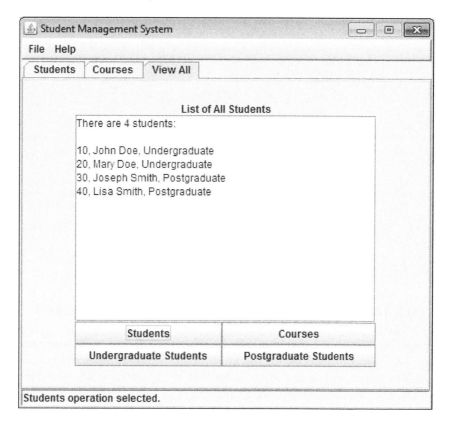

Figure 11.5: Screenshot of the `ViewAllPanel`

The `ViewAllPanel` does not require data to be input by the user. The user simply makes a selection by clicking on one of the buttons. The `StudentPanel` and `CoursePanel` allow the user to perform operations using the same set of buttons. The data to be input for each operation is given in Table 11.13:

Operation	Input Data for StudentPanel	Input Data for CoursePanel
Clear	None	None
Query	Student ID	Course code
New	If *Undergraduate Student* radio button selected, first five fields plus *Major* and *Minor*; otherwise, first five fields plus *Thesis Title* and *Supervisor*.	First four fields.
Update	Same as for the *New* operation.	Same as for the *New* operation.
Register	Student ID and course code.	Course code and student ID.
De-register	Same as for the *Register* operation.	Same as for the *Register* operation.

Table 11.13: Data to be Input in StudentPanel and CoursePanel

It should be mentioned that the user interface is not very sophisticated or robust. No validation is done on the input fields. So, if an integer is expected and a set of alphanumeric characters is entered, the application will generate an error. The GUI has been deliberately kept simple in appearance and features so that it will be consistent with the material on GUI development presented in Chapter 17.

11.4 Creating Source Files and Compiling

The code for each domain class should be written in a separate source file and compiled in the following order:

```
Course
Student
UndergraduateStudent
PostgraduateStudent
Registration
TooManyCoursesException
CourseFullException
University
```

The user interface classes should be compiled in the following order:

```
StudentPanel
CoursePanel
```

Chapter 11: Third Programming Project

```
ViewAllPanel
StudentApplication
```

It should be mentioned that the compiler generates the following warning when **University** is compiled:

```
Note: University.java uses unchecked or unsafe operations.
```

The warning can be ignored for this programming project. It is due to the way in which the **ArrayList** class is used by the **University** class. Chapter 13 explains how to use the **ArrayList** class as well as other collection classes so that this warning will not be generated.

Once **StudentApplication** compiles successfully, the application is ready to run. When the application is run, the **StudentPanel** is displayed. To switch between panels, click on the tab at the top of the window. The system is pre-loaded with four students (with IDs 10, 20, 30, and 40) and four courses (with codes COMP1100, COMP1200, COMP2500, and COMP3100). You can query for these students and courses using the *Query* operation. You can also create new students and courses and register/de-register students from courses.

Chapter 12

Interfaces

An interface allows a group of unrelated objects to be treated in a similar manner. This simplifies the writing of code which processes the objects in some way. This chapter describes the concept of an interface and shows how it is implemented in Java. It also gives an appreciation of the kinds of polymorphic behavior that are possible when multiple interfaces are implemented.

12.1 The Concept of an Interface

In order to understand the concept of an interface in object-oriented programming, it is helpful to consider the following question, what do the following objects have in common?

- A door
- A bank account
- A book
- A drawer in a filing cabinet

It is clear that the four objects above are not structurally related. However, they are related through a set of common behaviors namely, `open()` and `close()`. This set of behaviors can be grouped into a concept called `Openable`. In object-oriented programming, the concept `Openable` is referred to as an *interface*.

It should be noted that `open()` and `close()` specify behaviors that are common to the objects above but these behaviors take place in different ways. For example, opening an account is a very different operation from opening a door.

12.2 A Real-World Example

Consider an alarm clock. There are hundreds of models of alarm clocks available on the market produced by different manufacturers. These models have a wide variety of shapes and sizes yet they provide the same basic functionality to users:

- Set current time
- Set alarm time
- Set alarm (radio or alarm ring)
- Display current time
- Sound alarm

The above functionality can be considered the interface of an alarm clock. Manufacturers of alarm clocks have the freedom to use different technology to design their alarm clocks. They may also choose to include features in addition to those that are required by the interface. However, manufacturers always ensure that the functionality of the interface is provided.

The user of an alarm clock expects to find features to set the current time, the alarm time, and the type of alarm to wake up to. They also expect the alarm clock to display the current time and to sound the alarm when the specified time is reached. Because manufacturers ensure that the functionality of the interface is provided, persons can use different models and brands of alarm clocks without being concerned that they will be able to set the current time, the alarm time, and the type of alarm to wake up to.

A similar benefit is derived in object-oriented programming by using interfaces. A group of classes that agree to provide features based on an agreed protocol (interface) simplifies the work of client objects which can now deal with instances of these classes in a standard way without being concerned about the differences in implementation.

12.3 Defining an Interface

As mentioned earlier, an *interface* specifies a set of common behaviors or a *protocol* for classes. The interface does not specify how the behavior is provided; this is the responsibility of the classes that implement the interface. A class that implements the interface must provide method implementations for all the behaviors specified in the protocol, unless that class is abstract.

Chapter 12: Interfaces

In Java, an interface is defined using a special structure known as an `interface`. The behaviors of an interface are specified using a set of abstract methods.

To define the `Openable` interface in Java, the following code should be used:

```
public interface Openable
{
   public abstract void open();   // abstract keyword can be omitted
   public abstract void close();  // abstract keyword can be omitted
}
```

12.4 Implementing an Interface

Any class that wishes to obey the protocol specified by an interface must provide method implementations for all the abstract methods in the interface (unless that class is abstract). There is no restriction on how the methods are implemented in the class. The only requirement is that the method signatures of the interface are maintained. Thus, an interface is a "method signature contract" and there is no guarantee that the methods are implemented in any given manner. Note that a class that implements an interface can have additional methods of its own.

Consider the `Door` class. If the `Door` class wishes to conform to the `Openable` interface, it must first indicate that it `implements` the `Openable` interface. Next, it must provide method implementations for the `open()` and `close()` methods. Methods can also be written which provide behaviors for the `Door` class which are not required by the interface, e.g., `knock()`. An outline of the code for the `Door` class is given below:

```
public class Door implements Openable
{  // indicates that Door will conform to the Openable interface

   // instance variables of Door

   // constructor/s of Door

   // other methods of Door

   public void knock(int times) {
      // method implementation
   }
```

```
    public void open() {
       // method implementation
    }

    public void close() {
       // method implementation
    }
}
```

implementation of methods from **Openable** interface

To correctly implement the **Openable** interface, the **open()** and **close()** methods in **Door** must have the same signatures as specified in the interface. If **Door** claims to implement the **Openable** interface (by means of the **implements** keyword) and does not provide method implementations for one or more methods in the interface, it must be declared as an abstract class. Like any other abstract class, one or more descendants of **Door** (abstract or concrete subclass) will now be expected to provide the missing method implementations.

It is possible for **Door** to have other **open()** or **close()** methods with different signatures. For example,

```
public void open(int count) {
   // method implementation
}
```

This is an example of method overloading and is not related to the interface mechanism discussed in this chapter.

12.5 UML Notation for Interfaces

There are two ways to depict interfaces in the UML. One way is to draw an interface using a rectangular symbol similar to a class except that a *stereotype descriptor* <<interface>> is added above the interface name. If a class implements an interface, a line with a closed arrow tip is used to connect the class to the interface. This line is similar to the one used to depict an inheritance relationship, except that the line is broken.

Figure 12.1 is a UML diagram of the **Openable** interface and the **Door**, **Account**, and **Book** classes that implement the interface.

Chapter 12: Interfaces

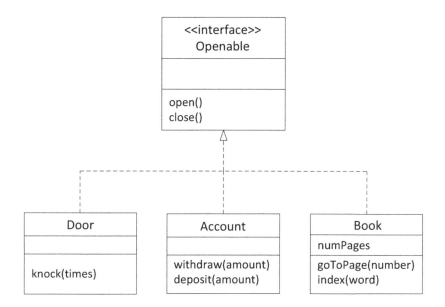

Figure 12.1 Depicting Interfaces in the UML

Another way to depict an interface in the UML is to use a circle to denote the interface. A class that implements the interface connects to the circle with a straight line. Figure 12.2 shows this notation:

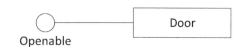

Figure 12.2: Another Way to Depict Interfaces in the UML

12.6 Properties of Interfaces

It is possible for an abstract class to have only abstract methods. It is also possible for an abstract class to have neither instance variables nor class variables. Under these two circumstances, an interface is identical to an abstract class. A method declared in an interface is implicitly abstract; also, any variable declared is implicitly a **static final** variable (i.e., a constant).

A constant **MAX_TRIES** can be explicitly declared in an interface as follows:

```
public static final int MAX_TRIES = 3;
        // declares MAX_TRIES as a constant (type is int)
```

The constant **MAX_TRIES** then becomes available to any class implementing the interface.

Like an abstract class, it is not possible to create an instance of an interface. However, unlike an abstract class, an interface cannot contain instance variables, class variables, or method implementations.

An interface and a concrete class can be viewed as two opposite ends of an implementation continuum. The interface is highly abstract and declares methods but provides no implementation of these methods. On the other hand, a concrete class must have method implementations of all its methods (directly or indirectly through inheritance). An abstract class is like a bridge between these two concepts in the continuum and may have method implementations as required.

An interface defines a new type and this type can be used to refer to objects created from classes implementing the interface, directly or indirectly. For example, the following code is legal in a client:

```
Openable o;   // declare variable of type Openable (interface name)
Door d;       // declare object variable of type Door (class name)

d = new Door();
              // create instance of Door

o = d;        // variable of type Openable refers to Door instance
```

In the above example, after assigning the variable of type **Door**, d, to a variable of type **Openable**, o, only methods declared in the **Openable** interface and those of the **Object** class[1] can be invoked on o. In other words, it is only possible to use the methods **open()** and **close()** and those of the **Object** class:

```
o.toString();  // OK, as well as other methods of Object
o.open();      // OK, since open() is a method in Openable
o.close();     // OK, since close() is a method in Openable
```

An attempt to invoke the **knock()** method on o will generate a compilation error since the **knock()** method is not present in the **Object** class and it is not declared in the **Openable** interface:

---

[1] Implicitly, the **Openable** object is at least an instance of **Object**, so all the methods of the **Object** class can be used.

Chapter 12: Interfaces

```
o.knock(3);    // will generate a compilation error
```

Note that the error will be generated even though `o` is currently referring to an instance of `Door` which has a `knock()` method implemented. Since the interface defines a type, the compiler will only allow method invocations on `o` that are defined in the `Object` class or are declared in the *static* type, i.e., the method invocations that obey the interface specification.

12.7 The Comparable Interface

Consider the `Comparable` interface in Java[2]. This interface declares a single method, `compareTo()`, that is responsible for comparing one object with another and determining their relative order, according to some specified ordering for that class of objects. The following is the signature of the `compareTo()` method:

```
public abstract int compareTo (Object o);
```

The `compareTo()` method compares the current object (`this`) with the object passed as a parameter (`o`). If the current object is less than the supplied object or should appear before the supplied object in a sorted list, `compareTo()` should return a negative number. If it is greater than the supplied object or should come after the supplied object in a sorted list, `compareTo()` should return a positive integer. If the two objects are equivalent or their relative order in a sorted list does not matter, `compareTo()` should return zero. If `compareTo()` returns zero with a supplied object, the `equals()` method should typically return `true` with the supplied object.

To allow `Account` objects to be compared with each other (e.g., to allow sorting of accounts in a report), the `Account` class must implement the `Comparable` interface. This requires the `Account` class to provide a method implementation for the `compareTo()` method, in addition to its usual set of methods. The `compareTo()` method in `Account` can be implemented as follows.

```
public class Account implements Comparable
{
   // instance variables
```

---

[2] The `Comparable` interface is discussed in this chapter without the use of generics. In Chapter 13, a version of the `Comparable` interface using parameterized types is presented.

```
// Account methods

public int compareTo(Object o) {
    if (o instanceof Account) {
        Account a = (Account) o;
        if (this.num < a.num)
            return -1;
        else {
            if (this.num == a.num)
                return 0;
            else
                return 1;
        }
    }
    else
        throw new IllegalArgumentException ("Expected an Account");
}
}
```

Since the `compareTo()` method accepts objects of the general type **Object**, it is necessary to check that the object being compared is indeed an instance of **Account** before proceeding with the comparison. If this is the case, the object is cast to an **Account** object and the comparison is then made.

The **Comparable** interface defines a type so the following code is legal in a client:

```
Comparable c1, c2;

Account a1 = new Account(10, 1000.00);
Account a2 = new Account(20, 2000.00);

c1 = a1;
c2 = a2;

int compare = c1.compareTo(c2);
```

Since the `compareTo()` method is present in the **Account** class, it is also possible to do the following in a client, without using a variable of type **Comparable**:

```
compare = a1.compareTo(a2);
```

Chapter 12: Interfaces

The `Comparable` type makes it possible to take advantage of pre-defined methods that work on only `Comparable` objects. For example, the class `Collections` in Java provides a class method `sort()` that sorts the objects in a collection. An `ArrayList`, `al`, can be populated with a set of `Account` instances implementing the `Comparable` interface as shown above. It is easy to sort this `ArrayList` using the `sort()` method:

```
Collections.sort(al);
```

Now, assume that a set of `Door` instances implementing the `Comparable` interface is stored in the `ArrayList` instead of the set of `Account` instances. These instances can be sorted (based on the implementation of the `compareTo()` method in `Door`) using a similar method invocation:

```
Collections.sort(al);
```

Since the `sort()` method operates on objects of type `Comparable`, it is possible to sort a collection containing objects of any type, without knowing anything about the objects to be sorted. The only requirement is that the corresponding object class must implement the `compareTo()` method of `Comparable` interface. This is one of the most powerful uses of interfaces: being able to write code to deal with objects which are not known but which are guaranteed to provide a minimal set of behavior specified by an interface.

12.8 Polymorphism with Interfaces

Suppose that the `Door` and `Book` classes mentioned earlier implement the `Openable` interface together with the `Account` class. Next, assume that an instance of each class is created as follows:

```
Door d = new Door();
Book b = new Book();
Account a = new Account(10, 1000.00);
```

Now, suppose that these three instances are inserted into an array of type `Openable`:

```
Openable[] o = new Openable[3];
o[0] = d;
o[1] = b;
o[2] = a;
```

It is now possible to go through the collection of objects in the array and treat the objects as if they were all `Openable`, ignoring the fact that they are really a `Door`, a `Book`, and an `Account`:

```
for (int i=0; i<o.length; i++) {
   o[i].open();
   o[i].close();
}
```

This is similar to the case where `B` and `C` are subclasses of a superclass `A`, and variables of type `A` are used to refer to instances of `B` and `C` (based on the Principle of Substitutability).

It is another example of polymorphism at work since it allows objects of matching interfaces to be substituted for one another at run-time (using a common interface type such as `Openable` in the above example).

12.9 Implementing Multiple Interfaces

A class can implement more than one interface by simply separating the interfaces with commas after the `implements` keyword. For example, the `Account` class can implement both the `Comparable` interface and the `Openable` interface as follows:

```
public class Account implements Comparable, Openable
{
    :
}
```

If the `Account` class is not abstract, it must provide method implementations for the only method in the `Comparable` interface (`compareTo()`) and the two methods in the `Openable` interface (`open()` and `close()`), as discussed before. Assuming that this is the case, it is possible to create an `Account` object and assign its reference to variables of type `Comparable` and `Openable`, respectively:

```
Account a = new Account(10, 1000.00);

Comparable c = a;
Openable o = a;
```

The variable `c` can now be used wherever a variable of type `Comparable` is expected. Similarly, the variable `o` can be used wherever a variable of type `Openable` is expected. Of course, the variable `a` can be used wherever a variable of type `Account` is expected (including situations where a variable of type `Object` is expected). Thus, there are at least four situations where the single `Account` instance can be used, each one having a different view of the `Account` object. In essence, if a class implements multiple interfaces, instances of the class can be viewed in different ways at different times, depending on the "lens" (i.e., interface type) being used. This feature allows instances of a class to perform different roles at different times.

12.10 Inheritance of Interfaces

Some object-oriented programming languages such as Java only allow single inheritance, i.e., a child class can have at most one parent class. However, as mentioned in the previous section, it is possible for a class to implement more than one interface, allowing a restricted form of multiple inheritance. It is also possible to define an interface which inherits from more than one parent interface. For example,

```
public interface Multiple extends   Interface1,
                                    Interface2,
                                    Interface3 {
   // declaration of methods in Multiple
}
```

Suppose a concrete class `MultipleImpl` implements the `Multiple` interface. `MultipleImpl` must provide method implementations for all the methods declared in the `Multiple` interface as well as all the methods declared in `Interface1`, `Interface2`, and `Interface3`. Using substitutability, it will then be possible to assign a variable of type `MultipleImpl` to a variable of type `Multiple`, `Interface1`, `Interface2`, or `Interface3`. Of course, only the methods of the latter types can be used when this is done.

Consider the UML diagram of Figure 12.3 which shows the relationship between three interfaces, `I1`, `I2`, and `I3`, and three concrete classes, `A`, `B`, and `C`.

Fundamentals of Object-Oriented Programming in Java

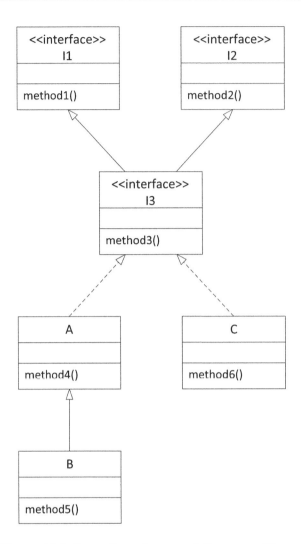

Figure 12.3: Some Interfaces and Concrete Classes

I1 and I2 are interfaces which declare the methods method1() and method2(), respectively. I3 is an interface that inherits from both I1 and I2 and declares an additional method, method3(). A, B, and C are concrete classes. Both A and C implement the I3 interface, providing methods of their own. B is a concrete subclass of A and adds a method of its own.

Consider the following segment of code based on Figure 12.3:

Line 1:
I3 b = new B();

Chapter 12: Interfaces

Line 2:
```
b.method1();
```

Line 3:
```
b.method3();
```

Line 4:
```
b.method4();
```

We would like to determine if the code above will compile and run successfully. There is no problem in Line 1 since A implements I3 and B is a concrete subclass of A. This is normal polymorphic assignment with interfaces described in Section 12.8. Now, I3 extends I1 and I2. Thus, the type I3 is associated with the methods of I3 (i.e., method3()) as well as those of I1 and I2 (method1() and method2()). Since b is of type I3, it is legal to invoke method1() on b as well as method3(). Thus, there is no problem in Line 2 and Line 3.

Finally, it should be noted that method4() is a valid operation on an instance of B since B inherits this method from class A. However, even though the dynamic type of b is B, only the methods of the *static* type of b (i.e., I3) can be used. Since method4() is not present in I3 (or any of its inherited interfaces), Line 4 will not compile.

Consider also the following segment of code:

Line 1:
```
I1 c = new C();
```

Line 2:
```
I2 i = (I2) c;
```

Now, C implements I3 which extends I1 and I2. So, C must implement the methods of I2 and I2 since it is a concrete class. By the polymorphic assignment of interface types, it is legal to assign a concrete instance of C to one of its interface types such as I1. So, Line 1 will compile and run. At run time, the dynamic type of c is C. Since C implements I1, I2, and I3, it is legal to cast c to one of the interface types such as I2. So, Line 2 will also compile and run.

Exercises

1. What does it mean to implement an interface?

2. What are the benefits of an interface?

3. Discuss two situations where it might be better to use an interface instead of an abstract class.

4. A certain interface declares three methods. A is an abstract class which implements the interface and C is a concrete class which also implements the interface. Is it necessary to implement the three methods in both A and C? Explain.

5. A class C implements an interface I. What are three types of object variables that can be used to refer to an instance of C? Are there any other possibilities?

6. A concrete class C implements the Comparable interface. Suppose the implementation of the compareTo() methods returns zero when a certain object is passed as an argument to the method. Why is it a good idea to override the equals() method in C? Explain how the equals() method should be implemented.

7. Two interfaces I1 and I2 declare a method with the same signature. A class C intends to implement the two interfaces. Investigate if there will be any problem writing the code for C, given the common method in both interfaces. What conclusion can you make about situations like these?

8. Chapter 9 explains how to use delegation to achieve a limited form of multiple inheritance in an object-oriented application. Compare this approach with implementing multiple interfaces.

Chapter 13

Container Classes

As mentioned in Chapter 7, one-to-many and many-to-many associations between objects are common in object-oriented programming. These types of associations are best implemented using classes that allow groups or collections of objects to be stored. Object-oriented programming languages typically provide a number of classes that can be used for storing collections of objects. For example, the Java *Collections* framework provides several containers for storing objects in linked lists, trees, hash tables, and other structures. These containers are referred to as *collection classes*.

Two important issues with collection classes is generalizing the type of objects that can be stored and providing type safety. The chapter starts off by showing how the *generics* feature in Java addresses these two issues in an elegant way. This is followed by a discussion of the Iterator Design Pattern which prescribes a way for the elements of different types of containers to be traversed in a uniform manner. Next, the chapter describes the classes in the Java *Collections* framework. Finally, the chapter concludes with some guidelines for choosing the right collection class to implement an association between two classes.

The chapter gives a good overview of the Java *Collections* framework since it provides an excellent example of how fundamental object-oriented concepts such as interfaces, abstract classes, and inheritance can be applied to build a set of general-purpose classes. To fully appreciate the material discussed in this chapter, it will be helpful if you have a good background in data structures such as linked lists, binary trees, and hash tables. However, the material is presented from an object-oriented perspective and the internal details of the data structures are mostly ignored.

13.1 The Need for Generics

The Java *Collections* framework uses a feature known as *generics* which allows a container class to be specified in such a way that it is possible to store any type of object in a container and yet be type safe. This section explains why generics are important by comparing linked lists that can store different types of data. It also shows how a linked list can be implemented using generics.

13.1.1 Linked Lists

A *linked list* is a data structure consisting of a set of nodes in a sequence where each node is linked to the next node in the sequence. A node has two components, `element` and `next`. The `element` component stores data associated with the node. The `next` component stores a reference to the next node in the sequence. The `next` reference of the last node in the sequence is `null`. A variable `head` is used to keep track of the first node in the list. From `head`, it is possible to find all the nodes in the linked list by following the links in the `next` component of each node. Figure 13.1 is a diagram of a linked list which stores integer values.

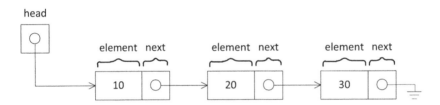

Figure 13.1: A Linked List

13.1.2 A Linked List of Integers

To implement the linked list shown in Figure 13.1, an inner class `Node` can be used to store the information on each node. `Node` is an inner class since it is highly unlikely that it will be used by other classes. The `LinkedList` class has two instance variables: `head`, which keeps track of the first node in the list, and `count`, which keeps track of the amount of nodes in the list. A portion of the code for the `LinkedList` class is as follows:

```
public class LinkedList {

    private Node head; // first node of the linked list
    private int count; // amount of nodes in the linked list
```

Chapter 13: Container Classes

```
    public LinkedList() {
       head = null;
       count = 0;
    }

    public void addFirst(int element) {
       Node newNode = new Node(element);
       newNode.next = head;
       head = newNode;
       count++;
    }

    public int getFirst() {
       if (count > 0)
          return head.element;
       else
          throw new LinkedListException("List is empty.");
    }

    // other linked list methods

    // Node inner class

    private class Node {
       private int element;
       private Node next;

       private Node(int element) {
          this.element = element;
       }
    }

}
```

The important thing to observe in the code above is the declaration of the instance variable **element** as an **int** in the **Node** inner class:

```
private int element;
```

Since **element** is explicitly declared to be of type **int**, it is impossible to use the linked list to store values of other types such as **double**, **char**, **boolean**, etc. Thus, if a linked list is required to store other types of data, a new **LinkedList** class must be written where the **element** type in **Node** is changed to the type required. In addition, all the linked list methods that refer to element (e.g., addFirst()) must be also be changed to accommodate the new type. For these reasons, the LinkedList class above is not a very practical container.

13.1.3 A Linked List of Objects

An improvement on the linked list is to declare the element type as Object. Wherever element is used in the class definition, its type is changed to Object. The code for the revised version of LinkedList is given below.

```java
public class LinkedList {

   private Node head; // first node of the linked list
   private int count; // amount of nodes in the linked list

   public LinkedList() {
      head = null;
      count = 0;
   }

   public void addFirst(Object element) {
      Node newNode = new Node(element);
      newNode.next = head;
      head = newNode;
      count++;
   }

   public Object getFirst() {
      if (count > 0)
         return head.element;
      else
         throw new LinkedListException("List is empty.");
   }


   // other linked list methods

   :
```

Chapter 13: Container Classes

```
// Node inner class

private class Node {
   private Object element;
   private Node next;

   private Node(Object element) {
      this.element = element;
   }
}
}
```

Node inner class

The **element** type of **Node** is declared to be of type **Object** as follows:

```
private Object element;
```

Since the **Object** class is the superclass of all classes in Java, by substitutability this means that instances of any class can be stored in the linked list.

Suppose **linkedList** is an instance of the revised version of the **LinkedList** class. Also, suppose that **account** is an instance of the **Account** class. We can insert **account** at the top of the linked list as follows:

```
linkedList.addFirst(account);
```

Now, suppose that **student** is an instance of the **Student** class. We can insert **student** in the linked list as follows:

```
linkedList.addFirst(student);
```

This reveals one important weakness when **element** is declared to be of type **Object**: it is not possible to prevent objects of different types from being stored in the linked list at the same time. This is because an instance of any class in Java is of type **Object**, by substitutability.

Using **Object** as the **element** type presents another problem when dealing with the reverse polymorphism problem. Suppose we legitimately store a set of objects of different types in the linked list (e.g., **Account**, **Student**). Any retrieval method (e.g., **getFirst()**) will return an object of type **Object** despite what it really is at run-time.

For example, consider the following code:

```
Object o = linkedList.getFirst();
```

Although `o` can either be an `Account` instance or a `Student` instance, the most we know about `o` after the call to `getFirst()` is that it is of type `Object`. To obtain the object actually stored in the container, the `instanceof` operator must be used to determine if the object is an `Account` or a `Student`; the object must then be cast to its specific type before any class-specific processing takes place:

```
if (o instanceof Account) {
   Account a = (Account) o;
   // process a
}
else
if (o instanceof Student) {
   Student s = (Student) o;
   // process s
}
```

This can become tedious when retrieving the objects from a container.

13.1.4 A Linked List with Generic Types

The previous section highlighted two problems with using `Object` as the `element` type in the linked list container. These problems are solved in an elegant manner by using Java *generics*. Generics make it possible to parameterize the type of objects to be stored in a container when the container class is being defined. When an instance of the container is created, the programmer can specify the actual type of objects to be stored. The code below shows how the linked list can be parameterized using generics:

```
public class LinkedList<T>
{
   private Node head;
   private int count;

   public LinkedList() {
      head = null;
      count = 0;
   }

   public void addFirst(T element) {
      Node newNode = new Node(element);
      newNode.next = head;
```

Chapter 13: Container Classes

```
         head = newNode;
         count++;
      }

      public T getFirst() {
         if (count > 0)
            return head.element;
         else
            throw new LinkedListException("List is empty.");
      }

      // other linked list methods

      // Node inner class

      private class Node
      {
         private T element;
         private Node next;

         private Node(T element) {
            this.element = element;
         }
      }
   }
```

Notice how the class is parameterized with the type T in the first line:

```
public class LinkedList<T>
```

It is normal to use a single letter such as T when parameterizing a container class (however, longer names can be used). The type T is then used to refer to the objects of the container throughout the class definition. For example, in the Node inner class, the element of a Node is declared to be of type T:

```
private T element;
```

In addFirst() and other methods, the type T is used to specify the input parameters and return values. Thus, no commitment is made as to the exact type of the values that will be stored in the linked list.

When creating an instance of the linked list, the type of object to be stored is specified using angle brackets which are written *before* the argument list of the constructor. For example,

```java
LinkedList linkedList = new LinkedList<Account>();
```

Once the linked list is created this way, it can only contain objects of type `Account` since `Account` replaces T in the class definition. An attempt to store any other type of object in the linked list will result in a compilation error. Note that by substitutability, the linked list above can store instances of `Account` as well as instances of any of its subclasses. It should also be noted that the call to `getFirst()` now returns an object of the specified type and there is no need to use the `instanceof` operator and casting to obtain the actual object:

```java
Account a = linkedList.getFirst();
```

To create a linked list to store `Student` objects, the following code can be used:

```java
LinkedList linkedList = new LinkedList<Student>();
```

Thus, by using the parameterized type T, the container class only has to be defined once.

The containers in the Java *Collections* framework use generics and thus benefit from the advantages of using parameterized types.

It should be noted that if no type is specified when the container is created, the container behaves as if it stores objects of type `Object` (which is the type of all objects in Java, through substitutability). For example, the container created using the following code will be able to store objects of any type:

```java
LinkedList linkedList = new LinkedList();
```

In this case, the compiler generates a warning about type safety.

13.2 Iterators

Different containers store objects in different ways. For example, a linked list consists of a set of nodes where each node stores an object and contains a reference to the next node in the list. A binary tree uses a tree-like structure to store objects ordered in some way. A hash table stores its objects based on a *key* value.

It is highly desirable to enumerate the objects stored in any container without knowing the internal implementation details of that container. This makes it possible to access objects from different containers in a uniform manner. This is the purpose of an iterator. This section describes the Iterator Design Pattern and shows how it is implemented in Java. It also gives an iterator for the linked list described in the previous section.

13.2.1 Iterator Design Pattern

When the *Iterator Design Pattern* is employed, a container object is no longer responsible for accessing and traversing its elements. Instead, access and traversal becomes the responsibility of an iterator object. An iterator object is responsible for keeping track of the current element in the container; thus, an iterator must know which elements have been traversed already.

An iterator defines the interface for accessing the objects from the underlying container. The iterator interface specifies the following methods: `first()`, `next()`, `isDone()`, and `currentItem()`. The `currentItem()` method returns the current element in the container; `first()` initializes the current element to the first element; `next()` advances the current element to the next element; and `isDone()` checks to see if we have advanced beyond the last element, i.e., whether the traversal has come to an end.

13.2.2 Implementation in Java

The Java *Collections* framework defines an `Iterator` interface that accomplishes the design objectives of the Iterator Design Pattern. Thus, classes that implement the `Iterator` interface provide a standard way to traverse and access the objects in a container. The `Iterator` interface is slightly different from the one specified in the Iterator Design Pattern. It is defined as follows using generics:

```
public interface Iterator<T> {
   public abstract boolean hasNext();
   public abstract <T> next();
   public abstract void remove();
}
```

Typically, a container class will contain an inner class that implements the `Iterator` interface. The container class will provide a method `iterator()` that returns an instance of this class to a client object. So, if `c` is an instance of a container, an `Iterator` is obtained as follows:

```
Iterator<Account> i = c.iterator();
```

Notice the use of generics to specify the type of objects which will be iterated. This is the type of object which will be returned by the `next()` method. If no type is specified, the `next()` method will return objects of type `Object`; thus, type checking and casting will be necessary to obtain the actual objects from the container.

Once an instance of an `Iterator` is obtained, its `hasNext()` method can be invoked to determine if there are more elements to be enumerated. This method returns `true` if there are more elements to enumerate, and `false` if all the elements have already been returned. The `next()` method returns the next element in the container. These two methods make it easy to loop through the elements of a container with code such as the following:

```
while (i.hasNext())     // if more elements to enumerate
   process(i.next());   // get next object from iterator and process
```

The `remove()` method removes the object most recently returned by `next()` from the collection. However, support for `remove()` is optional; if an `Iterator` does not implement the `remove()` method, it should throw an `UnsupportedOperationException` when the method is invoked. While iterating through a container, the only way the container can be modified is by calling the `remove()` method of `Iterator`.

It should be noted that many of the concrete collection classes in the Java *Collections* framework provide an `iterator()` method. These include `ArrayList, Vector,` and `TreeSet`.

13.2.3 Linked List Iterator

An iterator for a container is typically implemented as an inner class that implements the `Iterator` interface. The code for an iterator class for `LinkedListGeneric` is given below.

```
public class ListIterator implements Iterator<T>
{
   private Node current;

   private ListIterator (Node head) {
      current = head;
   }

   public boolean hasNext() {
      return (current != null);
   }
```

Chapter 13: Container Classes

```
  public T next() {
    T save = current.element;
    current = current.next;
    return save;
  }

  public void remove() {
    throw new UnsupportedOperationException
      ("ListIterator does not support remove operation.");
  }
}
```

When an instance of `ListIterator` is created, the current element is positioned at the head of the list. Whenever `next()` is invoked, the current element advances to the next element in the linked list. The `hasNext()` method returns `true` as long as the current element is referring to an actual node of the linked list. When the end of the list is reached, `hasNext()` returns `false`.

The `iterator()` method of the linked list class creates and returns an instance of `ListIterator` when it is called:

```
public Iterator<T> iterator() {
   return new ListIterator(head);
}
```

Client objects can then use the methods of the `Iterator` interface to iterate over the elements in the linked list.

There are two ways to iterate over the objects in a container. The first way is to iterate on the objects exactly as they are stored in the container. `ListIterator` takes this approach. The second way is to copy the object references to another container (e.g., an array) and then iterate over the copied objects in the second container. This approach can be expensive due to copying of objects.

13.2.4 *foreach* Statement

Java provides a *foreach* statement which simplifies the traversal of an `Iterator`. Indeed, code is no longer required to declare an `Iterator` object and to manipulate the `Iterator` using the `hasNext()` and `next()` methods..

Consider the following code which inserts a few `Account` objects in an instance of the `LinkedListGeneric` class:

```
LinkedListGeneric<Account> linkedList =
   new LinkedListGeneric<Account>();

Account a1 = new Account(10, 1000.00);
Account a2 = new Account(20, 2000.00);
Account a3 = new Account(30, 3000.00);

linkedList.addFront(a1);
linkedList.addFront(a2);
linkedList.addFront(a3);
```

A *foreach* statement which traverses the linked list and prints out the information on each `Account` object is given below:

```
for (Account a : linkedList)
   System.out.println(a.toString());
```

The *foreach* statement says that for each `Account` object `a` in `linkedList`, display the contents of `a` using its `toString()` method. In order for this to work, the `LinkedListGeneric` class must implement the `Iterable<T>` interface. The `Iterable<T>` interface only declares one method `iterator()`:

```
Iterator<T> iterator();
```

Since this method was already implemented in `LinkedListGeneric` through the `ListIterator` inner class, all that has to be done is to indicate that it implements `Iterable<T>`:

```
public class LinkedListGeneric<T> implements Iterable<T> {
   :
}
```

Note that the *foreach* statement still uses the `Iterator` object in the background. All it does is simplify the code to declare and traverse the `Iterator`.

13.3 The Java *Collections* Framework

The Java *Collections* framework defines two types of containers: a `Collection`, which is a group of objects and a `Map`, which is a set of mappings between objects. Different types of containers in the *Collections* framework have

Chapter 13: Container Classes

different properties. For example, a `Set` is a type of `Collection` in which there are no duplicates, and a `List` is a `Collection` in which the elements are ordered in a sequence. This section describes the interfaces and classes in the Java *Collections* framework.

13.3.1 Interfaces in the Java *Collections* Framework

The Java *Collections* framework contains a set of interfaces such as `Collection`, `Set`, `List`, and `Map` that are used as a basis for creating concrete collection classes such as `ArrayList`, `LinkedList`, `HashSet`, and `TreeMap`. A class diagram showing the interfaces in the Java *Collections* framework that will be discussed in this chapter is given in Figure 13.2 below. It is important to understand the features of each interface in the diagram before studying the concrete classes that are derived from them. These interfaces will be described next.

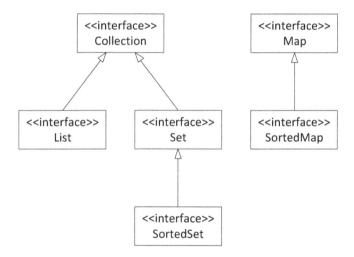

Figure 13.2: Interfaces in the Java *Collections* Framework

13.3.1.1 The `Collection` Interface

The `Collection` interface represents a group or collection of objects. The objects may or may not be ordered, and the collection may or may not contain duplicate objects. The `Collection` interface is not usually implemented directly. Instead, most concrete collection classes implement one of the more specific sub-interfaces. For example, `Set`, an ordered collection that does not allow duplicates, and `List`, an ordered collection that does allow duplicates, are both sub-interfaces of `Collection`. Some of the methods declared in the

`Collection` interface are listed in Table 13.1. Note that all the methods are `public` and `abstract`.

Method	Description
boolean add(E o)	Inserts the object of the specified type into the collection; returns `true` if the object was added to the collection; otherwise returns `false`.
boolean addAll(Collection c)	Inserts all the objects from the specified collection into the current collection.
void clear()	Removes all the elements from the collection.
boolean contains (Object o)	Returns `true` if the specified object is present in the collection and `false`, otherwise.
boolean isEmpty()	Returns `true` if there are no elements in the collection and `false`, otherwise.
boolean remove(Object o)	Deletes the specified object from the collection.
int size()	Returns the number of elements currently in the collection.

Table 13.1: Some Methods of the `Collection` Interface

It should be observed that the arguments for methods such as `contains()` and `remove()` are of type `Object`. The `contains()` and `remove()` methods use the `equals()` method of the `Object` class to determine if two objects are the same. If the `equals()` method of `Object` is not overridden in the class of objects being stored in the collection, equality is based on object references and not on the contents of the objects being compared.

13.3.1.2 The `List` Interface

The `List` interface represents an ordered collection of objects (also known as a sequence). Users of the `List` interface have precise control over where in the list each element is inserted. Each element in a `List` has an index, or position, in the list, and elements can be inserted, queried, and removed by index. The first element of a `List` has an index of zero. The last element in a list has an index of `size()-1`. It should be noted that a `List` typically allows duplicate elements, unlike a `Set`.

In addition to the methods declared by its inherited interface, `Collection`, `List` declares a number of methods for working with its indexed elements. Some of these are listed in Table 13.2.

Chapter 13: Container Classes

Method	Description
void add(int index, E element)	Inserts the object supplied as an argument in position **index** of the **List**. The other elements in the **List** are shifted down one position.
E get(int index)	Returns the element at position **index** of the **List**.
int indexOf(Object o)	Returns the position of the object supplied as an argument in the **List**, or –1 if it does not find a match. **indexOf()** uses the **equals()** method of the contained objects to check for equality with the object supplied as an argument.
E remove(int index)	Removes the object at position **index** of the **List**.
E set(int index, E element)	Inserts the object supplied as **element** in position **index** of the **List**, overwriting the element that was there previously, if any. It returns the element that was previously stored at that position; otherwise, it returns **null**.

Table 13.2: Some Methods of the **List** Interface

13.3.1.3 The `Set` and `SortedSet` Interfaces

The `Set` interface represents an unordered collection of objects that contains no duplicate elements. That is, a `Set` cannot contain two elements, `e1` and `e2`, where `e1.equals(e2)`, and it can contain at most one `null` element. The `Set` interface declares the same methods as its super-interface, `Collection`. It does not allow the `add()` and `addAll()` methods to add duplicate elements to the `Set`. If a `Set` already contains the element being added, its `add()` and `addAll()` methods return `false`.

In order for a `Set` to determine if it already contains an element, it uses the `equals()` method of `Object` to check if this element is equal to an existing element in the `Set`. If the objects in the `Set` do not override the `equals()` method, equality is based on object identifiers. Thus, two objects with exactly the same contents will not be equal and the `Set` will not treat them as duplicates. It is therefore necessary to override the `equals()` method of the objects that will be inserted into the `Set` so that the comparison will be based on the contents of the objects rather than object identifiers.

The `SortedSet` interface is a `Set` that sorts its elements and guarantees that its `iterator()` method returns an `Iterator` that enumerates the elements of the set in sorted order. It declares a few methods of its own such as `first()` and `last()` which return the lowest and highest elements in the set, respectively (as determined by the sort order).

13.3.1.4 The `Map` and `SortedMap` Interface

The `Map` interface represents a collection of mappings between *key* objects and *value* objects. Hash tables are examples of maps. The set of *key* objects in a `Map` must not have any duplicates. However, the collection of *value* objects may contain duplicates. Table 13.3 contains a list of some of the methods in the `Map` interface.

Method	Description
boolean containsKey(Object key)	Returns `true` if the `Map` contains a mapping for the specified `key` and `false`, otherwise.
V get(Object key)	Returns the `value` object associated with the specified `key` or `null` if there is no mapping for the `key`.
Set<E> keySet()	Returns a `Set` of all the `key` objects in the `Map`.
V put(K key, V value)	Creates a `key`/`value` mapping in the `Map`. If the `key` already exists in the `Map`, `put()` replaces the `value` currently in the `Map` with the `value` supplied as an argument and returns the `value` replaced; otherwise, it returns the `value`.
Collection<V> values()	Returns a `Collection` of all the `value` objects in the `Map`.

Table 13.3: Some Methods of the `Map` Interface

To ensure that the set of `key` objects in a `Map` does not contain duplicates, it is important that the `key` objects override the `equals()` method of the `Object` class, based on the contents of the `key`. Note that duplicates depend on how the `equals()` method is defined. If the `equals()` method from `Object` is not overridden, there is a duplicate if two objects references are the same. Two objects might have the same set of values for the attributes but will not be considered to be duplicates if equality is based on object references. To ensure that equality is based on attribute values, the `equals()` method of the `key` object should be overridden.

Chapter 13: Container Classes

The `SortedMap` interface represents a `Map` object that keeps its set of `key` objects in sorted order. Its `keySet()` and `values()` methods inherited from `Map` return collections that can be iterated in sorted order of the `key`. It also declares methods of its own such as `firstKey()` and `lastKey()` that return the lowest and highest `key` values in the `SortedMap`.

13.3.2 Classes in the Java Collections Framework

The interfaces in the *Collections* framework have several methods that can be easily implemented. These interfaces are partially implemented in five abstract classes so that concrete collection classes can inherit these methods as a starting point. The five abstract classes are: `AbstractCollection`, `AbstractList`, `AbstractSequentialList`, `AbstractSet`, and `AbstractMap`. A concrete collection class can be implemented by inheriting from one of these abstract classes.

The class diagram in Figure 13.3 shows the concrete classes that are discussed in this chapter and their relationship to the abstract classes. The concrete classes are shaded in the diagram. Note that in addition to inheriting from the abstract classes shown, a concrete class will typically implement one of the interfaces in the Java *Collections* framework.

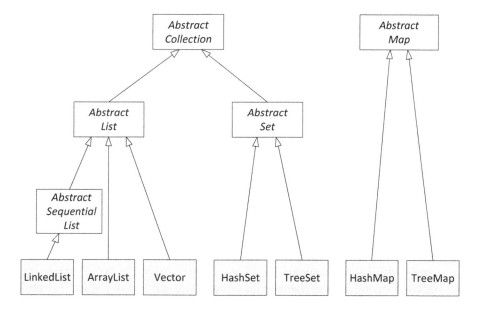

Figure 13.3: Classes in the Java *Collections* Framework

13.3.2.1 LinkedList

A `LinkedList` is a `List` implementation based on an underlying doubly linked list. Since it is implemented using a linked list data structure, each node in the list is connected to its immediate successor and predecessor. This makes its `add()` and `remove()` methods more efficient than an `ArrayList` since an `ArrayList` shifts its elements upwards or downwards whenever a new element is inserted or removed. However, the `get()` and `set()` methods of a `LinkedList` are substantially less efficient than the corresponding `get()` and `set()` methods of `ArrayList` and `Vector` (see next section), since they require traversal of the list from the beginning to find the element at the specified index.

13.3.2.2 ArrayList and Vector

An `ArrayList` is a general-purpose `List` implementation based on an array (that is re-created as necessary as the list grows or shrinks). Since an `ArrayList` is based on an array, its `get()` and `set()` methods are very efficient. A `Vector` is similar to an `ArrayList`, except that its methods are guaranteed that no concurrency control problems will arise. There are additional methods in `Vector` that have the same functionality as some of the methods in `List` described above, to maintain compatibility with earlier versions of Java. These include methods such as `elementAt()` and `setElementAt()`.

An `ArrayList` can be used to store a collection of `Account` objects as follows:

```
ArrayList<Account> accounts = new ArrayList<Account>();
                  // create instance of ArrayList

Account a1 = new Account(10, 1000.00);
Account a2 = new Account(20, 2000.00);
                  // create two Account objects

accounts.add(a1);    // insert a1 into collection
accounts.add(a2);    // insert a2 into collection
```

Since an `ArrayList` implements the `List` interface (which in turn, extends the `Collection` interface), the client of an `ArrayList` can use all the index-based methods of the `List` interface as well as all the methods of the `Collection` interface. A client can choose any method from the `ArrayList` that is appropriate for its needs. For, example, if a client wishes to remove the

Chapter 13: Container Classes

`Account` instance, `a`, at position `i` of the `ArrayList`, it could use the index-based `remove()` method of `List`:

```
accounts.remove(i);   // remove Account at position i
```

However, it could also use the `remove()` method from the `Collection` interface:

```
accounts.remove(a);   // remove Account referred to by a
```

The only difference is that the index-based `remove()` will be faster than the `remove()` in `Collection` since there is no need to search for the given object in the `ArrayList`.

Since `ArrayList` implements the `Collection` interface, the following declaration can also be used:

```
Collection<Account> accounts = new ArrayList<Account>();
```

This means that an instance of an `ArrayList` can be used wherever an object of type `Collection` is expected. It is preferable to specify the general type `Collection` in method signatures rather than specific types such as `ArrayList` and `TreeSet` since it allows the signatures to stay the same, even though the underlying implementation of the collection may change for some reason (e.g., replacing an `ArrayList` with a `TreeSet`). However, when this is done, clients will only be able to use the methods of the `Collection` interface.

Before concluding this section, it should be noted that the code given above could be used without change if a `Vector` was used to store the accounts instead of an `ArrayList`, since both `Vector` and `ArrayList` implement the `List` interface.

13.3.2.3 HashSet

The `HashSet` class implements the `Set` interface using an internal hash table. Because `HashSet` is based on a hash table, its `add()`, `remove()`, and `contains()` methods are very efficient. However, a `HashSet` makes no guarantee about the order in which the set elements are enumerated by the `Iterator` returned by the `iterator()` method. In the previous section, an example was given showing how to insert elements in an `ArrayList`. No change to this code is required when a `HashSet` is used.

The `Object` class provides a `hashCode()` method that generates a hash code for an object based on its memory address. The `HashSet` uses this method to determine where to place an object in the hash table. However, the `hashCode()` method of the `Object` class is generally not very useful since it would generate different hash codes for objects with identical contents. Thus, in order to store objects efficiently in a `HashSet`, the preferred technique is to override the `hashCode()` method to generate a (possibly) unique hash code based on the contents of the objects.

The following code is a fragment of an `Account` class that overrides the `hashCode()` method of `Object`:

```java
public class Account {
   private int num;
   private double balance;

   // usual Account methods

   public int hashCode() {
      return 13 * num;
   }
}
```

Many of the built-in classes in Java override the `hashCode()` method to generate more useful hash codes. These hash codes are normally derived from the contents of the objects.

Since a `HashSet` is a `Set`, it does not allow duplicates. It is useful to understand how a duplicate is detected. Consider two objects of the `Account` class which are created as follows:

```java
Account a1 = new Account(10, 1000.00);
Account a2 = new Account(10, 1000.00);
```

Notice that `a1` and `a2` have the same value for `number` (which is the primary key for `Account` objects). They also have the same value for the `balance` attribute. So, `a2` can be considered a duplicate of `a1`.

Now, suppose that `a1` and `a2` are inserted in the `HashSet` using its `add()` method. If the `Account` class does not override the `hashCode()` method, there is a strong possibility that `a1` and `a2` will hash to different locations in the `HashSet` since the hash code is based on the memory address of `a1` and `a2`. Even if the `Account` class overrides the `equals()` method in `Object` which specifies that two `Account` objects are equal if they have the same `number`, `a1` and `a2` will still hash to different locations and will be both inserted in the `HashSet`. In other words, it is important to override both the `hashCode()`

Chapter 13: Container Classes

method and the equals() method to ensure that duplicates are not inserted in a HashSet.

13.3.2.4 TreeSet

A TreeSet implements the Set interface using an internal red-black tree so that its elements are maintained in sorted order. Every time an element is added to a TreeSet, it is placed in a position determined by its sort order. Therefore, its iterator() method returns an Iterator that traverses the elements in the TreeSet in sorted order.

Consider the following code:

```
TreeSet<String> names = new TreeSet<String>();

names.add("Shellyann");
names.add("Diana");
names.add("Keshav");

Iterator <String> i = names.iterator();
while (i.hasNext())
   System.out.println(i.next());
```

When run, this code will generate the names in sorted order as follows:

```
Diana
Keshav
Shellyann
```

In order to determine the sort order of the elements in a TreeSet, the objects to be inserted must implement the Comparable interface[1]. In other words, they must supply an implementation of the compareTo() method which specifies how to order two elements in the TreeSet.

It should be noted that since the Collection interface inherits from the Iterable interface, the *foreach* statement can be used to traverse the TreeSet as follows:

```
for (String n : names)
   System.out.println(n);
```

---

[1] Later in this chapter, an alternative approach to using the *Comparable* interface is discussed.

The *foreach* statement can also be used to traverse the other collections that implement the `Collection` interface.

13.3.2.5 HashMap

The `HashMap` class implements the `Map` interface using an internal hash table. Since it is based on a hash table, its `get()` and `put()` methods are very efficient. The following code shows how a `HashMap` can be used for storing accounts:

```
HashMap <Integer, Account> accounts =
    new HashMap<Integer, Account>();

Account a1 = new Account(10, 1000.00);
Account a2 = new Account(20, 2000.00);
Account a3 = new Account(30, 3000.00);

accounts.put(new Integer(a1.getNum()), a1);
accounts.put(new Integer(a2.getNum()), a2);
accounts.put(new Integer(a3.getNum()), a3);
```

In this example, the account number is used as the *key* (an `Integer` object) and the entire account object (`Account`) is used as the value in the `HashMap`. However, since the account number is of the primitive type `int`, it cannot be used directly, since the `put()` method expects the *key* to be of type `Integer`. So, the account number is first converted to an `Integer` object (which overrides the `hashCode()` and `equals()` methods of `Object`, like many of the other Java classes).

Figure 13.4 is a diagram showing how a `HashMap` can be used to store `Account` objects. The *key* is the account `number` (converted to an `Integer` object) and the *value* is the `Account` object itself.

Chapter 13: Container Classes

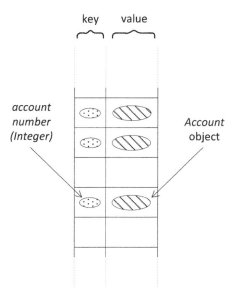

Figure 13.4: HashMap of `Account` Objects

It should be noted that there is no problem with having a duplicate *value* in the `HashMap` (or in a `TreeMap` for that matter), as long as it is associated with a different *key*. For example,

```
accounts.put(new Integer(40), a3);
```

To find the account in the `HashMap` with the account number 10, the following code can be used:

```
Account a = accounts.get(new Integer(10));
```

If there is no element in the `HashMap` with the given *key*, the `get()` method returns `null`.

13.3.2.6 TreeMap

The `TreeMap` class implements the `SortedMap` interface using an internal red-black tree data structure. It guarantees that the *keys* and *values* of the mapping can be enumerated based on the order of the *keys*. The objects being used as *keys* in a `TreeMap` must implement the `Comparable` interface.

Consider the following example:

```
TreeMap<Integer, Account> accounts =
```

```
    new TreeMap<Integer, Account>();

Account a1 = new Account(10, 1000.00);
Account a2 = new Account(40, 4000.00);
Account a3 = new Account(30, 3000.00);

accounts.put(new Integer(a1.getNum()), a1);
accounts.put(new Integer(a2.getNum()), a2);
accounts.put(new Integer(a3.getNum()), a3);

Set<Integer> keys = accounts.keySet();
Iterator<Integer> i = keys.iterator();

while (i.hasNext()) {
   Integer key = i.next();
   System.out.println(key.toString());
}
```

When run, the code is guaranteed to generate a list of the *keys* in sorted order (based on the implementation of the `compareTo()` method in the `Integer` class):

```
10
30
40
```

This is different from when a `HashMap` is used since a `HashMap` does not guarantee how the *keys* will be ordered.

Next, consider what happens when the following code is executed on a `TreeMap` of `Account` objects:

```
Collection<Account> c = accounts.values();
Iterator<Account> i = c.iterator();

while (i.hasNext()) {
   Account a = i.next();
   System.out.println(a.toString());
}
```

This code will generate a listing of the accounts, in the order **a1, a3, a2**. This is because the *values* are sorted based on the *key*.

Chapter 13: Container Classes

13.4 The Comparable Interface (Generics Version)

In the previous chapter, it was shown how the **Comparable** interface can be implemented in the **Account** class. The generics version of the implementation will now be presented. First, the **Account** class must indicate that it implements the **Comparable<T>** interface, replacing T with the type **Account**:

```
public class Account implements Comparable<Account>
{
   :
}
```

Next, the **compareTo()** method is implemented. The implementation is very similar to the one previously described except that it is not necessary to use **instanceof** and casting to retrieve the **Account** object passed as an argument. This is because the parameter of the **compareTo()** method is already specified to be of type **Account**. The code is given below.

```
public int compareTo(Account a) {
   if (this.number < a.number)
      return -1;
   else
   if (this.number == a.number)
      return 0;
   else
      return 1;
}
```

13.5 The Comparator Interface

A **TreeSet** requires its elements to implement the **Comparable** interface. Similarly, a **TreeMap** requires its keys to implement the **Comparable** interface. One limitation of this approach is that a particular class can only implement the **Comparable** interface once. So based on this approach, it is not possible to store, say, **Account** objects in one **TreeSet** sorted by **number** and in another **TreeSet**, sorted by **balance**. However, there is another approach that can be used to specify multiple sort orders. This approach requires the use of the **Comparator** interface (from **java.util.***).

Like the **Comparable** interface, the **Comparator** interface has a single method:

```
public interface Comparator<T> {
```

```
   public int compare (T o1, T o2);
}
```

The `compare()` method is similar to the `compareTo()` method except that both objects to be compared are supplied as arguments to the method.

To specify a sort order, a class must be created that implements the `Comparator` interface. For example, to specify a sort order for `Account` objects based on account numbers, the following class can be created:

```
public class AccountComparatorNum implements Comparator<Account> {
   public int compare(Account a1, Account a2) {
      return (a1.getNum() - a2.getNum());
   }
}
```

To specify a sort order for `Account` objects based on account balances, the following class can be created:

```
public class AccountComparatorBalance implements Comparator<Account>
{
   public int compare(Account a1, Account a2) {
      return (int) (a1.getBalance() - a2.getBalance());
   }
}
```

Collection classes that depend on a sort order (such as `TreeSet` and `TreeMap`) provide a constructor that accepts a `Comparator` object. To specify that the elements of a `TreeSet` are to be sorted by account number, an instance of `AccountComparatorNum` is created and supplied to the constructor of the `TreeSet` as an argument:

```
Comparator<Account> comparator = new AccountComparatorNum();
TreeSet<Account>accounts = new TreeSet<Account>(comparator);
```

If instead, the accounts are to be sorted by account balance, an instance of `AccountComparatorBalance` is created and supplied to the constructor:

```
Comparator<Account> comparator = new AccountComparatorBalance();
TreeSet<Account> accounts = new TreeSet<Account>(comparator);
```

Thus, a `Comparator` class can be written to define a particular sort order for a class of objects. An instance of the `Comparator` is supplied when creating a collection. This approach is not restricted to collection classes alone. A class that depends on its objects implementing the `Comparable` interface could provide a constructor allowing a `Comparator` to be specified at run-time. In this way, clients can specify one of several sort orders at run-time, by creating and sending an appropriate `Comparator` object.

Both the `AccountComparatorNum` and the `AccountComparatorBalance` classes have no attributes. These classes provide a single method to perform the comparison based on the `Comparator` interface. For that reason, an instance of a class such as `AccountComparatorNum` is known as a *function object*. However, more flexibility can be achieved if instance variables are used. For example, the `AccountComparatorBalance` class can use an instance variable, *ascending*, to specify whether the accounts are to be sorted in ascending order or descending order by balance. A client can then specify a value for this attribute at run-time, according to its needs.

13.6 Which Collection to Use?

This chapter has discussed several concrete collection classes, each with their own features and performance characteristics. In an object-oriented application, you must choose the collection classes that best meet your needs. All the collection classes allow objects to be stored, some based on sorted order, while others are based on no particular order. Some allow index-based access while others enable random access based on hash codes.

Before concluding this discussion on the classes of the Java *Collections* framework, a brief comparison will be given of the performance characteristics of the different containers.

For insertion and deletion of elements, a `LinkedList` is more efficient than an `ArrayList` or a `Vector`. However, for index-based retrieval, the latter two are more efficient and the operation takes place in constant time. The performance of index-based retrieval on a `LinkedList` is of the order n ($O(n)$).

Inserting an element in a `HashSet` or `HashMap` takes place in constant time compared to a `TreeSet` or `TreeMap` where the time complexity is of the order $\log_2 n$ ($O(\log_2 n)$), where n is the number of elements already in the `TreeSet`. Searching for an element in a `HashSet` or `HashMap` also takes place in constant time compared to a `TreeSet` or `TreeMap` where it takes place in ($O(\log_2 n)$) time. So, generally, a `HashSet` or a `HashMap` should be used instead of a `TreeSet` or a `TreeMap`, unless there is a need to maintain elements in sorted order.

Exercises

1. Explain how the generics feature in Java solves the problem of generalizing the type of objects that can be stored in a container while providing type safety at the same time.

2. In a certain human resource application, it is necessary to generate reports of employees sorted in different ways. For example, the employees sometimes need to be sorted by their **last name** and sometimes by their **position**. An **Employee** class represents the concept of an employee in the application. Explain how the different sort orders can be implemented in the application. How can ascending and descending sort orders be accommodated?

3. A class **C** does not override the **equals()** method of the **Object** class but it overrides the **hashCode()** method by generating a value based on the attributes of the class. Two instances of **C** are created where the values of the attributes are the same. Explain what happens if an attempt is made to insert both instances of **C** in a **HashSet**.

4. Explain how you would choose between a **TreeMap** and a **HashMap** for storing a certain collection of objects.

5. Suppose you need to store a collection of objects for which index-based retrieval is important. Compare the use of an **ArrayList**, a **LinkedList**, and a **HashSet** for storing the objects.

6. An **ArrayList** implements the **List** interface which extends the **Collection** interface. How does this affect the operations that a client can perform on an **ArrayList**? Which operations will be more efficient?

7. You are planning to write a new container class, **C**, which will store collections of objects. Will you use the **Collection** interface, the **Map** interface, or neither? Give reasons for your answer.

8. Suppose you have written a collection class, **C**. You would like clients to be able to use the *foreach* statement to traverse the collection. Explain the additional features that should be implemented in **C** to accommodate this functionality. Assuming that **Account** objects are stored in an instance of **C**, write the code to find the sum of all the **Account** balances using a *foreach* statement.

9. How do client objects benefit when a collection class provides an `Iterator` object to its underlying elements?

10. Objects of a certain class `C` must be must be stored in a `TreeSet`. Describe two features that must be implemented in `C` in order for instances of `C` to be stored in a `TreeSet`.

Chapter 14

Fourth Programming Project

This chapter shows how to enhance the code from the third programming project in various ways. It explains how to make the code more efficient by replacing the `ArrayList` collections with collections that are more suitable for the type of access required. It also shows how to organize the classes of the application into packages, as described in Chapter 3. The chapter explains how to implement the constraint that only one instance of a class should exist at run-time. For example, in the Student Management System, it is important that only one instance of the `University` class should exist at run-time.

The chapter introduces a new concept called a *role object*. A role object enables a particular object to have many roles over the lifespan of that object. For example, a `Student` object can have an `UndergraduateStudent` role and later, a `PostgraduateStudent` role, and indeed, any combination of these roles. If inheritance is used, separate objects such as `UndergraduateStudent` and `PostgraduateStudent` will have to be created. It then becomes a challenge to link these different objects together and to treat them as different aspects of the same `Student` object. It is also difficult to enforce constraints such as ensuring that the related objects have the same student ID. This chapter shows how it is more convenient to use role objects for the different roles rather than use inheritance.

14.1 Requirements of the Application

The requirements of the application are the same as in the third programming project. The application manages information on undergraduate students and postgraduate students and the courses they register for at a certain university.

However, there are some new implementation requirements:

- The application should allow at most one instance of the `University` class to be created.

- The `ArrayList` collections in the `University` class should be replaced with collections that are more appropriate for the type of access required in the application.

- Instead of using inheritance to create `UndergraduateStudent` and `PostgraduateStudent` objects, role objects should be used.

- The application should be organized into packages.

14.2 Ensuring that at Most One Instance of the University Class Exists

If two instances of the `University` class are allowed to exist while the application is running, some `Student` objects and some `Course` objects will belong to one instance and some will belong to the other. This is a serious application error. Thus, it is important to ensure that only one instance of the `University` class is created and that this instance is easily accessible to client classes.

In order to solve the problem, the following must be done:

- Allow a client to create one instance of the `University` class
- Prevent the same client or other clients from creating another instance of `University`
- Provide a way for clients to access the single instance of `University`

Ensuring that only instance of a class is created is not as straightforward as it seems. A client class (e.g., one belonging to the user interface) can create an instance of `University` whenever it wants by using the `new` keyword:

```
University university =
    new University ("The University of Computing");
```

The first step towards a solution is to make the constructor of the `University` class private as follows:

```
private University(String name) {
    :
}
```

Chapter 14: Fourth Programming Project

Since private methods are inaccessible to other classes, it is not possible for a client to create an instance of University using the new keyword. This effectively solves the problem of clients being able to create instances of University. However, it solves the problem so well that it is not possible for a client to create even *one* instance of University!

The next step in the solution is to modify the University class so that it is responsible for creating an instance of itself. Assume that the method to do this is called createInstance(). The createInstance() method must be a class method and not an instance method since it must be possible to invoke createInstance() when no instance of University exists.

The following is a first version of the createInstance() method:

```
public static University createInstance() {
    University university =
        new University("The University of Computing");
    return university;
}
```

The createInstance() method creates an instance of University and returns the instance to its caller. Thus, a client can get an instance of University by making the following call:

```
University university = University.createInstance();
```

However, clients can do this as many times as they please and receive different instances of University from the createInstance() method. So, we are right back to the original problem.

It is therefore necessary to modify the createInstance() method so that it creates only one instance of University. In order to do so, it must know whether an instance was already created. A boolean variable, instanceExists can be used for this purpose. So, if no instance already exists (instanceExists is false), one is created and returned to the client (and instanceExists is set to true). Otherwise, the already created instance is returned:

```
public static University createInstance() {
    if (!instanceExists) {
        university = new University("The University of Computing");
        instanceExists = true;
    }
    return university;
```

```
}
```

The **university** and **instanceExists** variables must be declared outside the **createInstance()** method so that they will persist from one invocation to the next. These variables must be declared as class variables since, as mentioned in Chapter 3, class methods cannot access instance variables. The declarations are done as follows in the **University** class:

```
private static University university;
private static boolean instanceExists = false;
```

The solution given above for solving the problem of ensuring that at most one instance of a class is created is known as the *Singleton Design Pattern* (Gamma et al, 1994). The **createInstance()** method is typically called **instance()** or **getInstance()** in the literature. Also, there is no real need to use the **boolean** variable **instanceExists** since the **university** variable can be set to **null** to indicate that no instance exists. Thus, the method is typically implemented as follows:

```
public static University getInstance() {
   if (university == null)
      university = new University("The University of Computing");

   return university;
}
```

14.3 Using More Efficient Collections to Manage Data in the **University** Class

In the third programming project, instances of **ArrayList** are used to store collections of objects such as **Student**, **Course**, and **Registration**. Figure 14.1 shows the three **ArrayList** collections which are used for storing **Student**, **Course**, and **Registration** objects.

Chapter 14: Fourth Programming Project

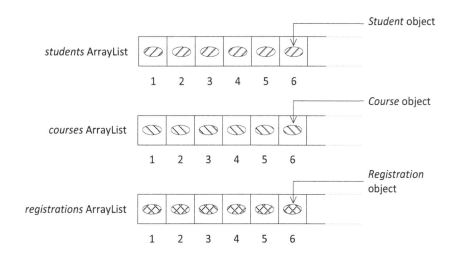

Figure 14.1: **ArrayLists** Used in Third Programming Project

An **ArrayList** is a sequential structure and its performance on linear searches is $O(n)$ where n is number of elements in the **ArrayList**. Since its performance depends on the number of elements stored in the **ArrayList**, the search time increases as more and more elements are added to the **ArrayList**. This problem can be solved by using collection classes that are more suitable for the type of access desired.

This section explains how to improve the performance of the Student Management System by using instances of **HashMap** and **TreeSet**. As explained in Chapter 13, it is often convenient to specify a sort order when using a **TreeSet**. This can be achieved using **Comparator** objects. This section presents two **Comparator** objects for specifying the sort order of **Student** objects. The code given in this section also demonstrates how generics can be used for the respective collections.

14.3.1 Comparators for Student Objects

The Student Management System uses a **TreeSet** to sort the collection of **Student** objects before generating output for the user interface. For example, when the user clicks on the "Students" button in the *View All* screen, the **Student** objects are copied into an instance of **TreeSet** and returned to the user interface. A **Comparator** object is used to determine the sort order. The **TreeSet** can then be traversed using an **Iterator** to produce a list of the **Student** objects in the sort order specified.

The first `Comparator` is `StudentNameComparator`. It compares two `Student` objects based on the value of the `name` instance variable. The code for the `Comparator` class is given below:

```java
import java.util.Comparator;

public class StudentNameComparator implements Comparator<Student> {

    public int compare(Student student1, Student student2) {
        return student1.getName().compareTo(student2.getName());
    }
}
```

As explained in Chapter 13, writing a `Comparator` class simply involves implementing the `Comparator` interface and providing a method implementation for the `compare()` method. Since we are comparing based on the `name` instance variable which is a string, we can use the `compareTo()` method of the `String` class to perform the comparison.

The second `Comparator` is `StudentIDComparator`. This `Comparator` is almost identical to the `StudentNameComparator` except that it compares two `Student` objects based on the value of the `ID` instance variable:

```java
public int compare(Student student1, Student student2) {
    return (int) student1.getID() - student2.getID();
}
```

Later in this section, it will be shown how these two `Comparator`s can be used to obtain a `TreeSet` sorted by `name` and `ID`, respectively.

14.3.2 New Collections for `Course`, `Student`, and `Registration`

It is important in the Student Management System to be able to find out as quickly as possible if a particular course or a particular student exists in the system. It is also important to be able to quickly retrieve all the courses a particular student has registered for. The `HashMap` collection permits retrieval in constant time and is thus more appropriate than an `ArrayList`. Objects in a `HashMap` are stored as (*key, value*) pairs where the *key* and the *value* are themselves objects.

For the `HashMap` of `Student` objects, the *key* is the student `ID` and the *value* is the corresponding `Student` object. However, since the student `ID` has the primitive type `long`, it must first be converted to an object using an instance of

Chapter 14: Fourth Programming Project

the wrapper class, **Long**. The **HashMap** of **Student** objects is declared as follows:

```
private HashMap<Long, Student> students;   // changed from ArrayList
```

For the **HashMap** of **Course** objects, the *key* is the course **code** and the *value* is the corresponding **Course** object. The *key* is already an object since it is an instance of **String** so there is no need to use a wrapper class. The **HashMap** of **Course** objects is declared as follows:

```
private HashMap<String, Course> courses;   // changed from ArrayList
```

Figure 14.2 is a pictorial representation of the **HashMap**s that are used for storing **Student** objects and **Course** objects. For simplicity, the **HashMap**s are drawn as if they contain actual objects; however, as noted in the previous chapter, only object references are stored.

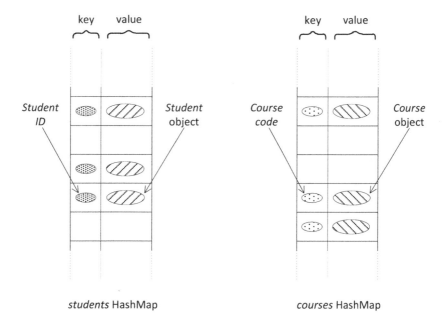

Figure 14.2: HashMaps for Student Objects and Course Objects

In the third programming project, each **Registration** object is stored in an **ArrayList**. To find the **Registration** objects corresponding to a particular student, it is necessary to traverse the entire **ArrayList** and look for all the **Registration** objects with the same **Student** object as the one being searched for. This is very inefficient. In this project, each student has its own

ArrayList of Registration objects. The ArrayList objects are themselves stored in a HashMap as *values* with the Student object as the *key*. The HashMap of Registration objects is declared as follows:

registrations = new HashMap<Student, ArrayList<Registration>>();

Figure 14.3 is a pictorial representation of the registrations HashMap. Since a Student object is the *key*, we can say that the HashMap is indexed by Student.

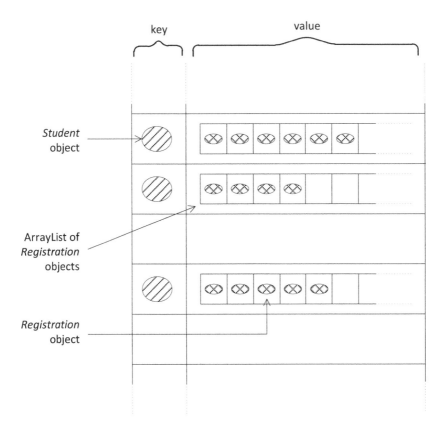

Figure 14.3: HashMap of Registration Objects Indexed by Student

However, while it is possible to use the registrations HashMap to quickly obtain the list of courses for which a student has registered, it is now a challenge to find the set of students who have registered for a particular course. This requires traversing each ArrayList in the HashMap to find out if it contains the course specified. A simple solution is to use another HashMap

Chapter 14: Fourth Programming Project

where the *key* is a `Course` object and the *value* is an `ArrayList` of `Registration` objects corresponding to the registrations for that course.

The two `HashMap`s can be declared as follows:

```
registrations1 = new HashMap<Student, ArrayList<Registration>>();
registrations2 = new HashMap<Course, ArrayList<Registration>>();
```

Using two `HashMap`s to store the same information introduces another problem of maintaining the integrity of the data stored in both `HashMap`s. Thus, if a student registers for a particular course, the instance of `Registration` has to be added to the `ArrayList` associated with that student as well as the `ArrayList` associated with the particular course. If one of them is not updated, the system becomes inconsistent.

It should be noted that since `Student` and `Course` objects are now being used as *keys* for the different `HashMap`s, it is a good idea to override the `hashCode()` method of `Student` and `Course`. The `hashCode()` method should generate hash codes which achieve a reasonable spread of the underlying hash table.

14.3.3 Using the New Collections

The signature of the methods for accessing `Student`, `Course` or `Registration` objects remain the same as in the third programming project when the `ArrayList` collections were used. This is one of the advantages of object-oriented programming: the ability to change the underlying implementation without affecting the publicly available interface. The implementation has to change to deal with the new `HashMap` collections which replaced the `ArrayList` collections.

The code to insert a new `Course` object is as follows:

```
course = new Course(code, title, numCredits, maxStudents);
courses.put(code, course);    // only change for HashMap
```

After creating the `Course` object, it is added to the `courses` HashMap using its `put()` method. Here the *key* is the course *code* and the *value* is the newly created `Course` object.

The code to insert a new `Student` object in the `students` HashMap is similar. It first creates an instance of `UndergraduateStudent` or `PostgraduateStudent` and adds the instance to the `HashMap`. However, in order to use the student ID as the *key*, a `Long` object must first be created from the student ID using the Long wrapper class. The *key* and corresponding Student object are then added to the students HashMap using the put() method:

```
students.put(new Long(ID), student);
```

The code to register a student for a course is a little more complicated since two collections, registrations1 and registrations2, must be updated. Also, since each collection is a HashMap where the *value* associated with the *key* is itself an ArrayList, more work has to be done in order to add a new Registration object to the two collections.

Consider what is involved in adding a new Registration object to the registrations1 collection where the *key* is the Student object. If the student has not previously registered for a course, there will be no entry for that Student object in the HashMap. Thus, a new ArrayList has to be created and the Registration object must be inserted in this ArrayList. The ArrayList is then added to the HashMap using the Student object as the *key*. However, if the student has previously registered for a course, there will already be an entry for that student in the HashMap with a corresponding ArrayList as the *value*. All that has to be done is to insert the new Registration object in the ArrayList.

The code for adding a new Registration object to the registrations1 collection is given below:

```
Collection<Registration> existingListStudent;

existingListStudent = registrations1.get(student);
  // obtain list of Registration objects corresponding to student

if (existingListStudent == null) {
  // no Registration objects for this student as yet

  ArrayList<Registration> newListStudent =
      new ArrayList<Registration>();
  // create new ArrayList to store Registration objects

  newListStudent.add(registration);
  // add Registration object to list

  registrations1.put(student, newListStudent);
  // put list of Registration objects in HashMap with Student as key
}
```

Chapter 14: Fourth Programming Project

```
else {
  // there is already a list of Registration objects

   existingListStudent.add(registration);
  // just add Registration object to list
}
```

After adding the `Registration` object to the `registrations1` collection it must be added to the `registrations2` collection which is indexed by `Course`. If no student has previously registered for the course, there will be no entry for that `Course` object in the `courses HashMap`. Thus, a new `ArrayList` has to be created and the `Registration` object must be inserted in this `ArrayList`. The `ArrayList` is then added to the `HashMap` using the `Course` object as the *key*. However, if students have previously registered for the course, there will already be an entry for that course in the `HashMap` with a corresponding `ArrayList` as the value. All that has to be done is to insert the new `Registration` object in the `ArrayList`. The code is similar to that given for `registrations1` so it is not repeated.

De-registering a student from a course is a lot easier. Once it is determined that a student was indeed registered for the given course, all that has to be done is to remove the corresponding `Registration` object from both `registrations1` and `registrations2`:

```
registrationsStudent = registrations1.get(student);
            // find ArrayList containing Course objects

registrationsCourse = registrations2.get(course);
            // find ArrayList containing Student objects

registration = getRegistration(registrationsStudent, course);
            // find Registration object corresponding to course

registrationsStudent.remove(registration);
registrationsCourse.remove(registration);
            // remove Registration object from both collections
```

The first line in the code above shows how to retrieve the `ArrayList` of `Registration` objects corresponding to a particular `Student` object from the `registrations1 HashMap`. The `Student` object is supplied as the *key* in the `get()` method and the *value* returned is the `ArrayList` of `Registration` objects.

The second line shows how to retrieve the `ArrayList` of `Registration` objects corresponding to a particular `Course` object from the `registrations2 HashMap`. The `Course` object is supplied as the *key* in the `get()` method and an `ArrayList` of `Registration` objects is returned. The `Student` object can be extracted from each `Registration` object to obtain the list of students registered for a course.

If the list of students should be in sorted order, a `TreeSet` can be used to insert the `Student` objects extracted from the `Registration` objects. The `TreeSet` should be created using one of the `Comparator` objects for `Student` previously discussed. For example, the following code extracts the `Student` objects and stores them in a `TreeSet` sorted by the name of the student:

```
Collection<Registration> registrations = registrations2.get(course);
   // find collection of Registration objects for course

regStudents = new TreeSet<Student>(new StudentNameComparator());
   // sort order in TreeSet is determined by the name of the student

Iterator<Registration>i = registrations.iterator();
while (i.hasNext()) {
   Registration r = i.next();
   regStudents.add(r.getStudent());
   // insert the Student object in the TreeSet
}
```

The code above is used in the `getStudents()` method of `University` which returns a collection of `Student` objects registered for a given course where the `Student` objects are sorted by the `name` of the student. If the application requires the `Student` objects to be sorted by student `ID`, the `StudentIDComparator` should be used when creating the `TreeSet`:

```
regStudents = new TreeSet<Student>(new StudentIDComparator());
   // sort order in TreeSet is determined by the student ID
```

14.3.4 Overriding the `hashCode()` and `equals()` Methods

Since a `HashMap` is used to store `Registration` objects indexed by `Course` objects and `Student` objects, it is a good idea to override the `hashCode()` and `equals()` methods of these two classes. If the `hashCode()` method is not overridden, the default `hashCode()` method of the `Object` class is used which generates hash codes based on the memory address of a `Course` object or a `Student` object. Overriding the `equals()` method allows explicit criteria to be

Chapter 14: Fourth Programming Project

specified for checking whether two *keys* are the same instead of relying on the equality of memory addresses.

14.4 Using Roles Instead of Inheritance

The first version of the code for the fourth programming project incorporates the changes discussed in the previous two sections. It ensures that only one instance of the University class is created and it uses more efficient collections that take advantage of the generics feature in Java. In this section, the code is enhanced further to deal with the concept of a *role object*.

14.4.1 Problem with Inheritance and a Solution Using Role Objects

Consider the two inheritance hierarchies shown in Figure 14.4. In Figure 14.4 (a), a Circle class and a Rectangle class inherit from a Shape class. In Figure 14.4 (b), a SavingsAccount class and a ChequingAccount class inherit from an Account class. Inheritance can be used in both cases to implement the child classes since it allows the parent class to specify attributes and behavior that can be inherited by the child classes. This is an important benefit of inheritance and was discussed in Chapter 9.

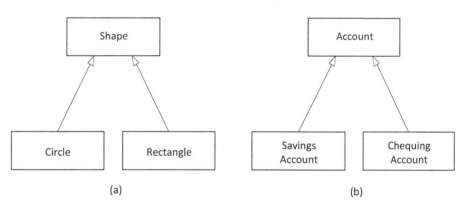

Figure 14.4: Inheritance Hierarchies (a) Shape (b) Account

Given the inheritance hierarchy in Figure 14.4 (a), it is hardly likely that a particular shape which is a rectangle could be a circle at some point in the future. Similarly, given the inheritance hierarchy in Figure 14.4 (b), it is hardly likely that a particular account which is a savings account could be a chequing account at some point in the future.

Now, consider the inheritance hierarchies shown in Figure 14.5. In the `Employee` hierarchy, it is possible for an employee who is an hourly employee to become a salaried employee in the future. In the `Student` hierarchy, it is possible for an undergraduate student to later become a postgraduate student and yet later, become an undergraduate student for some other academic discipline. The challenge in these two situations is how to use inheritance to handle the different roles that an employee or a student can play in the application over time. Even though instances of the subclasses can be created, it becomes a challenge to link these different objects together and treat them as different aspects of the same `Employee` or `Student` object. It is also difficult to enforce constraints such as ensuring that the instances of the subclasses have the same unique identifier.

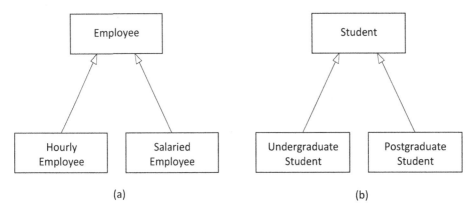

Figure 14.5: Inheritance Hierarchies (a) `Employee` (b) `Student`

There are different ways to solve this problem. One fairly straightforward technique is to use *role objects* for the different roles and to aggregate the role objects in the parent class. For example, when role objects are used, the `UndergraduateStudent` and `PostgraduateStudent` classes will no longer be subclasses of `Student`. Rather, they will now be independent classes representing roles that a student can play.

To represent the fact that a student is an undergraduate student, an instance of `UndergraduateStudent` is created and stored in an instance of `Student`. Similarly, to represent the fact that a student is a postgraduate student, an instance of `PostgraduateStudent` is created and stored in an instance of `Student`. Thus, there is only one instance of `Student`. This instance can have many roles over the lifetime of the application. Whenever a role is required, an instance of the appropriate role is created and stored in the instance of `Student`. Thus, the `Student` object contains a collection of role objects. Note that aggregation rather than inheritance is used to solve the problem so that `Student` is no longer a superclass.

Chapter 14: Fourth Programming Project

Figure 14.6 shows how **Student** contains a collection of roles. This solution makes it possible for a **Student** to have multiple instances of the same role if this was required. For example, a student can have two **UndergraduateStudent** roles in different academic disciplines.

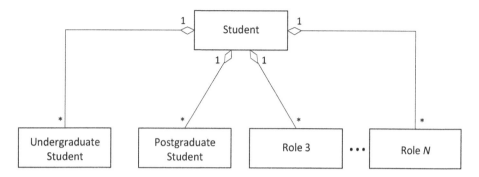

Figure 14.6: Student Contains a Collection of Roles

Consider again the UML diagram in Figure 14.6. It is clear that the **Student** class must be aware of the existence of each potential role that a student can play. If there is need to introduce a new role, the **Student** class must be modified accordingly. An important goal in software development is to reduce the amount of changes required of existing code since code modification is costly. Thus, a solution is required which minimizes code changes.

An abstract class, **StudentRole**, can be introduced so that no modification of the **Student** class is required. This solution requires the **Student** class to maintain a collection of objects whose type is **StudentRole**. Each role inherits from **StudentRole**. So, if a new role is introduced, it will inherit from **StudentRole** and since its type will be **StudentRole** by substitutability, it can be inserted into the collection of roles in **Student**. Figure 14.7 shows the classes involved:

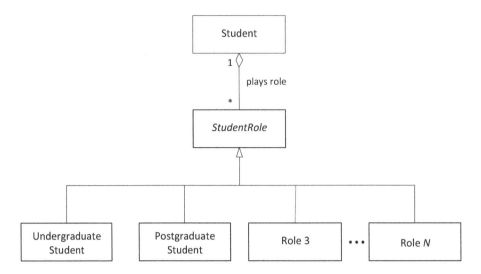

Figure 14.7: Using a **StudentRole** Abstract Class

14.4.2 Implementation of Role Objects

The second version of the code for the fourth programming project uses role objects instead of inheritance for **Student**, **UndergraduateStudent**, and **PostgraduateStudent**. As indicated in Figure 14.7, a new abstract class **StudentRole** is part of the solution. **StudentRole** is a simple class and is shown in the UML diagram in Figure 14.8:

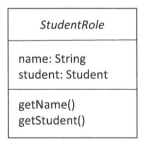

Figure 14.8: **StudentRole** Class

The **name** attribute is the name of the role, for example "UndergraduateStudent" or "PostgraduateStudent". The **student** attribute is a reference to the **Student** object which contains the role.

Chapter 14: Fourth Programming Project

A new exception class is introduced in this version of the programming project. It is called `NoSuchRoleException` and is thrown if a client (e.g., the user interface) requests a particular role that is not available.

The `Student` class is no longer an abstract class. It is basically the same as the previous version except that it now contains a collection of `StudentRole` objects and a set of role management operations. The collection of `StudentRole` objects is declared as follows:

```
private ArrayList<StudentRole> roles;
```

An `ArrayList` is a suitable collection for storing roles since a student is not likely to have too many roles over the lifetime of the application.

The role management operations are listed in Table 14.1.

Operation	Purpose
void addRole(StudentRole newRole)	Adds a new role to the `Student`.
StudentRole getRole(String roleName)	Returns the role object corresponding to a particular role name or `null` if none exists.
Iterator<StudentRole> getRoles()	Returns an iterator for all the roles of the `Student`.
String getRoleNames()	Returns a string representation of all the role names of the `Student`.

Table 14.1: Role Management Operations

It should be noted that the `getRole()` method assumes that a `Student` object will have at most one role with the given role name. This was done to simplify the implementation; the code can be modified to deal with multiple role objects with the same name.

The `UndergraduateStudent` and `PostgraduateStudent` classes remain almost unchanged from the previous version. However, since these classes are now roles, they inherit from `StudentRole` rather than `Student` (see Figure 14.7). Also, in the previous version, it was necessary to supply information for the superclass attributes of `Student` in the constructor of these two classes. Since instances of these classes will now be contained within a particular `Student` object, the constructor only needs information for the `StudentRole` superclass and the attributes that are declared in each class. The constructor for the `UndergraduateStudent` class is given below:

```
public UndergraduateStudent (Student student, String roleName,
```

```
    String major, String minor) {

    super(roleName, student);
    this.major = major;
    this.minor = minor;
}
```

The constructor takes a reference to the **Student** object which will contain the role as well as the name of the role. These values are stored in the attributes of **StudentRole**.

The **University** class has to be modified to deal with the concept of role objects instead of inheritance. All the methods that manipulate instances of **UndergraduateStudent** and **PostgraduateStudent** have to be changed. It also has to provide methods to create and update instances of **Student** since **Student** was not a separate entity in the previous version of the code. It should be noted that the methods of **University** which previously referred only to the **Student** class do not need to be changed (e.g., **registerStudent()**, **deRegisterStudent()**). Thus, registration for a course is not tied to a particular role but to the student who is registering for the course.

The following is the code to add the role of **UndergraduateStudent** to an already existing **Student**:

```
public UndergraduateStudent addUndergraduateStudent(long ID,
    String major, String minor) {

    Student student = getStudent(ID);
    if (student == null)      // student for role does not exist
        return null;

    UndergraduateStudent ugStudent =
        new UndergraduateStudent(student, "UndergraduateStudent",
            major, minor);

    student.addRole(ugStudent);
    return ugStudent;

}
```

The method first searches for the **Student** object with the given student **ID** to find the **Student** object which will contain the role. If the **Student** object is found, an instance of the role is created and added to the **Student** using its

Chapter 14: Fourth Programming Project

addRole() method. The update method behaves in a similar manner by searching for the role in the containing **Student** object.

The query methods in **University** which return a list of undergraduate students and a list of postgraduate students have to be modified to search for roles instead of instances of **UndergraduateStudent** or **PostgraduateStudent**. Each **Student** object is examined one by one to determine if it plays the role being searched for (as a string). If so, the student **ID** and **name** is concatenated to the result list. The code for searching for the role of **PostgraduateStudent** in a given **Student** object is given below:

```
String roleNames = student.getRoleNames();
                // list of all roles

int index = roleNames.indexOf("PostgraduateStudent");
                // check if list contains PG student

if (index >= 0) {    // list contains PG student
   output = output + student.getID() + ", " +
      student.getName() + "\n";
   :
}
```

The code for the second version of this programming project which uses role objects can be downloaded from the book Web site.

14.4.3 Re-design of the Graphical User Interface

The user interface of the application must be re-designed to deal with the concept of a role object. Since a **Student** object is distinct from the roles it can play, the user interface must allow a **Student** object to be created and updated independently from its roles. The user interface must also allow the roles to be added to an existing **Student** object at different points in time. Because of this, the **StudentPanel** was divided into two sections, one to manipulate student information and the other to manipulate role information. Figure 14.9 is a screenshot of the new **StudentPanel**. The other windows in the user interface remain unchanged from the previous version.

Figure 14.9: Screenshot of Re-designed `StudentPanel`

The code for the user interface as well as an updated User's Guide is available at the book Web site.

14.5 Organizing the Application into Packages

Chapter 4 explained how to organize an object-oriented application into packages. The second version of this programming project contains sixteen classes so that it is a good idea to consider organizing the application into packages. In this section, it will be shown how the application can be organized into the `UserServices` and `BusinessServices` packages described in Chapter 4. Figure 14.10 shows the package structure of the new application:

Chapter 14: Fourth Programming Project

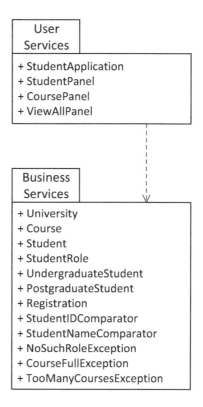

Figure 14.10: Package Structure of Student Management System

To implement the package structure, two folders must be created on the storage medium used for development. One folder is called **user** and the other is called **business**. They are created as sub-folders of a folder called **project4**. Next, the source code for the **BusinessServices** package is placed in the **business** folder and the source code for the **UserServices** package is placed in the **user** folder. Figure 14.11 shows the folder structure:

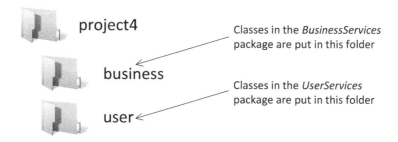

Figure 14.11: Folder Structure for Packages

The following line must be placed at the top of each source file in the **business** folder to indicate that it belongs to the **BusinessServices** package:

```
package business;
```

Similarly, the following line must be placed at the top of each source file in the **user** folder to indicate that it belongs to the **UserServices** package:

```
package user;
```

The classes in the **BusinessServices** package do not interact with the classes in the **UserServices** package. However, the classes in the **UserServices** package must necessarily know about the classes in the **BusinessServices** package (there is a dependency symbol from the **UserServices** package to the **BusinessServices** package in Figure 14.10). Thus, an **import** statement must be used in each class of the **UserServices** package to indicate that it needs to access the classes in the **BusinessServices** package. The **import** statement is written as follows:

```
import business.*;
```

These are all the changes that are required to organize the application in the two packages. The code for the third version of this programming project which uses packages can be downloaded from the book Web site. Instructions for using packages in specific development environments are also available at the book Web site.

Chapter 15

Object Persistence

The programs discussed so far in the book create and manipulate objects in various ways; however, when the programs terminate, the objects are lost since they were created in random access memory. A computer program typically stores data in some persistence medium so that the data is available to the program the next time it runs. This chapter explains how the objects in an object-oriented program can be made persistent. Three different approaches are discussed: storing the objects in a plain text file, storing the objects in a special file using a technique called object serialization, and storing the objects in a relational database. The suitability of each type of persistence storage is also discussed. The chapter does not provide a theoretical description of object persistence. Rather, it uses a practical example to show how it is achieved.

15.1 Objects to Be Made Persistent

This chapter uses a practical example to explain how the objects in an object-oriented application can be made persistent. The example deals with making the account objects in a banking application persistent. A UML class diagram of the **Bank** and **Account** classes in the application is given in Figure 15.1.

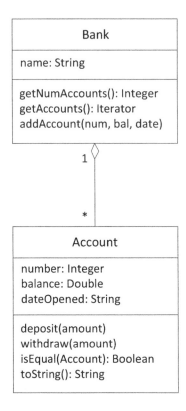

Figure 15.1: Bank and Account Classes

In order to make the **Account** objects persistent, sufficient information must be stored about their state so that they can be restored to this state at some point in the future. Three approaches are used to store the **Account** objects: a text file, a relational database, and object serialization. The three approaches essentially provide a means for storing the values of the instance variables in each **Account** object. However, object serialization is the most "object-oriented" of the three approaches since it provides capabilities for dealing with the objects exactly as they are in the application.

15.2 Classes Used to Describe Object Persistence

In this chapter, eight classes are used to show how the **Account** objects in the banking application can be made persistent. These classes are described in Table 15.1.

Chapter 15: Object Persistence

Class	Purpose
Account	Instances of this class are the objects to be made persistent.
Bank	An instance of **Bank** contains a collection of Account instances to be made persistent.
Persistence	An abstract class that specifies two abstract methods for reading and saving **Account** objects from/to the persistence medium. It also contains methods which create the **Bank** and associated **Account** objects.
PersistenceText PersistenceRDB PersistenceSerial	These are three concrete subclasses of the **Persistence** class. They implement the abstract **read()** and **save()** methods in the **Persistence** class. The suffix "Text", "RDB", or "Serial" indicates whether a text file, a relational database, or serialization is used for persistence, respectively.
TestPersistenceRead	This class is used to test the reading of the **Account** objects from the persistence medium.
TestPersistenceRead	This class is used to test the saving of the **Account** objects to the persistence medium.

Table 15.1: Classes Used To Describe Object Persistence

A UML diagram showing the **Persistence** class and its three subclasses is given in Figure 15.2 below.

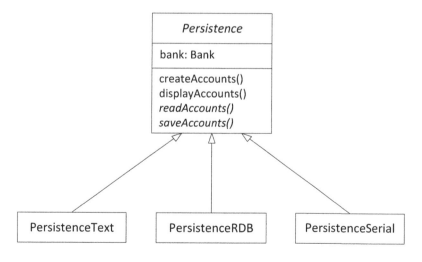

Figure 15.2: **Persistence** Class and its Subclasses

The `Persistence` class creates an instance of `Bank` and then uses the methods of `Bank` to manage the accounts in the application. The methods of the `Persistence` class are described in Table 15.2:

Method	Purpose
createAccounts()	Creates a set of `Account` objects to be made persistent.
displayAccounts()	Displays all the `Account` objects.
readAccounts()	Restores the `Account` objects from the type of persistence storage used.
saveAccounts()	Saves the `Account` objects to the type of persistence storage used.

Table 15.2: Methods of `Persistence` Class

The `readAccounts()` and `saveAccounts()` methods of `Persistence` are abstract and need to be implemented differently for each type of persistence medium used. `PersistenceText`, `PersistenceRDB`, and `PersistenceSerial` are concrete classes which inherit from `Persistence` and implement the `readAccounts()` and `saveAccounts()` methods.

The `TestPersistenceRead` class creates an instance of the appropriate `Persistence` subclass (depending on the persistence medium being used) and displays the `Account` objects in the system (there should be none since the system is now starting up). The accounts are then restored from persistence storage using the `readAccounts()` method. After that, the `Account` objects are displayed using the `displayAccounts()` method.

The `TestPersistenceSave` class creates an instance of the appropriate `Persistence` subclass (depending on the persistence medium being used) and creates and displays a set of `Account` objects which will be saved to the persistence medium. The `saveAccounts()` method is then called to save all the `Account` objects to the type of persistence storage used. The `readAccounts()` and `saveAccounts()` methods are called within a `try` block since a number of exceptions can occur when using persistence storage such as a file not being found in the persistence medium.

To test the sample programs, the `TestPersistenceSave` class should be executed first so that the `Account` objects will be saved to the persistence medium. Then, the `TestPersistenceRead` class should be executed to verify that the `Account` objects have indeed been restored from the persistence storage.

Chapter 15: Object Persistence

`PersistenceText` and `PersistenceSerial` use a file for object persistence. In Java, a file is a specialization of a concept known as an *input/output stream*. So, before discussing how the `readAcounts()` and `saveAccounts()` methods are implemented in the three `Persistence` subclasses, input/output streams will be explained.

15.3 Input / Output Streams in Java

In Java, an input/output (I/O) stream is used to represent an input source or an output destination. Streams can represent many different kinds of sources and destinations including disk files, devices, or other programs. Conceptually, a stream is simply a sequence of data that is used for either input or output. In this chapter, when a text file or serialization is used for persistence, the input source and output destination is a file stored on a disk or some other storage medium.

In order to read data from the file, an *input stream* must be created. Conversely, in order to save data to the file, an *output stream* must be created. It should be noted that streams are not used when accessing a relational database. Instead, a direct connection to the database is made using the Java Database Connectivity (JDBC) application programming interface (API).

The next three sections of this chapter discuss the details of the implementation of the `readAcounts()` and `saveAccounts()` methods in `PersistenceText`, `PersistenceRDB`, and `PersistenceSerial`. Each section discusses `saveAccounts()` before `readAccounts()` since this is the natural order in which objects are made persistent and then restored to their original state.

15.4 Using a Text File

`FileReader` and `FileWriter` are two character streams in Java. `FileReader` is an input stream and can be used for reading characters from a text file. `FileWriter` is an output stream and can be used for writing characters to a text file. These two streams support the reading and writing of only single characters at a time. To read or write larger units of characters from a text file (e.g., an entire line of characters with a line terminator at the end), the buffered streams, `BufferedReader` and `BufferedWriter` can be used.

15.4.1 Saving Account Objects to a Text File

To save `Account` objects to a file, the `saveAccounts()` method in `PersistenceText` first creates an instance of `FileWriter`, specifying the name of the file, "Accounts.txt". The constructor for FileWriter used in the example below creates a new file; if a file with that name already exists, it is erased. The FileWriter instance is then used to create an instance of BufferedWriter:

```
FileWriter fileWriter = null;
BufferedWriter bufferedWriter = null;

fileWriter = new FileWriter("Accounts.txt");
bufferedWriter = new BufferedWriter(fileWriter);
```

The saveAccounts() method then obtains an Iterator of Account objects from the Bank object by calling its getAccounts() method. The Iterator is traversed one by one, obtaining the corresponding Account object. A string line is created consisting of the values of the account number, balance, and dateOpened instance variables concatenated together. Each value in the string is separated by a comma. The string is then written to the BufferedWriter followed by a line terminator. The code is as follows:

```
Iterator<Account> i = bank.getAccounts();
while (i.hasNext()) {
    Account a = i.next();
    String line = a.getNumber() + "," + a.getBalance() + "," +
        a.getDateOpened();
    bufferedWriter.write(line);
    bufferedWriter.newLine();
}
```

Saving the Account objects to a text file essentially involves generating a string corresponding to the values of the instance variables and writing that string to a line of the file. Since the values in each line are separated by commas, the file is referred to as a "comma delimited text file". The process is depicted in Figure 15.3.

Chapter 15: Object Persistence

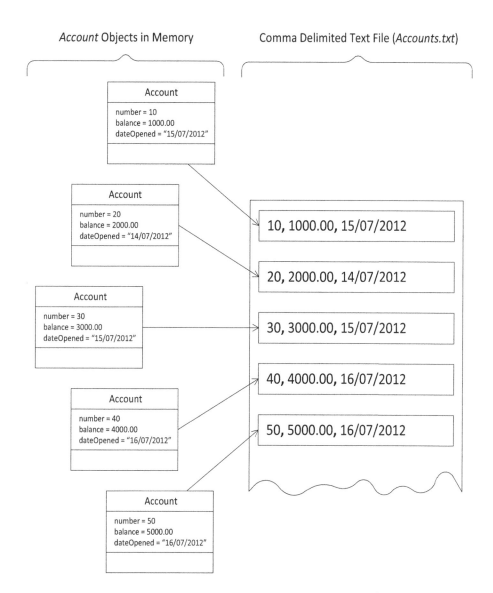

Figure 15.3: Saving **Account** Objects to a Text File

The code for creating the output streams and writing to the **BufferedWriter** is enclosed in a **try** block since reading and writing to an I/O stream can generate a number of exceptions (e.g., the file is not found or it is not in the required format). If something goes wrong during the process, a **finally** block is used to ensure that resources are released before exiting the **saveAccounts()** method. It is written as follows:

```
try {
   /* code for saving Account objects to text file */
}
finally {
   if (bufferedWriter != null)
      bufferedWriter.close();

   if (fileWriter != null)
      fileWriter.close();
}
```

The test for "not null" in the `finally` block is required since the streams may not have been created at the time when the exception occurred. It should be noted that the `finally` block is executed even if the code executes normally so that in all cases, the output streams are closed before the method terminates.

15.4.2 Reading Data for Account Objects from a Text File

The `readAccounts()` method creates an instance of `FileReader` specifying the name of the file to open. The `FileReader` instance is then used to create an instance of `BufferedReader`:

```
FileReader fileReader = null;
BufferedReader bufferedReader = null;

fileReader = new FileReader("Accounts.txt");
bufferedReader = new BufferedReader(fileReader);
```

The `readAccounts()` method must then read each line from the text file, separate the line into the data for each instance variable, and re-create the corresponding `Account` objects in memory. Reading a line of data is straightforward using the `readLine()` method of `BufferedReader`:

```
String line = bufferedReader.readLine();
```

The problem now is how to extract the data for the instance variables from the line. The `StringTokenizer` class solves this problem by splitting a line into sections based on a delimiter symbol. Since the values in the text file are delimited using a comma, an instance of `StringTokenizer` can be created for the line using the comma as the delimiter:

```
StringTokenizer st = new StringTokenizer(line, ",");
```

Chapter 15: Object Persistence

Starting from the left, the `nextToken()` method of `StringTokenizer` can be used to obtain the corresponding section of the string referred to as a *token*. The token is a string, so if necessary, it must be converted into the appropriate type using methods such as `Integer.parseInt()` or `Double.parseDouble()`. Figure 15.4 is a diagrammatic representation of the process.

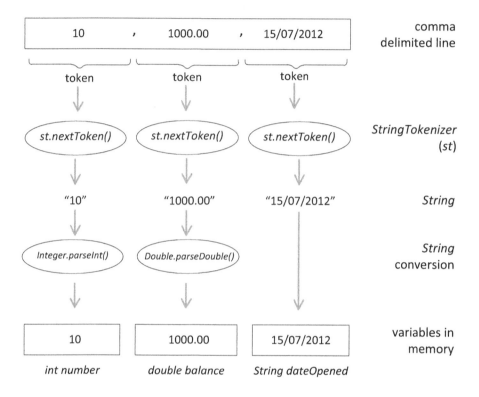

Figure 15.4: Reading Object Data from a Line of Text

The code to implement the reading of object data from a line of text is given below:

```
StringTokenizer st = new StringTokenizer(line, ",");
int number = Integer.parseInt(st.nextToken());
double balance = Double.parseDouble(st.nextToken());
String dateOpened = st.nextToken();
```

Once the data from a line has been extracted, the corresponding `Account` object can be re-created in memory by calling the `addAccount()` method from the `Bank` instance:

```
bank.addAccount(number, balance, dateOpened);
```

The above code must be repeated until there are no more lines in the file. This is easy to detect since the `readLine()` method of `BufferedReader` returns `null` when the end of file is reached.

Similar to the `saveAccounts()` method, a `finally` block is used to close the input streams before exiting the method.

15.4.3 Suitability of Text Files for Object Persistence

Using a text file is a simple approach for making the objects in an application persistent. This approach is feasible in an application where there are not many different types of objects. It is also feasible in environments where resources are low (e.g., devices with limited processing power, memory, or disk space). In these situations, a small collection of text files can perform the role of a database without the overhead of a database management system. However, text files have several disadvantages. For example, they can be easily viewed by anyone. To increase the level of security when using a text file, techniques such as encryption can be employed.

15.5 Using a Relational Database

This section explains how `Account` objects can be saved to a relational database and how they can be retrieved from the database. It gives an overview of a relational database and then discusses how the Java Database Connectivity API can be used to save and retrieve `Account` objects from the database. Similar to when a text file is used, only the attribute values of the `Account` objects are stored in the database.

15.5.1 Relational Databases

A relational database consists of a collection of *tables* for storing data on entities. A table has a set of *columns* which correspond to the attributes of an entity being stored (similar to the attributes of a class). Each *row* in the table contains the data for one entity (similar to the values of the instance variables of a single object). Figure 15.5 shows an `Account` table for storing data on accounts such as `number`, `balance`, and `dateOpened`.

Chapter 15: Object Persistence

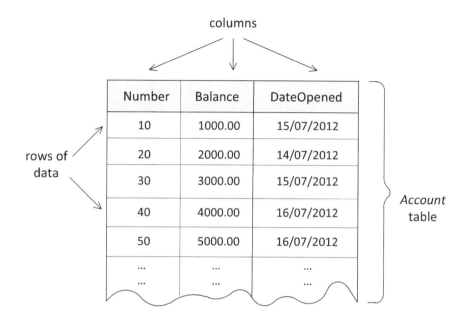

Figure 15.5: The **Account** Table in a Relational Database

A relational database management system (RDBMS) is software responsible for the storage, maintenance, and retrieval of data in a relational database. RDBMSs are widely used in businesses and organizations around the world. Typical examples include SQL Server®, Access®, MySQL®, and Oracle®.

SQL is a language that is commonly used to access data in a relational database. To insert a row in the **Account** table, the following SQL statement can be used:

```
INSERT INTO Account (number, balance, dateOpened) VALUES
(10, 1000.00, '15/07/2012/')
```

To list the values of the attributes of each row in the **Account** table, the following SQL statement can be used:

```
SELECT number, balance, dateOpened FROM Account
```

In order for a Java application to store and retrieve data from an RDBMS, it must first be able to connect to the database as an authorized user. Next, it must be able to send SQL statements to the RDBMS and receive data from the RDBMS. These tasks can be accomplished through the Java Database Connectivity API.

15.5.2 Java Database Connectivity (JDBC) API

The Java Database Connectivity (JDBC) API provides a means for a Java application to connect to a relational database and perform operations on the database. The JDBC API classes are in two packages, `java.sql` and `javax.sql`. The JDBC API specifies a `DriverManager` class which is responsible for setting up connections to the relational database. In order to do so, a *JDBC driver* must be available for the target RDBMS. This JDBC driver will translate calls to the JDBC API to calls to the specific RDBMS.

The Java application must first inform the `DriverManager` about the JDBC driver that will be used to access the RDBMS. Next, it must supply a *connection string* to the `DriverManager`. The `DriverManager` will use this string to connect to the RDBMS and logon on to the database using the user name and password supplied in the string. Table 15.3 gives an example of a JDBC driver and connection string for SQL Server®.

JDBC Driver	"com.microsoft.sqlserver.jdbc.SQLServerDriver"
Connection String	"jdbc:sqlserver://localhost:1433;databaseName=Bank;user=Oopbook;password=Oopb00k2013"

Table 15.3: JDBC Driver and Connection String for SQL Server®

It is possible to change the JDBC driver and RDBMS by changing only the information supplied to the `DriverManager`. Also, the same application can connect to multiple heterogeneous RDBMSs using different connection strings.

The JDBC architecture is shown in Figure 15.6.

Chapter 15: Object Persistence

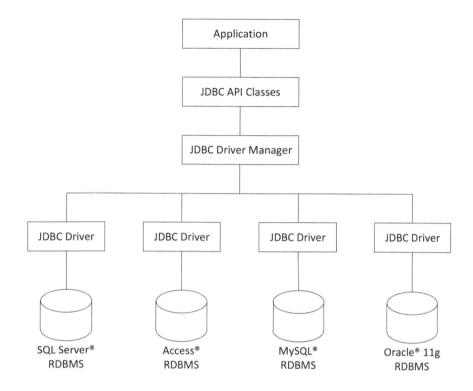

Figure 15.6: JDBC Architecture

15.5.3 Saving Account Objects to a Database

Before **Account** objects can be saved to a database, both the database and the **Account** table must have already been created. Typically, this will be done using tools provided by the vendor of the RDBMS. Of the four RDBMSs shown in Figure 15.6, only Access® permits the actual database files to be used independently of the DBMS. An Access® database with the **Account** table already created can be downloaded from the book Web site.

An important aspect of using a database is obtaining a connection to the database (which is stored in a **Connection** object) and creating a **Statement** object which provides a means to create and execute SQL statements. These objects are declared as follows in the **saveAccounts()** method:

```
Connection connection = null;
Statement stmt = null;
```

To save `Account` objects to the `Account` table, the `saveAccounts()` method in `PersistenceRDB` first informs the JDBC `DriverManager` about the JDBC driver using the `Class.forName()` method:

```
Class.forName(JdbcDriver);
```

It then supplies the connection string to the `DriverManager` using its `getConnection()` method (a class method). This causes the `DriverManager` to connect to the RDBMS using the JDBC driver and it then logs on to the database using the user name and password supplied in the connection string:

```
connection = DriverManager.getConnection(connectionStr);
```

Once the `DriverManager` connects successfully to the RDBMS, it returns a `Connection` object. This `Connection` object can be used to create a `Statement` object which is the conduit through which SQL statements can be sent to the RDBMS using its `execute()`, `executeQuery()`, and `executeUpdate()` methods:

```
stmt = connection.createStatement();
```

Similar to `PersistenceText`, the `saveAccounts()` method obtains an `Iterator` of `Account` objects from the `Bank` object by calling its `getAccounts()` method. The `Iterator` is traversed one by one, obtaining the corresponding `Account` object. An SQL INSERT statement is then composed, consisting of the values of the account `number`, `balance`, and `dateOpened` instance variables. The INSERT statement is then sent to the RDBMS by invoking the `executeQuery()` method of the `Statement` object. The code is as follows:

```
Iterator<Account> i = bank.getAccounts();
while (i.hasNext()) {
   Account a = i.next();
   String insertRow = "INSERT INTO Account
      (number, balance, dateOpened) VALUES (" +
         a.getNumber() + ", " +
         a.getBalance() + ", '" +
         a.getDateOpened() + "'" +
      ")";

   stmt.execute(insertRow);
}
```

Chapter 15: Object Persistence

Figure 15.7 shows the SQL INSERT statement that is generated for a given Account object.

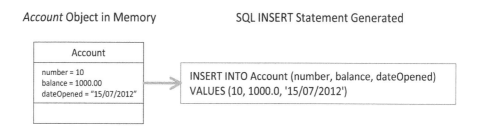

Figure 15.7: SQL Statement to Insert an **Account** Object

Thus, saving an **Account** object to a relational database essentially involves generating an SQL INSERT statement corresponding to the values of its instance variables and then executing the INSERT statement using the appropriate method from the **Statement** object. Each **Account** object becomes a row in the **Account** table. The process is depicted in Figure 15.8.

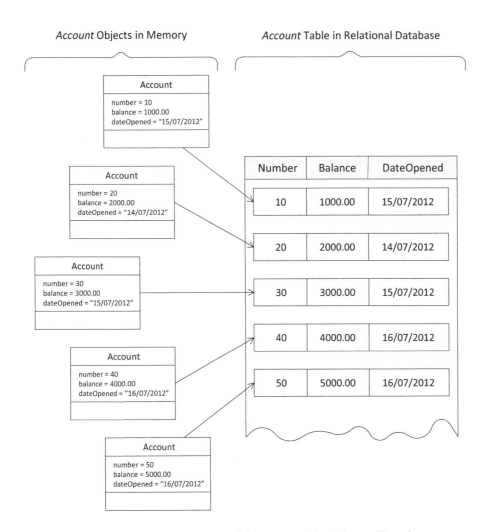

Figure 15.8: Saving **Account** Objects to a Relational Database

The code for creating the JDBC objects and saving to the database is enclosed in a **try** block since reading and writing to the database can generate a number of exceptions (e.g., incorrect SQL syntax). If something goes wrong during the process, a **finally** block is used to ensure that database resources are released before exiting the **saveAccounts()** method. The code for the **saveAccounts()** method is given below:

```
public void saveAccounts() throws Exception {

  Connection connection = null;
  Statement stmt = null;
```

Chapter 15: Object Persistence

```
try {
   Class.forName(JdbcDriver);
   connection = DriverManager.getConnection(connectionStr);

   stmt = connection.createStatement();

   :

   int numAccounts = 0;

   Iterator<Account> i = bank.getAccounts();
   while (i.hasNext()) {
      Account a = i.next();
      String insertRow = "INSERT INTO Account
         (number, balance, dateOpened) VALUES (" +
            a.getNumber() + ", " +
            a.getBalance() + ", '" +
            a.getDateOpened() + "'" +
         ")";

      stmt.execute(insertRow);
      numAccounts++;
   }

   System.out.println
      ("# rows inserted in Account table: " + numAccounts);
}

finally {

   if (stmt != null)
      stmt.close();

   if (connection != null)
      connection.close();
}
}
```

The test for "not **null**" in the **finally** block is required since the JDBC objects may not have been created at the time when the exception occurred. It should be noted that the **finally** block is executed even if the code executes normally so that the JDBC objects are always closed before the method terminates.

In the code available for download, the existing rows of the `Account` table are first deleted using the `executeUpdate()` method on the `Statement` object:

```
int rowsDeleted = stmt.executeUpdate("DELETE FROM Account");
```

The `executeUpdate()` method returns the amount of rows affected by the SQL statement. The rows are deleted simply for testing purposes since a user may run `TestPersistenceSave` several times and insert duplicates in the database if the `Account` table is not set up properly. This problem does not occur with `PersistenceText` since the file is re-created each time the program is executed.

15.5.4 Reading Data for `Account` Objects from a Database

In order to read data from a relational database, it is necessary to first obtain a `Connection` object and a `Statement` object as described in the preceding subsection.

To obtain all the rows of data in the `Account` table, the method `executeQuery()` is invoked on the `Statement` object with the SQL statement as a parameter:

```
ResultObject rs = null;
:
rs = stmt.executeQuery
     ("SELECT number, balance, dateOpened FROM Account");
```

The rows from the `Account` table which satisfy the query are returned in a `ResultSet` object, `rs`. A `ResultSet` object can be viewed as a table of rows satisfying the query. The `ResultSet` object is in some way similar to an `Iterator` and has a pointer indicating the next row of data to be returned. Initially, this pointer is positioned before the first row. The `ResultSet` object returned by the `executeQuery()` method above is shown in Figure 15.9.

Chapter 15: Object Persistence

	Number	Balance	DateOpened
pointer is initially just before first row	10	1000.00	15/07/2012
	20	2000.00	14/07/2012
	30	3000.00	15/07/2012
	40	4000.00	16/07/2012
	50	5000.00	16/07/2012

ResultSet

Figure 15.9: ResultSet Returned from Query

The next() method advances the pointer to the next row. If there are no more rows in the ResultSet, the next() method returns false. If the pointer is currently positioned on a valid row of the ResultSet, methods such as getInt(), getDouble(), getString(), etc. can be used to obtain the data from the row by specifying the name of the column as a parameter.

For example, to find the number attribute of the row (which is an integer), the getInt() method of the ResultSet can be used. The code for obtaining the values of all the instance variables of an Account object is as follows:

```
int number = rs.getInt("number");
double balance = rs.getDouble("balance");
String dateOpened = rs.getString("dateOpened");
```

Once the data from a row in the ResultSet has been extracted, the corresponding Account object can be re-created in memory by calling the addAccount() method on the Bank instance.

```
bank.addAccount(number, balance, dateOpened);
```

This code is repeated as long as there are more rows of data in the ResultSet object (i.e., as long as rs.next() is true).

Just like with the saveAccounts() method, before exiting, a finally block is used to close the objects from the JDBC API which were used to access the database. Here is the complete code for restoring the Account objects from the rows of the Account table:

```
public void readAccounts() throws Exception {
```

```java
Connection connection = null;
Statement stmt = null;
ResultSet rs = null;

try {
   Class.forName(JdbcDriver);
   connection = DriverManager.getConnection(connectionStr);

   stmt = connection.createStatement();

   rs = stmt.executeQuery
      ("SELECT number, balance, dateOpened FROM Account");

   while (rs.next()) {
      int number = rs.getInt("number");
      double balance = rs.getDouble("balance");
      String dateOpened = rs.getString("dateOpened");
      bank.addAccount(number, balance, dateOpened);
   }
}

finally {

   if (rs != null)
      rs.close();

   if (stmt != null)
      stmt.close();

   if (connection != null)
      connection.close();
   }
}
```

15.5.5 Test Programs

In the `TestPersistenceRead` and `TestPersistenceSave` classes, the JDBC driver information and connection string information must be supplied. For the SQL Server® RDBMS, the JDBC driver is specified as follows:

```
private static final String JdbcDriver;
JdbcDriver = "com.microsoft.sqlserver.jdbc.SQLServerDriver";
```

Chapter 15: Object Persistence

The connection string can be specified as follows:

```
private static final String connectionStr;

connectionStr =

"jdbc:sqlserver://localhost:1433;databaseName=Bank;user=Oopbook;password=Oopb00k2012";
```

Note that the `databaseName`, `user`, and `password` fields have to be changed to suit the specifics of database being used. The string "`localhost:1433`" may also have to be changed depending on where the database is located (e.g., standalone or networked). More information about this is available at the book Web site.

To use another RDBMS such as one of those shown in Figure 15.6, all that has to be done is to change the JDBC driver information and connection string to what is required for accessing that RDBMS. The book Web site provides the necessary driver information and connection strings for the four database management systems shown in Figure 15.6.

15.5.6 Suitability of Relational Database for Object Persistence

Relational databases are widely used in businesses and organizations. Thus, it is a feasible approach for storing objects since the object data is then available to the wide range of applications that are able to access a relational database. The JDBC API also makes it possible to switch the RDBMS being used according the needs of the application or other business constraints. However, one disadvantage is that it requires a mapping between Java and the SQL language used by relational databases.

15.6 Using Object Serialization

In order to save `Account` objects using serialization, the `Account` class must implement the `Serializable` interface (which is available in the `java.io` package). Interestingly, this interface does not declare any methods; its sole purpose is to indicate that `Account` objects can be made persistent using serialization. Thus, the `Account` class is declared as follows:

```
import java.io.Serializable;
public class Account implements Serializable {
    :
```

}

It is possible to serialize different types of objects in the same file. However, to correctly restore the objects when de-serializing, they must be read in the same order that they were written to the file.

Also, when using serialization, end-of-file cannot be checked as with a text file. If an attempt is made to read an `Account` object from a file and the file has come to an end, the run-time system generates an exception, `EOFException`. Instead of relying on an exception to be generated, it is better to first write a value to the file to indicate how many `Account` objects are stored.

The implementation of `saveAccounts()` and `readAccounts()` will now be discussed.

15.6.1 Saving `Account` Objects using Serialization

In order to save objects to a file using serialization, a `FileOutputStream` to the underlying file must first be created. A `FileInputStream` provides byte-level access to the data in a file. The `FileOutputStream` is then wrapped around an `ObjectOutputStream` which allows entire objects to be saved to the file. These two streams are declared and created as follows:

```
FileOutputStream fos = null;
ObjectOutputStream oos = null;

fos = new FileOutputStream("Accounts.ser");
oos = new ObjectOutputStream(fos);
```

To write an `Account` object to the file, "`Accounts.ser`", the `writeObject()` method is invoked on `oos`, supplying an `Account` object as the parameter. For example,

```
Account a;
:
oos.writeObject(a);
```

To save all the `Account` objects to the file, an `Iterator` for the `Account` objects is obtained and traversed. Each `Account` object is written to the file using the `writeObject()` method. However, before saving the first `Account` object, the number of `Account` objects to be saved (an integer value) is written to the file using the `writeInt()` method. The code for the `saveAccounts()` method is given below:

```
public void saveAccounts() throws Exception {

   FileOutputStream fos = null;
   ObjectOutputStream oos = null;

   try {
      fos = new FileOutputStream("Accounts.ser");
      oos = new ObjectOutputStream(fos);

      int numAccounts = bank.getNumAccounts();
      oos.writeInt(numAccounts);
         // write number of accounts first to the file

      Iterator<Account> i = bank.getAccounts();
      while (i.hasNext()) {
         Account a = i.next();
         oos.writeObject(a);
      }
   }
   finally {
      if (oos != null)
         oos.close();

      if (fos != null)
         fos.close();
   }
}
```

15.6.2 Reading Account Objects using Serialization

To restore the **Account** objects from the serialized file, a **FileInputStream** to the underlying file must first be created. This must then be wrapped around an **ObjectInputStream**. These two streams are declared and created as follows:

```
FileInputStream fis = null;
ObjectInputStream ois = null;

fis = new FileInputStream("Accounts.ser");
ois = new ObjectInputStream(fis);
```

The amount of **Account** objects in the file is first obtained using **readInt()**:

```
int numAccounts = ois.readInt();
```

Each `Account` object can be read from the file, one at a time, using the `readObject()` method of the `ObjectInputStream`. However, the `readObject()` method does not know the type of the object (since the serialized file may have been created by another program) so it returns the object as type `Object`. This needs to be cast to an `Account` object:

```
Account a = (Account) ois.readObject();
```

Now, the `Bank` class does not have a method to add an `Account` object to its collection of `Account` objects (see Figure 15.1). The `addAccount()` method of `Bank` takes a number, balance, and dateOpened values as parameters and then proceeds to create an instance of `Account` and insert it in its collection of `Account` objects.

One solution to this problem is to obtain the values for number, balance, and dateOpened from the `Account` object and then call the `addAccount()` method of bank to create and insert the new `Account`:

```
bank.addAccount(number, balance, dateOpened);
```

This approach is similar to that used when reading from a text file or a relational database. However, it does not take advantage of the ability to read entire objects from an `ObjectInputStream`. A much simpler approach is to serialize the entire `ArrayList` of `Account` objects (which is managed by the `Bank` instance). This is discussed in the next sub-section.

15.6.3 Alternative Approach for Serializing `Account` Objects

Since an `ArrayList` is an object and `ArrayList` implements the `Serializable` interface (as indeed, many of the classes in Java), it can be saved to a file using the `writeObject()` method. The serialization process stores not only the `ArrayList` but all the `Account` objects that are contained in the `ArrayList`.

It should be noted that the class that is responsible for saving the objects, `PersistenceSerial`, does not have access to the `ArrayList` of `Account` objects, which is maintained by the instance of `Bank`. It is possible for `Bank` to provide public access to the `ArrayList`. However, giving uncontrolled public access to collections of data is not recommended in an object-oriented application. One solution is to let the `Bank` class be responsible for saving and

Chapter 15: Object Persistence

reading its own collection of **Account** objects. This requires the **Bank** class to implement the **saveAccounts()** and **readAccounts()** methods.

An outline of the **saveAccounts()** method in **Bank** is given below:

```
public void saveAccounts() throws IOException {
    :
    try {
        :
        oos.writeObject(accounts);
    }

    finally {
        :
    }
}
```

Note that the **accounts** variable refers to the **ArrayList** of **Account** objects managed by the **Bank** instance. As can be seen, all that has to be done to serialize the **Account** objects in the **ArrayList** is to call **writeObject()** with the **ArrayList** itself! Restoring the **ArrayList** of **Account** objects from the file is just as straightforward:

```
public void readAccounts() throws IOException,
    ClassNotFoundException {

    :
    try {
        :
        accounts = (ArrayList<Account>) ois.readObject();
    }

    finally {
        :
    }
}
```

Since the instance of **Bank** has its own implementation of **saveAccounts()** and **readAccounts()**, the corresponding methods in **PersistenceSerial** simply invoke these methods on the **Bank** instance. This is another example of delegation. The **saveAccounts()** method in **PersistenceSerial** can be implemented as follows:

```
public void saveAccounts() throws Exception {
```

```
    bank.saveAccounts();
}
```

One might wonder if it is possible to the store the instance of **Bank** that was created in **PersistenceSerial**? This is indeed possible and enables the instance of **Bank** to be saved together with all its data including the value of its **name** instance variable and the **ArrayList** of **Account** objects. The example code contains two methods **saveBank()** and **readBank()** that are responsible for serializing and de-serializing the instance of **Bank**. However, in order to do so, the **Bank** class must implement the **Serializable** interface.

Before closing, it should be noted that in order to test the different approaches for object serialization discussed in this sub-section, it is necessary to modify certain parts of the code in **PersistenceSerial**, **TestPersistenceRead**, and **TestPersistenceSave**. These modifications are indicated in the respective source files.

15.6.4 Suitability of Serialization for Object Persistence

Of the three approaches discussed for object persistence, serialization is the most powerful since it enables objects to be stored exactly as they are in memory without the conversions required when text files or a relational database is used. Object serialization also makes it easy to store objects that refer to other objects as explained in the preceding sub-section. However, serialized files are not portable. They can only be understood by Java applications which know how the objects are stored in the file.

15.7 Objects that Contain Other Objects

Consider the case where a bank contains accounts and customers, and a customer can have one or more account. This scenario is depicted in the UML diagram shown in Figure 15.10:

Chapter 15: Object Persistence

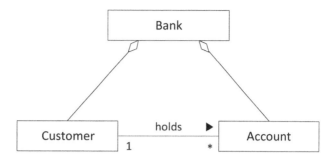

Figure 15.10: Classes in Banking Application

Suppose that we are given an **Account** object and we wish to find the customer who owns or holds the account. From Figure 15.10, we observe that one **Account** object is related to exactly one **Customer** object (and one **Customer** object is related to zero or more **Account** objects). To implement the relationship between **Account** and **Customer**, we can keep a reference to the associated **Customer** object in each **Account** object, as explained in Chapter 7. Thus, given an **Account** object, we can use the reference to find the corresponding **Customer** object.

Now, suppose that **Account** objects and **Customer** objects have to be saved to a relational database, but in different tables. To do this, we have to find a way to save **Account** objects in one table and **Customer** objects in another table yet maintain the link between **Account** objects and **Customer** objects.

In the world of relational databases, links between two tables such as **Account** and **Customer** are established through the use of a *foreign key*. So, each row in the **Account** table will contain data for an account (such as **number**, **balance**, and **dateOpened**) as well as the foreign key for the customer owning the account (this is normally the *primary key* of the corresponding row in the **Customer** table). When an **Account** object is being restored during **readAccounts()**, the associated **Customer** object is found by looking up the foreign key; the **Customer** object is then stored as an attribute of the **Account** object. This implies that the **Customer** objects must be restored first from the database. A similar approach has to be taken if a text file is used for object persistence.

However, if serialization is used and the instance of **Bank** is serialized, all these issues are automatically taken care of by the **writeObject()** method. Nevertheless, if the collection of **Customer** objects is serialized to a different file than the **Account** objects, the issue of duplicate objects must be dealt with. This is because when **Account** objects are serialized to a file, **Customer** objects end up in the file also, since **Account** objects contain references to

Customer objects. Thus, the same Customer objects will be present in both files and the de-serialization mechanism cannot look across files to remove duplicates.

In the next chapter, the objects from the fourth programming project will be made persistent using the three approaches described in this chapter. There are a number of cases where one object contains several other objects so it is instructive to study how they are stored using each of the three approaches.

15.8 Applying Persistence Techniques to Other Applications

This chapter has shown how objects can be made persistent using three different approaches. To digress a little from the main theme of the book, it is possible to use these same techniques in ways that are not object-oriented. For example, one can read data from a text file and store it in a relational database. One can also read data from a relational database and store it in a text file. By extension, it is possible to read data from a relational database and generate Web pages (which is a text file marked up with tags written in the Hypertext Markup Language, HTML). This is the essence of Java technology such as Java Server Pages and Java Servlets. Thus, the techniques covered in this chapter can also be applied to a wide variety of interesting applications which need to access data from sources such as text files and relational databases.

Exercises

1. Explain how a `FileWriter` object and a `BufferedWriter` object can be used to write a line of text to a file. Conversely, explain how a `FileReader` object and a `BufferedReader` object can be used to read a line of text from a file.

2. Explain how the `StringTokenizer` class can be used to extract different types of data items from a string, where the data items are separated by spaces.

3. SQL is a data manipulation language for relational databases. In order to access a relational database, a user must first supply information needed to connect to the database; the user can then proceed to issue SQL statements to the database. Explain how these tasks are accomplished using the Java JDBC API.

Chapter 15: Object Persistence

4. Suppose that the `executeQuery()` method is invoked on a `Statement` object with a valid SQL statement as the argument. Explain how a client object can retrieve the data from the `ResultSet` object returned by the `executeQuery()` method.

5. A `Customer` class consists of the following attributes: `number`, `first name`, `last name`, `address`, and `contact number`. The first attribute is an integer quantity while the remaining four attributes are strings. Explain what is involved in:

    (a) Saving a collection of `Customer` objects to a text file and retrieving the `Customer` objects from the text file.

    (b) Saving a collection of `Customer` objects to a relational database and retrieving the `Customer` objects from the database.

    (c) Saving a collection of `Customer` objects using object serialization and de-serializing the `Customer` objects from the serialized file.

6. Explain why it is necessary to place the code for saving or retrieving object data from a persistence medium in a `try` block.

7. The `finally` block checks to see whether an input stream or an output stream is not `null` before closing the stream. When a relational database is used, the `finally` block checks to see if the `Connection` or `Statement` objects are not `null` before closing them. Why is there is a need to check that the objects are not `null` before closing them in all three cases?

8. An instance of an `Agent` class is associated in a one-to-many manner with instances of the `Customer` class in (5) above through a "supports" relationship. Thus, the `Customer` class has an additional attribute, `agent`, which is a reference to the agent who supports the customer. The `Agent` class has a unique identifier, `agentID` (of type `int`) as well as other attributes. Explain how the link between a `Customer` object and an `Agent` object is maintained when the objects are made persistent using (a) a text file (b) a relational database and (c) object serialization.

9. Give one advantage and one disadvantage of using each of the following for object persistence: (a) a text file (b) a relational database and (c) object serialization.

10. Explain how the JDBC API makes it possible for the same application to be used with different relational databases. How can different relational databases be used *simultaneously* in an application?

Chapter 16

Fifth Programming Project

This chapter shows how the objects from the fourth programming project can be made persistent using the three approaches discussed in Chapter 15. In particular, it shows how to store the objects in a text file, how to store the objects using object serialization, and how to store the objects in a relational database. The chapter also explains how to restore the state of the objects from each type of persistence medium. A simple `Persistence` interface is defined to standardize the access to each type of storage medium so that it is easy to switch the medium used for storing objects. The code examples are particularly valuable for this programming project and are available for download at the book Web site. Detailed instructions for connecting to several popular relational databases are also available at the book Web site.

16.1 Objects to be Made Persistent

In the fourth programming project, a singleton `University` object contains a collection of `Student` objects and a collection of `Course` objects. A student can have different roles at different times. Thus, a `Student` object consists of a collection of `StudentRole` objects. There are two roles, `UndergraduateStudent` and `PostgraduateStudent`. Each role inherits from `StudentRole`. Whenever a student registers for a course, an instance of the association class `Registration` is created, representing a link between the particular student and the particular course. Two collections are used to store the `Registration` objects in the system; one is indexed by `Student` and the other is indexed by `Course`.

In the previous chapter, a `Persistence` abstract class was defined which provides two abstract methods `read()` and `save()` for reading from and saving to the persistence medium. `PersistenceText`, `PersistenceRDB`, and `PersistenceSerial` are concrete subclasses of `Persistence` and provide method implementations for `read()` and `save()`. The `Persistence` class also provides concrete implementations of two methods, `createAccounts()` and `displayAccounts()`. The `createAccounts()` method creates the `Account` objects for saving to the persistence medium and the `displayAccounts()` method displays the `Account` objects on the console.

In this programming project, there is no need to create objects for saving to the persistence medium; there is also no need to display objects on the console. Both of these operations are handled through the graphical user interface. Thus, only the `read()` and `save()` methods are required in the `Persistence` class. Since these methods are abstract anyway, it is better to define `Persistence` as an interface. The `Persistence` interface is defined as follows:

```java
public interface Persistence {
    public abstract void read() throws Exception;
    public abstract void save() throws Exception;
}
```

Combining the domain classes from the fourth programming project with the `Persistence` classes, the UML diagram in Figure 16.1 is obtained. This chapter shows how the domain classes on the left side of the diagram can be made persistent using the `Persistence` classes on the right side.

Chapter 16: Fifth Programming Project

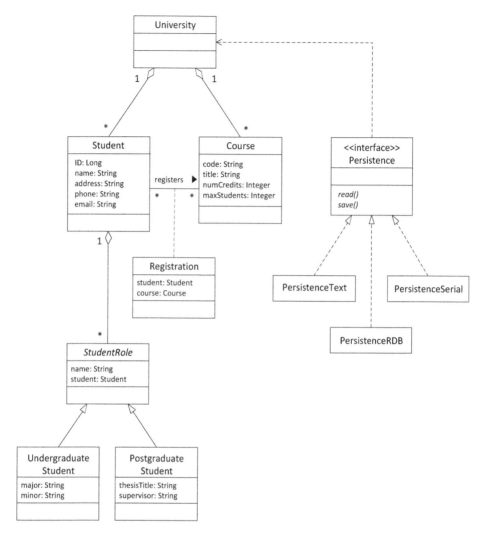

Figure 16.1: Classes in Fifth Programming Project

16.2 Changes to `StudentApplication`

The main class in the graphical user interface, `StudentApplication`, has been modified to automatically create an instance of the appropriate concrete subclass of `Persistence` when the application starts. The `read()` method is then invoked to populate all the collections in the `University` object with the data read from the persistence medium:

```
try {
    Persistence p = new ...  // constructor of Persistence subclass
```

```
      p.read();
}
catch (Exception e) {
   setStatus("Error in reading: " + e);
}
```

A new menu option, "*Save and Exit*" has also been added to the graphical user interface. It is shown in Figure 16.2.

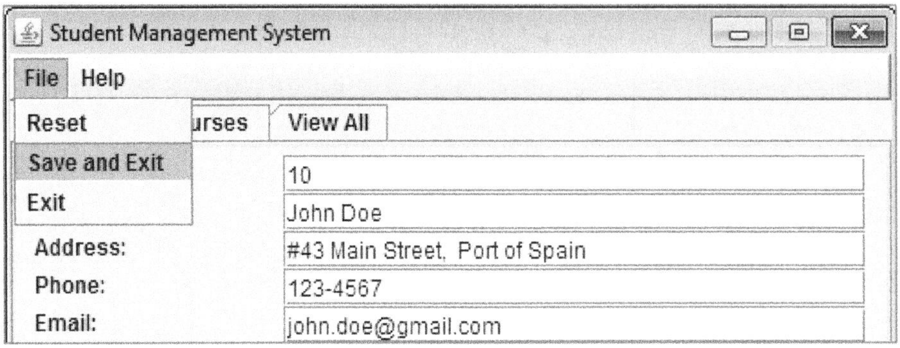

Figure 16.2: New Menu Option to Save Objects

When the "*Save and Exit*" menu option is selected, the following code invokes the `save()` method:

```
if (command.equals("Save and Exit")) {
   try {
      Persistence p = new ...  // constructor of Persistence subclass
      p.save();
      System.exit(0);          // exit application
   }
   catch (Exception e) {
      setStatus("Error in saving: " + e);
   }
}
```

Table 16.1 shows how to create an instance of each of the `Persistence` subclasses, where `university` is the singleton instance of `University` created by the graphical user interface.

Persistence Subclass	Constructor Call
PersistenceText	new PersistenceText(university)
PersistenceRDB	new PersistenceRDB(university, JdbcDriver, connectionStr)
PersistenceSerial	new PersistenceSerial(university)

Table 16.1: Creating an Instance of the **Persistence** Subclasses

Note that for `PersistenceRDB`, the `JdbcDriver` and `connectionStr` must be set in `StudentApplication` depending on the particular RDBMS being used. Chapter 15 provides more information on this. Information on the JDBC Driver and connection string for several databases can also be obtained at the book Web site. Once the values for `JdbcDriver` and `connectionStr` are set correctly, the code in `PersistenceRDB` can be used without modification to access any RDBMS for which a JDBC driver is available.

It should also be noted that the Student Management System can use any of the three types of media for persistence discussed in this chapter by simply changing the subclass of `Persistence` that is created in `StudentApplication`.

16.3 Using a Text File

Five comma-delimited text files are used to save data on the five different types of domain objects in the application. The data stored on an object is its state information, i.e., the values of its instance variables. The mapping between the domain classes and the text files is shown in Figure 16.3. The figure also shows the layout of the lines in each text file.

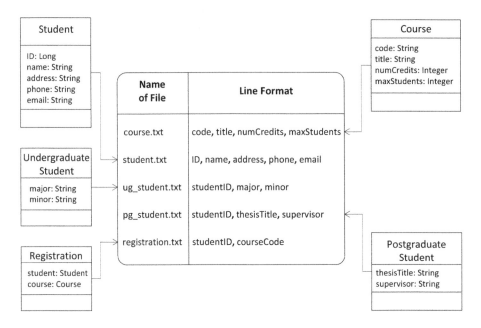

Figure 16.3: Text Files Corresponding to Domain Classes

16.3.1 Saving Objects to a Text File

The `save()` method of `PersistenceText` is implemented by calling methods to save objects from each domain class to its corresponding text file. The code is as follows:

```
public void save() throws Exception {

    saveCourses();
    saveStudents();
    saveUndergraduateStudents();
    savePostgraduateStudents();
    saveRegistrations();
}
```

Each of the methods called in `save()` is similar to the `saveAccounts()` method described in Chapter 15. It creates a `BufferedWriter` object and then composes a string consisting of the values of the relevant instance variables concatenated together with a comma delimiter. The string is then written to the text file.

Chapter 16: Fifth Programming Project

Saving data from a `Student` object or a `Course` object to a file is identical to saving data from an `Account` object to a file, as discussed in Chapter 15. Saving data from the other objects is a little different since `UndergraduateStudent` and `PostgraduateStudent` contain a `Student` object as a reference and `Registration` contain both a `Student` object and a `Course` object as references. An important question to ask when saving these objects is this: what data is required to re-create them? Table 16.2 gives the relevant methods from the `University` class that are required to create these objects and the arguments required for each one.

Method name	Arguments
addUndergraduateStudent()	long ID, String major, String minor
addPostgraduateStudent()	long ID, String thesisTitle, String supervisor
registerStudent()	long studentID, String courseCode

Table 16.2: Data Required for Creating Instances of
`UndergraduateStudent`, `PostgraduateStudent`, and `Registration`

Based on the information listed in Table 16.2, it is only necessary to save the data listed in the *Arguments* column of the table when saving data on `UndergraduateStudent`, `PostgraduateStudent`, and `Registration` objects, despite the object references they contain. The object references are used to extract the primitive values required for the comma-delimited line. For example, the following is the line generation code for `Registration` objects, where `registration` is an instance of `Registration`:

```
String line = registration.getStudent().getID() + "," +
    registration.getCourse().getCode();
```

16.3.2 Reading Data for Objects from a Text File

The `read()` method of `PersistenceText` is implemented as follows:

```
public void read() throws Exception {

    readCourses();
    readStudents();
    readUndergraduateStudents();
    readPostgraduateStudents();
    readRegistrations();
}
```

Each of the methods called in `read()` is similar to the `readAccounts()` method described in Chapter 15. It creates a `BufferedReader` object to read a line from the relevant text file. After using a `StringTokenizer` instance to extract the data for the instance variables, an appropriate `add()` method from `University` is called to re-create the object. For example, the code to obtain the data and re-create an `UndergraduateStudent` object is given below:

```
StringTokenizer st = new StringTokenizer(line, ",");
long id = Long.parseLong(st.nextToken());
String major = st.nextToken();
String minor = st.nextToken();
university.addUndergraduateStudent(id, major, minor);
```

Since `addUndergraduateStudent()` requires the student ID to correspond to an already existing `Student` object, it is important to execute `readStudents()` before `readUndergraduateStudents()` in `PersistenceText`.

16.4 Using a Relational Database

As discussed in Chapter 15, using a relational database for object persistence is similar to using a text file except that objects from the JDBC API are used to save and retrieve the domain objects. Five tables are used to save data on the domain objects, similar to the case with text files. The data corresponds to instance data from five of the domain classes. The mapping between the domain classes and the tables in the database is shown in Figure 16.4. The figure also shows the column names and SQL data types of each table (in brackets).

Chapter 16: Fifth Programming Project

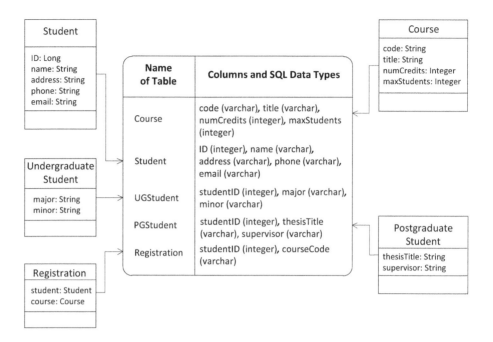

Figure 16.4: Tables Corresponding to Domain Classes

Before reading from or saving to the database, the database and the five tables shown in Figure 16.4 must be created. Figure 16.5 shows a model of the five tables generated by the *Relationship* tool in Microsoft Access®.

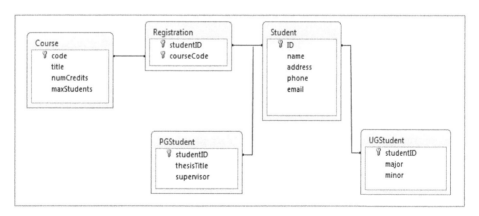

Figure 16.5: Tables in Microsoft Access®

The key symbol next to an attribute in a table indicates that this attribute is either the *primary key* (e.g., ID is the primary key of Student) or one component of the primary key (e.g., courseCode is one component of the primary key of **Registration**). The line from one table to another indicates that there is a relationship between the two tables (similar to the line drawn between classes in the UML).

A Microsoft Access® database already created with the five tables above is available for download at the book Web site. Microsoft Access® is not required to use the database.

16.4.1 Saving Objects to a Database

The data saved in each text file in **PersistenceText** corresponds exactly to the data that needs to be saved in each table of the relational database. The **save()** method in **PersistenceRDB** is implemented exactly as in **PersistenceText** except that it first creates a **Connection** object to the database:

```
public void save() throws Exception {

  Class.forName(JdbcDriver);
  connection = DriverManager.getConnection(connectionStr);

  saveCourses();
  saveStudents();
  saveUndergraduateStudents();
  savePostgraduateStudents();
  saveRegistrations();
}
```

JdbcDriver and **connectionStr** are instance variables of **PersistenceRDB** which get their values when **PersistenceRDB** is instantiated by the **StudentApplication** class. **connection** is an instance variable of **PersistenceRDB** and is thus available to all the methods called in **save()**.

The methods called by **save()** are implemented in a similar fashion to the **saveAccounts()** method in Chapter 15. Each method creates a **Statement** object and for each object to be saved, it composes an SQL INSERT statement using the values of the relevant instance variables. This SQL statement is executed using the **execute()** method of the **Statement** object.

16.4.2 Reading Data for Objects from a Database

The data to be read from each table in **PersistenceRDB** corresponds exactly to the data in each text file read by **PersistenceText**. The **read()** method in

`PersistenceRDB` is implemented exactly as in `PersistenceText` except that it first creates a `Connection` object to the database:

```
public void read() throws Exception {

  Class.forName(JDBCDriver);
  connection = DriverManager.getConnection(connectionStr);

  readCourses();
  readStudents();
  readUndergraduateStudents();
  readPostgraduateStudents();
  readRegistrations();
}
```

The methods in `read()` are implemented in a similar fashion to the `readAccounts()` method in Chapter 15. Each method creates a `Statement` object; the rows from the relevant table are then obtained by calling the `execute()` method of the `Statement` object with an appropriate SQL SELECT statement. The rows satisfying the query are returned in a `ResultSet` object. Data from each row in the `ResultSet` is extracted and used to re-create the corresponding objects in memory just like when text files are used.

16.5 Using Object Serialization

As indicated in Chapter 15, it is easier to save and restore collections of objects rather than individual objects using object serialization. This is the approach that will be taken to store the collections of objects managed by the singleton `University` instance. There are four collections of objects to be serialized:

```
private HashMap<Long, Student> students;
private HashMap<String, Course> courses;
private HashMap<Student, ArrayList<Registration>> registrations1;
private HashMap<Course, ArrayList<Registration>> registrations2;
```

As explained in Chapter 15, it is better for `University` to save and restore its own collections instead of giving `public` access to its collections. Thus, the `University` class also implements the `Persistence` interface and provides method implementations for `read()` and `save()`. As a result, the `PersistenceSerial` class doesn't have much work to do; its `read()` and `save()` methods simply invoke the `read()` and `save()` methods on `University`, respectively.

16.5.1 Saving Objects using Serialization

The four collections of objects are serialized to a single file, "University.ser". A FileOutputStream to this file is first created and then it is wrapped around an ObjectOutputStream. Each collection is then written to the ObjectOutputStream using its writeObject() method. The code is as follows:

```
FileOutputStream fos = null;
ObjectOutputStream oos = null;

fos = new FileOutputStream("University.ser");
oos = new ObjectOutputStream(fos);

oos.writeObject(students);
oos.writeObject(courses);
oos.writeObject(registrations1);
oos.writeObject(registrations2);
```

16.5.2 Reading Objects Using Serialization

The "University.ser" file is de-serialized by first creating a FileInputStream from the file and then wrapping the FileInputStream around an ObjectInputStream. Each collection is then restored from the ObjectInputStream using its readObject() method. The collections must be read in the same order that they were saved to the file. The code is as follows:

```
FileInputStream fis = null;
ObjectInputStream ois = null;

fis = new FileInputStream("University.ser");
ois = new ObjectInputStream(fis);

students = (HashMap<Long, Student>) ois.readObject();
courses = (HashMap<String, Course>) ois.readObject();
registrations1 = (HashMap<Student, ArrayList<Registration>>)
ois.readObject();
registrations2 = (HashMap<Course, ArrayList<Registration>>)
ois.readObject();
```

It should be noted that the readObject() method does not know the type of objects that are being read from the ObjectInputStream. Thus, the object returned must be cast to the appropriate type.

Chapter 16: Fifth Programming Project

16.5.3 Alternative Approaches for Serialization

It is possible to serialize the singleton instance of University either from the University class itself (using the this keyword to refer to the instance) or from the PersistenceSerial class. However, the de-serialization process fails. This is because the constructor of the University class is private and thus the readObject() method cannot re-create an instance of University.

Another possibility is to serialize the four collections to separate files. Table 16.3 shows the collections and the files in which they are saved.

Collection	Serialized File	Contents of Serialized File
students	Student.ser	HashMap of Student objects
courses	Course.ser	HashMap of Course objects
registrations1	Registration1.ser	HashMap of Registration objects; Student objects and Course objects
registrations2	Registration2.ser	HashMap of Registration objects; Student objects and Course objects

Table 16.3: Serializing Collections in Separate Files

Note that the serialized Registration files contain not only a HashMap of Registration objects but also Student objects and Course objects because these are needed in order to correctly restore Registration objects in memory.

Consider what happens when the objects are de-serialized from their respective files. First, the students HashMap is restored; this results in the Student objects being re-created in memory. This is followed by restoring the courses HashMap; this results in the Course objects being re-created.

When the "Registration1.ser" file is de-serialized, the Student objects and Course objects in the file are re-created. However, these objects already exist in memory due to the previous de-serialization of students and courses. The de-serialization process doesn't know that the same Student objects and Course objects are already in memory since different files are involved. So, it proceeds by re-creating the HashMap of Registration objects. However, the Registration objects refer to the newly created Student and Course objects, not those that were earlier serialized from students and courses.

Because of the duplicate `Student` objects and `Course` objects in memory, a `Student` object in the `students` `HashMap` will not have a corresponding list of registrations in the `registrations1` `HashMap`. Although the corresponding `Student` object is identical in terms of state, it has a different object reference. Therefore, it will be treated as if it is a different `Student` object and may even hash to different locations in the `HashMap`.

To solve this problem, the `hashCode()` method of `Student` and `Course` should be overridden so that the hash code will not be generated based on object references. Instead, the hash code should be generated based on the state of the objects. As a result, `Student` and `Course` objects which have the same state will now hash to the same location in their respective `HashMap`s. However, this is not enough. Even if two objects hash to the same location, they could still be considered different since a hash table permits more than one object to hash to the same location.

In order for the `HashMap` to know that two `Student` objects or two `Course` objects are the same, it is important to override the `equals()` method in these two classes as well. Thus, when two objects which are identical in state hash to the same location, the `equals()` method will tell the `HashMap` that they are the "same". This approach solves the problem of linking `Student` objects and `Course` objects with their related `Registration` objects in the `registrations1` and `registrations2` `HashMap`s; however, it should be noted that the duplicate `Student` and `Course` objects still exist in memory.

16.6 Packaging the Application

One more task needs to be undertaken before we complete the fifth programming project. At the end of the fourth programming project, the classes for the Student Management System were separated into two packages, `UserServices` and `BusinessServices`. The `Persistence` classes can now be placed in a `DataServices` package to complete all three tiers of the object-oriented application. Figure 16.6 shows the three packages that comprise the Student Management System.

Chapter 16: Fifth Programming Project

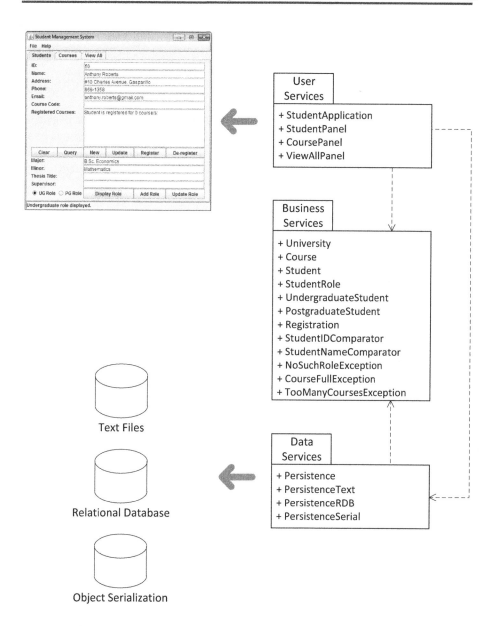

Figure 16.6: Three Tiers of the Student Management System

The `UserServices` package contains the classes which generate the graphical user interface. The `DataServices` package contains the classes which save the domain objects to a persistence medium. Since these two packages must have knowledge about the classes in the `BusinessServices` package, a dependency arrow is drawn to connect them to the `BusinessServices` package. The dependency is implemented in code by placing the following `import` statement in each class of the `UserServices` and `DataServices` packages:

```
import business.*;
```

There is also a dependency relationship between the `UserServices` package and the `DataServices` package. This is because classes in the `DataServices` package (e.g., `PersistenceRDB`) are invoked by the `StudentApplication` class in the `UserServices` package. Thus, the `StudentApplication` class has an additional `import` statement:

```
import data.*;
```

Note that the classes in the `BusinessServices` package do not know about the classes in either the `UserServices` package or the `DataServices` package. Thus, they can be re-used in different applications which employ different user interfaces or persistence media.

Chapter 17

Introduction to Graphical User Interface Programming

This chapter explains how to build a graphical user interface (GUI) for an object-oriented program. In Chapter 4, the three tiers of a typical object-oriented program were presented. These comprise *Business Services*, *Data Services*, and *User Services*. The Business Services tier has been discussed throughout the book. Three ways to implement the Data Services tier were discussed in the fifth programming project. In the first two programming projects, the User Services tier was written as a text-based user interface that interacts with the objects in the Business Services tier. In the third, fourth and fifth programming projects, the User Services tier consisted of a set of GUI components; however, apart from a UML diagram in Chapter 11, no explanations were given on how to develop the GUI. Now, in order to facilitate a complete understanding of all three tiers of an object-oriented program, this chapter describes how to develop the User Services tier using a small set of GUI components.

This chapter is essentially a simplification of the knowledge and skills required to develop a GUI for an object-oriented program. It only touches the surface of the large set of GUI components that can be used to build the User Services tier of a Java application. At the end of the chapter, readers will understand how to develop the user interface code that will produce a GUI that is almost identical to the one used in the third, fourth and fifth programming projects. The chapter reinforces many of the object-oriented concepts covered in this book by describing the object-oriented nature of the GUI components in Java. Once readers are familiar with the basic concepts of GUI programming, there are many good resources that can be consulted for building more sophisticated GUIs.

17.1 The Swing Toolkit

The Swing Toolkit can be used for building graphical user interfaces and adding interactivity to Java programs. It provides a wide variety of components such as labels, text fields, buttons, check boxes and list boxes. To use components from the Swing Toolkit, the following `import` statement is required:

```
import javax.swing.*;
```

In addition to the Swing components, it is often necessary to use packages from the Java Abstract Windowing Toolkit (AWT) to provide functionality related to the GUI. The following `import` statements are usually required to use these packages:

```
import java.awt.*;
import java.awt.event.*;
```

The remainder of this chapter shows how to build an increasingly complex GUI using a minimal set of Swing components. Detailed explanations of the Swing components will not be provided since the objective of this chapter is to focus on the object-oriented aspects of the GUI. The Swing and AWT APIs can be consulted to obtain more detailed explanations of the GUI components mentioned in this chapter. The book Web site also contains instructions for using the Java API from a local computer or from the Internet.

17.2 An Empty Window

The first step in building a GUI is to create a top-level window. This section explains how to write the code to generate a top-level window. Two versions of the code are presented.

17.2.1 First Version

A fundamental concept in GUI programming is that of a *window*. A window is usually a rectangular portion of the monitor screen that can operate independently of the rest of the screen. A window has a width and a height. It also has a title and a border. `JFrame` is a Swing component that is used for creating top-level windows. To create a top-level window for a Java GUI, a class can be written that inherits from `JFrame`.

The first application we will look at in this chapter is `EmptyWindow`. This application creates a window and does nothing else. The window does not

Chapter 17: Introduction to Graphical User Interface Programming

contain any other components. A UML diagram of the classes in the application is given in Figure 17.1.

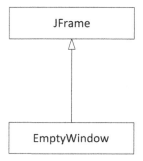

Figure 17.1: Classes in `EmptyWindow` Application

The `EmptyWindow` class inherits from `JFrame` and invokes some of its methods. It is written as follows:

```java
import javax.swing.*;

public class EmptyWindow extends JFrame
{
   public EmptyWindow() {
      setTitle("An Empty Window");
      setDefaultCloseOperation(EXIT_ON_CLOSE);
      setSize(300, 150);
      setVisible(true);
   }
}
```

The methods called in the constructor of `EmptyWindow` are either present in the `JFrame` class or are inherited from one of its ancestors (e.g., `Container` and `Component`). Since these methods are inherited, they can be used like any other method belonging to the `EmptyWindow` class. The methods called in the constructor of `EmptyWindow` are described in Table 17.1.

Method	Description
setTitle()	Puts a value on the title bar of the window.
setSize()	Establishes the dimensions of the window (width by height).
setVisible()	Makes the window disappear or reappear.
setDefaultCloseOperation()	Tells the application what to do when the user clicks on the "*Close*" button.

Table 17.1: Methods Used in `EmptyWindow`

The first argument of the `setSize()` method is the width of the window in pixels and the second argument is the height of the window in pixels. A newly created window is not visible on the desktop; to make the window visible, the `setVisible()` method must be used with an argument of `true`. Finally, the `setDefaultCloseOperation()` method tells the application what to do when the user clicks on the "*Close*" button at the top right hand corner of the window. The `EXIT_ON_CLOSE` argument tells the application to exit when the user clicks on "*Close*".

To create an instance of `EmptyWindow`, a `main()` method is written as follows:

```
public static void main(String[] args) {
   JFrame window = new EmptyWindow();
            // EmptyWindow "is-a" JFrame, by inheritance
}
```

The `main()` method can be written in a separate class or in the `EmptyWindow` class itself. Figure 17.2 gives a labeled screenshot of the window that is displayed when an instance of `EmptyWindow` is created.

Chapter 17: Introduction to Graphical User Interface Programming

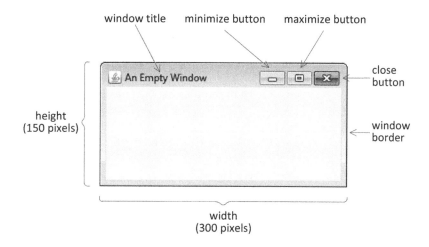

Figure 17.2: Window Displayed by `EmptyWindow`

Note that the window behaves just like the windows from other applications. For example, it can be re-sized by dragging the mouse at the borders. The window can be enlarged to occupy the entire desktop by clicking on the maximize button. The window can be made to temporarily "disappear" from the desktop by clicking on the minimize button. Finally, the application can be shut down by clicking on the close button.

17.2.2 Second Version

The simple `EmptyWindow` class can be enhanced by calling methods from its parent class `JFrame` or from the ancestors of `JFrame`. The Java API provides a detailed listing of the methods that are available in `JFrame` and its ancestor classes. Two enhancements to the constructor of `EmptyWindow` can easily be made. `EmptyWindow` presently positions the window at the top left hand corner of the screen. The `setLocationRelativeTo()` method of `Window` (an ancestor of `JFrame`) can be used to position the window at the center of the screen using an argument of `null`. Alternatively, the `setLocation()` method of `Component` can be used to position the window at some (x, y) location on the screen. Another change is to make it impossible for a user to adjust the size of the window by dragging on its borders. This is done by calling the `setResizable()` method of `Frame` (the direct superclass of `JFrame`) with a value of `false`.

The code for the enhanced constructor of `EmptyWindow` is given below:

```
public EmptyWindow() {
```

```
setTitle("An Empty Window: Version 2");
setDefaultCloseOperation(EXIT_ON_CLOSE);
setSize(300, 150);

setResizable(false);
                    // ensure that window cannot be resized

setLocationRelativeTo(null);
                    // position window at center of screen

setVisible(true);   // make the window visible
}
```

Now that we can display a window and manipulate the window in various ways, it is time to place some GUI components on the surface of the window. In the next section, we will learn how to do this using some simple GUI components.

17.3 Some Simple GUI Components

Consider the window shown in Figure 17.3. As the labels indicate, the surface of the window is populated with four types of visible GUI components: *labels*, *text fields*, *command buttons*, and a *text area*. This section describes each of these components. In the next section, it will be explained how these components can be put together to produce the GUI shown in Figure 17.3.

Chapter 17: Introduction to Graphical User Interface Programming

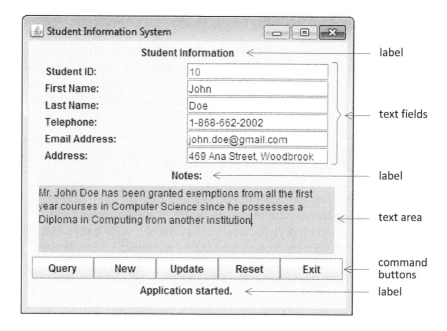

Figure 17.3: Window with Four Types of Visible GUI Components

17.3.1 Label

A *label* is a GUI component for displaying a short string or an image or both. It does not respond to input events such as clicking of the mouse or pressing a key on the keyboard. The Swing class corresponding to a label is `JLabel`. To create a label with the string "*Student Information*", an instance of `JLabel` is created as follows:

```
JLabel headingL;
headingL = new JLabel("Student Information");
```

A `JLabel` has methods such as `getText()` and `setText()` which can be used to retrieve or modify the label at any time. For example, to find out the textual label of a `JLabel` object, the following statement can be used:

```
String label = headingL.getText();
```

To change the text of the label, the following statements can be used:

```
String newLabel = "Student Personal Information";
headingL.setText(newLabel);
```

17.3.2 Text Field

A *text field* is a GUI component that can be used for editing a single line of text. Typically, it is used for data entry and data modification. The Swing class corresponding to a text field is `JTextField`. To create a text field that will enable a user to type the first name of a student, an instance of `JTextField` is declared and created as follows:

```
JTextField firstNameTF;
firstNameTF = new JTextField(15);
```

The argument 15 specifies the amount of columns that the text field should have. The amount of columns determines the width of the text field and this in turn determines the amount of characters that are visible. A `JTextField` will normally allow more characters to be typed than are visible. Like a `JLabel`, a `JTextField` has methods such as `getText()` and `setText()` which can be used to retrieve or modify the data in the text field at any time.

17.3.3 Text Area

A *text area* is a GUI component that facilitates the editing of several lines of text. It can be used in situations where the amount of characters to be typed by the user is difficult to predict. The Swing class corresponding to a text area is `JTextArea`. Arrow keys or the mouse can be used to position the cursor at any location inside the `JTextArea`.

To create a `JTextArea` that will enable a user to enter notes (or comments) on a student, a new empty `JTextArea` is declared and created as follows:

```
JTextArea notesTA;
notesTA = new JTextArea(5, 32);
```

The first argument of the constructor specifies the number of rows of the `JTextArea` and the second argument specifies the number of columns of the `JTextArea`.

Like a `JTextField`, a `JTextArea` has methods such as `getText()` and `setText()` which can be used to retrieve or modify the data in the `JTextArea` at any time.

17.3.4 Command Button

Command buttons are commonly used in GUI applications. They can be "pushed" by a user to perform a particular action. The Swing component for a

Chapter 17: Introduction to Graphical User Interface Programming

command button is `JButton`. A simple command button can be declared and created as follows:

```
JButton queryB;
queryB = new JButton("Query");
```

The string "*Query*" becomes the label that is displayed on the surface of the button. It can be modified at any time using the `setText()` method of `JButton`. Responding to a mouse click on the button is a little more complicated and will be discussed in a later section.

17.3.5 Layout Manager

GUI components must be placed at some location on a window (or other GUI container). In Java, a *layout manager* is responsible for positioning GUI components on a window or other container. There are several layout managers in Swing. In keeping with the object-oriented theme of the book, we are more interested in understanding the object-oriented nature of the GUI rather than the design and layout of the GUI. Thus, in this chapter, we will look at two of the simplest layout managers, `FlowLayout` and `GridLayout`.

`FlowLayout` is a very simple layout manager. It positions components in rows. If a component cannot fit on a row, it creates a new row and puts it there. When using `FlowLayout`, the width of a row is approximately the width of the window or container. GUI components are simply added to the container. The `FlowLayout` manager automatically positions the components by causing them to "flow" from one row to the next. If the user resizes the window or container, the `FlowLayout` manager re-positions the components based on the new width of the window or container. A `FlowLayout` manager is created as follows:

```
FlowLayout flowLayout = new FlowLayout();
```

`GridLayout` is another simple layout manager which uses a rectangular grid to position GUI components. A grid consists of a number of rows and columns, like a table. The rows and columns are specified when the `GridLayout` manager is created. The following statement creates a `GridLayout` manager for a grid that is 6 rows by 2 columns.

```
GridLayout gridLayout = new GridLayout(6, 2);   // 6 rows x 2 columns
```

The `GridLayout` manager positions the GUI components on the cells of the grid starting from the cell at the first row and first column. Figure 17.4 shows how components are positioned by the `GridLayout` manager; the numbers in the cells indicate the order in which components are placed on the grid (starting from 1 and ending at 12):

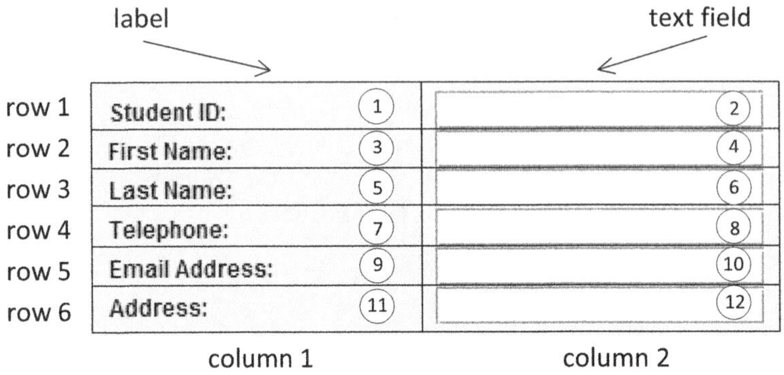

	label			text field	
row 1	Student ID:	1			2
row 2	First Name:	3			4
row 3	Last Name:	5			6
row 4	Telephone:	7			8
row 5	Email Address:	9			10
row 6	Address:	11			12
	column 1			column 2	

Figure 17.4: Placement of Components by **GridLayout** Manager

After creating an instance of the layout manager, it must be assigned to a window or container using the `setLayout()` method of the window or container. For example, to attach the `GridLayout` manager above to a window, the following statement is used:

```
setLayout(gridLayout);
```

17.4 StudentWindow

This section describes the code which generates the GUI shown in Figure 17.3. The GUI is used to enter, query, and update information on students. It uses the four visible GUI components discussed in the previous section. Two versions of the code are described. The first version uses the `FlowLayout` manager and the second version uses the `GridLayout` manager.

17.4.1 First Version of **StudentWindow**

Figure 17.5 shows the GUI generated by the first version of the code. A UML diagram of the components that generate the GUI is given in Figure 17.6. The UML diagram uses a different kind of labeling from what we have seen so far. Some of the rectangles contain a label which is underlined. The label consists of a class name prefixed with a colon, e.g., :JLabel, :JTextArea. This notation is used to represent an instance of a class rather than the class itself. For example, :JLabel inside a rectangle represents a single instance of the class, `JLabel`. If more instances are required, this is specified at the end of the relationship line. For example, the "5" at the end of the relationship line which connects

Chapter 17: Introduction to Graphical User Interface Programming

`StudentWindow` to `:JButton` indicates that `StudentWindow` contains five instances of `JButton`.

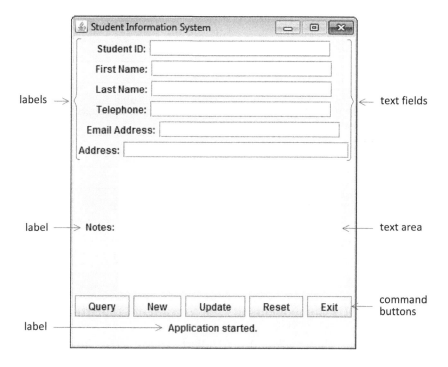

Figure 17.5 First Version of **StudentWindow** (using **FlowLayout**)

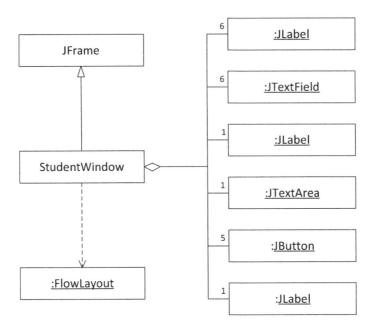

Figure 17.6: GUI Components in First Version of StudentWindow

The UML diagram shows that the StudentWindow class inherits from JFrame. StudentWindow contains six labels, six text fields, one label and a text area, five command buttons, and another label. StudentWindow uses an instance of the FlowLayout manager to position the GUI components on the window. The GUI components are positioned in the order shown in Figure 17.6, from top to bottom, except for the six labels and six text fields which are positioned in pairs.

All the GUI components are declared as instance variables of the StudentWindow class. In the constructor of StudentWindow, the components are created as discussed in the previous section. An instance of the FlowLayout manager is created and assigned to the window. The GUI components are simply added to the window in the order desired using the add() method of JFrame:

```
add(IDL);          // add ID label to the window
add(IDTF);         // add ID text field to the window

// repeat above code for next five labels and text fields

add(notesL);       // add label for text area
```

Chapter 17: Introduction to Graphical User Interface Programming

```
add(notesTA);          // add text area

add(queryB);           // add query command button

// repeat above code for next four command buttons

add(statusBarL);       // add status bar label
statusBarL.setText("Application started.");
                       // display message in status bar
```

Apart from the basic windowing statements discussed in Section 17.2, nothing more is required to generate the GUI shown in Figure 17.5. The complete code is available at the book Web site.

The **FlowLayout** manager produces a simple layout; however, it is generally not neat or attractive. The **GridLayout** manager can be used to produce a neater layout than the one shown in Figure 17.5. It is discussed in the next sub-section.

17.4.2 Second Version of **StudentWindow**

In this sub-section, the **StudentWindow** from the previous sub-section is enhanced so that it will generate the GUI shown in Figure 17.7. Incidentally, this is the same GUI shown in Figure 17.3. A UML diagram of the components that are used to generate the second version of the GUI is shown in Figure 17.8.

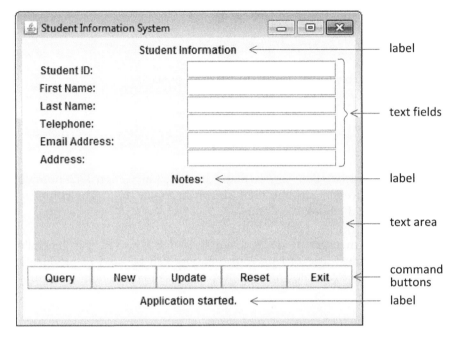

Figure 17.7 Second Version of **StudentWindow** (using **GridLayout**)

Chapter 17: Introduction to Graphical User Interface Programming

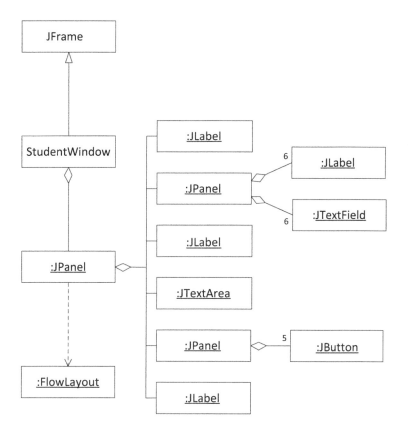

Figure 17.8: GUI Components in Second Version of StudentWindow

The two major differences in this version of the GUI are:

(1) The GridLayout manager is used to arrange the labels and text fields to give a neater appearance of the GUI components on the window, and

(2) Two panels are used to group GUI components together. The first panel groups together the six labels and six text fields at the top of the window. The second panel groups together the five command buttons.

A *panel* is a container that can contain other GUI components. Each panel can use its own layout manager. The Swing class corresponding to a panel is JPanel. The first JPanel uses the GridLayout manager; the dimensions of the grid are 6 rows by 2 columns (see Figure 17.4). Each row contains a label followed by a text field. The second `JPanel` also uses the `GridLayout` manager; the dimensions of the grid are 1 row by 5 columns. This causes the command buttons to be neatly displayed in one row.

The following code shows how the two `JPanel`s are created and how the layout managers are created and assigned to each one:

```
GridLayout gridLayout;

JPanel topPanel = new JPanel();
                         // JPanel for labels/textfields at top

gridLayout = new GridLayout(6, 2);
                         // grid is 6 rows x 2 columns

topPanel.setLayout(gridLayout);
                         // assign layout manager to JPanel
:

JPanel buttonPanel = new JPanel();
                         // JPanel for buttons at bottom

gridLayout = new GridLayout(1, 5);
                         // grid is 1 row x 5 columns

buttonPanel.setLayout(gridLayout);
                         // assign layout manager to JPanel
```

After creating the `JPanel`s, the GUI components are added to each `JPanel` using the `add()` method of `JPanel`.

As shown in Figure 17.8, all the GUI components are themselves grouped together in another `JPanel` which is attached to the `StudentWindow`. This `JPanel` uses a `FlowLayout` manager to position the sub-panels, labels, and text area on the surface of the panel.

17.5 Three Advanced GUI Components

This section explains how to use three advanced GUI components: *combo boxes*, *radio buttons*, and *check boxes*. These GUI components make it easier for the user to enter data and reduce the risk of data-entry errors. Each component is explained in the context of creating and updating a `Student` object and displaying data from an existing `Student` object. The section concludes by

Chapter 17: Introduction to Graphical User Interface Programming

showing how to enhance the `StudentWindow` from the previous section with these three components.

17.5.1 Combo Box

A *combo box* combines a button with a drop-down list. If the user clicks on the button, a drop-down list is displayed. The user can scroll down the drop-down list and select a value which is then displayed. Figure 17.9 shows a combo box which allows a user to choose from a list of countries.

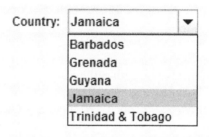

Figure 17.9: Combo Box with List of Countries

The functionality of a combo box is provided in Swing by `JComboBox`. A `JComboBox` must be supplied with the set of items to populate the drop-down list (this is referred to as the *data model*). The data model can be supplied as an array of `Object`s when the `JComboBox` is created; the `Object`s in the array must implement the `toString()` method. For example, to create a `JComboBox` to display the list of five countries shown in Figure 17.9, the following code can be used:

```
String[] countries = new String
   {"Barbados", "Grenada", "Guyana", "Jamaica",
   "Trinidad & Tobago"};

JComboBox countriesCB = new JComboBox(countries);
```

Alternatively, the `JComboBox` can be created with an empty data model and then the items for the data model can be supplied using its `addItem()` method:

```
JComboBox countriesCB = new JComboBox();
countriesCB.addItem("Barbados");
countriesCB.addItem("Grenada");
countriesCB.addItem("Guyana");
countriesCB.addItem("Jamaica");
```

```
countriesCB.addItem("Trinidad & Tobago");
```

To automatically position the combo box at a particular country, the index of that country can be specified as the argument of the `setSelectedIndex()` method. For example, to position the combo box on *"Jamaica"* when it is initially displayed, the following code can be used:

```
countriesCB.setSelectedIndex(3);          // index of Jamaica is 3
```

Alternatively, the name of the country can be specified as the argument of the `setSelectedItem()` method of the `JComboBox`. For example,

```
countriesCB.setSelectedItem("Jamaica");   // use name of country
```

If the index of the country is not within the range of valid indices of the data model (or -1), an `IllegalArgumentException` is thrown when the `setSelectedIndex()` method is called. On the other hand, if the name of the country supplied as an argument to the `setSelectedItem()` method is not present in the data model, the combo box is positioned at the first item in the data model.

To create a new `Student` object (or update an existing one), we must find out which of the items in the drop-down list is currently selected by the user. To do so, the `getSelectedItem()` method can be used:

```
String country = countriesCB.getSelectedItem().toString();
```

The `getSelectedItem()` method returns an `Object` so the `toString()` method should be used to get a string representation of the object displayed. The `country` string is then stored as an attribute of the new or updated `Student` object.

To display the `country` attribute of an existing `Student` object, the combo box must position the drop-down list at the given country. To do this, the data model of the `JComboBox` must be searched to find the index of the country in its list of countries. The index obtained is used with the `setSelectedIndex()` method to cause the combo box to display the given country:

```
String country = student.getCountry();
        // obtain value of country attribute from Student object

int countryIndex = getCountryIndex(country);
        // obtain index corresponding to country
```

Chapter 17: Introduction to Graphical User Interface Programming

```
if (countryIndex >= 0)
       // index is valid

   countriesCB.setSelectedIndex(countryIndex);
       // combo box displays country at given index
```

Note that `getCountryIndex()` is a method which searches the data model of the `JComboBox` to find the index of the given country.

17.5.2 Radio Button

A *radio button* is a GUI component that can be selected or de-selected by the user. It is available in Swing as `JRadioButton`. A `ButtonGroup` object can be used to group together a set of `JRadioButton` objects so that only one `JRadioButton` at a time can be selected.

Figure 17.10 shows a set of `JRadioButton` objects which allow the user to specify the attendance `status` of a student:

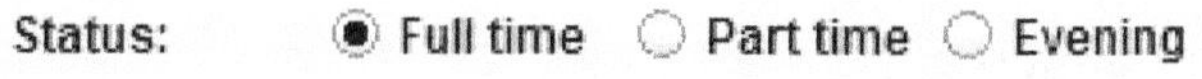

Status: ● Full time   ○ Part time   ○ Evening

Figure 17.10: Radio Buttons for Attendance Status

To create the `JRadioButton` objects, the following code can be used:

```
// declare radio buttons

JRadioButton status1, status2, status3;
ButtonGroup statusGroup;          // to group radio buttons together

// create radio buttons

status1 = new JRadioButton("Full time");
status2 = new JRadioButton("Part time");
status3 = new JRadioButton("Evening");
statusGroup = new ButtonGroup();// create instance of ButtonGroup
```

The `JRadioButton` objects are then grouped together by the `ButtonGroup` object:

```
statusGroup.add(status1);
statusGroup.add(status2);
statusGroup.add(status3);
```

Once the three `JRadioButton` objects are added to the `ButtonGroup`, only one at a time can be selected. If they are not added to the `ButtonGroup`, any combination of the three can be selected.

When displayed for the first-time, all the `JRadioButton` objects are de-selected. To automatically select one of the `JRadioButton` objects, the `setSelected()` method can be used. For example, since "*Full time*" students are the most common, the "*Full time*" `JRadioButton` can be pre-selected with the following code:

```
status1.setSelected(true);
```

To find out at any time if a `JRadioButton` is selected or de-selected, its `isSelected()` method can be invoked. For example, the following code can be used to determine which of the three radio buttons is selected:

```
String status;
if (status1.isSelected())
   status = status1.getText();
else
if (status2.isSelected())
   status = status2.getText();
else
if (status3.isSelected())
   status = status3.getText();
```

At the end of the `if` statement, the `status` string will contain the label of the `JRadioButton` that is currently selected. The label of a `JRadioButton` is the string that was supplied to the constructor (e.g., "*Part time*"). The `status` string can then be used to update the `status` attribute of a `Student` object.

To display the `status` attribute of a given `Student` object on the GUI, it is necessary to select the appropriate `JRadioButton` from the `ButtonGroup`. The following code can be used for this purpose:

```
String status = student.getStatus();
if (status1.getText().equals(status))
   status1.setSelected(true);
else
if (status2.getText().equals(status))
   status2.setSelected(true);
else
if (status3.getText().equals(status))
   status3.setSelected(true);
```

Chapter 17: Introduction to Graphical User Interface Programming

The code checks to see which of the `JRadioButton`s corresponds to the `status` attribute. The `JRadioButton` with the same label as the `status` attribute is selected through its `setSelected()` method.

17.5.3 Check Box

A *check box* is similar to a radio button and can be selected or de-selected by the user. A check mark is usually placed inside the check box to indicate that it has been selected. If a group of check boxes is used, the user can select as many of them as required. The Swing component corresponding to a check box is `JCheckBox`. In the example Student Information System, six check boxes are used to specify the extra-curricular activities a student is engaged in. They are shown in Figure 6.11.

>   Extra-Curricular ☐ Cricket   ☐ Football   ☐ Basketball
>   Activities   ☐ Athletics   ☐ Swimming   ☐ Hiking

Figure 6.11: Check Boxes for Extra-Curricular Activities

Check boxes can be created and manipulated individually like radio buttons. However, when there are many check boxes, the coding becomes tedious so it is more effective to create an array of check boxes. So, the six check boxes in the Student Information System can be declared and created as follows:

```
JCheckBox[] ecActivities = new JCheckBox[6];
                   // array of 6 check boxes

ecActivities[0] = new JCheckBox("Cricket");
ecActivities[1] = new JCheckBox("Football");
ecActivities[2] = new JCheckBox("Basketball");
ecActivities[3] = new JCheckBox("Athletics");
ecActivities[4] = new JCheckBox("Swimming");
ecActivities[5] = new JCheckBox("Hiking");
```

Unlike a combo box or `ButtonGroup` of radio buttons, a container rather than a single variable is needed to store the currently selected set of check boxes. Assuming that an `ArrayList` is used, the code to store the selections is as follows:

```
ArrayList<String> ecActivitiesSelected = new ArrayList<String>();
for (int i=0; i<ecActivities.length; i++) {
        // examine each check box
```

```
if (ecActivities[i].isSelected()) {
    // is check box selected?

    String label = ecActivities[i].getText();
        // get label of check box

    ecActivitiesSelected.add(label);
        // store label in ArrayList
    }
}
```

The code examines each check box to determine if it is selected. If so, the label of the checkbox is added to the `ArrayList` of selections. After the loop exits, the `ArrayList` of selections is used to update the corresponding attribute in a new or existing `Student` object. Note that the `ArrayList` stores the string that was used in the constructor of the `JCheckBox`. However, it might be more efficient to store indexes rather than an entire string.

To display the `ArrayList` of selections from a given `Student` object, the reverse process occurs. For each `JCheckBox` in the `ecActivities` array, we must check to see if its label is stored in the `ArrayList` (which indicates that this `JCheckBox` was selected for the given `Student`). If so, the `setSelected()` method is used to automatically select that `JCheckBox`. The code is as follows:

```
for (int i=0; i<ecActivities.length; i++) {
    if (ecActivitiesSelected.contains(ecActivities[i].getText())) {
        ecActivities[i].setSelected(true);
    }
}
```

17.5.4 Final Version of StudentWindow

We would now like to add the following GUI components to the `StudentWindow` shown in Figure 17.7:

- A combo box, to allow selection from a list of countries of the world
- Three radio buttons, to allow selection of one of the three different possibilities for attendance status
- Six check boxes, to allow selection of extra-curricular activities

The radio buttons and check boxes used in the final version of `StudentWindow` are exactly as described in the previous two sub-sections. However, the combo box must display a list of all the countries in the world

Chapter 17: Introduction to Graphical User Interface Programming

instead of only five countries. This is accomplished by storing a list of the countries in a text file, `Countries.txt`. As explained in Chapter 15, a `BufferedReader` can be used to read the text file, line by line. The countries are stored in an `ArrayList`. Next, the elements of the `ArrayList` are inserted into the combo box using the `addItem()` method of `JComboBox`.

The combo box, radio buttons, and check boxes are inserted at the appropriate positions in the GUI. Figure 17.12 is a screenshot of the actual window generated. Figure 17.13 is a UML diagram of the classes and objects in the final version of `StudentWindow`.

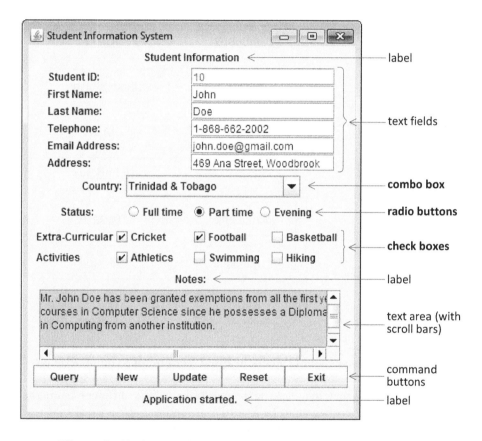

Figure 17.12: Screenshot of Final Version of `StudentWindow`

Fundamentals of Object-Oriented Programming in Java

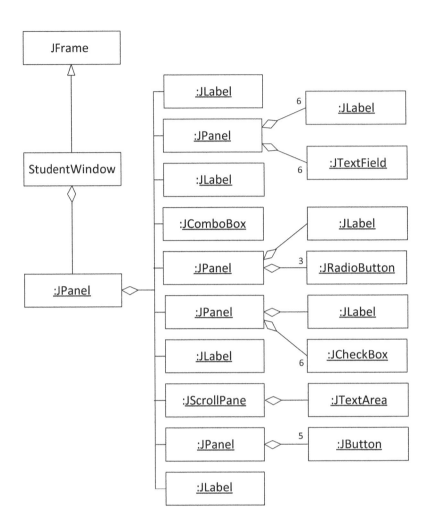

Figure 17.13: Classes and Objects in Final Version of StudentWindow

It can be observed that the *Notes* text area looks a little different from the previous version. There seems to be a border around the text area; also, if text is typed in the text area and it goes beyond the width or height of the text area, scroll bars automatically appear. The scroll bars operate just like the scroll bars in other applications. To get scroll bars around the text area, a JScrollPane must be used. The following is the code required to use a JScrollPane:

```
JScrollPane notesScroller;
notesScroller = new JScrollPane();
            // create instance of JScrollPane
```

Chapter 17: Introduction to Graphical User Interface Programming

```
notesScroller.getViewport().add(notesTA);
                // insert text area in JScrollPane
```

Note that the scroll bars only appear when the text goes beyond the viewable area of the text area.

At this point in time, the GUI is exactly as we want it in terms of its physical appearance. However, if we click on any of the command buttons, nothing happens. Clicking on the combo boxes and other GUI components causes some action to take place that is specific to the GUI component. However, no application-specific behavior takes place. In the next section, we will learn how to get the GUI to respond to events such as clicking of the mouse or pressing *Enter* on the command buttons.

17.6 Responding to Events on the `StudentWindow`

Command buttons and other user interface components are built-in components that provide a wide variety of functionality depending on the requirements of a given application. A very important issue in developing a graphical user interface is how to respond to an event such as a click on a command button. This is known as *event-driven programming*. Event-driven programming involves writing application-specific code to take some action when a pre-determined event occurs. This code is referred to as an *event handler*. This section describes the event handling mechanism in Java and explains how three main types of events are handled.

17.6.1 Event Handling Mechanism

In writing event handling code, a basic problem is how to connect application-specific code to a built-in GUI component that has no prior knowledge of the application-specific code. This problem is solved in Java by using the concept of an interface. Recall that an interface makes it possible to deal with objects which are not known except that they implement a minimum set of behaviors specified by the interface. In order to respond to an event occurring in a built-in GUI component, the class that contains the event-handling code must implement a specific interface defined by the designers of the GUI component. Table 17.2 lists the interfaces for some common events on a GUI component (there are many more).

Event	Interface
Clicking on a command button or pressing the Enter key on a command button	`ActionListener`
Pressing a key on the keyboard	`KeyListener`
Clicking the mouse on the window surface	`MouseListener`

Table 17.2: Common Events on a GUI

The event handler for a particular event must be written in a class that implements the appropriate interface. Indeed, the event handlers *are* the methods implemented from the interface together with any other helper methods. For example, to specify what to do when a user clicks on a command button, a class must be written that implements the *ActionListener* interface. Table 17.3 lists the methods that must be implemented for each of the interfaces given in Table 17.2.

Interface	Methods of Interface	Event Class
ActionListener	**void actionPerformed(ActionEvent e)**	ActionEvent
KeyListener	**void keyPressed(KeyEvent e)** void keyReleased(KeyEvent e) void keyTyped(KeyEvent e)	KeyEvent
MouseListener	**void mouseClicked(MouseEvent e)** void mouseEntered(MouseEvent e) void mouseExited(MouseEvent e) void mousePressed(MouseEvent e) void mouseReleased(MouseEvent e)	MouseEvent

Table 17.3: Event Handling Methods

Each of the three interfaces in Table 17.3 has an associated `Event` class. An instance of this `Event` class is passed as an argument to the method/s implementing the interface. The `Event` object provides detailed information about the event that occurred. For example, an instance of `ActionEvent` is passed as an argument to the `actionPerformed()` method. It provides information such as the title of the command button which generated the event.

Only the three methods highlighted in bold in Table 17.3 will be discussed in this chapter. Empty method bodies will be provided for the remaining

Chapter 17: Introduction to Graphical User Interface Programming

methods since a concrete class implementing an interface must provide an implementation for all the methods declared in the interface.

It is convenient for the class that generates the window to implement the relevant interface itself. So, to respond to a button click on any of its buttons, the `StudentWindow` class can itself implement the `ActionListener` interface.

17.6.2 Clicking on a Command Button

In order to respond to a click on a command button, the `ActionListener` interface must be implemented. This interface has only one method, `actionPerformed()`. The implementation of the `actionPerformed()` method must specify what to do when the user clicks on one of the command buttons.

A simple example of the implementation of the `actionPerformed()` method is as follows:

```
public void actionPerformed(ActionEvent e) {
   String command = e.getActionCommand();
   statusBarL.setText(command + " button clicked.");
}
```

The `ActionEvent` object passed to the `actionPerformed()` method can be queried to find out more information about the event that occurred. For example, its `getActionCommand()` method returns the label of the button which the user clicked on. In the example above, the `actionPerformed()` method simply displays the label together with a short string on the status bar. Clicking or pressing *Enter* on any of the five buttons causes a message to be displayed on the status bar indicating which button was pressed.

The `actionPerformed()` method may need to refer to GUI components on the window. In the example above, it needs to refer to the status bar. In other cases, it may need to refer to the text fields and other GUI components on the window. For this reason, the GUI components should be declared as instance variables rather than local variables in the class implementing the `ActionListener` interface (in this case, `StudentWindow`).

17.6.3 Pressing a Key on the Keyboard

If we wanted to know when the user pressed a key on the keyboard, the `KeyListener` interface should be implemented. This interface has three methods as shown in Table 17.3. A simple `keyPressed()` method can be written as follows:

```
public void keyPressed(KeyEvent e) {
    int keyCode = e.getKeyCode();
    String keyText = e.getKeyText(keyCode);
    statusBarL.setText(keyText + " pressed.");
}
```

Like the `ActionEvent` object passed to the `actionPerformed()` method, the `KeyEvent` object passed to the `keyPressed()` method can be queried to get more information on the keyboard event that occurred. In the example above, the `getKeyCode()` method of `KeyEvent` returns an integer code representing the key that was pressed. The `getKeyText()` method returns a string representation of the integer code such as "*A*", "*F1*", "*Escape*", etc. The string is displayed on the status bar.

Empty method bodies are written for the remaining methods in the interface. For example,

```
public void keyReleased(KeyEvent e) {

}
```

Of course, if you wish to take some action when a key is released, event handling code should be written for the `keyReleased()` method.

17.6.4 Clicking the Mouse

To find out if the user clicked the mouse somewhere on the window (in an area not occupied by a GUI component), the `MouseListener` interface should be implemented. There are five methods in the `MouseListener` interface. In the following example, only the `mouseClicked()` method is implemented. Empty method bodies are provided for the remaining four methods declared in the interface.

```
public void mouseClicked(MouseEvent e) {
    int x = e.getX();
    int y = e.getY();
    statusBarL.setText("Mouse click at (" + x +", " + y + ")");
}
```

In the above example, the `MouseEvent` object passed to the `mouseClicked()` method gives more information about the mouse click event. It can be queried

Chapter 17: Introduction to Graphical User Interface Programming

to find out the (x, y) coordinates of the point at which the mouse was clicked. After finding out the coordinates, the `mouseClicked()` event handler simply displays the coordinates on the status bar.

An important point to note about event handlers is that they are not called explicitly. Whenever an event occurs on a GUI component, the Java run-time system creates an instance of the appropriate event and passes it to an event handler connected to that GUI component (if one exists). For example, if a user clicks on a command button, the Java run-time system creates an instance of `ActionEvent` and passes it to the `actionPerformed()` method. If the `actionPerformed()` method is not implemented, the event will not be handled and nothing happens. This is exactly what happened in the previous versions of `StudentWindow`.

17.6.5 Attaching Event Handlers to GUI Components

Besides implementing the relevant `Listener` interface, there is one more task that must be done to complete the event handling process. This involves attaching the event handler to the appropriate GUI component or components. If this is not done, the event handler will not be activated by the Java run-time system when the event of interest occurs on the GUI component. Table 17.4 gives some examples of attaching an event handler to a GUI component for the three types of events listed in Table 17.2.

Event	GUI Component	Declaration of Component	Code to attach event handler
Mouse click or pressing *Enter* on a command button	JButton	JButton queryB; JButton newB;	queryB.addActionListener(this); newB.addActionListener(this);
Pressing a key on the keyboard	JTextArea	JTextArea notesTA;	notesTA.addKeyListener(this);
Clicking the mouse on the surface of a panel	JPanel	JPanel mainPanel;	mainPanel.addMouseListener(this).

Table 17.4: Attaching Event Handlers to GUI Components

The `this` argument of the `addListener()` methods listed in Table 17.4 indicates that the current class contains the event handler. If the event handler is implemented in another class, an instance of this class must be supplied to the `addListener()` methods in Table 17.4. Note that the same event handler can be attached to more than one GUI component. For example, all the command buttons can have the same event handler.

17.7 Communicating with Domain Objects in `StudentWindow`

In Chapter 4, the three-tier architecture of an object-oriented application was presented. It was mentioned that the User Services tier is relatively free of application processing and forwards task requests to the Business Services tier. In Chapter 16, it was shown how the User Services tier may also forward task requests related to persistence to the Data Services tier. An important question is this: how should the objects in the Business Services tier communicate with objects in the User Services tier? In other words, how should domain objects communicate with user interface objects?

17.7.1 Model-View Separation

The *Model-View Separation* design pattern states that model objects (i.e., domain objects or objects in the Business Services tier) should *not* have direct knowledge of or be directly coupled to view objects (i.e., the user interface objects) (Larman, 1997). Thus, a model class should not have knowledge or code related to user interfaces. In order for the objects in the view to display information, methods must be invoked on the relevant objects in the model. The data is then displayed via GUI components such as those we have already seen in this chapter. This approach is called the *pull-from-above* method. In support of this principle, none of the domain classes in this book contains code that directly communicates with the user interface (text-based or otherwise).

There are several advantages that are gained by using the Model-View Separation design pattern. For example,

- The model can be developed independently of the user interface
- New views can be easily connected to an existing model without affecting the objects in the model
- Multiple, simultaneous views of the same model can be developed (e.g., a desktop view, a smart phone view, a Web form view)
- The classes in the model can easily be ported to another user interface

17.7.2 Writing Code that Implements Pull-From-Above

The `StudentWindow` (the view) has buttons to enable the querying of students, inserting new students, and updating the information on students. The classes of the model (or the domain classes) are `Student` and `University`. A UML diagram of the model classes is given in Figure 17.14.

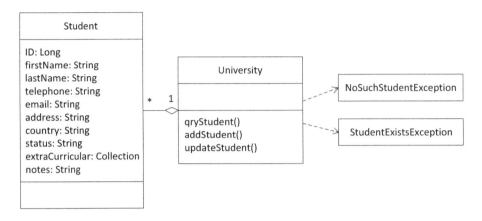

Figure 17.14: Model Classes Accessed by StudentWindow

Essentially, the view will use pull-from-above to communicate with the model classes. The event handler for the *Query* button will invoke the qryStudent() method on a University instance, supplying the value of the ID text field as an argument. Similarly, the event handler for the *New* button will invoke the addStudent() method on a University instance, supplying the values from the different GUI components which accept input as arguments. The event handler for the *Update* button will invoke the updateStudent() method on a University instance, again supplying the values from the different GUI components as arguments. The addStudent() method will throw an exception if a student with the given ID already exists. The updateStudent() method will also throw an exception if a student with the given ID cannot be found. In both cases, the view (i.e., the instance of StudentWindow) must catch the exception and do something with it.

The same actionPerformed() method handles events from all the command buttons. However, a helper method performs task-specific event handling for each command button. The actionPerformed() method determines which button was pushed and then calls the appropriate helper method:

```
public void actionPerformed(ActionEvent e) {

   String command = e.getActionCommand();

   if (command.equals(queryB.getText())) {  // Query button clicked
      queryStudent();
   }
   else
   if (command.equals(newB.getText())) {    // New button clicked
      newStudent();
```

Chapter 17: Introduction to Graphical User Interface Programming

```
    }
    else
    if (command.equals(updateB.getText())) { // Update button clicked
        updateStudent();
    }
    else
    if (command.equals(resetB.getText())) {  // Reset button clicked
        clearFields();
    }
    else
    if (command.equals(exitB.getText()))     // Exit button clicked
        System.exit(0);
}
```

The queryStudent(), newStudent(), and updateStudent() helper methods invoke methods on the University instance to get their work done. However, there is some additional work that must be done by the helper methods. This is described in Table 17.5.

Event handler helper method	Additional work before calling relevant method of University	Additional work after calling relevant method of University
queryStudent()	Obtains studentID from ID text field and ensures that it is not null. Converts studentID to a long value and invokes qryStudent() on the University instance.	If a valid Student object is returned, invokes accessor methods on the Student object to obtain data. This data is displayed on the GUI components.
addStudent(), updateStudent()	Obtains studentID from ID text field and ensures that it is not null. Obtains data from the GUI components that accept input and invokes addStudent() or updateStudent() on the University instance.	Displays error message if exception is generated.

Table 17.5: Work Done by Event Handler Helper Methods

The following code shows how the newStudent() helper method is implemented:

```java
private void newStudent() {

   String ID = IDTF.getText();
                // obtain ID string

   if (ID.length() == 0) {
                // check if the string has anything in it

      statusBarL.setText("Student ID must be specified.");
      return;
   }

   try {
      Student student;
      String country = countriesCB.getSelectedItem().toString();
                // find which country is currently selected

      String status = null;

      if (status1.isSelected())
                // find which status button is selected

         status = status1.getText();
      else
      if (status2.isSelected())
         status = status2.getText();
      else
      if (status3.isSelected())
         status = status3.getText();

                // request University to create Student
      student = university.addStudent(Long.parseLong(Id),
                firstNameTF.getText(),
                lastNameTF.getText(),
                addressTF.getText(),
                country,
                telephoneTF.getText(),
                emailTF.getText(),
                status);

      ArrayList<String> ecActivitiesSelected =
         new ArrayList<String>();

      for (int i=0; i<ecActivities.length; i++) {
                // examine each check box
```

```java
            if (ecActivities[i].isSelected()  {
                    // is check box selected?

                String label = ecActivities[i].getText();
                    // get label of check box

                ecActivitiesSelected.add(label);
                    // store label in ArrayList
            }

            student.setExtraCurricular(ecActivitiesSelected);
                    // set extraCurricular attribute

            student.setNotes(notesTA.getText());
                    // set notes attribute

            statusBarL.setText("Student successfully added.");
                    // display message on status bar

        }
    }
    catch (StudentExistsException see) {
                    // catch exception

        statusBarL.setText
            ("Error: A student with this ID already exists.");
    }
}
```

At this stage, the **StudentWindow** has the appearance that we want and it can also respond to mouse clicks on the buttons in a meaningful way. However, a few enhancements will be made before the chapter concludes.

17.8 Enhancing the GUI

In this section, we will show how to enhance the GUI so that it will resemble the one used in the third, fourth, and fifth programming projects. First, a *tabbed pane* is used so that several views can be accommodated on the same window by clicking on a tab. Next, a *menu bar* is added to the window. Finally, several *popup windows* will be used to display different kinds of information.

17.8.1 Supporting Multiple Windows

A JTabbedPane is a Swing component that allows different components to be displayed on the same window by clicking on a tab. The tab appears at the top of the window. The StudentWindow from the previous sections is a subclass of JFrame. In all the examples except the first one, a JPanel called mainPanel is used to arrange all the GUI components to be displayed on the StudentWindow. We can easily modify StudentWindow so that it *becomes* the mainPanel. Four things must be done to modify StudentWindow and use a JTabbedPane:

(1) StudentWindow must inherit from JPanel rather than JFrame. Since it is now a JPanel, it is renamed StudentPanel.

(2) Instead of adding components to the mainPanel using its add() method (e.g., mainPanel.add()), the components are simply added to the StudentPanel using its add() method (e.g., add()), since the StudentPanel object now performs the role of mainPanel.

(3) A new class must be written to create the JFrame and attach the JTabbedPane to the JFrame. The class must also create the StudentPanel and add it to the JTabbedPane. This class is called StudentApplication, just as in the programming projects.

(4) The *Exit* button is removed from StudentPanel since it is better for the main window, StudentApplication, to manage the closing of the application.

To illustrate how the JTabbedPane works, it is necessary to create another JPanel called CoursePanel, which enables course information to be entered and edited. CoursePanel inherits from JPanel and uses a subset of the GUI components in StudentPanel. StudentPanel and CoursePanel use pull-from-above to access the domain objects. Figure 17.15 is a UML diagram of the main classes involved in generating the enhanced GUI. Figure 17.16 shows the classes in the domain layer.

Chapter 17: Introduction to Graphical User Interface Programming

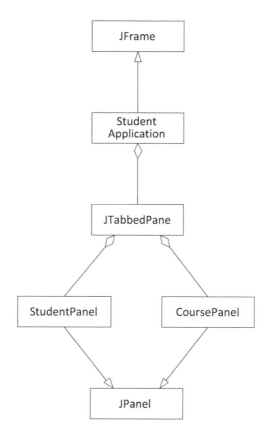

Figure 17.15: Main Classes in Enhanced GUI

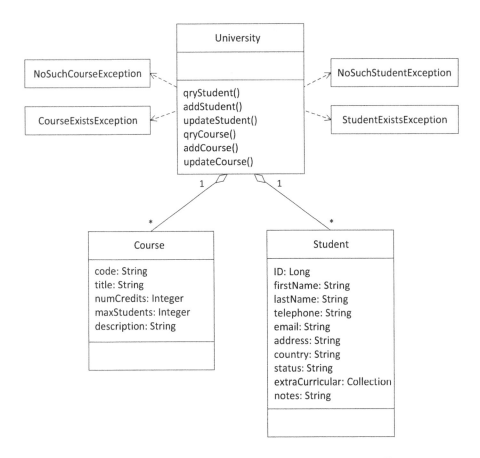

Figure 17.16: Domain Classes in Enhanced Student Application

The UML diagram of Figure 17.15 shows that `StudentApplication` is the main window and it inherits from `JFrame`. `StudentApplication` contains a `JTabbedPane` which contains two `JPanel`s, `StudentPanel` and `CoursePanel`. Both `StudentPanel` and `CoursePanel` are subclasses of `JPanel`.

The `StudentPanel` needs access to the `University` instance in order to manipulate `Student` objects. The `CoursePanel` also needs access to the `University` instance in order to manipulate `Course` objects. Thus, the `StudentApplication` also creates the single `University` instance and passes this instance as an argument to the `StudentPanel` and the `CoursePanel`.

The status bar in the main window displays informational messages generated from the main window and from `StudentPanel` and `CoursePanel`. Thus, `StudentPanel` and `CoursePanel` must be able to access the status bar in the main window. The `StudentApplication` provides a method, `setStatus()` which can be used to set the status bar. A reference to the `StudentApplication` is passed to both `StudentPanel` and `CoursePanel` so that they can invoke the `setStatus()` method (and perhaps, make modifications to the GUI components in the main window displayed by `StudentApplication`).

17.8.2 Including Menus on the Main Window

The Swing component for a menu bar is `JMenuBar`. A menu bar can contain zero or more menus and each menu can contain zero or more menu items. The Swing component for a menu and menu item are `JMenu` and `JMenuItem`, respectively. Figure 17.17 shows a menu bar consisting of two menus, one of which contains three menu items.

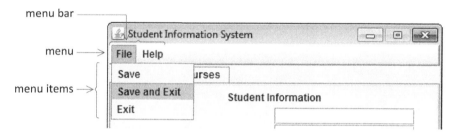

Figure 17.17 Menu Bar with Two Menus

To create the menu bar, the following code is used:

```
JMenuBar menuBar = new JMenuBar();
```

To create a menu called "File", the following code is used:

```
JMenu fileMenu = new JMenu("File");
```

Menu items are then created and attached to the menu:

```
JMenuItem saveMI = new JMenuItem("Save");
JMenuItem saveExitMI = new JMenuItem("Save and Exit");
JMenuItem exitMI = new JMenuItem("Exit");

fileMenu.add(saveMI);
fileMenu.add(saveExitMI);
fileMenu.add(exitMI);
```

Finally, the menu is attached to the menu bar:

menuBar.add(fileMenu);

When all the menus have been created and attached to the menu bar, the menu bar is attached to the JFrame using the following statement:

setJMenuBar(menuBar);

Note that it is not possible to attach a menu bar to a JPanel.

Figure 17.18 is a UML diagram showing the objects that are involved in producing the menu bar of the enhanced GUI.

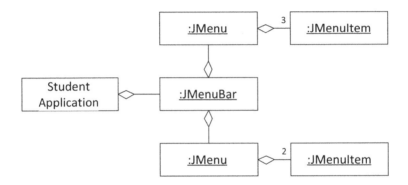

Figure 17.18: Objects that Produce Menu Bar in Student Application

Writing an event handler for a menu item is identical to writing one for a command button. Thus, in order to respond to the user clicking on a particular menu item, the ActionListener interface must be implemented. The actionPerformed() method can perform event handling just like with a command button. The getActionCommand() method of the ActionEvent parameter returns the text label of the menu item that was selected. Appropriate action can then be taken. If the menu item has the same text label as a command button, the same event handling code can work for both of them.

17.8.3 Popup Windows

Consider the popup window shown in Figure 17.19. This window can be generated using the class method showMessageDialog() from the

Chapter 17: Introduction to Graphical User Interface Programming

JOptionPane class. A popup() method can be used to generate a popup window whenever one is required. It is written as follows:

```
private void popup (String title, String message) {
   JOptionPane.showMessageDialog
      (null, message, title, JOptionPane.INFORMATION_MESSAGE);
}
```

There are several overloaded versions of the showMessageDialog() method; the Java API can be consulted for more information on each one.

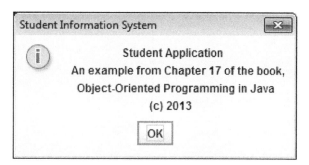

Figure 17.19: Popup Window

17.8.4 Completed Student Application

Figure 17.20 shows two screens from the final student application. Two menus are visible on the menu bar at the top. Two tabs are also visible at the top. Clicking on the "*Students*" tab causes the StudentPanel to be displayed. Clicking on the "*Courses*" tab causes the CoursePanel to be displayed. Most of the menu options cause a popup window to be displayed. To exit the application, the user can select the menu item "*Exit*" from the *File* menu. Alternatively, the user can click on the *Close* button.

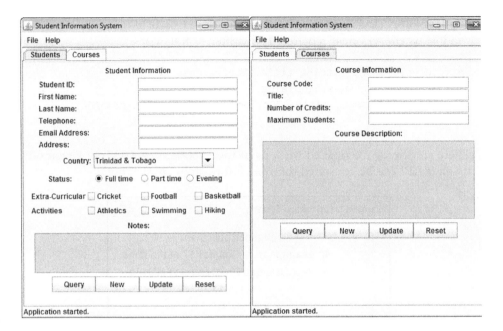

Figure 17.20: Windows of Completed Student Application

17.9 Is There a Better Way to Develop a GUI?

This chapter has described how to develop a GUI from scratch. The process can quickly become very tedious and error-prone when there are several GUI components and/or windows. Typically, a GUI developer would not follow the steps described in this chapter. Rather, a GUI developer will use a tool which simplifies the process of designing windows and populating them with the GUI components that are available. One such tool is *NetBeans GUI Builder*. This tool has features which make it easy to select GUI components from a palette and position them on a window. The tool also generates some of the code required for using the GUI components in a Java application. Of course, the event handling code is application-specific so it will have to be written by the developers of an application.

The objective of this chapter was not to describe an efficient way of developing a GUI for a Java application. Rather, the chapter sought to explain the object-oriented nature of GUI components and to show how they can be integrated with domain objects and objects in the persistence tier to achieve the functionality of an application. A good understanding of this process is important in order to design and build the software for the different layers of an object-oriented application.

Chapter 17: Introduction to Graphical User Interface Programming

Exercises

1. A GUI consists of one main window and several other child windows that are launched from the main window. The child windows occupy too much space on the monitor and it is convenient to display only the main window and one other window at any point in time. Explain how this can be achieved as efficiently as possible.

2. A GUI contains a menu bar with several menus. One of the menu items is "*Save*". It also has a button labeled "*Save*" which provides the same functionality as the menu item. Explain how the event handler for the "*Save*" feature should be implemented.

3. Should the domain objects in an object-oriented application contain user interface code? If not, explain how domain objects are created and manipulated via the user interface.

4. Suppose you wanted to design your own table for a GUI where the header and at most five rows of data should be displayed. The table should have three columns and at most 20 rows of data. It should be scrollable to permit the user to view the entire table. Using only the GUI objects discussed in this chapter, explain how you would implement the table.

5. Suppose you wanted the table component in (4) above to be available to other applications. Explain how you would go about creating the table as a reusable component so that a client can create the component by using only the new operator with the constructor, supplying arguments such as a data model (similar to a `JComboBox`) and a list of headings.

6. A certain GUI implements the `MouseListener` interface to trap mouse events on a window. However, whenever the mouse is clicked on the window, nothing happens. Explain what could be the reason for this.

7. Certain applications require two keys to be pressed in order to trigger the appropriate response from the domain objects. For example, in a game, pressing the right arrow with the up arrow indicates that the player would like to move in a northeasterly manner. However, the `keyPressed()` event handler is called *each* time a key is pressed on the keyboard (i.e., it is called once for each key press). Explain how the key combination can be detected by the event handler.

8. The getGraphics() method of the JFrame class returns a Graphics object which you can use to draw things on the window. The Graphics class has a method drawLine() which takes four arguments representing the beginning and ending coordinates of the line and draws the line between the two points:

```
void drawLine(int x1, int y1, int x2, int y2)
//(x1, y1) and (x2, y2) are the end-points of the line
```

Extend the SimpleWindow class so that it displays a line from (0, 0) to the coordinates where the mouse is first clicked. After that, whenever the mouse is clicked, a line should be drawn from the previous mouse position to the current mouse position. Note that the current (x, y) coordinates of the mouse as well as the Graphics object should be instance variables of the SimpleWindow class.

9. Suppose that you wanted to design a special text field of your own. The Graphics class has a drawRect() method which takes four arguments to draw a rectangle: the top left hand coordinates of the rectangle and the width and height of the rectangle:

```
void drawRect (int x, int y, int width, int height)
//(x, y) is the upper left-hand coordinates of the rectangle
```

The Graphics class also has a drawString() method which draws a string at a certain (x, y) location on a window:

```
drawString(String s, int x, int y);
// draws s at the coordinates (x, y)
```

Use these two methods to design your own text field (as simple as possible). You will need to implement the KeyListener interface. Characters should be displayed on the text field as they are typed on the keyboard. The backspace key should be used to delete characters from the right.

10. The top-level windows in this chapter inherit from JFrame. Another approach is to let the top-level windows *contain* a JFrame (i.e., use composition rather than inheritance). Evaluate the strengths and weaknesses of both approaches.

Appendix A

Questions on Object-Oriented Programming

This appendix contains twenty questions designed to test your understanding of the object-oriented concepts covered in the book. The questions generally require an understanding of several related topics so it is better to attempt these questions after you have studied the relevant material in the book. Answers for the first fifteen questions are given in Appendix B. Answers for the remaining questions are available at the book Web site.

A.1 Questions with Answers

1. When writing a user-defined class, it is normal to override the following methods of the `Object` class:

   ```
   public String toString()
   public boolean equals(Object o)
   public int hashCode()
   ```

   It is also common for user-defined classes to implement the `Comparable` interface as well as the `Serializable` interface.

   (a) For each of the three methods above, explain the benefits of overriding the method and state the implications of not doing so.

   (b) Describe clearly what must be done in order to implement the `Comparable` interface and the `Serializable` interface.

   (c) What are the benefits of implementing the `Comparable` interface and the `Serializable` interface?

2. (a) A digital counter is a bounded counter that starts from a minimum value and increments by one until its integer value reaches a certain maximum. At this point, it restarts from the minimum value. Examples include the numbers in a digital clock and the odometer in a car.

Write the code for a class **Counter** that provides the functionality of a bounded counter. **Counter** should allow clients to set the minimum and maximum value of the counter when it is created, increment its value (by one), and obtain its current value at any time.

(b) Consider the following:

A variable is passed by *value* to a method if changes made to the variable inside the method do not affect its value outside the method call. A variable is passed by *reference* to a method if changes made inside the method affect its value outside the method call.

In Java, a variable of a primitive type such as **int, float**, or **boolean** is passed to a method by *value*. Propose a general object-oriented technique for passing a primitive variable by *reference* from a method **A** to a method **B** and explain how the technique works.

3. Discuss the validity of each of the following statements:

(a) A public setter method (mutator) is just as bad as a public instance variable since in both cases, client objects can modify the instance variable as they please.

(b) There is no need for the *interface* feature in Java. An abstract class can be used whenever an *interface* is required.

(c) There is no need for generics in Java since **Object** parameters already make it possible for containers to store any kind of object.

(d) A class **Meeny** has a constructor which accepts two parameters. Suppose **Eeny** is a subclass of **Meeny** with no constructor. **Eeny** will compile successfully.

(e) The class **Miny** is a subclass of **Mo** and has a method of its own, **newMethod()**. It is legal to create an instance of **Miny**, assign it to **m** (an object variable of type **Mo**), and then do the following:

Appendix A: Questions on Object Oriented Programming

```
m.newMethod();
```

4. Determine the correctness of each of the following statements. If a statement is incorrect, explain how it can be corrected.

   (a) Constructors are used to create instances of a class.

   (b) A `private` instance variable can be accessed directly by all instances of the same class.

   (c) A `public` abstract method, `m()`, with no parameters and with return type `void`, can be declared as follows:

   ```
   public abstract void m() {

   };
   ```

   (d) Suppose that a method, `m()`, with no parameters and with return type `void` is declared in an interface, `I`. This method must be defined in every class that implements `I`.

   (e) If a `HashSet` is to be used for storing instances of a class `C`, it is necessary for `C` to implement the `Comparable` interface.

5. Determine if each of the following statements is true or false. Justify your answer.

   (a) If a class has a `public` instance variable, `v`, there is only one copy of `v`, which is shared among all instances of the class.

   (b) An abstract class must contain at least one abstract method.

   (c) A `protected` instance variable in a class `C` can be accessed directly by all subclasses of `C` and by all classes which are in the same package as `C`.

   (d) If a `try-catch` statement contains a `finally` block, the `finally` block is only executed if an exception in generated in the `try` block.

   (e) An unchecked exception can be caught and thrown just like a checked exception.

6. Suppose B is a child class of A. A has a method m() and a `protected` instance variable v.

   (a) Suppose m() is `private` in A. Determine if m() can be overridden in B and made `public`.

   (b) Suppose m() is `public` in A. Determine if m() can be overridden in B and made `private`.

   (c) Suppose B has a class method, cm(). Determine if cm() can access v directly.

   (d) Is it possible for B to declare and manipulate a `private` instance variable of its own named v? If so, explain how B will be able to access the `protected` instance variable v declared in A.

   (e) Suppose that b is an object variable referring to an instance of B. What is the value of the following expression?

   `(b instanceof A && b instanceof B)`

7. A certain inheritance hierarchy consists of three classes, `Person`, `Student`, and `Employee`, where `Student` and `Employee` are subclasses of `Person`. The `Person` class contains a method, m() which is declared as follows:

```
public boolean m (int param) {
    :
};
```

   (a) Explain how each of the following can be achieved in the `Employee` class:

   - using m(), exactly as defined in `Person`,
   - *refinement* of m(), and
   - *replacement* of m().

   (b) Using an appropriate example based on the hierarchy, explain what is meant by the *Principle of Substitutability*.

   (c) Using appropriate examples based on the hierarchy, distinguish between the *static type* and the *dynamic type* of an object variable.

Appendix A: Questions on Object Oriented Programming

(d) Using a polymorphic variable based on the hierarchy, explain how *method selection* takes place at run time.

8. Two techniques of object-oriented software reuse are inheritance ("is-a") and composition ("has-a"). Suppose we wish to reuse the functionality of class **A** in a class **B**. **B** can either inherit from **A** or use composition and create an instance of **A** and invoke its methods.

   Discuss two advantages and two disadvantages of using inheritance instead of composition for reuse.

9. A thesaurus is a listing of words with their synonyms (i.e., words which are similar in meaning). Table A.1 shows three words and their synonyms.

Word	Synonyms (In Sorted Order)
class	breed, category, clan, domain, family, species, subtype
object	article, body, entity, fact, item, thing
relationship	association, bond, correlation, dependency, interconnection, link, network

   Table A.1: Words and Their Synonyms

   (a) Describe clearly the storage structure you would use to store a thesaurus in an object-oriented Java application.

   (b) Write the code to accomplish the following:

   - Create the storage structure,
   - Insert the word "relationship" and two of its synonyms in the storage structure, and
   - Find a given word, w, in the storage structure and display its synonyms on the monitor.

10. (a) Describe each layer in the 3-tier architecture for object-oriented software applications.

    (b) State two benefits of using the *Model-View Separation* design pattern to build an object-oriented application.

(c) When using the *Model-View Separation* design pattern, explain how communication takes place between objects in the top two layers of the application.

(d) Discuss three techniques that can be used for making objects persistent in an object-oriented application. Which is the most "object-oriented" of the three techniques?

11. (a) c is an instance of a certain container class, C, which implements the Collection interface. Thus, it provides an iterator() method which returns an Iterator to its underlying data.

   (i) What is the benefit of including the Iterator interface in the Collection interface?

   (ii) Explain how an object of type Iterator can be used by clients to access the data from c. (Assume that generics are not used.)

   (iii) Suppose we wish to find out if a certain object belongs to c. Describe two ways this can be done.

(b) Generics make it possible for clients that use container classes to specify the type of objects that will be stored in the container when it is declared and created.

   (i) Explain how the container class, C, from (a) above can be declared and created using generics.

   (ii) How is the client access code different when generics are used?

(c) In a flight reservation system, a list of all the international airports located in each country must be stored. The airports in each country must be maintained in sorted order. A list of airports in three countries is shown in Table A.2.

Appendix A: Questions on Object Oriented Programming

Country	International Airports (In Sorted Order)
Jamaica	Ian Fleming International Airport (OCJ), Sangster International Airport (MBJ), Normal Manley International Airport (KIN)
Taiwan	Kaohsiung International Airport (KHH), Taoyuan International Airport (TPE)
Trinidad and Tobago	Crown Point International Airport (TAB), Piarco International Airport (POS)

Table A.2: International Airports of Certain Countries

(i) Describe clearly how you would go about storing the airport information using one or more container classes.

(ii) Write a segment of code which:
- Creates the container class (or classes) you specified in (i) above.
- Stores the airport information for Trinidad and Tobago given in the table above.
- Finds and displays all the airports in a given country, c, on the monitor.

12. An object-oriented software application is being developed for a patient healthcare system. A key part of the system is getting readings from medical devices at different times of the day. At present, readings must be obtained from three types of devices (there can be many more in the future):

- A blood pressure meter (*BPMeter*)
- A glucose meter (*GLMeter*)
- A peak flow meter (*PFMeter*)

The readings have some common attributes:

- `ID`, a unique integer which is generated whenever a reading is taken
- `dateTaken`, a `Date` object indicating the date/time when the reading was taken by the device (NB: `Date` is a built-in class in the `java.util` package)
- `dateTransferred`, a `Date` object indicating the date/time when the reading was transferred from the device to the application

- `unit`, a `String` indicating the unit of measurement

The readings from the devices differ in several ways. For example, a glucose meter reading and a peak flow meter reading is comprised of a single integer value; however, a blood pressure reading is comprised of four integer values. A reading should also provide a string representation of its state regardless of which device it comes from.

(a) Explain how you would model the *readings* obtained from the different devices in an object-oriented manner. Draw a UML diagram of the class or classes in your design.

(b) A `TransferAgent` object is being designed to control the transfer of the readings from each device to the application. The program code to establish a connection to the device is the same in all cases. Also, the `TransferAgent` uses the same program code to store the readings once they are obtained from each device. However, the program code required to obtain the readings from each device is different since they are stored in different formats and the data is different.

Suggest an approach that may be used to simplify the writing of the program code for the different devices. This approach should take advantage of the similarity of the code to connect to the devices and to store the readings obtained. (Hint: Consider how different `Comparator` objects can be employed in the same sort method.)

NB: It is not necessary to specify the technical details of obtaining the readings from a particular device.

(c) The program code to obtain readings from each device might fail to obtain the reading/s after a connection is made. For example, the device may take too long to supply the data or the data may not be in the required format due to device errors. Explain how the data access code can deal gracefully with these kinds of situations in an object-oriented manner and explain how the `TransferAgent` in turn will know about them. Give details of any new classes or interfaces you create.

(d) The designers of the application are planning to put a button on the user interface which patients can press to initiate the transfer of the reading/s from the device to the application. Clicking on this button results in an instance of `TransferAgent` being created

Appendix A: Questions on Object Oriented Programming

which then begins the transfer process. However, because of error situations, a patient may inadvertently press the button again. Explain how the `TransferAgent` can be implemented to prevent more than one instance from being created.

(e) `TransferAgent` needs to store the readings from the devices. Because of the nature of the application, the readings must be stored in order of the most current to the least current.

   (i) Choose an appropriate `Collection` class to use and give details of any additional code that may have to be written to provide the desired functionality.

   (ii) Using generics, give sample code showing how the instance of the `Collection` class is created and how readings are inserted into the collection.

   (iii) The user interface of the application has several screens to display the readings from the different devices. Suppose we wanted to get a list of all the blood pressure readings. Write a method, `BPToString()` which returns a string representation of all the blood pressure readings from the collection of readings.

   (iv) The graphical user interface in Figure A.1 is being built to display all the blood pressure readings in a `JTextArea`, when the "Blood Pressure Readings" button is clicked.

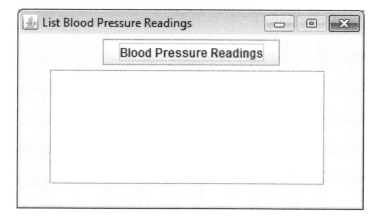

Figure A.1: GUI to Display Blood Pressure Readings

Write the code for the method that will process the click on the button. Assume that references for the TransferAgent, JButton, and the JTextArea are available and are transferAgent, button, and textArea, respectively.

13. Consider the UML diagram shown in Figure A.2. In this diagram, BPMeter and GLMeter are subclasses of a class Device.

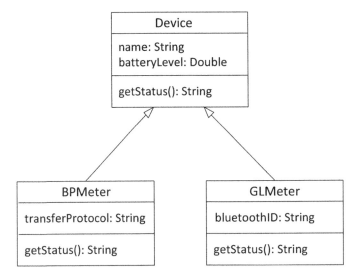

Figure A.2: UML Diagram of **Device** Class and Subclasses

You should note the following:

- name and batteryLevel are private instance variables of Device.

- Accessors are available for the instance variables in all three classes and a mutator is available for the batteryLevel instance variable of Device.

- The Device class has a single constructor implemented as follows:

```
public Device (String n) {
    name = n;
}
```

- The GLMeter class does not have a constructor but uses a mutator to modify its instance variable. The BPMeter class has a constructor

Appendix A: Questions on Object Oriented Programming

which takes the name and transfer protocol as parameters.

- The `Device` class does not have an `equals()` method, but the `GLMeter` class has an `equals()` method written as follows:

```
public boolean equals (Object o) {
   if (o instanceof GLMeter) {
      GLMeter glm = (GLMeter) o;
      return getName().equals(glm.getName());
   }
   else throw new IllegalArgumentException
      ("Need a GLMeter to compare.");
}
```

(a) Determine if the `GLMeter` class will compile successfully.

(b) Write a constructor for the `GLMeter` class that takes `name` and `bluetoothID` as parameters (both of type `String`).

(c) Assuming that there are no more compilation errors in `Device`, determine what kind of errors, if any, the following statements will generate in a client class.

   (i)   `GLMeter glm = new Device ("One Touch Ultra 2");`

   (ii) `Device d = new GLMeter`
         `          ("Bayer Contour", "T350320011");`

   (iii) `Device d = new GLMeter`
         `          ("Bayer Contour", "T350320011");`
         `System.out.println (d.getBluetoothID());`

(d) Suppose the following statements are written in a client class:

```
GLMeter glm = new GLMeter
            ("Bayer Contour", "T350320011");

Device d1 = new GLMeter("Bayer Contour", "T798820990");
Device d2 = new BPMeter("Bayer Contour", "USB");
Device d3 = new GLMeter("Bayer Contour", "T350320011");
Object o = d1;
```

What is the value of the following expressions? Clearly explain each answer. If an exception is thrown, you should explain why it is thrown.

(i) `d1.equals (glm)`

(ii) `o.equals (d2)`

(iii) `d2.equals (o)`

(iv) Suppose the `o` parameter of the `equals()` method in `GLMeter` was of type `GLMeter`. What is the value of the following expression? Explain your answer.

`glm.equals (d3)`

14. In a flight reservation system, one of the most important concepts is a flight which departs from a certain airport and arrives at another airport. Airports are located in cities. Each flight is administered by a particular airline and has a pilot assigned to it. A flight uses an aircraft and there are different types of aircrafts (e.g., Airbus A-380, Boeing 787, Embraer 195). Each aircraft has a set of seats. When a passenger books a flight, a reservation is made for that passenger to occupy a seat on that flight.

Draw a UML diagram showing the classes and relationships described in the narrative above. Only important attributes of classes should be included in the UML diagram. Behaviors can be omitted. Also, do not consider flights which have multiple segments (i.e., flights which go to more than one city).

15. An object-oriented application is being designed for a company in the financial services industry. The key item managed by the company is an asset which represents an item that has monetary value. There are different types of assets such as bank accounts, real estate, and securities. Stocks and bonds are specific types of securities.

The attributes of an asset are:

- A unique ID for the asset
- A description of the asset
- The date the asset was created

Appendix A: Questions on Object Oriented Programming

An asset must provide methods such as `toString()` which returns a string representation of the asset and `presentValue()` which returns the present value of the asset.

Table A.3 lists the attributes of the different types of assets in the system.

Asset	Attributes
Bank account	a collection of assessments of the market value of the property
Stocks	number of shares, share price
Bonds	face value, interest rate, current yield

Table A.3: Attributes for each Type of Asset

Draw a UML diagram showing the classes and relationships described in the narrative above.

A.2 Questions without Answers

16. Some of the methods of the `Iterator` interface and the `Collection` interface are listed in the Table A.4

Iterator	Collection
public boolean hasNext();	public int size();
public Object next();	public boolean add(Object o);
	public void clear();
	public boolean remove(Object o);
	public Iterator iterator();

Table A.4: Methods of the `Iterator` and `Collection` Interfaces

(a) Write the code for a new collection class known as `MoneyBag`. The `MoneyBag` class must implement the `Collection` interface using a one-dimensional array to manage the objects in its collection. Only the methods in the table above are to be implemented.

Note 1: In order to implement the `iterator()` method, you must write another class that implements the `Iterator` interface. An instance of this class must be returned when the `iterator()` method of the `MoneyBag` is invoked.

Note 2: To implement the remove() method, you must remove the object from the MoneyBag without leaving gaps in the underlying array.

(b) Write a code segment to:

(i) Create a MoneyBag and insert the following values into the MoneyBag:

19.95
100
24.25

(ii) Find and display the sum of all the values stored in the MoneyBag.

(c) How would the code segment in (b) above be different if the generics feature of Java was used?

17. Customised Fabricators is a manufacturing company that fabricates many different kinds of products for the energy industry. These products are made from parts that are stored and managed in an inventory. A part may be supplied by more than one supplier, and a given supplier may supply more than one part. Every time a part is supplied, information such as the date, amount supplied and unit cost is recorded. A class diagram of the relevant classes is shown in Figure A.3.

Appendix A: Questions on Object Oriented Programming

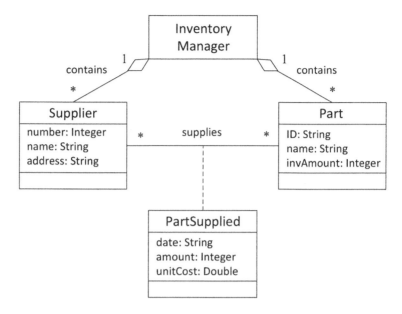

Figure A.3: UML Diagram of Classes in Inventory Application

Write Java code to implement all the classes shown in the diagram above, subject to the following:

(a) At most one instance of the **InventoryManager** can exist at any point in time.

(b) **Part** objects must be stored in a **HashMap**, based on **Part ID**. **Supplier** objects must be stored in a **TreeSet**, in ascending order of **Supplier name**. **Supplier** numbers are generated automatically for each **Supplier** object, starting from 1000 and incrementing by 10.

(c) Use a suitable container for the association class **PartSupplied**, such that given any **Part** instance, its related instances of **PartSupplied** are efficiently retrieved. Whenever a part is supplied, its inventory amount (**invAmount**) is updated by the amount supplied.

(d) Assume that accessors, mutators, and a **toString()** method have already been written for each class.

(e) **InventoryManager** must supply the methods listed in Table A.5:

Method	Purpose
public void addPart (String ID, String name)	Adds a part to its collection of Part objects
public void addSupplier (String name, String address)	Adds a supplier to its collection of Supplier objects
public Part getPart (String ID)	Returns the Part object with the given ID, or null if no such part exists
public Supplier getSupplier (int number)	Returns the Supplier object with the given number, or null if no such supplier exists
public void addPartSupplied (String partID, int supplierNumber, String date, int amount, double unitCost)	Adds an instance of the association class to the collection of PartSupplied objects
public Collection getPartSuppliers(Part p)	Returns a collection of Supplier objects that supply the given part. No duplicates should be present.
public int amountSupplied (Part p, Supplier s)	Returns the total number of the given part supplied by the given supplier over time.

Table A.5: Methods of InventoryManager

18. An object-oriented Vehicle Management System is being written in Java. In the application, Car is a subclass of Vehicle. The Vehicle class contains a private instance variable name with an accessor method getName(). The constructor for Vehicle is as follows:

```
public Vehicle (String n) {
    name = n;
}
```

The Car class does not have any instance variables of its own neither does it have a constructor; however, it has a method "public void accelerate()". The Vehicle class does not have an equals() method, but the Car class has an equals() method written as follows:

```
public boolean equals (Object o) {
    if (o instanceof Car) {
        Car c = (Car) o;
        return getName().equals(c.getName());
```

Appendix A: Questions on Object Oriented Programming

```
    }
    else throw new IllegalArgumentException
        ("Need a Car to compare.");
}
```

(a) Assuming that there are no other potential sources of compilation errors in Car, determine if the Car class will compile successfully, clearly explaining your answer.

(b) Write a constructor for the Car class that takes a string n as a parameter, representing the name of the Car.

(c) Determine what kind of errors, if any, are generated by the following statements in a client class:

```
Car c = new Vehicle("Yaris");
Vehicle v = new Car("Corolla");
v.accelerate();
```

(d) Suppose the following statements are written in a client class:

```
Car c = new Car("Corolla");
Vehicle v1 = new Car("Corolla");
Vehicle v2 = new Vehicle("Corolla");
```

What is the value of the following expressions? Clearly explain each answer. If an exception is thrown, explain why it is thrown.

(i) (c == v1)
(ii) c.equals(c)
(iii) c.equals(v1)
(iv) v1.equals(c)
(v) v2.equals(c)
(vi) c.equals(v2)

(e) Suppose the o parameter of the equals() method in Car was of type Car. What is the value of (d)(iii) above? Explain your answer.

19. (a) In the UML, *relationships* are used to model the ways that things can connect to one another, either logically or physically. In object-oriented modeling, the three most important kinds of relationships are *dependencies*, *generalizations*, and *associations*. Briefly discuss each of these relationships, and by means of an example,

show how each is drawn in a UML diagram.

(b) By means of suitable examples, clearly differentiate between *aggregation* relationships and *composition* relationships.

(c) Categorize the following relationships as dependency, generalization, aggregation, composition, or association. If two categories are possible, give the one that provides more information:

   (i) A country has a capital city
   (ii) A student registers for a course
   (iii) A file is an ordinary file or a directory file
   (iv) A student registers for a course
   (v) A software engineer uses a programming language on a project
   (vi) A route connects two cities
   (vii) Object classes may have several attributes

(d) In an employer/employee relationship between a Company and a Person, a Job (with attributes such as description, dateHired, and salary) pertains to exactly one pairing of Person and Company. Explain how this relationship can be modeled. Draw a UML diagram to illustrate your answer.

20. In a hospital system, a hospital manages several patients. A patient is prescribed drugs over time to deal with his/her ailments. Figure A.4 is a UML diagram showing the relevant classes in the system.

Appendix A: Questions on Object Oriented Programming

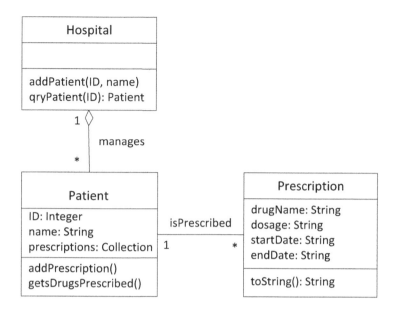

Figure A.4: UML Diagram of Classes in Hospital System

(a) Write the code for the Prescription class.

(b) Write the code for the Patient class. Note that the Patient class must manage a collection of Prescription objects in prescriptions. The addPrescription() method accepts data to create a Prescription object, creates the Prescription object, and stores it in the prescriptions collection. The getDrugsPrescribed() method returns a string representation of all the Prescription objects in prescriptions.

(c) Write the code for the Hospital class using an appropriate collection to store the Patient objects. The addPatient() method accepts data to create a Patient object, creates the Patient object, and stores it in its collection of Patient objects. The qryPatient() method searches for the Patient object with the ID supplied as a parameter; if it is not found, it returns null.

(d) Write the code to generate the user interface shown in Figure A.5 (*Patient Window*) and Figure A.6 (*Prescription Window*). The windows should be built as follows:

Patient Window

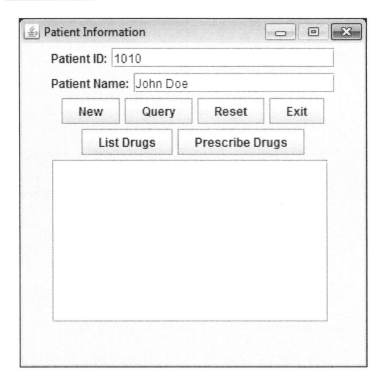

Figure A.5: GUI to Enter Patient Information and List Prescribed Drugs

When the *New* button is clicked, a new patient is added to the `Hospital` by invoking its `addPatient()` method with the data entered in the *ID* and *Name* fields. When the *Query* button is clicked, a query is performed for a patient matching the `ID` entered in the *ID* field. The *Reset* button causes all the fields of the form to be cleared. When the *List Drugs* button is clicked, a list of all the drugs prescribed for the patient is displayed. When the *Prescribe Drugs* button is clicked, the *Prescription Window* should be displayed with the corresponding patient `ID` moved across to the patient *ID* field. The *Exit* button shuts down the application.

Appendix A: Questions on Object Oriented Programming

Prescription Window

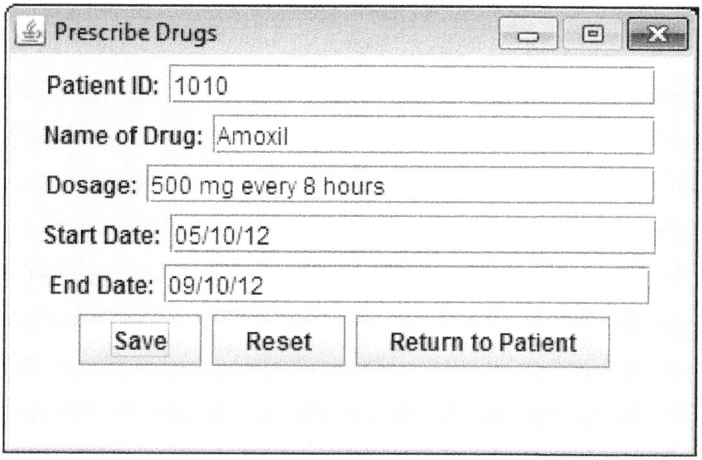

Figure A.6: GUI to Enter Drugs Prescribed

When the *Save* button is clicked, the data from the form is used to create a new `Prescription` object which is saved in the corresponding `Patient` object (using its `addPrescription()` method). When the *Reset* button is clicked, the fields in the form are cleared. When the *Return to Patient* button is clicked, the window should disappear.

Appendix B

Answers to Questions

This appendix gives answers to the first set of questions in Appendix A. These are only suggested responses and in some of the free-form questions, there may be alternative answers that are equally correct. In general, the answers provided are derived directly from the material presented in the book. The answers for the remaining questions are available at the book Web site.

1. (a) **toString()**: allows the object to display a string representation of its state.

    If not overridden, the method from **Object** will be used which displays an "@" symbol followed by the memory address of the object, which is not useful to humans.

    equals(): allows the object to specify what it means to be equal to another object so that methods that do insertion, deletion etc., can operate based on this definition.

    If not overridden, the method from **Object** will be used which returns **true** if the two objects being compared are stored at the same memory address. This is a very restricted form of equality.

    hashCode(): allows the object to specify a hash function if there is the possibility that the object may have to be stored in a structure such as a hash table.

    If not overridden, the method from **Object** will be used which generates hash codes based on the memory address of the object. This may not be as effective as a user-defined hash code.

(b) In order to implement the `Serializable` interface a class must simply declare that it implements the `Serializable` interface. No methods have to be implemented.

In order to implement the `Comparable` interface, a class must implement the `compareTo()` method which has the following signature:

```
public int compareTo(Object o)
```

`compareTo()` must check that the current object is the same type as `o`, the one supplied as an argument. After casting `o` to its own type, it must then compare its own attributes with those of `o` to determine whether it is less than, equal to, or greater than `o` in some ordering scheme.

Note that if generics is used, type checking and casting are unnecessary since the parameter of the `compareTo()` method can be of the same type as the class.

(c) If the `Comparable` interface is implemented, the object can be stored in container classes which require an ordering of objects (e.g., `TreeSet`) or it can be used in algorithms which depend on the ordering of objects (e.g., sort algorithms). If the `Serializable` interface is implemented, the object can be serialized to a file for permanent storage.

2. (a)
```
public class Counter
{
    private int min, max;
    private int value;

    public Counter(int min, int max) {
        this.min = min;
        this.max = max;
        this.value = min;       // starting value of
        counter is min
    }

    public int getValue() {
        return value;
```

Appendix B: Answers to Questions

```
    }

    public void increment() {
        if (value == max)         // max is reached
            value = min;          // reset counter to min
        else
            value++;              // increment counter
    }
}
```

(b) For each primitive type, write a class such as `IntHolder`, `FloatHolder`, `BooleanHolder`, etc., as follows:

```
public class IntHolder
{
    private int intValue;

    public IntHolder(int intValue) {
        this.intValue = intValue;
    }

    public int getInt() {
        return intValue;
    }

    public void setInt(int intValue) {
        this.intValue = intValue;
    }
}
```

Note that the accessor and mutator methods are specific to the class. So, the `IntHolder` class will use variables of type `int`, and `FloatHolder` will use variables of type `float`, etc.

If method `a()` needs to pass an integer `i` by reference to a method `b()`, it first creates an instance of `IntHolder`, passing the integer value to the constructor. For example,

```
IntHolder ih = new IntHolder(i);
```

It then passes `ih` to method `b()`. If method `b()` needs to obtain the value of the integer, it invokes `getInt()` on `ih`. If it needs to modify the integer value, it invokes `setInt()` on `ih`. After method `b()` is invoked, method `a()` can obtain the modified value by invoking `getInt()` on `ih`.

Note that the object variable referring to the `IntHolder` object is unchanged, but the `IntHolder` object itself has been modified. It should also be noted that the wrapper classes in Java (e.g., `Integer`, `Double`, etc.) cannot provide the functionality required since objects of these classes are immutable.

3. (a) This is not true. A `public` setter method (mutator) can perform validation checks before modifying the instance variable, protecting the integrity of the object. This cannot be done if the instance variable is modified directly.

   (b) It is true that an abstract class with only abstract methods and no instance variables can be used whenever an interface is required. However, the interface structure enforces the requirements that all the methods are abstract and that there are no instance variables. It should also be noted that a class can inherit from only one class; however, a class can implement multiple interfaces.

   (c) It is true that `Object` parameters make it possible for containers to store any kind of object. However, there is no type checking performed when objects are inserted into a container. The use of *generics* ensures that a container is created for only a specific type of object. It also simplifies the retrieval process.

   (d) The `Eeny` class will not compile successfully. Since it has no constructors of its own, the compiler attempts to provide a default no-argument constructor for `Eeny` that invokes a no-argument constructor for `Meeny`. But, no such constructor exists in `Meeny` (since a two-argument constructor was already provided, the compiler did not provide a default no-argument constructor for `Meeny`).

   (e) Although the assignment to `m()` is legal because of the Principle of Substitutability, only methods of the static type (i.e., `Mo`) can be used. Since `newMethod()` is declared in the dynamic type but not in the static type, it is not legal to invoke `newMethod()` as shown.

4. (a) Incorrect. Constructors are used to *initialise* instances of a class.

Appendix B: Answers to Questions

(b) Correct. A `private` instance variable can be accessed directly by instances of the same class.

(c) Incorrect. A `public` abstract method, `m()`, with no parameters and with return type `void`, can be declared as follows:

```
public abstract void m();
```

(d) Incorrect. This method must be defined in every class that implements `IF`, *unless that class is abstract*.

(e) Incorrect. If a `TreeSet` is to be used for storing instances of a class `C`, it is necessary for `C` to implement the `Comparable` interface.

5. (a) False. The statement is true for a *class* variable rather than a `public` *instance* variable.

   (b) False. An abstract class can contain *zero* or more abstract methods.

   (c) True. Note that package access can result in uncontrolled access by classes in the same package.

   (d) False. The `finally` block is executed just before the method exits, regardless of what happens inside the method.

   (e) True. Although it is not required, an unchecked exception can be caught and thrown just like a checked exception.

6. (a) Yes. A child class can provide more functionality than its parent class.

   (b) No. A child classes cannot provide less functionality than its parent class.

   (c) No. A class method cannot access an instance variable.

   (d) Yes. This can be done by simply declaring the instance variable when writing the class `B`. To access the `protected` instance variable `v` declared in `A`, `B` must use `super.v`.

Note that the above approach is referred to as *shadowing* the instance variable v declared in A. The approach is not recommended since it is considered bad programming practice.

(e) The expression evaluates to true. An instance of B satisfies a type check for a parent of B (in this case, A) by the Principle of Substitutability.

7. (a) Using m(): nothing has to be done in Employee.

Refinement of m(): a method m() must be written in Employee with the same signature given. In Employee, the parent's version of m() must be called somewhere using the keyword super as follows: super.m(x) where x is a variable of type int. The result of the call must then be augmented with additional behavior specified in the version of m() in Employee.

Replacement of m(): a method m() must be written in Employee with the same signature given. In Employee, a new method implementation must be written for m(), one that does not use the parent's version.

(b) The Principle of Substitutability says that it should be possible to replace instances of Person with instances of Student or Employee, with no observable effect.

(c)
```
Person p = new Student(…);      // Line 1
boolean b = p.m();              // Line 2
```

In Line 2, the static type of p is Person, since this is what p was declared to be in Line 1. However, the dynamic type of p is Student, since p is actually referring to a Student instance at run-time.

(d) The variable p in (c) above is a polymorphic variable since it can refer to both Person instances and Student instances. In Line 2, method selection takes place by invoking the method m() of the dynamic type, i.e., Student. If Student did not refine or replace m(), then the method defined in the static type, i.e., Person is chosen. If the method was not found in the static type, search for the method continues up the inheritance hierarchy, until Object is reached. If the Object class does not have the method m(), a

Appendix B: Answers to Questions

compilation error is generated.

8. Advantages:

   The inherited class **B** automatically embodies all the functionality of its parent, **A**. If composition is used, code has to be written to create an instance of **A** and invoke its methods when necessary.

   Inheritance makes it possible to use an instance of **B** where an instance of **A** is expected (e.g., in an existing polymorphic method). This is not possible if composition was used.

   Disadvantages:

   When inheritance is used, it is only possible to inherit from one class. However, with composition, it is possible to compose the behavior of objects from as many classes as required.

   When inheritance is used, all the methods of **A** are automatically available to clients even if they are not appropriate in **B**. When composition is used, only the required methods from **A** can be invoked.

9. (a) A `HashMap` can be used where the *key* is the word (stored as a string) and the *value* is a `TreeMap` which stores the alternative meanings (as strings) in sorted order.

   (b)
   ```
   HashMap thesaurus = new HashMap();
   TreeSet value = new TreeSet();
   value.add("association");
   value.add("bond");
   thesaurus.put("relationship", value);

   TreeSet output = thesaurus.get(w);
   Iterator i;

   i = output.iterator();
   while (i.hasNext())
      System.out.println (i.next());
   ```

10. (a) Presentation layer: contains the objects that are responsible for

generating the user interface and interacting with the user.

Application or domain layer: contains the objects that perform the business processing related to the application.

Persistence layer: contains the objects that manage the storage of the domain objects in a persistent medium such as a database.

(b) Many different views can be attached to a model.

A new view can be easily added to the system without the model knowing about it.

Since the model is not coupled to its views, it can be reused independently.

(c) View objects communicate with model objects by pull-from-above, where methods are invoked on model objects when necessary. Model objects communicate with view objects indirectly using a technique known as *push-from-below*, which can be implemented using the *Observer Design Pattern* (Gamma et al, 1995).

(d) Three techniques than can be used to make the objects in an object-oriented application persistent are (1) using a text file (2) using a relational database and (3) using object serialization. Using a text file involves saving the values of the instance variables of objects as lines of a text file which are delimited in some way (e.g., using a space or a comma). Using a relational database is similar to using a text file except that the values are saved to the tables of a relational database using the Java Database Connectivity (JDBC) API. In both cases, references to other objects must be replaced with the primary keys to these objects. Object serialization involves saving the objects exactly as they are to a file. If an object contains other objects, these are automatically saved to the file. Conversely, entire objects (and any contained objects) are retrieved from the file.

Object serialization is the most object-oriented of the three approaches since it is able to save and retrieve objects exactly as they are in memory without any conversions or mappings.

11. (a) (i) The `Iterator` interface makes it possible to access the underlying data stored in concrete classes which implement

Appendix B: Answers to Questions

the `Collection` interface in a standard way. So, even if the concrete collections are fundamentally different (e.g., `TreeSet`, `HashSet`), the code to traverse and access the elements is the same.

(ii) First, an object of type `Iterator` is obtained by invoking the `iterator()` method on `c`. The `hasNext()` method of the `Iterator` is used in a `while` loop to determine if there are more elements to enumerate. If so, the `next()` method of the `Iterator` object is used to retrieve the next element. This element is returned as an object of type `Object`. It is cast to its appropriate type and the client can then invoke operations on this object as required. The code is given below:

```
Iterator i = c.iterator();
while (i.hasNext()) {
  // if more elements to enumerate

  Object o = i.next();
  // cast o to object of appropriate type and process
}
```

Alternatively, the *foreach* statement can be used as follows:

```
for (element : c)
  // process element
```

(iii) (1) Use the `contains()` method of the `Collection` interface which returns `true` if an object is present in the collection and `false` otherwise. (2) Use an `Iterator` to traverse the elements of the collection and check each object to see if it is equal to the object being compared.

(b) (i) The container class, `C`, can be made "generic" by using parameterized types. So, when defining the class, the type of objects to be stored is expressed as a parameter, `T`:

```
public class C <T> {
  :
}
```

The methods of `C` operate on objects of type `T` instead of a specific type. For example, the signature of the `add()` method is:

```
public boolean add(T o)
```

(ii) When a client creates an instance of the collection, the type of objects to be stored in the container is specified. For example,

```
C collection = new C<Student>();
```

The client can then call methods of collection using the specific type when required (in this case, Student). Also, when using an Iterator, the type of object is specified when the Iterator is created so that there is no need to cast when the objects are returned by the next() method.

(c) (i) A HashMap can be used where the *key* is the country (stored as a string) and the *value* is a TreeSet which stores the airports (as strings) in sorted order.

(ii)
```
HashMap allAirports = new HashMap();
TreeSet value = new TreeSet();
value.add
   ("Crown Point International Airport (TAB)");

value.add("Piarco International Airport (POS)");
allAirports.put("Trinidad and Tobago", value);

TreeSet output = (TreeSet) allAirports.get(c);
Iterator i;

i = output.iterator();
while (i.hasNext())
   System.out.println (i.next());
```

12. (a) A UML diagram for the given scenario is shown in Figure B.1.

Appendix B: Answers to Questions

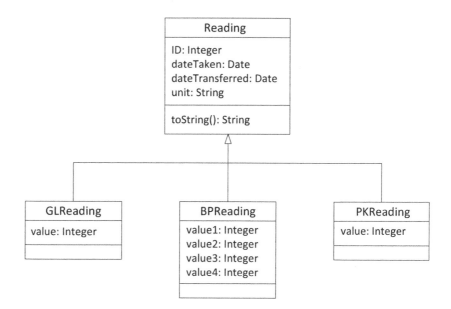

Figure B.1: UML Diagram of Readings in Healthcare System

(b) It should be noted that the methods `connectToDevice()` and `storeReadings()` are the same in all cases. The first step towards a solution is to write an interface, `ReadingsInterface` that has a single method, `getReadings()`. The signature of this method is not important in obtaining a solution to the problem.

The next step is to write three classes that implement the method `getReadings()`, one for each device. Each implementation will provide behavior that is specific to the device in question. For example,

```
public class BP implements ReadingsInterface {
    // device specific behavior for getReadings()
}
```

An instance of the class implementing the `ReadingsInterface` is created and stored in an object variable of type `ReadingsInterface`. For example,

```
ReadingsInterface ri = new BP();
```

When creating the `TransferAgent`, `ri` is passed to the constructor of `TransferAgent`. To transfer data, the following is done in `TransferAgent`:

```
connectToDevice();
ri.getReadings();
storeReadings();
```

Since `TransferAgent` stores a reference to an object of type `ReadingsInterface`, it can accept objects of any class that implements `ReadingsInterface`. Thus, the code above can work unchanged for any of the devices supported.

(c) Create an exception class for each of the two situations mentioned by inheriting from the `Exception` class.

When the situation occurs, throw an instance of the specific `Exception` class (it must be declared in the method header that an `Exception` will be thrown).

In `TransferAgent`, put the following code in a `try-catch` block:

```
try {
    r.getReading();
}
catch (TimeOutException toe) {
    // do something
}
```

(d) `TransferAgent` must be implemented as a *Singleton* to prevent more than one instance from being created. Chapter 14 explains how to create a Singleton using the Singleton Design Pattern. Essentially, the constructor of `TransferAgent` is made `private` and a class method `getInstance()` is used to determine if an instance already exists. If not, an instance of `TransferAgent` is created and returned; otherwise, the existing instance of `TransferAgent` is returned. The reference to the instance must be stored in a class variable since class methods cannot access instance variables.

(e) (i) `TreeSet`, since it is able to keep its contained objects in sorted order.

Reading must implement the `Comparable` interface, based on dateTaken, i.e., the `compareTo()` method must be implemented comparing the dateTaken instance variables.

Appendix B: Answers to Questions

However, the `compareTo()` method must be written to arrange the objects descending order.

(ii)
```
TreeSet<Reading> readings = new TreeSet<Reading>();
readings.add(r); // r is an instance of Reading
```

(iii)
```
String output = "";
Iterator i = readings.iterator();
while (i.hasNext()) {
  Reading r = i.next();
  if (i instanceof BPReading)
     output = output + "\n" + r.toString)();
}
return output;
```

(iv) The `actionPerformed()` method of the Graphical User Interface is written as follows:

```
public void actionPerformed (ActionEvent e) {
  String readings;
  String command = e.getActionCommand();
  if (command.equals("Blood Pressure Readings")) {
     readings = transferAgent.BPToString();
     textArea.setText(readings);
  }
}
```

13. (a) The `GLMeter` class will not compile successfully. Since it has no constructors of its own, the compiler attempts to provide a default no-argument constructor for `GLMeter` that invokes a no-argument constructor for `Device`. But, no such constructor exists in `Device` (since a one-argument constructor was already provided, the compiler did not provide a default no-argument constructor for `Device`).

(b)
```
public GLMeter (String name, String bluetoothID) {
  super (name);
  this.bluetoothID = bluetoothID;
}
```

(e) (i) It is not possible to assign an instance of a parent class (Device) to a variable declared to refer to an instance of a child class (GLMeter) so a type conversion compilation error will occur.

(ii) No problems occur here since it is permitted by the Principle of Substitutability.

(iii) As indicated in (ii) above, the first line does not cause any problems. However, the second line generates an error since the method is not present in the static type of d which is Device.

(d) (i) d1.equals(glm) is true, since the equals() method of GLMeter will be used by dynamic binding, and when glm is cast to a GLMeter, the cast will be successful since glm is really a GLMeter. The test for equality then yields true since the names are equal (although belonging to different objects).

(ii) o.equals(d2) will generate an IllegalArgumentException. o is really a GLMeter so the equals() method of GLMeter will be used. However, d2 is a BPMeter so the instanceof test will fail, causing the IllegalArgumentException to be generated.

(iii) d2.equals(o) is false, since at run time, the equals() method of BPMeter will be used since d2 is a BPMeter. However, BPMeter does not override the equals() method of Object, which returns true if the object identifiers are the same. Since this is not the case, false is returned.

(iv) The type Device cannot take the place of GLMeter. Thus, when the equals() method is invoked on the GLMeter instance with d3 as parameter, the equals() method does not bind to the one defined for the GLMeter class since this one takes a GLMeter as parameter. The compiler looks up the hierarchy and finds the equals() method of the Object class which takes an Object as parameter. Since the type of d3 is Device which is an Object, this is the method that is bound to the call, glm.equals (d3). Since the object identifiers are different, the call returns false.

14. A UML diagram based on the information provided is shown in Figure

Appendix B: Answers to Questions

B.2.

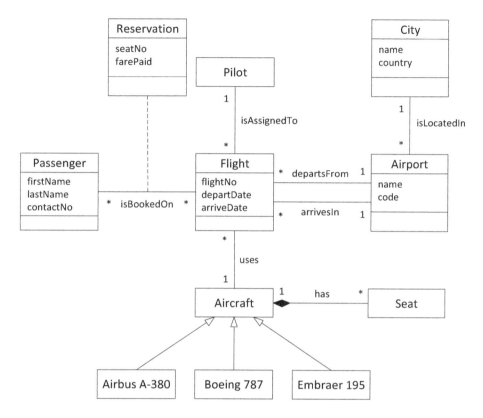

Figure B.2: UML Diagram of Classes in Flight Reservation System

15. A UML diagram based on the information provided is shown in Figure B.3. Note that **Asset** is an abstract class and that **presentValue()** is an abstract method that is implemented in the concrete subclasses of **Asset**. **Security** is also an abstract class.

Fundamentals of Object-Oriented Programming in Java

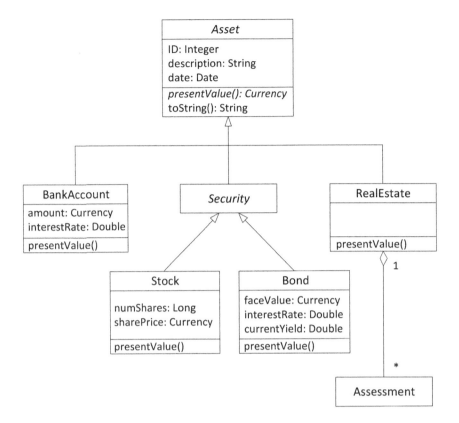

Figure B.3: UML Diagram of Classes in Financial System

Glossary

abstract class	A class from which instances cannot be created. It can only be used as the superclass or parent class of some other class.
access modifier	A keyword used to control access to the individual members of a class such as its attributes and methods. The access modifiers in Java are `private`, `protected`, and `public`.
accessor method	A method which returns the value of an attribute.
aggregation relationship	A relationship which models a "whole/part" relationship between two classes A and B, in which an instance of A (the "whole") consists of instances of B (the "parts").
annotation	A programming feature that allows metadata to be provided about the source code of a class. In Java, annotations are written using the '@' symbol.
assert statement	A statement that evaluates to `true` or `false`. If the statement evaluates to `true`, the test passes; otherwise, the test fails.
associations	A structural relationship between two classes that specifies that objects of one class are connected to objects of the other class.
attribute	A property of an object which has a type. It is implemented as an instance variable.
checked exception	An exception that must be handled by a client object.

class	*1.* A type of object which specifies the attributes and behavior which apply to all objects of that type.
	2. The mechanism used in object-oriented programming to define and implement the attributes and methods of a particular type.
class member	A feature of a class such as its attributes and methods.
class method	A method which can be invoked without an instance of a class being present. It cannot access the instance variables of a class.
class variable	A variable that is shared among all the instances of a class. It declared with the `static` keyword.
client object	An object which uses the services of another object. The object providing the service is referred to as a *server object*.
cohesion	A measure of the internal strength of a class, i.e., how strongly related the parts of the class are. Strong cohesion is desirable in object-oriented programming.
collection class	See **container class**.
composition relationship	A form of aggregation with strong ownership between the "whole" and its "parts". The "whole" is responsible for the creation and destruction of the "parts". The "parts" of the composition live and die with the "whole".
constructor method	A method that is used to initialize an instance of a class after it has been created with the `new` keyword. It has the same name as the name of the class.
container class	A class which is designed to contain objects of another class. Typical examples in Java include `ArrayList`, `HashSet`, `TreeSet`, `HashMap`, and `TreeMap`.
coupling	The degree or strength of interconnection

Glossary

	among classes. Loosely coupled classes are desirable in object-oriented programming since they can be handled in a relatively independent manner.
dependency	A class **A** depends on a class **B** if objects of class **A** manipulate objects of class **B** in any way.
design pattern	A reusable solution to a commonly occurring problem in object-oriented programming in a given context.
domain object	An object belonging to the Business Services tier of an object-oriented application. It is responsible for performing tasks related to the problem being solved by the application.
dynamic type	The actual type of an object referred to by an object variable at run-time.
encapsulation	Hiding the secrets of an object that do not contribute to its essential characteristics.
event-driven programming	Writing application-specific code that performs some action when a pre-determined event occurs on a GUI; for example, clicking on a button.
exception	An unexpected event that occurs in an application that is not expected or is not part of the application's normal operations.
exception handling	The process of responding to the occurrence of exceptions while an application is executing; it can be achieved in Java through the use of a `try-catch` block.
generalization	A relationship between a general class called the *superclass* or *parent class* and a more specific class called the *subclass* or *child class*; it is often referred to as an "is-a" or "is-a-kind-of" relationship.
generics	A programming language feature which generalizes the type of objects that can be stored in a container while providing type

	safety at the same time.
GUI component	An object that can be used to build a GUI. For example, buttons, labels, text fields, and text areas.
immutable object	An object whose state cannot be changed after it has been created.
import statement	A statement which uses the `import` keyword to indicate that a required class or set of classes belongs to another package.
inheritance	A characteristic of object-oriented programming languages which allows a class to acquire the features (attributes and methods) from another class referred to as a *parent class* or *superclass*.
inheritance hierarchy	A set of classes connected by generalization relationships. It can be arbitrarily deep.
inner classes	A class that is written inside another class. It has access to the attributes and methods of the containing class.
input stream	Data being read from an input source such as a file or a device.
instance	A programming entity that has both state and behavior which are characterized by the class that the instance belongs to.
instance method	A method which can be invoked on an instance of a class. It can perform operations on the attributes of the instance.
instance variable	An instance variable is a variable associated with an instance of a class. The set of values of the instance variables of an object determines the state of an object.
integrated development environment	Software that provides facilities for editing, compiling, and running an application from within a single environment.
interface	*1.* A programming language feature in Java

Glossary

	that specifies a set of common behaviors or protocol for classes.
	2. The set of public services provided by an object.
iterator design pattern	A design pattern which specifies an interface for accessing the elements from a container in a standard way.
JDBC driver	Software which serves as a bridge between a Java application and a relational database management system.
Law of Demeter	A guideline for reducing the coupling among classes. It restricts the kinds of objects on which methods can be invoked.
layout manager	An object responsible for positioning GUI components on a window or other container.
method overloading	The process of writing methods with the same name in a class but with different signatures.
method overriding	Defining a method in a child class with the same signature as its parent class.
method refinement	This is when a child class overrides a method of its parent class but still uses the functionality of the parent's method.
method replacement	This is when a child class overrides a method of its parent class but does not utilize the functionality of the parent's method in any way.
method signature	When declaring a method, the method signature refers to the name of the method and the number, types, and order of its parameters.
model-view separation design pattern	A design pattern which states that the *model* or *domain objects* should not have direct knowledge of, or be directly coupled to *view* objects.

multiple inheritance	A feature which allows a class to acquire the features (attributes and methods) from two or more classes. Some programming languages such as Java do not support multiple inheritance.
multiplicity	The number of objects that are allowed to participate in an association. Typical multiplicities are one-to-one, one-to-many and many-to-many.
mutator method	A method which changes the value of an attribute.
object	See **instance**.
object persistence	Storing objects in a persistence medium (e.g., file or database) so that they are available for future use.
object serialization	A Java technique that is used to save objects to a file exactly as they are in an application.
object variable	A variable that is used to refer to an actual object in memory.
object-oriented programming	A style of computer programming where the code consists of a set of objects which collaborate to achieve the functionality of the application.
output stream	Data being written to an output source such as a file or a device.
package	A way of grouping related classes into a single unit. In Java, classes can be placed in a package using the `package` keyword.
Principle of Substitutability	A principle which states that if **B** is a subclass of **A** (even indirectly), it should be possible to substitute instances of **B** for instances of **A** in any situation, *with no observable effect*.
procedural programming	A style of computer programming where the code is (hierarchically) structured according to the processes taking place in the application.

Glossary

programming paradigm	A fundamental style of computer programming; two of the most common paradigms are the object-oriented paradigm and the procedural (imperative) paradigm.
pull-from-above	A technique that is used with the Model-View Separation design pattern to enable user interface objects to obtain data and services from the model objects (i.e., objects in the Business Services layer).
relational database	A collection of *tables* for storing data on entities. A table has a set of *columns* which correspond to the attributes of an entity.
relational database management system (RDBMS)	Software that manages the operations of a relational database. It provides services such as data definition, data manipulation, and user authentication.
relationships	A connection among objects. The three most important relationships in an object-oriented program are dependencies, associations, and generalizations.
role object	An object that can take the place of an instance of a subclass as an alternative to using inheritance.
server object	An object which provides a service to another object. The object requesting the service is referred to as a *client object*.
singleton design pattern	A design pattern which ensures that at most instance of a class is created at run-time.
specialization	A different viewpoint of the generalization relationship where a subclass or child class is viewed as a specialization of the superclass or parent class.
SQL	A language that is used for data definition and data manipulation in a relational database.
static type	The type that is used to declare an object variable.

test	A statement written using one of the *assert* methods in JUnit.
test class	A class which contains a set of test methods. It is supplied as input to the unit testing framework which runs the test methods one by one.
test method	A method that is preceded by the "@Test" annotation and provides a means for a test to be executed. It can contain any number of tests.
test suite	A collection of test classes which are executed as one unit.
text file	A file that consists of a set of characters.
three-tier architecture	A way of organizing an object-oriented application into three vertical tiers: User services (which interacts with the user), Business Services (application processing), and Data Services (persistent storage mechanism).
unchecked exception	An exception which may or may not be handled by a client object.
Unified Modelling Language	A graphical language that is widely used for modelling object-oriented applications.
unit test	An automated piece of code which invokes the methods or a class being tested and checks some assumptions about the logical behavior of that method or class.
user interface object	An object belonging to the User Services tier of an object-oriented application. It is responsible for interacting with the user and communicating with the objects in the Business Services tier. It can be a GUI object such as a button or text field or it can be an object that processes user input in some way.

Bibliography

Booch, G. (1994). *Object-Oriented Analysis and Design with Applications, Second Edition*. Reading, Massachusetts: Addison-Wesley.

Booch, G., Rumbaugh, J., and Jacobson, I. (1999). *The Unified Modeling Language User Guide*. Reading, Massachusetts: Addison-Wesley.

Budd, T. (1998). *An Introduction to Object-Oriented Programming, Second Edition*. Reading, Massachusetts: Addison Wesley.

Date, C.J. (1994). *An Introduction to Database Systems, Sixth Edition*. Reading, Massachusetts: Addison Wesley.

Doshi, G. (2003). *Best Practices for Exception Handling*. Available from: http://www.onjava.com/pub/a/onjava/2003/11/19/exceptions.html

Gamma, E., Helm, R., Johnson, R., and Vlissides, J. (1995). *Design Patterns: Elements of Reusable Object-Oriented Software*. Reading, Massachusetts: Addison Wesley.

Horstmann, C. (2002). *Object-Oriented Design and Patterns*. New Jersey: John Wiley and Sons, Inc.

Larman, C. (1998). *Applying UML and Patterns*. Upper Saddle River, New Jersey: Prentice Hall.

Poo, D., Kiong, D., and Ashok, S. (2008). *Object-Oriented Programming Java, Second Edition*. London: Springer-Verlag.

Rumbaugh, J., Blaha, M., Premerlani, W., Eddy, F., and Lorensen, W. (1991). *Object-Oriented Modeling and Design*. Englewood Cliffs, New Jersey: Prentice-Hall.

Shelton, C.P. *Exception Handling*. Available from: http://www.ece.cmu.edu/~koopman/des_s99/exceptions/

Tremblay, J-P., and Cheston, G.A. (2003). *Data Structures and Software Development in an Object-Oriented Domain*. New Jersey: Pearson Education, Inc.

Index

A

Abstract class	186, 433
Abstract method	187
Abstract methods	187
Access Modifier	59, 433
Accessor method	64
Aggregation implementation	143
Aggregation relationship	433
Annotation	433
Arithmetic Operators	18
ArrayList	270
Arrays	
declaring	*28*
length	*28*
assert statement	433
associations	433
attribute	433
Attributes	33

B

boolean primitive	16

C

case statements	25-26
catch-block	201
Checked exception	
catching	*200*
declaring	*198*
definition	*196, 433*
implementation	*197*
not handling	*204*
throwing	*198*
Child classes	170
Class	
access modifiers	*81*
associations	
definition	*132*
implementation	*137*
attributes	*33*
client class	*40*
construct	*35*
definition	*33, 434*
dependencies	
implementation	*136*
instances	*38*
member	*434*
method	*434*
objects	*38*
UML notation	*37*
variables	*52, 434*
Class generalizations	135
Class methods	52
client object	434
Code Commenting	15
Cohesion	71-72, 434
Collection classes	253
Collection Interface	265
Comparable interface	245

Comparator interface	277-278	throwing an exception	198
Comparison Operators	19	unchecked	206-207
Composition relationship	434		
Concrete class	187	**F**	
Concrete method	187	false, boolean value	16
Conditional Statements	25	File manipulations, in Java	309
Constructor method	45, 434	FileReader	309
Container class	434	FileWriter	309
Coupling	70, 434	finally-block	203
		float, primitive type	16
D		for loop	27
		foreach statement	263
Database			
connectivity	316	**G**	
relational	314-315		
retrieving	322		
saving	317	Garbage collector	45
Delegation, in Java	190	Generalization	168, 435
Demeter, law of	71	Generics	435
Dependency	131, 435	Generics, Java	254
Design pattern	11, 435	Graphical User Interface	351
Domain object	435	GUI	351
Dynamic type	179	GUI component	436
E		**I**	
Encapsulation	59, 435	Immutability	67
Event-driven programming	435	Immutable object	436
Exception handling	435	Import statement	436
Exception handling, in Java	196	Information hiding, concept of	7
Exceptions		Inheritance	
catching an exception	200-202	benefits	189
checked	197-198	definition	167-169, 436
definition	195-196, 435	drawbacks	189

Index

forms	188	comparison operators	19
implementation	171	exception handling	196
multiple	189	foreach	263
prevention	185-186	HashMap	274

Inheritance hierarchy 436

Inner class 81-82, 436

Input and output operation

scanner class	24	iterators	261
system.out	22	LinkedList	270

Input stream 436

Instance 436

Instance method 436

Instance variable 55

Integrated development environment 436

Interface(s)

concept	239-240	JFrame	352
definition	436	label	357
implementation	241-242	layout manager	359
inheritance of	249-251	text area	358
multiple interfaces	248-249	text field	358
properties	243	switch statement	25
UML notation	242	TreeMap	275

Interface, comparable 245

Iterator design pattern 437

Iterator implementation, Java 261-262

Iterators 261

- HashSet 271
- input
  - scanner class 24
  - input and output 22
  - input stream 309
- list interface 266
- logical operators 19-20
- map, sorted map 268
- output stream 309
- primitive data types 16
- repetition and loops 27
- set, sorted set 267
- string API 20
- swing toolkit 352
  - command button 358
- TreeSet 273
- variables 17

Java Development Environment 13

Java IDE 13

JDBC 316

JDBC driver 437

JUnit 99-106, 128

test suite 122

J

Java

annotations	108
arithmetic operators	18
ArrayList	270
collection interface	265
collections	253
collections framework	264
comments	15

L

Law of Demeter 437

Layout manager 437

Linked list

definition	254	creation of	38
generic types	258	definition	35
iterator	262	in memory	41
of integers	254	instantiation	38
of objects	256	persistence	305, 438

Local variable	55
Logical operators	19
long, primitive type	16

M

Method binding	181

Methods

definition	34
overloading	50, 437
overriding	437
refinement	437
replacement	175, 437
signature	50, 437

Model-View separation design pattern	381, 437

Multiple Inheritance

concept of	189, 438
problems associated with	190

Multiplicity	438
Mutator method	64, 438
MySQL Database	315

O

Object Class	176
Object de-serialization	327
Object instantiation	38
Object serialization	325, 438
Object variable	39, 438
Object(s)	

Object-Oriented Programming 438

basic concept

client object	3
server object	3
design patterns	11
three-tier architecture	74

Operators

arithmetic	18
comparison	18
logical	18

Oracle Database	315
Output stream	438

P

Package

accessing attributes	80
accessing methods	80
creation	76
definition	73, 438
nesting	78
usage	77

Polymorphism	180
Polymorphism, reverse polymorphism problem	183
Polymorphism, with interfaces	247
Principle of Substitutability	438

Programming Paradigms

object-oriented paradigm	1-2
procedural paradigm	1-3, 438

pull-from-above	439

Index

R

Relational database	439
Relational database management system (RDBMS)	315, 439
Relationships	439
Role object	439

S

Serializable interface	325
Serialization	
object	*325*
Server object	439
Shared variable	53
short, primitive type	16
Singleton design pattern	439
Software engineering	11, 59
Specialization, concept	439
Specialization, of classes	188
SQL	315, 439
SQL Server Database	315
State, of the object	33
Static type	179, 439
Strings	20
Subclass	168-170
Subtype	178

T

test	440
Test class	107, 440
test method	440
test suite	440
text file	440
Three-tier architecture	440
true, boolean value	16
try-block	203
try-catch statement	203

U

UML Diagrams	10
UML Diagrams, of class	37
unchecked exception	196, 440
implementation	*206*
Unified Modelling Language (UML)	440
Unit test	440
Unit testing	
definition	*99*
guidelines	*127*
User interface object	440

V

Variable, declaration	17

W

while loop	27

CPSIA information can be obtained at www.ICGtesting.com
Printed in the USA
LVOW03s0227030414

380036LV00016B/418/P